W9-BBC-113

BLUES FELL THIS MORNING

PERFECT RACE RECORDS

"SLOPPY DRUNK"

0230 { I'm Still Sloppy Drunk
{ Man Of My Own

0225 { New Blue Heaven
{ Stopped Clock Blues

0226 { In A Shanty In Old Shanty Town
{ Sweet Evening Breeze

0207 { How You Want It Done?
{ M & O Blues

0217 { Worrying You Off My Mind No. 1
{ Worrying You Off My Mind No. 2

0218 { How Long How Long Blues
{ Mama Don't Allow No Easy Riders
{ Here

0215 { How Long How Long Blues No. 1
{ How Long How Long Blues No. 2

181 { New Huntsville Jail
{ John Henry Blues

180 { I'm Sitting On Top Of The World
{ Take A Look At That Baby

"DESERTED MAN"

0224 { Deserted Man Blues
{ Motherless Boy

"DO IT AGAIN"

0227 { Do It Again
{ Water Trough Blues

"GRAVEYARD DIGGER"

0222 { Graveyard Diggers' Blues
{ Lonesome Road Blues

0216 { New Strangers Blues
{ Georgia Hound Blues

195 { You're Going To Leave The Old
{ Home Jim
{ Careless Love Blues

193 { Slow Mama Slow
{ New Salty Dog

198 { Sloppy Drunk Blues
{ Alley Boogie

0208 { Bad Depression Blues
{ Howling Wolf Blues

0212 { You Rascal You No. 1
{ You Rascal You No. 2

0214 { I'm Talkin' 'Bout You No. 1
{ I'm Talkin' 'Bout You No. 2

0211 { Bumble Bee No. 1
{ Bumble Bee No. 2

 25c

FOR SALE BY

 25c

(OVER)

PRINTED IN U. S A

BLUES FELL THIS MORNING

MEANING IN THE BLUES

PAUL OLIVER

with a foreword by Richard Wright

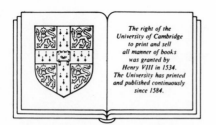

The right of the
University of Cambridge
to print and sell
all manner of books
was granted by
Henry VIII in 1534.
The University has printed
and published continuously
since 1584.

CAMBRIDGE UNIVERSITY PRESS

CAMBRIDGE

NEW YORK   PORT CHESTER

MELBOURNE   SYDNEY

ARNULFO L. OLIVEIRA MEMORIAL LIBRARY
1825 MAY STREET
BROWNSVILLE, TEXAS 78520

Published by the Press Syndicate of the University of Cambridge
The Pitt Building, Trumpington Street, Cambridge CB2 1RP
40 West 20th Street, New York, NY 10011, USA
10 Stamford Road, Oakleigh, Melbourne 3166, Australia

First edition © Paul Oliver 1960
Second edition © Cambridge University Press 1990

First published 1960 by Cassell & Company Ltd, London
Second edition published by Cambridge University Press 1990
Reprinted 1990

Printed in Great Britain at the University Press, Cambridge

British Library cataloguing in publication data
Oliver, Paul, *1927–*
Blues fell this morning: meaning in the blues – 2nd
rev. ed.
1. Blues
I. Title
784.5'3

Library of Congress cataloguing in publication data
Oliver, Paul.
Blues fell this morning: the meaning of the blues / by Paul
Oliver: with a foreword by Richard Wright. – 2nd rev. ed.
    p.   cm.
Includes bibliographical references and discography.
ISBN 0 521 37437 5 (U.S.). – ISBN 0 521 37793 5 (U.S.: pbk.)
1. Blues (Music) – History and criticism.   I. Title.
ML3521.O42   1990
781.643'09 – dc20   89-25402   CIP

ISBN 0 521 37437 5 hardback
ISBN 0 521 37793 5 paperback

SE

To Valerie

Contents

Illustrations

Contemporary advertisements for blues records are listed with the year of the advertisement, and not that of the record issue.

Author's note and acknowledgments to the first edition (1960)

When the present work was originally undertaken it had been my intention to write not only on the meaning of vocal blues, but also on the historical development of the blues forms with summaries of the lives and work of principal singers. With this end in view I circulated a number of blues enthusiasts with a draft scheme requesting the assistance of those interested. Though many were fully occupied with their own researches the response from collectors was very generous, with the result that the information gathered from many sources far exceeded my expectations. To attempt to do some justice both to the subject and to the work of contributors I found that it was necessary drastically to reduce the original plan. Accordingly, I have devoted the present book solely to the meaning and content of blues, but a study of its form and history is now in preparation.

Though possibly no further removed from my subject in distance than the historian is removed from his in time, I am acutely aware of my remoteness from the environment that nurtured the blues. The help given me by visiting blues singers has therefore been invaluable and I would like to express to them my heartfelt thanks for their patient interest and kindly forbearance of my endless questions. In many hours of conversation Big Bill Broonzy drew from his inexhaustible fund of memories of half a century; Jimmy Rushing recalled at length the hey-day of the twenties; Brownie McGhee and Sonny Terry reminisced on blues and blues singers of the thirties and forties, demonstrating many points, and Brother John Sellers gave me the benefit of his wide knowledge of the blues in the post-war years.

The preliminary work for this book involved the written transcription of several thousand blues recordings from my own collection and from the record libraries of many collectors who generously put them at my disposal. A number of collectors also undertook the laborious task of transcribing records on my behalf and, though only a small proportion of these texts could be used in the final work, they all helped me to obtain a picture of the blues on record. For their help in transcribing records and for the information that they supplied my very sincere gratitude to Brian Davis; M. Jacques Demetre, blues columnist of *Jazz-Hot*, Paris; D. J. Parsons, who also checked numerous items; Max Vreede of Holland, Race Research columnist to *Matrix*, and J. R. T. Davies who assisted him.

For the loan of records and the resources of their files my warmest thanks to Sam Benjamin, U.K. representative of the International Jazz Club; jazz and blues singer Beryl Bryden; Derek Coller, editor of the *Discophile* from 1948–1958, who also kindly solicited help through his magazine; J. R. Davis who taped innumerable items; Brian Rust of the B.B.C. Gramophone Department; Derrick Stewart-Baxter, blues columnist of *Jazz Journal*; and Michael Wyler of *Jazz Publications* and Paramount specialist of *Jazz Monthly*.

Sincere thanks for many enjoyable record playing and transcribing sessions and for the loan of valuable items from their collections to Roy Crawford Ansell who also joined me in research on Negro terminology; Graham Boatfield, *Jazz Journal* columnist; Peter Gammond of Decca Record Company; Gerry Grounsell and John Jack, Columbia Race catalogue specialists; Norman Jenkinson; John Langmead; Vic Schuler; and Eric Townley, *Jazz Journal* columnist.

Though the major proportion of the blues quoted in this book is of traditional and folk blues items, every attempt has been made to trace possible holders of copyright. In making this search I have been given every possible assistance by the Mechanical-Copyright Protection Society and in particular Miss M. D. Jarvis and members of her department who have been unstinting in their efforts and time. To them and to the publishing companies who have so kindly given permission for the quotation of items under their control, my warmest appreciation of their generosity. In this connection I would like to express my thanks to the Directors of Cromwell Music, Ltd.; Empress Music, Inc.; Essex Music, Ltd.; Leeds Music, Ltd.; Milton 'Mezz' Mezzrow; Pickwick Music, Ltd., and Southern Music Publishing Company, Ltd. Full details of the items held in copyright by these companies are given under the appropriate titles in the appendix, Acknowledgments in Discography. As far as is known, all holders of copyright have been traced, but the author requests the indulgence of any publishing companies whose copyright of a quoted blues and permission so to quote have been inadvertently overlooked.

I am greatly indebted to the distinguished authority on American folk song, Alan Lomax, and to the eminent Negro writer Richard Wright for their advice and encouragement. Likewise I am deeply appreciative of the interest and help of John Ball, Professor of English at Miami University, Oxford, Ohio, and Director of the Archive of Ohio Folklore, and of his wife, Mrs. Helen C. Ball, Special Services Librarian at Miami University; and of the valuable information on Negro affairs given me by Ralph H. Turner, Associate Professor of Sociology, University of California, and Philip H. Wikelund, Associate Professor of English, Indiana University.

To Richard C. Wootton, Cultural Affairs Officer of the United States Embassy, my grateful thanks for his help and advice, and to the Staff of the American Library for the loan of innumerable books and recordings from the Archives of the Library of Congress. Sincere thanks also to B. Bennett, Librarian of the Greenford Branch, Ealing Libraries, and his staff, for their trouble in obtaining many rare books for my use. Doug Dobell, Brian Harvey, and Bill Colyer of Dobell's Record Shops have also loaned me books and recordings for which I am most grateful, and I have been greatly encouraged by the continued interest of Doug Dobell in the progress of this work.

Many other persons have helped me in divers ways. I would especially like to thank Sam Charters for information on singers; Tom Cundall, Editorial Director, and Jack Higgins, past editor of *Music Mirror*, in which magazine appeared the series of articles on which the idea of this book was based; Nat Hentoff, co-editor of *The Jazz Review* and late of *Downbeat*, who kindly solicited help through his column; Max Jones of *Melody Maker* for much advice and aid; Donald Kincaid and Alexis Korner for technical information; Robert Koester, editor of the *St. Louis Jazz Report*, for his interest and generous notice in his magazine; Albert McCarthy, editor of *Jazz Monthly* and compiler of *Jazz Directory*, for his great help in enabling me to trace obscure discographical data; Anthony Rotante, columnist of *Record Research*, for discographical information, and Bert Whyatt, assistant editor of the *Discophile*, for the loan of Race Record publicity sheets. My warm thanks to all the other persons who have helped in different ways and who, by letter or in person, have expressed their interest in the project. In expressing my appreciation of the great help that I have received from all these persons, I would add that the selection of relevant material, the opinions stated and the conclusions drawn in the content of the book are entirely my own and do not necessarily represent those that might be made by any persons who have assisted me.

To no one do I owe a greater debt of gratitude, however, than to my wife Valerie, who has endured for many months the constant upheaval caused by sheaves of notes, stacks of books and piles of discs; who has nobly transcribed recordings, typed and filed transcriptions; who has checked discographies and typed the final manuscript; who has heard blues records incessantly and repeatedly; who has given me the right encouragement when enthusiasm has flagged, and who has somehow developed a passion for blues herself.

Foreword by Richard Wright

Millions in this our twentieth century have danced with abandonment and sensuous joy to jigs that had their birth in suffering: I'm alluding to those tunes and lyrics known under the rubric of the blues, those starkly brutal, haunting folk songs created by millions of nameless and illiterate American Negroes in their confused wanderings over the American southland and in their intrusion into the northern American industrial cities.

The blues are fantastically paradoxical and, by all logical and historical odds, they ought not have come into being. I'm absolutely certain that no one predicted their advent. If I may indulge in an imaginative flight, I can hear a white Christian Virginia planter, say, in 1623, debating thus with his conscience while examining a batch of the first slaves brought from Africa:

"Now, these black animals have human form, but they are not really human, for God would not have made men to look like that. So, I'm free to buy them and work them on my tobacco plantation without incurring the wrath of God. Moreover, these odd black creatures will die early in our harsh climate and will leave no record behind of any possible sufferings that they might undergo. Yes, I'll buy five of these to be used as slaves . . ."

But that mythical Virginia planter would have been tragically deluded. Not only did those Blacks, torn from their tribal moorings in Africa, transported across the Atlantic, survive under hostile conditions of life, but they left a vivid record of their sufferings and longings in those astounding religious songs known as the spirituals, and their descendants, freed and cast upon their own in an alien culture, created the blues, a form of exuberantly melancholy folk song that has circled the globe. In Buenos Aires, Stockholm, Copenhagen, London, Berlin, Paris, Rome, in fact, in every large city of the earth where lonely, disinherited men congregate for pleasure or amusement, the orgiastic wail of the blues, and their strident offspring, jazz, can be heard.

How was that possible? I stated above that the possibility of those shackled, transplanted Blacks ever leaving behind a record of their feelings about their experiences in the New World ran smack against historical odds. What were some of those odds?

First, those Blacks were illiterate and it was not until some three centuries later that their illiteracy diminished to any appreciable degree.

Second, how could tribal men, whose values differed drastically from those of the Puritan Christian environment into which they were injected as slaves, ever arrive at an estimate or judgment of their experiences? How could they determine whether their lives were better or worse in America than in Africa?

Third, upon being sold into slavery, many tribes were deliberately separated one from another, so that the possibility of tribal inter-communication would be nullified, and, thus, the likelihood of revolt eliminated.

Fourth, not only were slaves bought and sold, employed as commodity-mediums of exchange, but they were intentionally bred as livestock, thereby augmenting the wealth of the planters.

Fifth, the spur to obtain the slaves' labor was brutality; the effort of the slave to learn merited punishment; self-assertion on the slaves' part met with rebuff; the penalty of escape, death.

How could such men, then, speak of what they underwent? Yet they did. In a vocabulary terser than Basic English, shorn of all hyperbole, purged of metaphysical implications, wedded to a frankly atheistic vision of life, and excluding almost all references to nature and her various moods, they sang:

> Whistle keeps on blowin' an' I got my debts to pay,
> I've got a mind to leave my baby an' I've got a mind to stay.

This volume contains three hundred and fifty fragments (a fraction of the material extant) of the blues, and I believe that this is the first time that so many blues, differing in mood, range, theme, and approach, have been gathered together. We thus have here a chance to cast a bird's-eye view upon the meaning and implication of the blues. Certain salient characteristics of the blues present themselves at once.

The most striking feature of these songs is that a submerged theme of guilt, psychological in nature, seems to run through them. Could this guilt have stemmed from the burden of renounced rebellious impulses?

There is a certain degree of passivity, almost masochistic in quality and seemingly allied to sex in origin, that appears as part of the meaning of the blues. Could this emotional stance have been derived from a protracted inability to act, of a fear of acting?

The theme of spirituality, of other-worldliness is banned. Was this consciously done? Did it imply reflection upon the reigning American religious values?

Though constant reference is made to loved ones, little or no mention is made of the family as such. Was this because family life was impossible under slavery? (Family life among American Negroes has remained relatively weak until the present day!)

The locale of these songs shifts continuously and very seldom is a home site hymned or celebrated. Instead, the environmental items extolled are saw-mills, cotton-gins, lumber-camps, levee-banks, floods, swamps, jails, highways, trains, buses, tools, depressed states of mind, voyages, accidents, and various forms of violence.

Yet the most astonishing aspect of the blues is that, though replete with a sense of defeat and down-heartedness, they are not intrinsically pessimistic; their burden of woe and melancholy is dialectically redeemed through sheer force of sensuality, into an almost exultant affirmation of life, of love, of sex, of movement, of hope. No matter how repressive was the American environment, the Negro never lost faith in or doubted his deeply endemic capacity to live. All blues are a lusty, lyrical realism charged with taut sensibility. (Was this hope that sprang always phoenix-like from the ashes of frustration something that the Negro absorbed from the oppressive yet optimistic American environment in which he lived and had his being?)

All American Negroes do not sing the blues. These songs are not the expression of the Negro people in America as a whole. I'd surmise that the spirituals, so dearly beloved of the southern American Whites, came from those slaves who were closest to the Big Houses of the plantations where they caught vestiges of Christianity whiffed to them from the southern Whites' cruder forms of Baptist or Methodist religions. If the plantations' house slaves were somewhat remote from Christianity, the field slaves were almost completely beyond the pale. And it was from them and their descendants that the devil songs called the blues came – that confounding triptych of the convict, the migrant, the rambler, the steel driver, the ditch digger, the roustabout, the pimp, the prostitute, the urban or rural illiterate outsider.

This volume is the first history of those devil songs; it tells how fortuitously they came to be preserved, how their influence spread magically among America's black population, and what their probable emotional and psychological meaning is. It would be very appropriate to recount that an American Negro was the first person to attempt a history of the blues and their meaning. But, like the blues themselves, this volume is paradoxical in its origin. It was written neither by a Negro nor an American nor by a man who had ever seen America and her teeming Black Belts.

Paul Oliver, the author of this interpretation of the blues, an interpretation that cuts across such categories as anthropology, economics, and sociology, first heard the Negro's devil songs on phonograph records when he was a child living in London. Those songs haunted that English boy. They spoke to him and he was resolved to understand them. For twenty years, as a student, a teacher, a lecturer, Paul Oliver studied the blues, collected records, pored over the literature relating to the Negro and created by the Negro, interviewed blues singers and jazz players, and has finally presented us with this interesting and challenging documentary volume.

As a southern-born American Negro, I can testify that Paul Oliver is drenched in his subject; his frame of reference is as accurate and concrete as though he himself had been born in the environment of the blues. Can an alien, who has never visited the *milieu* from which a family of songs has sprung, write about them? In the instance of such a highly charged realm as the blues, I answer a categoric and emphatic Yes. Indeed, I see certain psychological advantages in an outsider examining these songs and their meaning: his passionate interest in these songs is proof that the songs spoke to him across racial and cultural distances; he is geographically far enough from the broiling scene of America's racial strife to seize upon that which he, conditioned by British culture, feels to be abiding in them; and, in turn, whatever he finds enduring in those songs he can, and with easy conscience, relate to that in his culture which he feels to be humanly valid. In short, to the meaning of the blues, Paul Oliver brings, in the fullest human sense, what courts of law term "corroborative evidence."

I'm aware of certain possible difficulties. The Cold War climate in which this non-political book will appear might well militate in some quarters against its being received in the same warm, impartial, and generous spirit in which the author conceived and wrote it. Much of the material, factual and authenticated, and drawn from official sources, upon which Paul Oliver floats his interpretations of the blues, no longer "officially" exists: that is, American Negro middle-class writers as well as some American Whites with psychological vested interests might not only decry the material, but may seek to cast doubt upon its validity. If such were the case, it would be tragic indeed that material relating to aesthetics should come under the racial or political hammer.

Yet the contents of the 1954 Supreme Court decision regarding the integration of black and white children in American schools ought, at least, to open our minds a bit on this subject, and Paul Oliver's book, directly and indirectly, deals with that psychological area of tension and depression consequent upon social exclusion, documenting it, illustrating it.

Recently, when commenting upon the death of Big Bill Broonzy, a well-known Negro blues singer, a powerful and popular American Negro magazine announced the "death of the blues." But can anyone or anything hand down an edict stating when the blues will or should be dead? Ought not the contraction or enlargement of the environment in which the blues were cradled be the calendar by which the death of the blues can be predicted?

The American environment which produced the blues is still with us, though we all labor to render it progressively smaller. The total elimination of that area might take longer than we now suspect, hence it is well that we examine the meaning of the blues while they are still falling upon us.

Paris 1959   RICHARD WRIGHT

Preface to the revised edition

Within a few months of the publication of *Blues Fell This Morning* my wife Valerie and I made our first trip to the United States, specifically to do research and field recording in the blues. It took us to cities like Washington, New York, Detroit, Chicago, St. Louis, Memphis, Dallas, and New Orleans, to small towns and rural communities in Tennessee, Arkansas, Mississippi, Louisiana, Texas, and California. We went with considerable trepidation, not for our safety – though it was a difficult time in the South – but fearing that the world described in the book would prove to be misleading. As it turned out though, we found that it was often too painfully accurate, as we encountered the humiliation of racial discrimination, the poverty and deprivation of Blacks in the urban ghettoes and the country, the conditions in which many blues singers lived.

Of course we learned much more: that was the purpose of the trip. We heard, interviewed, and recorded blues singers and musicians, record promoters, veterans of the shows; black writers, historians, and Civil Rights leaders too. The details of that trip, the substance of many of the interviews, and the field recordings I made were incorporated in a later book, *Conversation with the Blues*, and in a number of long-play record releases. Thirty years have passed since then; thirty years of change in the United States, in black culture, in the blues; thirty years of further research and writing about the blues, including my own. In that time I have spent several weeks, sometimes months, in the United States every year, on average, and my visits have taken me to every region in the South and to some two-thirds of the states in the country as a whole. These visits have enabled me to note the persistence of many aspects of American life, as well as to witness the many changes as they have occurred. Together, they have led me to make a number of amendments to the text of *Blues Fell This Morning* which require some words of explanation.

At the time of publication the lunch-counter sit-ins were just commencing, and Martin Luther King led the meeting in Raleigh, North Carolina which resulted in the forming of the Student Non-Violent Coordinating Committee, whose Freedom Rides commenced the following year. The formation of the Black Panther Party was still half a dozen years away. For many rural Blacks they were stressful years but eventually the effects of the non-violent demonstrations, the Washington March of August 1963, the Civil Rights Law, 1964, the 1965 Watts riots, the trials of the militant black activists, the martyrdom of Martin Luther King, the passing of the Civil Rights Bill of 1967 and its implementation, the ebb and flow of prejudice and justice, repression and freedom ultimately led to remarkable social change.

It seemed inconceivable when I made that first field trip that I would one day see a black leader be a serious contender for party nomination in a presidential campaign. I would not have anticipated that numerous cities, in the South as well as in the North and West, would have black mayors, that schools and public facilities would be desegregated throughout the country – or that the problems and squalor of the black ghettoes of New York, Washington, and Chicago would be as intractable after three decades as ever they were.

Change in the world of black people was not only the outcome of shifts in political power and Civil Rights legislation, nor the eventual end of discriminatory practice throughout the country, fundamentally important though these were. It was also brought about by the conjunction of many other factors – the decline in the cotton economy as synthetic fabrics became universal, the industrialization of the South which brought field labor to an end, reductions in relief payments for the poor, and much else. Yet the complex effects of political, industrial, commercial, and social decisions taken at levels far removed from them have left millions of Blacks without a share in the benefits of overall economic prosperity.

Blues in this period of upheaval has had a curious history. To a large extent it failed the campaigns of the non-violent demonstrators, the Civil Rights activists and the black militants: in the marches in Alabama and Mississippi, gospel song found a new role, but blues did not. Through the aggressive amplification of the Chicago blues bands of the late 1950s the sounds of protest could be heard, but the social commitment of the vocal blues of the 1930s was passed to James Brown and a few soul singers. By the early 1960s I had already seen indications that blues as an active force within the black community was showing signs of decline; the graph fell steeply soon after.

This was not the perception of listeners in general, for blues in the 1960s gained an international audience. Record labels and specialist magazines started up to cater for an expanding market for blues, field research uncovered a remarkable succession of veteran blues singers, among them many celebrated names. But now their audiences were white and largely middle-class; many singers followed the path staked out by Big Bill Broonzy in the 1950s. "Folk Blues Festivals" toured Europe in the 1960s and 1970s, blues singers went on State Department tours, star performers from Muddy Waters to B. B. King played for concerts and festivals. Rock musicians from both sides of the Atlantic paid homage to blues singers, exploited their techniques, recorded hit versions of their songs and made a lot of money of which little, and in many cases nothing at all, filtered back to the surviving blues singers in royalties. Small wonder that Blacks largely gave up the blues as Whites took over.

Throughout these eventful decades blues scholarship has grown, though regrettably, not often among black writers and researchers. The bulk of the work, whether historical or discographical, empirical or theoretical, has been done by white writers from outside the culture, European as much as American. Much of it is based on interviews with singers and musicians so that today we know far more about the lives of the singers, their sources and their influences, the work they did and the places where they performed. The history of regional styles has been pieced together, the role of the recording of the music is now better understood. Record collecting has become the obsession of many enthusiasts and some have made rare recordings available on their own long-play (LP) reissues. The LP revolution had begun in the 1950s, when I was writing this book, but it gained momentum after its publication.

An important aspect of all this activity has been recording in the field. The routes across the South had been way-marked by the early field units of the commercial companies, and the folklorists employed by the Archives of Folk Music of the Library of Congress. In the 1950s one or two field studies of folk forms of black music were done, especially in Alabama. But in the 1960s the emphasis was almost wholly on blues. Surprising numbers of singers were traced and recorded, adding to the now vast documentation of the subject. So much so that the relationship of blues to earlier forms of black music was in danger of being forgotten or ignored.

In the 1970s valuable contributions to the study of blues were made by many writers, even if theoretical and thematic books were rather fewer than the historical and biographical works. From such writings and further studies of my own I have come to modify my views about some aspects of the blues: its function as entertainment, the personalizing of the lyrics, the interaction between vocal expression and instrumental techniques. In the past I attached more importance to improvisation and the novelty of poetic invention in blues stanzas, than to the exchange and transfer of images and lyric fragments between singers. Yet the significance of the subjects about which blues artists sang, and which their audiences clearly wished to hear in person or through the purchase of their records, still remains of great importance to the understanding of the role of blues in black society.

Little, however, has been developed on the lyric content of blues since *Screening the Blues* (1968) where I sought to examine in depth some of the themes opened up in *Blues Fell This Morning*. The more liberal climate of the late 1960s enabled me to discuss freely the sexual emphasis of a large number of blues and black songs. Changes in social attitudes are evident when the discussion of the "blue blues" is compared with its treatment in the earlier book. In *Blues Fell This Morning* I had felt obliged to justify the consideration of certain themes – homosexuality and lesbianism for instance, sensitive subjects in those pre-Wolfenden days. Writing of the breakdown of the family, common-law liasons, desertion, or of alcoholism and drug addiction in a period which was less frank and less tolerant than the present, it was necessary to explain them in terms of social pressures. But a certain moralistic tone crept in, which I now regret. Some passages no longer require the kind of explanation that they did thirty years ago; others were over-written and have been simplified.

In revising the book, a number of other decisions had to be made. One was a matter of nomenclature: at the time of writing, "Negro" was a preferred term, but in the late 1960s "Black" generally replaced it. "Afro-American" was occasionally used, and in the late 1980s "African American," as an equivalent to, say, "Italian American," has gained some support. I have settled for "Black" and "White" when employed as nouns, and "black" and "white" when used as adjectives, though for relief, or to avoid anachronisms, other terms have been used a few times.

Further decisions were not about style. An important one was related to the period of time to which the book referred, now that so many more years of singing and recording the blues have passed. In theory, the large body of commercially recorded blues, the extensive field work and recording undertaken by researchers, and the greater accessibility of recordings drawn from a total span of seventy years, makes this a rich mine of material. Indeed it does, but the popularization of the blues in the 1960s, and its considerable popularity today, has been principally a reflection of the growing taste for the music among white enthusiasts. This has meant that blues has been shaped by their preferences, and singers have frequently responded to them as new, appreciative, but different audiences.

Commercial recording of blues that was addressed and sold to black audiences spans some forty years – roughly 1920–60. From the advent of rural blues singers on record in the mid-1920s to the decline of the 78 rpm disc in the Rhythm and Blues epoch was a period of thirty or so years. During this time the blues on record was essentially by and for Blacks, apart from Library of Congress recordings and a few minority collector labels of the post-war years. Often the men who were responsible for the recording of blues singers were Whites who frequently had local knowledge. But many talent scouts were black and quite a few were blues singers themselves. They responded to black preferences, identified most of the major singers and gave many minor ones a chance to record. To some extent they undoubtedly shaped taste, emphasizing "originals," or new compositions which could be copyrighted, and probably influenced the development of blues with a story-line. They also overlooked some aspects of black music, most regrettably the string bands that were still popular in the 1930s.

With all these factors borne in mind it is still my opinion that commercially recorded 78s, made between the mid-1920s and the mid-1950s, give us the most accurate picture we are likely to have of the blues when it was solely the music of the black community. Consequently, I have deleted from the book some blues which were recorded on the relatively new LPs and others that were issued on 78s which were marketed primarily for white collectors; where possible, I have made appropriate substitutions. In some other instances I have replaced the blues quoted with an example which better illustrates the point that I wished to make.

Transcribing blues, which involves coping with surface noise, comprehending the parochialisms of local accents, a knowledge of black idioms of the past, and a working understanding of the themes about which blues performers sing, can never be an exact science. It is a form of gestalt process, of fitting hypotheses about what is sung against the evidence of recorded sounds. Numerous readers have commented over the years on the blues quoted, suggesting alternative transcriptions of the words or interpretations of their meaning. They are too numerous to list, but I wish to express my gratitude to blues collectors and writers Alan Balfour and Chris Smith for the immense amount of trouble they have taken in checking transcriptions and debating others. Whatever improvements there are in the accuracy of the transcriptions is in very large measure due to them. I am also greatly indebted to Johnny Parth for his help with records and to John Cowley for many items of relevance.

Finally, there is the matter of interpretation. *Blues Fell This Morning* was subtitled (and published in the United States) as *The Meaning of the Blues*, though my preference had been for *Meaning in the Blues*, which more accurately described its purpose. Clearly, there are levels of meaning which are symbolic and abstract, and some of these I endeavored to unravel in *Screening the Blues*. There are also qualities of meaning which emanate from the instrumental accompaniments to the lyrics, which defy notation and which are best experienced through hearing the records. My intention in writing this book was more direct: I wished to show that the thematic content of the blues related to many aspects of black experience during the period in question. Always I started from the lyrics of the blues, rather from sociology or history, but in order to do so I had to consult many references. Apart from my conversations with the author Richard Wright, and with a number of blues singers, I was largely dependent on the work of black historians, sociologists and authors. Details of my principal sources and substantiating texts are given in the notes to the chapters.

In 1960 there were still young blues singers in their thirties around: today they are in their sixties. There were some that were younger, who had been playing since childhood, and they are still featured in the European blues clubs and festivals. Very few came after them, for the black blues clubs had dwindled in the cities. Rock and soul, and later, hip-hop and rap, filled the space that the blues had left. In the country districts, blues remained as the old folks' music, regarded by some young Blacks somewhat condescendingly, and by the more militant with impatience. Blues represented the values of another era, values which they did not share. This I rather expected. What I did not expect was the growing interest among some young Blacks today in the culture of what is now their grandparents' (or great-grandparents') generation. How widespread and how lasting this may be we can only wait and see, but perhaps this revised edition of a book written at the end of an era, will provide one means of access to the socio-historical background of that generation's blues songs.

Introduction

A full-featured, curly haired colored woman from Cincinnati, Ohio, in her thirtieth year stood before the horn of the recording machine in the New York Studios of the Okeh Record Company. At the signal of the recording engineer, the group of five musicians beside her, with their instruments pointed down the bells of similar horns, commenced to play an introduction, and then, in a clear voice, pitched a shade too high for comfort, she began to sing:

> 1 I'm worried in my mind, I'm worried all the time,
> My friend he told me to-day, that he was going away to stay,
> Now I love him deep down in my heart,
> But the best of friends must part . . .

Perry Bradford, the composer of her song, stood near. It was he who had secured this recording date for February 14, 1920, when Sophie Tucker had been unable to record. Neither the occasion nor the recording seemed unduly auspicious, but the sale of the first disc to be made by a colored singer, *That Thing Called Love*, backed by *You Can't Keep A Good Man Down*, sung by Mamie Smith, "contralto, with Rega Orchestra" on Okeh 4113 was sufficiently great to secure for the singer a second date on August 10 the same year. This time she cut Bradford's *Crazy Blues* with its choruses based on a twelve-bar structure, the first vocal recording to employ a blues form. For months the disc sold some 7,500 copies a week, revealing the existence of a market that the record companies were not slow to exploit. In Alberta Hunter's words, Mamie Smith had "made it possible for all of us."

If Mamie Smith had never entered a recording studio, if the blues had never been recorded in any form, it would have thrived as a folk music. Mamie's songs were on the very fringe of the blues, half-Vaudeville performances which marked a late stage in the development of the blues from a simple folk music to a form of sophisticated entertainment. When the first "Race records" – those made specifically for black consumption –

1

were issued, the blues had a history of some thirty years and attempts to commit the music to musical notation had been made a decade before. But though the advent of recording was not necessary to the life of the blues, it did mark an important stage in its history for two reasons. In the first place Blacks throughout the United States were now able to hear the voices of blues singers who were not in their immediate field of acquaintance, and in the second place the blues as largely improvised folk music, that often depended on the inspiration of the moment, could now be preserved in permanent form.

Undoubtedly the issue of the records in itself moulded taste, stimulated attempts to sing in similar vein, and in turn increased the demand. But the remarkable sale of the first blues recordings indicated that the demand already existed and that the black populace was anxious to obtain its own music on wax. Examining the situation in the middle twenties, when the recording of black artists was still young, the sociologists Odum and Johnson assessed the combined annual sale of records made by and for Blacks at a figure between five and six million copies. At this time examples of folk blues musicians had scarcely appeared for, contrary to the process of development of the blues, it was the more sophisticated and more easily accessible forms that were first put on disc. As the record companies broadened their activities they found a similar demand in southern country districts and commenced to record rural singers, first bringing them north to the studios, then taking mobile vans to record them nearer home.

By the end of the twenties Vaudeville and tent-show singers, circus artists and barnstormers, medicine-show entertainers and wandering troubadours, street beggars and field hands, folk minstrels with guitars and gin-mill musicians at upright pianos, singers with boogie-woogie pianists, vocalists with washboard, jug and jazz bands were to be heard on record all singing and playing some form of the blues, and outside the phonograph stores Blacks would form in line, anxious to obtain the latest blues discs fresh from the presses. Saloon bars, barber shop parlours, drug stores, cigar stands, and black business establishments of every description sold the records and the companies were advertising for more representatives. Discs could be bought from vendors who sold them from the trunks of automobiles, or through mail-order catalogs of big shipping firms, and Blacks throughout the northern and southern states ground them to grey inaudibility on old Victrolas, heavy-armed table machines and hand-cranked portables. This was their music, the blues of their own race, and families that could ill afford to do so, bought their phonographs and surrendered their seventy-five cents a time for the records. Country "dog-trot" cabins and "shot-gun" houses, edge-of-town taverns and waterfront barrelhouses, red light honky-tonks and hole-in-the-wall cribs, music shops and street corner intersections, crowded tenements and apartment houses alike echoed to the rocking, moaning, hollering, singing of the blues throughout the black world of the United States.

Wider acceptance of the blues came much later and such recognition as it enjoyed was, and for the most part still is, limited to the synthetic "blue" compositions of the Broadway show and the commercial confections of 52nd Street that purported to be blues by the inclusion of the word in the titles. But apart from the blues specialist and the occasional folklorist, interest in authentic blues was confined for many years to the enthusiasts of jazz. In the public mind the imprecise use of the term, not only in the field of popular music but also in dictionary definition, sowed seeds of perplexity as to the nature of the blues. But within the music itself there is room for confusion, for it does not conform to a simple definition. Were the blues a simple folk music local to one area, native to a small social group and tied to a firm tradition of standardized form and instrumentation, as is the case with many forms of folk music in various parts of the world, the identification and appreciation of its peculiar properties would present no undue difficulty. But the blues was sung and played in districts that are literally thousands of miles apart where widely differing social, economic, physical, and climatic conditions prevailed: its distribution might be compared with a purely hypothetical folk music that flourished at once in Copenhagen and in Rome, in London and in Cairo though bonded by language and national unity. It was a music that was common to persons living under the most primitive rural circumstances and in the high pressure of modern city life. It was not the creation of a distinct troubadour group but was as common to the farmer as to the factory worker, to the hobo as to the union entertainer, to the lover as to the murderer. It had an ancestry that extended back into the nineteenth century and, some would contend, into the slavery period (though there is no evidence to support the contention). It continued to thrive during the migratory movements and social advancement of millions of people.

In form the blues eventually determined its unique twelve-bar, three-line pattern, but innumerable variants exist in stanzas of eight, ten, fourteen, sixteen bars amongst many others, while the instrumental and vocal improvisation which is a feature of the blues has proved an effective barrier against standardization. Blues vocals have been sung to the accompaniment of axes and hammers, home-made instruments, guitars and harmonicas, mandolins and banjos, pianos and organs, trumpets, clarinets and saxophones; to the small folk bands and improvising 'traditional'-styled jazz bands, large jazz orchestras, rhythm and blues combinations – and to no accompaniment at all.

Blues singers ranged in style and delivery from those whose voices were coarsely incomprehensible to those who sang in soft, burred, if not dulcet tones; unlike the flamenco singers with whom they are so often loosely compared they varied from the taut to the supremely relaxed, the negligent to the precise. Some murmured, some moaned, some hollered, some declaimed. Some there were who half-spoke their words; others would shout and cry. There were blues singers with deep, rich voices, with guttural, throaty voices; and others whose voices were high-pitched and shrill. And in the field of jazz there have been the purely non-vocal forms of the blues where the means of vocal expression have been transmuted into instrumental terms; where the jazz musician plays the blues. If there is one simple common denominator in all these aspects of the music it is that the blues is a folk form of expression that is by superficial appearances the product of a racial group: the African American in the United States. However, African origins have been so reduced through intermarriage and miscegenation during the centuries that it is doubtful if pure African blood can be found to any great extent in the United States. Cultural features inherited from Africa have been so modified and altered during that passage of time, ousted by compulsory, and later voluntary, absorption of a new culture, that their retentions are conjectural. Yet the apparent fact remains that only the American Black whether purple-black or so light-skinned as to be indistinguishable from his sun-tanned white neighbor, can sing the blues. If there is a conclusion to be drawn from this it is that the blues has grown with the development of black society on American soil; that it has evolved from the peculiar dilemma of a particular group, isolated by skin pigmentation or that of its ancestors, which was required to conform to a society and yet refused its full integration within it. This enforced partial isolation produced, in spite of black desires to be accepted on wholly equal terms within the social pattern of American life, a certain cultural separation which bore fruit in, amongst other things, the blues.

With some speculation on the origins of the blues, which are admittedly obscure, it has been possible to trace its process of evolution and change in a sequence which becomes progressively more clear after the turn of the century. Buried deep in the fertile ground of Revival hymns, spirituals, minstrel songs, banjo and guitar rags, mountain "ballits", folk ballads, work songs and field hollers lie the roots of the blues which began to take form at some indeterminate time in the late nineteenth century. Above all the meandering, interminable hollers, improvised by the field hands of a thousand southern plantations influenced the growth of this extempore song. They were sung by men at work but the blues evolved as a song primarily created by men at leisure, with the time and opportunity to play an instrumental accompaniment to their verses. With fiddle, banjo and most of all, guitar, they were able to add a second, answering voice which amplified the meaning of their own song. In accepting certain restrictions that an instrument imposed they fell back on the simple three-chord harmony – tonic, subdominant, and dominant of the hymnals and ballads. But the shadings, the bendings and the flattenings of notes which had so delighted the field-hand were preserved in the vocal delivery and found instrumental expression in the employment of flatted thirds, dominant seventh chords, and whining notes achieved by sliding the strings, and the use of other unorthodox guitar and piano techniques.

From such beginnings evolved the folk blues, which originally had eight- and sixteen-bar forms related to the spirituals and ballads, but ever more frequently took shape in a pattern of twelve-bar stanzas of three lines each, wherein the first line was repeated, giving the singer an opportunity to extemporize if he so wished, a third, rhyming line. With vocal lines of approximately two bars each the singer was able to play instrumental "breaks" between them that added greatly to the meaning and beauty of his creations. These folk blues of the rural South, strong, untutored but rich in textural variety, moving in expression and frequently accomplished, if unorthodox in their instrumental accompaniments, are often termed the "Country Blues," or the "Southern Blues," though in the different styles recognizable in the work of singers from the Carolinas, from Mississippi, from Georgia, or from Texas they merit more detailed identification.

Sometimes, the early rural blues singers were supported by other instrumentalists, playing stringed instruments in "juke bands" or the home-made instruments of the "jug band" and the "washboard band." These were popular in rural districts of the South but found ready support in the streets of Memphis or New Orleans in which latter city the similar "spasm bands" had more than a little influence on the development of jazz. In the cities and towns – Dallas, Birmingham, Atlanta – folk blues guitarists also worked, begging in the streets or playing in the saloons where "barrelhouse" pianists copied their rhythms and pounded out their versions of the blues. Some singers worked in the medicine shows and the touring carnivals, finding an audience for their blues in the "tank towns" and villages that they visited. In these shows the Vaudeville singers and tent-show burlesque entertainers met the blues singers and absorbed the elements of their folk music. Bringing to it the professional qualities of deliberate artistry they laid the foundations of the "Classic Blues" which bridged the gap between the folk blues and the world of entertainment. Whilst the classic blues singers, of whom the majority were women, brought the blues to the minstrel shows and the black theaters, the "City Blues" singers of the urban centers developed their harder, tougher forms which reflected the different character of their environment. Some were a shade slicker, yet a trifle less relaxed than the country singers and their somewhat more facile playing and singing was "dressed up" through their contact with a more sophisticated world.

From the honky-tonks of New Orleans came the "black butt" pianists who played powerful, aggressive blues in the tough dives of the "wide open" city and the oil towns. The lumber-camps and levee-camps of Texas, Louisiana, and Arkansas yielded the so-called "Fast Western" pianists who sang as they played, in imitation of the southern guitarists, rolling eight-to-the-bar rhythms in the bass, and improvised endless blues variations in the treble. As "boogie woogie," their music found a home in the Chicago of the twenties. During the years of the great black migration they and the country singers who risked the unknown life of the urban North, brought their blues styles to Chicago, Detroit, Cleveland, and New York where the classic blues singers joined forces with those of the New Orleans and mid-western jazz musicians who had also migrated. While the clubs, theaters, and dance halls rang to the blues of the classic singers, the tenements and speakeasies gave a home to the city blues and the rapidly urbanized country blues of the southern-born Blacks.

The years of the Depression did not kill the blues; rather, they gave good reason for singing them. In the South, where conditions scarcely could have been worse, the blues did not change greatly in character; the guitarists still made the strings cry with knife blades and bottle-necks on their fingers as they moaned the blues. But in the North, blues guitarists and pianists combined during the thirties to produce, as conditions improved, the brash, exciting "Urban Blues" of Harlem and Chicago's South Side. Boogie piano, guitar, bass and drums in support of the singer made a frequent combination, often augmented by harmonica and on occasion by saxophone or clarinet. By now the Classic Blues had virtually died: linked with the traditions of Vaudeville and New Orleans-style jazz, it passed with them. Those elements that survived did so in the sophisticated forms of the blues which reached the night clubs and cabarets of Harlem or which were sung by the blues-jazz singers who worked in front of the large orchestras of the late thirties. But the strongly manned, blues-based bands that emanated from Kansas City with their riffing brass and "powerhouse" rhythm sections produced full-throated, deep-lunged "blues shouters" who declaimed their blues above the compelling music. Though World War II put a temporary stop to recording, it did not stop the blues, and when peace came the jumping, small group music of the urban blues groups and the driving, swinging jazz of the big combinations were wedded in the development of "Rhythm and Blues." In the "R. & B. bands," as they were soon to be known, the guitars, basses, even the harmonicas were electrified or amplified, and the post-war spirit was reflected in the optimistic and aggressive music which supported the strong-voiced blues shouters. Boogie pianos and guitars, honking tenors and heavily accented off-beat drumming characterized the post-war music of the city blues, and even in the southern towns and the newly rapidly growing black communities on the West Coast the same music could be heard. But with the popularity of R. & B. on the radio networks came a demand for the southern country blues – now played on electric guitars.

Such might be a summary of the development of the blues to 1960, with all the faults and inaccuracies that so brief a history must inevitably include. Blues, it must be emphasized, is a very individualistic form of music and the arbitary classification of so personal an art must necessarily force singers into categories which do not adequately represent their particular merits, but rather tend to minimize them in the process of fitting them into a general pattern of conformity. But, just as the folk singer is influenced by his environment, and his work is very largely a reflection of it, so too is he a part of his own tradition, and in being so, bears certain elements of similarity with others working in the same idiom. Loose classifications can therefore be made which can justifiably distinguish the country blues singer from Texas or Georgia from the Chicago R. & B. singer or the Kansas City blues shouter. Through the work of them all ran certain qualities of expression that characterized the blues as no other music, though the degree of blues quality tended to diminish as the music inclined to more sophisticated artistry on the one hand, or to the narrative ballad, rag, or other form of black folk song on the other. For this reason the examples quoted in the present work are drawn primarily from the country and urban folk blues. Likewise, as this is not intended to be an historical analysis, few examples have been taken from the work of big band or rhythm and blues singers and jazz-blues vocalists. The omission of many great names is therefore in no way an indication of personal prejudice, nor the inclusion of others an indication of preference. The examples that are quoted are taken from gramophone recordings, for these are the only means whereby most of us can obtain any impression of the work of all but a few blues singers. Without the phonograph record the singing of scores of blues artists of the twenties and thirties would be unknown to us today and it is fortunate that the recording of the blues, if it did commence somewhat late, at least came within the lifetime of what may well have been the first generation of true blues singers.

To what extent the blues examples that are to be heard on record give a truly accurate picture of the whole field of the music is a matter of conjecture. In the almost total absence of any contemporary research in written or noted form let alone on record, the extent to which records illustrate the forms of the music that were prevalent in the first decades of the century cannot be ascertained. That there have been forms of the blues scarcely represented on record or entirely absent, and that some may still exist, seems likely enough, and the dangers of dependence on phonograph recordings are readily apparent. It seems almost indisputable that the field hollers had a major formative influence on the blues, but no examples were to be heard on record during the twenties, and until the late thirties none was committed to wax for public release, and then by the Library of Congress. Certain forms of primitive unaccompanied blues have been recorded only in the post-war years for specialist collections and even these may have undergone a process of change, for the work of singers who have been consistently recorded over a period of perhaps thirty years often shows changes that reflect the altering circumstances of their environment. Similarly, the considerations that determined if a singer ever appeared on disc are innumerable: whether he was in the vicinity when the recording engineers arrived; whether he was interested in being recorded, or like Sonny Boy Williamson No. 2 (Alec Miller), jealous of his material; whether his work appealed to the session supervisors; whether his name reached the talent scouts; whether he had sufficient personal drive to present himself; whether he kept the recording date; and so on. Again, the material that appears on wax, though in the case of the blues remarkably broad in scope and more uncompromising than in almost any other branch of song, still depended to a certain extent upon its possible appeal, and on its acceptability to the recording company.

It is evident that any examination of the blues on record must be made with the foregoing considerations borne in mind. Nevertheless, the gramophone record still remains the basis for any discussion upon the subject, for it is the only means whereby all who are interested can consider the merits of an identical example of the blues. Above all other forms of music, folk song is to be heard rather than read. It scarcely exists in a true sense in written musical notation though folk songs have been noted and adapted by musicians and collectors frequently enough. There are no fundamental standards in the manner of delivery, for this is essentially personal to the folk singer himself who is in no way striving after technical perfection and purity of tone. And of all folk song forms the blues may well be said to be the one which most requires to be heard.

Fortunately, its representation on phonograph recordings is truly remarkable and exceeds that of any other type of folk music. Though some singers are known by a single 78 r.p.m. recording – some in fact by reputation only – the examples of blues by Big Bill Broonzy, Lonnie Johnson, Bumble Bee Slim, and Leroy Carr, to take but four great and admittedly well-featured singers, exceed a thousand titles. The factors that decide why a great singer should only appear for a single recording session may well be bound up in the circumstances of his private affairs and his personality, but there are literally thousands of blues by other singers which merit examination. In view of the abundance of recordings, the paucity of published works on the subject of the blues before the late 1950s is surprising. It is probably true to say that in proportion to the numbers of examples available to the public no folk music has been so neglected and so little documented. If it is true that the blues is to be heard and not written, it is also equally true that the blues eminently deserves to be written about. Though it was fashionable in jazz circles in the 1950s to decry any suggestion that the blues had "significance" under the curious pretext that such a suggestion destroys the spirit of the music, the fact remains that the blues *is* socially significant. Failure to appreciate what the blues is about, failure to comprehend the implications of its content, is failure to appreciate the blues as a whole.

Not that the blues has been entirely neglected: it is customary to include in any anthology of American folk song a selection of blues verses. But the blues has not the traditional sequences of stanzas of the narrative ballad, and seldom chronicles an historical event exterior to the experience of the singer. Consequently, blues verses plucked out of context and entered unexplained in such an anthology have a certain appeal as emotive fragments, but as a whole seem strangely bleak. Only in the histories of jazz does the blues receive closer examination. It is an undeniable fact that, complex though the beginnings of jazz undoubtedly were, in the assimilation of the influences of the marching parade music, of ragtime, the spasm bands, and the popular music of the turn of the century, in its final emergence as a coherent art form the blues played a major part.

Because of the dependence of jazz upon blues – the acceptance of the fact that the blues has proved to be a basic element in every aspect of the music, traditional, mainstream, and modern (to use the current nomenclature) as no other single feature has proved to be – instrumental blues has been studied in some detail. Through the blues have been traced the links of jazz music with earlier black musical traditions of the spirituals, the work songs, and the hollers, and the history of the music itself has received diverse and at times contradictory attention. Nevertheless these studies were clearly made from the standpoint of the jazz enthusiast, historian, and critic. The influence of the blues on jazz was a musical one, eventually to be developed in a purely musical non-vocal form of expression. Though a jazz band sometimes accompanied the blues singer it could just as well play the blues without the singer's presence and in the course of time the importance of the singer became less as the jazz musicians used the blues form instrumentally. Perhaps naturally, if not wholly justifiably, such analyses, though making some incursions into the content of the blues, are primarily concerned with its musical elements and the relationship of the vocal blues to instrumental jazz.

For the majority of collectors the appeal of listening to blues records lay mainly in the appeal of their musical qualities, often quite apart from the meaning of the blues verses themselves. But the music is the vehicle of expression; blues singers did not sing needlessly and song is the medium by which they expressed what they intended to say. To appreciate the music without appreciating the content is to do an injustice to the blues singers and to fail to comprehend the full value of their work. In view of their peculiar social status and the complexities of the racial relations in the United States the world of the blues singers was circumscribed. Their blues had meaning for them and they had ideas to express; it is impossible either to enjoy or to understand the blues to the full through its musical qualities alone.

One may wonder why there was such a market for the blues when the records of Mamie Smith first appeared on the stands. Why did the blues recordings sell in such numbers for so many years? What was it that attracted the purchasers of the blues discs and caused them to spend hard-earned money on the blues as they would on no other art form? It was not for the music alone. It was because the music had meaning not only for the singer but for every African American who listened. In the blues were reflected the

25ᶜ· Oriole Records 25ᶜ·

GENUINE NEGRO RECORDINGS

— IN BIG DEMAND —

8254

RED CROSS BLUES

You're Gonna Need Me

Vocal—Piano

Alabama Sam

Records by
JOSHUA WHITE

8267	Blood Red River / Low Cotton
8268	Jesus Gonna Make Up My Dying Bed / Motherless Children
8240	Double Crossing Women / Crying Blues
8241	Baby Won't You Doodle-Doo-Doo / High Brown Cheater
8139	Bad Depression Blues / Howling Wolf Blues

CURLY WEAVER
and FRED McMULLEN

8253	Birmingham Gambler / Tippin' Tom
8238	Leg Iron Blues / De Kalb Chain Gang
8205	Poor Stranger Blues / Cold Country Blues

OTHER BIG SELLERS

8204	Some Cold Rainy Day / Just Can't Stand It
8243	Where Is My Good Man / Kind Treatment Blues
8159	Lazy Black Snake Blues / Downhearted Man Blues
8184	Black & Evil Blues / Little Brother Blues
8228	Mama's Doughnut / Make It Tight
8167	New Strangers Blues / Georgia Hound Blues
8206	No No Blues / Early Morning Blues
8205	Poor Stranger Blues / Cold Country Blues

BESSIE JACKSON
The Greatest Blues Singer
of the South

THE LATEST HITS

8258	SEABOARD BLUES / TROUBLED MIND
8263	HOUSE TOP BLUES / T N & O BLUES
8122	SLOPPY DRUNK BLUES / ALLEY BOOGIE

A GREAT RECORD
8257

EARLY THIS MORNING
('Bout Break Of Day)
HOUSE LADY BLUES
Vocal—Piano   Walter Roland

SACRED

8220	This Wicked Race / Some Day
8191	When The Saints Go Marching In / Who Is That Knocking?
8135	Everytime I Feel The Spirit / Shine On Me
8098	This Train / I Want To Be Ready

— THE LATEST —

8262

HIGHWAY No. 61 BLUES

Red Ripe Tomatoes

Vocal—Piano

Jack Kelly and So. Memphis Jug Band

Records by
BUDDY MOSS

8252	Bye Bye Mama / Jealous Hearted Man
8223	T B's Killing Me / Hard Times Blues
8207	When I'm Dead And Gone / Prowling Woman

BIG BILL

8190	Bull Cow Blues / Too-Too Train Blues
8197	Rukus Juice Blues / Shelby County Blues
8168	Worrying You Off My Mind No. 1 / Worrying You Off My Mind No. 2

OTHER BIG SELLERS

8266	President Blues / R.F.C. Blues
8244	Dead Cats On The Line / Reckless Man Blues
8245	You Can't Get That Stuff No More / Don't Leave Me Here
8242	Fishin' Blues / Outdoor Blues
8119	You're Going To Leave The Old Home Jim / Careless Love Blues
8138	How You Want It Done? / M & O Blues
8206	I'm Still Sloppy Drunk / Man Of My Own
8165	I'm Talkin' 'Bout You No. 1 / I'm Talkin' 'Bout You No. 2
8200	Deserted Man Blues / Motherless Boy

HOT DANCE

2754	Learn To Croon / I Cover The Waterfront
2755	Lazybones / Mississippi Basin
8229	Jockey Stomp / Stomp That Thing

➤ See Other Side For Old Time Tunes ◆

effects of the economic stress on the depleted plantations and the urban centres, where conditions of living still did not improve. In the blues were to be found the major catastrophes both personal and national, the triumphs and miseries that were shared by all, yet private to one. In the blues were reflected the family disputes, the violence and bitterness, the tears and the upheavals caused by poverty and migration. In the blues an unsettled, unwanted people during these periods of social unrest found the security, the unity, and the strength it so desperately desired.

The blues did not reflect the whole of black life in the United States, and a social study of black problems does not explain the blues. But in order to understand the blues singers it is necessary to explore the background of their themes, and to try to enter their world through them, distant and unapproachable though it may be.

1   *Got to work or leave*

For one reason alone are Blacks to be found on the American Continent: the enslavement of their ancestors. Their labor in bondage accounts for their presence, no matter what place in society they hold today. Over a period of three centuries men and women in their millions were torn from their African homeland, chained, shipped, sold, branded, and forced into a life of toil that only ceased when death froze their limbs. Their children worked in the fields from the day when they could lift a hoe to the day when they dropped between the shafts of the plow. Brutal planters there were, and humane ones too. Some Blacks were given their freedom, some managed to buy theirs and even that of their womenfolk; some gained positions in the households as personal servants, some became skilled artisans and craftsmen. But it was the great multitude of common laborers, uneducated, unskilled, deliberately kept in ignorance and held in perpetual, unrelenting bondage on whom the South relied. On the results of their sweat and toil depended its economy.

With the end of the Civil War came the "Day of Jubilo," the Liberation, but many slaves failed to grasp its meaning. There were tears on both sides, from the eyes of both slave and owner on many a plantation when the promised freedom came. Uncertain groups of Blacks stood in the gateways not knowing what to do. Some begged to be taken back, some stumbled off along the highways until hunger and helplessness forced them to return, whilst others walked on till they starved by the wayside. In the terrible years of the "carpet-bagger" administration many former slaves were given unfamiliar power under the sometimes unscrupulous direction of northern adventurer politicians. The South, both black and white, suffered, and the good that the many able and educated black legislators did for the country did not afford a sufficient salve for the wounds that were borne. With the Reconstruction, Blacks who were tilling the farms that they had been given when the plantations were abandoned, found themselves driven away as these were returned to former Confederates or claimed by the railroads. Ruthlessly and systematically the embittered Southerners deprived the black population of its Civil Rights, in open defiance of the Fourteenth Amendment and, embarking upon a succession of legal measures that enforced "Jim Crow" laws of segregation in every aspect of life, effectively disenfranchised them. On the plantations that were being re-established field hands found that they were again working under conditions of virtual slavery and that the share-cropping system, which had seemed a just method of dividing the labor amongst families employed by one owner, had become an iniquitous method of holding people in bondage. It was to persist in much of the South for nearly eighty years. Far from any legal constraints many plantation bosses were a law unto themselves, as Bessie Tucker, a Texas singer with one of the most dolorous voices in the blues, indicated on *Mean Old Master*, recorded in Dallas in 1929.

2 Our boss man may come here – we did not run, *(twice)*
   Oh master got a pistol, he have a great big gun.

   Master, Master aah-ah, please turn me a-loose, *(twice)*
   I ain't got no money; I got a good excuse.

Reconstruction brought new work in different spheres for those who had kept on walking when they stepped from the plantation gates to freedom, though it was work of the most strenuous kind. Railroads that had been destroyed were rebuilt and new ones constructed; the river levees were repaired and graded and the expansion of trade on river and railroad gave work to roustabouts and stevedores. Mines were opened, saw-mills built, and they attracted the black laborers who were being squeezed out of other occupations by the continual flow of immigrants from Europe and the closing ranks of segregated unions.

The last quarter of the nineteenth century saw an ever-increasing movement of black workers from state to state. By 1910 nearly one and three-quarter million had left their home states for others and of these some had moved West and half a million had gone to the North. As the pressure of hostile opinion and legislation became ever greater, they sought new employment and traveled long distances in order to find it. In the ensuing years they were to be followed by thousands more. Ramblin' Thomas, a blues singer from Texas, recorded one of the earliest blues to be collected in the field, one that reflects those times.

3 I was down in Louisiana doin' as I please
   Now I'm in Texas I got to work or leave.
      Poor boy, poor boy, poor boy long ways from home.*

* Here and in subsequent lyrics, a refrain is indicated by indentation.

"If your home is in Louisiana, what you doin' over here?"
"And my home ain't in Texas and I sure don't care."
Poor boy, [etc.]

I don't care if the boat don't never land,
I'd like to stay on water as long as any man,
Poor boy, [etc.]

When my boat comes a rockin' just like a drunken man,
Says my home's on the water and I sure don't like land,
Poor boy, [etc.]

Tied in permanent debt to the planters on whose lands they were share-croppers or tenants, a vast number of Blacks were still forced to remain, for the share-cropping system was flourishing in the twenties and was still in operation in the 1960s. A black farmer – or "poor White" – let his labor and that of his wife and family in return for "furnishings" of food and equipment, plow and mules and a percentage of the proceeds of the crop that he produced. These were hired to him on credit at the beginning of the year and were paid off when the crop had been gathered and "ginned," or compressed and cleaned of oil and foreign matter. The "cropper's" share seldom represented more than a fraction of the sum that his crop could realize, and when he had paid for the rent of his farm buildings and for the food that he had received, he generally found himself in debt to the landowner. To meet this debt he had to pay in labor and as the years passed he found himself more and more firmly enslaved to the "Boss man." He secretly called the white man Mister Tom, Mister Charlie, or Mister Eddie and tried to convince himself that he "gets along" and would one day earn enough to free himself and seek work elsewhere. In his broken, incoherent, but profoundly moving voice, Sleepy John Estes claimed ironically that "Mister Tom's all right with me" whilst he outlined the injustices of his situation in Brown' – Brownsville, Tennessee:

4   Tom is good, some say mean,
    Hauling his cotton, if he ain't got no team,

        Now tell me how's about it? Yes, tell me how's about it?
        Tell me how's about it, Mister Tom's all right with me.

    Tom ain't so tall, know he's kinda low,
    Everybody in Brown' say he got him plenty of dough.

He rides over his fields, givin' his hands a rule,
Ask him for a li'l money he says, "Boy, shed a mule."

Tom lives in the country, Mis' Robert live in town,
Soon every morn' Mis' Robert' hit that black lyin' down,

    Now tell me how's about it? Yes, tell me how's about it?
    Tell me how's about it, Mister Tom's all right with me.

In his "dog-trot" cabin with its crumbling foundations, leaking walls and wind-swept corridor dividing the rooms, the share-cropper raised as large a family as he was able, sometimes marrying a widow and taking her children into his home. For children meant labor: labor to dig, to plow, to hoe; labor to chop cotton, to "buck-jump" or weed cotton, to pick cotton. The plow-hand dreamt that one day he might break free, and vowed that he would no longer plow and hoe. But when the winter threatened he found himself once more in a harness as real as that which held his mules, as Big Bill Broonzy recalled.

5   I was a plow-hand for forty years, I swore I would never plow no
      more, (*twice*)
  Now I'm a married man now, oh Lord there ain't no more so and so.

  I'm going back to my plow, now a woman is the cause of it all, (*twice*)
  Now she said "If you don't raise no cotton, oh Lord, Bill we'll earn no
      money in the fall."

  "Farming is all right, little girl if you knows just what to do, (*twice*)
  'Cause it killed my old grandpap, oh Lord, I declare I'm going to make
      it kill me too."

  Every night, I'm calling John, Jake an' Pat. (Sing it boy, sing it.) (*twice*)
  Now I had a dream last night, oh Lord, there was a mule was in my
      hat.

The money he realized from his crop barely kept him and his family alive through the year. In theory the cropper received half of what he produced from the sales prices, but as the field hands so often sang:

  Ought's a ought, figger's a figger
  All for the white man, none for the nigger.

For those who "cain't read, cain't write" there was little protection against ruthless exploitation, and their rights were less than those of a peasant working under the conditions of medieval feudalism. A sharecropper was powerless to dispute the reckoning when the scales weighed against him and he had no means of legislation against the system that kept him in serfdom. His farming methods were not of the best, for he had to try to get the largest crop he could, and rotation farming meant a year or two of starvation. Thus even the most fertile lands could have farms of exceptionally low standard; the rain corrugated the land and washed away the top soil on the slopes, and the undernourished land was starved for fertilizer that the cropper could not afford. In the principal states producing cotton in 1930 there were a million and a half share-croppers working under the system and of some 225,000 tenant families in Mississippi at that time – of whom more than seventy per cent were black – over 135,000 were in the lowest economic category.

It was a little insect barely a quarter of an inch long that set the seal on the destruction of the South's cotton economy. In 1862 the boll-weevil was observed in the cotton fields of Mexico, and thirty years later it was ravishing the plantations of Texas. Within a few years it was to be found throughout the entire South where the warm, humid conditions were perfect for its propagation. Attacking the cotton bolls where the weevil laid its eggs, the grubs reduced them to empty shells and the dismayed planters and field hands alike were powerless to prevent the pest. Thousands of black share-croppers were thrown out of work, but not out of debt, as the weevil destroyed their crops. They composed a ballad about the indestructible insect, even paradoxically found some sympathy for it as they saw their own unbreakable spirit symbolized in its invincibility. Years later, in the particularly bad years of the mid-twenties, the ballad became a blues and the cotton worker would sing as did Kokomo Arnold from Georgia:

6   Boll-Weevil, Boll-Weevil come out of my flour barrel, (*twice*)
     Says there's the boll-weevil here mama, boll-weevil everywhere.

     Says I went to my captain, and I asked him for a peck of meal (*twice*)
     He said, "Leave here Kokomo, you got boll-weevils in yo' field'."

     Now Mister Weevil, how come your bill's so long? (*twice*)
     Done eat up all my cotton, started on my youngest corn.

Bo-Weavil Blues

No 7191

7.191

BO-WEAVIL BLUES and LET YOUR MONEY
TALK—Vocal-Guitar Acc. Kokomo Arnold ..59c

*"Don't you know you done me wrong,
Eat up all my corn; eat up all my corn"*

ARNULFO L. OLIVEIRA MEMORIAL LIBRARY
1825 MAY STREET
BROWNSVILLE, TEXAS 78520

Says the merchant to the doctor, "Don't sell no mo' C.C. Pills *(twice)*
'Cause the boll-weevil down here in Georgia done stopped all these
cotton mills."

Now Mister Boll-Weevil, if you can talk why don't you tell? *(twice)*
Say, you got poor Kokomo down here in Georgia catchin' a lot of hell.

A number of the larger plantations managed to survive the ravages of the
boll-weevil and continued to produce cotton on the old system of share-
cropping. Amongst the largest of these was that owned by the Delta and
Pine Land Company – a British Syndicate of mill-owners, the Fine
Spinners' Association of Manchester, whose 3,300 croppers in a thousand
families were earning in the late thirties an average of $525 a season, two-
thirds of which being expended on credit furnishings. Centered on Scott,
Mississippi, it was still, in the 1950s, the largest plantation in the South and
though attempts were made at social reforms it maintained its share-
cropping system.

When the recording of blues commenced, the cotton-boll economy of
the South had already virtually collapsed. Many of the small plantations
were forced to change their crop as the weevil, in the space of thirty years,
brought waste and destruction to every part of the cotton belt. A severe
drought in the summer of 1930 effectively eliminated the boll-weevil, but it
also damaged other crops. In the words of Son House from Mississippi, it
"put everybody on the killing floor."

7   Now the people down south soon will have no home, *(twice)*
    'Cause this dry spell has parched all their cotton and corn.

    Pork chops forty cents a pound, cotton is only ten, *(twice)*
    I don't keep no women – no, no, not one of them.

    So dry, old boll weevil turn up his toes and die, *(twice)*
    Now ain't nothin' to do – bootleg moonshine and rye.

Other districts further to the south-west demonstrated that they could
effectively produce cotton, and mechanization began to replace the manual
labour of the black cotton-worker. Though it was still grown in considerable quantities in the South many planters had turned to "goober peas" –
ground nuts – and to the eye crops – black-eyed peas and potatoes – for their

source of income. For many Blacks this meant a change of work but no change of status, for they were still in virtual bondage, whilst others working on tenant farms had to face penury and the competition of the dispossessed.

Lack of incentives, lack of opportunity, lack of hope could dispirit a man until he no longer wished to live or to work and so he might resort to protest that manifested itself in deliberate idleness. Knowing that he could not benefit from his labors, he was determined that no one else should do so either. Sang a Florida worker, Gabriel Brown:

8   Now I started at the bottom, and I stayed right there,
  Don't seem like I'm gonna get nowhere.

    Now I'm gonna take it easy, I'm gonna take it easy,
    I'm gonna take it easy, babe, that's what I'm gonna do.

  You can have a old job, maybe it's hard or soft,
  You try to save something and they lay you off,

  Now what your bosses are doing you can never tell,
  They's always trying to cut the personnel,

  I've got myself together, made my mind up now,
  I won't have a doggone thing nohow.

Powerless to act in open hostility the field hand resorts to more cunning methods, such as that mentioned by Big Bill Broonzy in his *Plough Hand Blues* when he declared that he was "always setting my back-band back, oh Lord, to prevent my little plow from going too deep." Such methods only spite the perpetrator, who does no one as much harm as he does to himself. So many a field-hand finally resigned himself to being "a steady-rolling man," and by working himself unstintingly throughout the year, and finding other occupations during the lay-off periods, eventually saved sufficient money to purchase his own mule and equipment and rose fractionally up the scale to the status of tenant-farmer.

Tenant-farmers had a small degree of independence in that they owned their equipment and livestock and therefore had less to hire from the plantation, or the company. Some might eventually gain complete freedom and, if they were fortunate, bought their own land, but the odds were heavily against a tenant-farmer becoming prosperous. He still had to sell his crop in the open market and was subject to discrimination that could force him to sell at a ridiculously low price. At the mercy of the weather, his livestock, and the efficiency of his tools, when the crops "gave out" he, his family, and his livestock suffered. Ernest Blunt, the "Florida Kid," summed up their dilemma.

> 9   Well, I'm a poor farmer, what am I gonna do? (*twice*)
>   When my corn done give out, whoo, I take a load on my mule.
>
>   Well my mule was named Jim, he was too lazy to wag his tail, (*twice*)
>   Police told me if I hit that mule again, well they would put me in jail.
>
>   Well that mule's back was sharp as a razor, 'cause he sure couldn't get
>   no corn, (*twice*)
>   When the middle of my face gets hairy, takes a shave off his back bone.
>
>   Well that old mule he sat down, like he had heard what the police said,
>   Eh-eeh-hoo, Lord, like he had heard what the police said,
>   That mule looked back at me and smiled, bucked his head and crossed
>   his legs.
>
>   I don't blame my old mule and neither could nobody else, (*twice*)
>   Because every time he would wiggle, woo Lord, I said I'm hauling
>   myself, – yes, to hauling myself.

Both share-cropper and tenant-farmer had to "stay in good" with their white landlords and no southern rural black worker dared raise his voice aloud in protest or assert his rights when he was the victim of racial discrimination. So he maintained an air of happy indolence, played up to the stereotypes that traditional jokes had molded for him, hid his sufferings, and struggled to survive. Blues singer Jimmy Gordon spoke for many when he sang:

> 10   Well I drink to keep from worrying and I laugh to keep from crying,
>   (*twice*)
>   I keep a smile on my face so the public won't know my mind.
>
>   Some people thinks I'm happy but they sure don't know my mind,
>   (*twice*)
>   They see this smile on my face, but my heart is bleeding all the time.

Frustrated and disillusioned by the conditions of work and the poor rewards for his labors, discouraged by discriminatory practices that lowered his receipts or threatened to put him out of work altogether, the farm-hand sought work elsewhere, hoping to find employment in a different district that would enable him to save sufficient to bring his family. Walter Davis moved to St. Louis from the South.

11 If I mistreat you, babe, I don't mean you no harm (*twice*)
  I'm just a little country boy, right out of the cotton farm.

  I'm just from the country, never been in your town before, (*twice*)
  Lord, I'm broke and hungry, ain't got no place to go.

  I was raised in the country, I been there all my life, (*twice*)
  Lord, I had to run off and leave my children and my wife.

Eventually many would find work on "the jobs." However fierce the competition was from white workers, from immigrants, and "poor buckra" – whites of the lowest economic class – there were certain occupations that were – in the superbly ironic euphemism currently employed – "protected" for Blacks. These were known simply as "the jobs" and their nature was such that none but the poorest white men were employed in them. The conditions of work were usually so appalling, so injurious to health, to life and limb that only the most underprivileged classes were to be found undertaking the tasks. Amongst these were the turpentine workers who "guttered" the slash pines with their knives, collected the resin and pressed and distilled the turpentine. Working often in unbearable heat and using material which was dangerous to health, they lived in camps under the crudest of conditions, fenced in by barbed wire and suffering miserable privations. Calling themselves Pigmeat Pete and Cat-juice Charlie, two entertainers brought many wry smiles when they sang in mock-contented tones:

12 The horse we had done seen his best,
  Walk four blocks and he sit down to rest,
  Sit down one day in some turpentine,
  Now the poor horse he done lost his mind,
    On our turpentine farm, umm-hmmm
    On our turpentine farm,
    Where the work ain't hard and the weather is warm.

Our boss man is a lazy hound,
Chew his tobacco, spits on the ground,
Smokes his pipe and he lays in the shade
Laziest man that ever was made.
        On our turpentine farm, [etc.]

From the turpentine-camps the migrant workers would move on to the logging-camps, where, however, conditions were very little better. Whereas three-quarters of the entire personnel employed by the turpentine industry were black, they represented in 1930 only some thirteen percent of the labor force in forestry throughout the country. In the South alone, however, they formed the majority of the workers employed. The logging companies had paid the lowest wages possible, restricting the workers to a forty-hour week and paying them from twenty-three to forty cents per hour. "Dummy lines" which could be easily lifted and relaid connected some of the remotely placed logging-camps with the main railroad lines, but the men were confined to their shack and tent townships and bought all their requisites from the company stores. And from the exploitation of loggers and public alike the Weyerhauser syndicate massed its hundreds of millions of dollars in profits. Though logging topped the list in industrial fatalities relative to the man-hours worked, the black lumberman sang of the "rainbow round ma shoulder" as his diamond-blade axe flashed in the sunlight. In the extreme South the loggers faced each other in their "pirogues" – their dug-out canoes – and without rocking their clumsy boats expertly felled the cypresses with their singing cross-cut saws.

Meanwhile, in thigh-boots and rubber coat the mule-skinner endured the suffocating heat and the sweet stench of rotting wood whilst he fought off the attacks of the mosquitoes, "gallynippers" that plagued him in his "shanty" home and wherever he went. "Mosquitoes worry me so," sang Blind Lemon Jefferson, "I cain't hardly stay on my feet."

13   I bought a spray last night 'n I sprayed all over my house, (*twice*)
     Mosquitoes all around my door won't let nobody come out.

     Mosquitoes all around me, mosquitoes everywhere I go, (*twice*)
     No matter where I go, they sticks their bills in me.

     I would say gallynipper, these gallynippers bites too hard, (*twice*)
     I stepped back in my kitchen and they springing up in my back yard.

Through the slime of the swamps in the river bottoms the mule-skinner urged his mule, drawing the "skiff" on which the logs were carried to the river. When the water was deep he floated his skiff, when it was shallow he dragged it behind him. Other mule-skinners pulled the logs that the "chokerman" hitched with a wire noose behind the mule; it was a brutalized life with the considerable and ever-present danger of being crushed by rolling timber, of sinking to a gruesome death in the swamps, of mutilation or even of murder at the hands of one of the loggers. But as he drove his mule to the levee he would sing a blues, as did Leadbelly – Huddie Ledbetter:

> 14 This man is a long way from home, an' he's got a brownskin woman,
> An' he knows pay-day's comin' pretty soon,
> An' the ole woman's shoutin' for some mo' pay-day.
> An' the ole mule is hongry and the sun is going down,
> An' the man wishes that pay-day would move off a little further
> So he wouldn't have to pay the woman nothin'.
> I'm goin' t' tell ma woman like the – Dago told the Jew,
> You don' wan' me, and honey I don' wan' you.

On the levee the overseers worked the women as they worked the men – tough women who could handle the mule teams and who fought with knives and single-trees (poles to which a harness was attached). Life was cheap, or at least the lives of men; the lives of the mules were more greatly prized. Murder could be committed with little fear of legal retribution – if the victim was black and if he was not a "rolling man," an exceptionally strong worker. Yet the levee-graders took pride in the hard lives that they led. As in the past the roustabouts boasted of the weals that scarred their backs and the punishments meted by the "mean mates" who handled the river men, so the levee-workers relished the stories of their more vicious captains. As the loading crewsmen boasted of the weights they could carry up the swaying gang-planks of the stern-wheelers – it was reckoned that one man could carry what two of the raising crew could lift on to his back – so too, the mule-skinners would vie with each other in their skill with skiffs and bull-whips, as Leadbelly implied in the same holler.

> 15 The women on the levee, honey, holler, "Whoa," "Haw," "Gee!"
> The man on the levee holler, "Don't you murder me,
> Please baby, please baby, please baby, please baby."
> "Honey! I'm a long way from home.

Honey! I'm down in the bottoms, skinnin' for Johnny Ryan,
Puttin' my initials, honey, on the mule's behind
With my line babe, with my line babe, with my line babe . . ."

From way up the Ohio, on the Mississippi and many a tributary to the Brazos Bottoms the work of laying the giant mattresses and building the artificial banks that held back the flood waters was continuous. The work commenced in the eighteenth century, and by 1828 the levees extended from the Delta to the Red River. During the Civil War they were damaged or neglected and the disastrous flood of 1874 proved their ineffectiveness. The Government made a grant of $5,000,000 towards the repair of levees improving navigation, though not for the protection of the land, and the Blacks whose homes were threatened cut the willow canes, wove the hurdles and constructed the mud walls, establishing a traditional source of work for the migrant laborers. The loaders filled the skiffs with clay and rubble; the skinners brought the carts to the levee where the dumper unloaded them for the graders' use. Levee contractors hired the laborers whose work was supervised by a "straw boss" or "walking boss." A Texas singer, Gene Campbell, hinted at the injustices of the system in a 1930 recording.

16   These contractors they are getting so slack, (*twice*)
They'll pay you half of your money and hold the other half back.

There ain't but two men that get paid off, (*twice*)
That's the commissary clerk and the walkin' boss.

I see somebody comin' down to the water trough, (*twice*)
I know it ain't the contractor, it's that dog-gone walkin' boss.

A levee camp mule and a levee camp man, (*twice*)
They works side by side, and it sure is man to a man.

A levee camp man ain't got but two legs you know, (*twice*)
But he puts in the same hours that a mule do on four.

Men on the levee hollerin' "Whoa," "Haw," "Gee," (*twice*)
And the women on the levee camp hollerin' "Who wants me?"

The system operated in such labor camps was not greatly dissimilar to that which bound the share-cropper, for the "fixin's" or "furnishings" were deducted by the companies from the total pay and the balance, if there was any, was paid to the worker at the end of the week. If he found himself in "debt" he would leave. No one would follow him, for there were men waiting in line to be taken on, as there were at the railroad camps, the road camps, and the rock and gravel camps. Similar in character, erected from temporary shacks, railroad wagons or tents, the camps housed the men who dug gravel, quarried and pounded the hard rock, and built up the highways and gradients from the rubble. Conditions of labor seldom varied; the men were worked "from sun to sun" – from daybreak to sunset – expecting, and receiving, harsh treatment if they failed in their tasks, and little commendation when they worked well. In a voice so rough, strong, and wild that his pronunciation is scarcely comprehensible one such worker recorded in Atlanta – Lewis Black – told of catching a fast train on the Chicago, Burlington, and Quincy line, the C. B and Q, and going in search of work.

17 Goin' out on the "Q,"
Says I'm goin' away now mama, goin' out on the "Q,"
An' if I find anythin', comin' back after you.

Mmmm – mm goin' out on the C. B. and Q (*twice*)
If I find anything gal, comin' back after you.

Soon one mornin', I heard a panther squall (*twice*)
Say your mama caught the local, you catch the Cannonball.

I caught on behin',
Say my mama caught the local, I caught on behin',
Say you can't leave me, t'ain't no need a-cryin'.

When I leave from here, goin' out on the "O" (*twice*)
If I don't find no log camp, I'll find a gravel camp, sure.

Mmmm-mmm, what's the matter here? (*twice*)
Ain't nothin' goin' on wrong, but mama I don't care.

The belief that the black worker was a brute animal more capable of standing such grueling work provided that it did not require mental effort was a legacy of the slavery period. Curiously it found some support from Blacks also who accepted the belief and found in it a source of racial pride, drawing satisfaction from the conviction that they could undertake work from which the white "crackers," their economic equivalent, were debarred by physical weakness. Some realized that the perpetuation of the fallacy kept them in perpetual servitude; that the work might break them, but that they would never break the work. Taking a lesson from the ballad of the self-destruction of John Henry which had been an incentive to work for innumerable steel-drivers and spike-drivers on the southern railroads, Mississippi John Hurt sang the blues of a spike-driver who has worked himself to breaking point:

18   Take this hammer an' carry it to the captain, tell him I'm gone,
      Tell him I'm gone, you can tell him I'm gone.
      Take this hammer an' carry it to the captain, an' tell him I'm gone,
      Jes' tell him I'm gone, I'm sure is goin'.

      This is the hammer that killed John Henry, but it won't kill me,
      But it won't kill me, but it won't kill me.
      This is the hammer that killed John Henry, but it won't kill me,
      But it won't kill me, ain't gonna kill me.

      John Henry's a steel-drivin' boy, but he went down,
      But he went down, but he went down;
      John Henry's a steel-drivin' boy, but he went down,
      But he went down, that's why I'm gone.

There were other jobs to which a southern black worker could go with a reasonable chance of securing work: the tobacco and fertilizer plants, the cement factories, and the saw-mills. In all of these the dust hung thick and heavy, and in the majority extractors were not a part of the fixtures. The owners were in the business for the purpose of making money and dust extractors were a needless expenditure when workers could be obtained who were prepared to suffer the inhalation of the injurious particles, and in the instances of the tobacco and fertilizer plants especially, the sickening odors that made the senses reel. But many a black worker accepted the conditions along with the regular pay-check, as "Pleasant Joe" from Louisiana declared.

19   I didn't build this world, but I sure can tear it down, (*twice*)
      An' when I'm on my job, mama, I don't want no man hangin' around.

      Yes I'm workin' on the saw-mill, sleepin' in a shack 'bout six feet wide
      (*twice*)
      I see my new gal every pay-day and I'm perfectly satisfied.

Whilst the loggers worked and the "short dog" trains on the "dummy lines" took them deeper into the woods, the process of felling and shipping timber to the saw-mills continued, but the avarice of the landowners often caused them to destroy timber at a rate far in excess of any attempts at reforestation. By 1933 there were eighty-three million acres of timberlands laid waste, leaving hills gullied and dry, infertile and scarred by the ugly wounds where trees had been uprooted or felled without thought of restocking. A further two hundred million acres were dangerously deteriorating, and in the ensuing years vast areas were irrevocably lost to future cultivation. When the logging company or the railroad had reduced the country to the "stump lands" the temporary lines were shifted, the landings in the bottoms fell into decay, and the saw-mills closed down leaving its workers with no employment.

> 20   I was lyin' in bed this mawnin', an' heard the mill whistle blow like it
>   was cryin'. (twice)
>   Ole saw-mill has cut all that timber, ain't no mo' work for that man of
>   mine,

sang Elzadie Robinson, who was also from Louisiana.

Industrialization came slowly to the South. The insecurity of southern rural economy which was so markedly to his disadvantage caused many a black worker to move from the country areas and gravitate to the towns and industrial centers where wages were better and more stable. From the North came reports of good prospects and better opportunities of obtaining employment, and by 1910 there was a steady stream of migrating colored men moving from state to state with the northern cities as their ultimate goal. In the steel factories many of the jobs were restricted, but the "open-hearth" sections offered ready employment for Blacks; few others would work under the almost insufferable heat from the furnaces. Field-hands weighed their chances against the disadvantages of severing themselves from their homes; the mills of Bessemer and Gary called and, like Charles Pertum, they were gone.

> 21   To-day, mama, to-day – to-morrow – I might be 'way, (twice)
>   Going back to Gary, that's where I intend to stay.
>
>   Not o'clock in the mornin', mama, not o'clock in the afternoon, (twice)
>   When I leave for Gary, some good man can have my room.

"ARKANSAS MILL BLUES"

by
Elzadie Robinson

"WHEN I hear that whistle blow, there'll be no more work for that man of mine," sings Elzadie Robinson in "Arkansas Mill Blues". The old pond dries up, the last steam blows the whistle, and everybody moves on to a new place. There's a lot of real good stuff in this Paramount Record No. 12701 (Will Ezell tickles the ivories for a mean piano accompaniment). Ask your dealer for it, or send us the coupon.

[12701—**Arkansas Mill Blues** and **Gold Mansion Blues**, Elzadie Robinson. Will Ezell at the piano.]

> Shine on harvest moon, harvest moon shine on, (*twice*)
> For you will be shinin' after the days I'm gone.

Work in the steel-mills was tough, demanding precision timing, great physical strength and considerable powers of endurance. Southern Blacks were used to strenuous work but employment in a semi-skilled capacity precluded many who had been used only to heavy menial, unskilled labor. The mills wanted men, and those who applied were eager enough to learn. Soon there were more Blacks employed in semi-skilled work than there had ever been before. But the hardening effect of the mills on both the men and their women was implicit in a blues by a singer whose chosen nickname of "Six-Cylinder" Smith revealed his pride in his own strength and sexual prowess.

> 22   Working in the steel-mills baby, handling red hot steel, (*twice*)
> Pennsylvania women think that old men cannot do.
>
> I think I heard that steel-mill whistle blow, (*twice*)
> She blowed just like she ain't gonna blow no more.

I'm goin away baby, won't be back at all, (*twice*)
If I win any money, won't be back at all.

Pennsylvania women got hearts like solid stone, (*twice*)
For they're so dog-gone evil, break up every woman's home.

The prestige attached to working in the mills, as indicated in a blues by Peetie Wheatstraw, was an effective if minor adjunct to the recruiting drive, and the representatives of the mill-owners exploited this as much as the more obvious inducement of financial gain, in order to draw conservative spirits from the South.

23 I used to have a woman that lived up on the hill, (*twice*)
She was crazy 'bout me, ooh well, well, 'cause I worked at the Chicago mill.

You can hear the women hollerin' when the Chicago mill whistle blows, (*twice*)
Cryin', "Turn loose my man, ooh well, well, please and let him go."

If you want to have plenty women, boys work at the Chicago mill, (*twice*)
You don't have to give them nothin', ooh well, jest tell them that you will.

In 1914 the continual flow of immigrants from Europe to the United States ceased and the northern industrialists, whose work was expanding with the demands of impending war, required cheap labor in quantity. Restricted immigration still operated in the 1960s, but by then it had no major influence on the national economy; during the years of World War I when the stream of European unskilled laborers was halted there was an acute labor shortage in the industrial North. Recruitment officers were sent South to draw workers from the plantations, and special freight cars were chartered to bring them to the North. Many of the labor officers were literally tarred and feathered or expelled from southern towns and villages at the point of a gun, and Blacks who left the plantations were forced back by county sheriffs who implemented hastily drawn laws designed to stem the tide of migrant colored workers. The extreme was reached in Macon, Georgia, where a labor agent was required to pay a license fee of $25,000 to operate, and only then if he had the recommendations of twenty-five businessmen, ten ministers, and ten manufacturers of goods. Elsewhere, heavy fees were demanded and operating agents were put into jail. Though they were often technically in debt through the perniciousness of share-cropping, countless numbers of Blacks left the country farms that had been their whole world for their entire lives and, having little or no conception of northern urban life, prepared to face the risks involved in the hopes of a better future.

The cessation of the influx of European immigrants coincided with Henry Ford's pronouncement, in 1914, that none of his workers would earn less than five dollars per day, and it was in that year also that he commenced to employ Blacks on his assembly lines. As his huge plants in Detroit continued to expand and more workers were taken on, the news reached the remotest corners of the South and attracted men who had been living in penury. Blind Blake, who followed them, sang on their behalf.

24   I'm goin' to Detroit, get myself a good job, (*twice*)
        Tried to stay around here with the starvation mob.

I'm goin' to get a job, up there in Mr. Ford's place, (*twice*)
Stop these eatless days from starin' me in the face.

When I start to makin' money, she don't need to come around, (*twice*)
'Cause I don't want her now, Lord, I'm Detroit bound.

Because they got wild women in Detroit, that's all I want to see, (*twice*)
Wild women and bad whisky would make a fool out of me.

The pictures that the recruiting men painted were bright and colorful, and to many a southern Black with his limited experience and his folk ways, the prospect of work in the North was infinitely attractive. If he questioned the employers' motives or stopped to consider what his ultimate destiny might be, he was too familiar with poverty and exploitation to let the thoughts deter him long. Ford, it is alleged, with a long and distasteful history of anti-Semitism in his industrial dealings, had his reasons for employing black workers. He put considerable sums of money in the black "Urban League," paid good wages to his southern employees, and used them to block the organization of labor unions within his firm. As the unions gained strength he employed more Blacks, but few were aware of these motives, though Bob Campbell's woman clearly suspected them.

25   I'm goin' to Detroit, build myself a job,
      Say, I'm goin' to Detroit, I'm gonna get myself a job.
      I'm tired of layin' around here workin' on the starvation farm.

      Say, I'm goin' down there and get me a job now, working in Mr.
          Ford's place, (*twice*)
      Say, that woman tol' me last night, that "you cannot even stand Mr.
          Ford's ways."

      Say I know my dog, baby when I hear him bark, (*twice*)
      And I know my woman if I feel her in the dark.

      Say, you better stop your woman from smilin' in my face (*twice*)
      Woman, if you keep on a-smilin' I'm sure gonna take your place.

In his latter verses Campbell expressed his distrust by analogy. But when the eruptions between Ford and the unions came to a head in the mid-thirties, it was to the unions that the Blacks gave their votes. In the ensuing years, nevertheless, there were many in all parts of the country who had good reason to be glad of the dependability of Henry Ford's products, and in particular the celebrated "Model T" when, like "Sleepy" John Estes, they could afford to purchase one of the ancient and out-of-date models.

26   Well, well, when you feed in the winter, please throw your wire over
          in the bin, (*twice*)
      Well, well, papa, next spring, eeh-yeah, I won't wreck up my T-Model
          again.

      Well, well, a T-Model Ford, I say is a poor man's friend, (*twice*)
      Well, well, it will help you out, yeah when your money is thin.

      Well, one thing about a T-Model, you don't have to shift no gear,
          (*twice*)
      Well, well, just lay down your brake and feed the gas, eeh-yeah, and
          the stuff is here . . .

Throughout the war and the immediate post-war years Blacks in the North were able to have a share in the general prosperity; there were jobs in plenty in Pittsburgh and Cleveland, New York and Chicago, and if one

source of employment failed, it was still possible to secure alternative work.
Sang Frank Tannehill:

> 27   I don't care, if the streets is covered with snow, (*twice*)
> I got to work at the warehouse and bring my baby the roll.
>
> The warehouse burnt down, got to wait till they build again, (*twice*)
> I'm cuttin' grass now but I'm still bringing money in.
>
> They build and build till they finally done got through, (*twice*)
> You know in the mornin' just what I got to do.
>
> I've got to get up every mornin' till I wear my poor self out, (*twice*)
> Going down town working at the new warehouse.

Blacks were getting a share in the national prosperity of the era, even if it
was only the small surplus that dribbled down the sides of the gigantic and
ill-founded structure of the commercial pyramid, rather than an integral
part of it. The orgy of speculation which the stockholders enjoyed during
the late 1920s was to bring a sudden and devastating collapse of that unhappy
erection: the index of common stock prices averaged a hundred in the year
1926; by September 1929 it had more than doubled to 216. The big profits
that accrued from this speculation went into the pockets of only a small
percentage of the nation, though it seemed that everyone who had a few
dollars to spare attempted to invest them to his profit, and in doing so
contributed to the nation's eventual loss. The crash came in October 1929
when the shareholders desperately tried to sell out. Sixteen million shares
were sold on the 29th of that month and the total loss exceeded the National
Debt. Factories closed; the whistles sounded for the last time and the
workers were laid off as the Depression settled on the land.

In Atlanta, street singer "Peg Leg" Howell gave a new topicality to an old
song with his *Rolling Mill Blues*. The original mine owner named Joe
Brown was probably Governor Joseph Emerson Brown who in the 1870s
owned coal-mines in Dade County, Georgia.

> 28   The rollin' mill baby, it's done broke down,
> They ain't shippin' no iron to town.
>
> The longest train I ever seen,
> Run round Joe Brown's coal-mine.

Her engine was at the coal-mine hill,
And the cab hadn't never left town.

A shocked nation stared at its shattered industry, beheld in stupefied horror the closure of the banks, the collapse of capital investment. Inevitably those who had been signed on last were the first to lose their jobs. Those Blacks who had streamed forth in happy anticipation a decade before, now found themselves workless, laid off with considerable fear and no regrets, no thanks. Men huddled together in mind-shattered despair on the street corners, stood with tin cups in the soup kitchens, and queued for long hours in the bread lines. Steel workers in Pennsylvania slept in the now cold ovens, while in Oakland, California, families lived in sewer pipes that had never been laid. On the outskirts of the cities crude shack towns sprang up where the homeless lived in shanties made of packing cases, metal advertisements, railroad ties, cardboard boxes, tar-paper – anything that could be salvaged from scrap heaps. Their settlements were termed "Hoovervilles" after the President whose apparent inactivity and complacency – "No one has starved" he claimed with pride – were held to be largely responsible for the destitution.

29   And it's hard time here, hard time everywhere, (*three times*)

     I went down to the factory where I worked three years or more, (*twice*)
     And the boss man told me "Man, I ain't hiring here no more."

     Now we have a little city, that we calls down in "Hooverville" (*twice*)
     Times have got so hard, people ain't got no place to live.

     Sun early rose this morning, I was lyin' out on the floor, (*twice*)
     Lord, I didn't have no teasin' brown, baby ain't no place for me to go.

J. D. Short had moved from Mississippi to St. Louis where he worked in a brass foundry until he was laid off, and was forced to join the workless men in the Hooverville. In conditions of mutual suffering White and Black lived side by side but there remained the perpetual fear that the latter might take any work that was available, and the sight of a dark-skinned face was an unwelcome one.

30   I know just how, baby Lord, a broke man feels, (*twice*)
     There's no one, baby, that will do him a real good deal.

> I've been broke all day, baby, did not have a lousy dime, (*twice*)
> I'll be all right, baby, I swear some other time.
>
> Lord, I don't feel welcome, mama, in St. Louis any more, (*twice*)
> 'Cause I have no friends, baby, and no place to go.

In fact, Sylvester Palmer died a few years later.

Workless Blacks begged in the streets, rummaged through the garbage-cans for scraps of food that they could salvage. Coats wore thin, trousers were patched with rags, and feet and knees were bound in gunny sacks as clothes fell apart and shoes broke at the seams. With the coming of winter many homeless and despairing men wished themselves back once more in the hostile South. Robert Hicks, or "Barbecue Bob," was another singer who died soon after.

> 31   Winter-time is coming, you can hear that howlin' wind, (*twice*)
> You better get ready 'cause the summer's done gone in.
>
> Cold wave make me shiver, cold wave gets my goat, (*twice*)
> I feel so disgusted, ain't got no overcoat.
>
> Shoes ain't got no bottom, feets pattin' on the ground, (*twice*)
> When it starts to snowin' be Alabama bound.
>
> Winter-time is comin', ain't got a single sou, (*twice*)
> With my pocket empty, tell me what I'm goin' to do?

This was a period when every man was for himself. There were twelve million unemployed in 1932. Consuming poverty ate into the hearts of men, and human feelings were wrung dry. With the election to the presidency of Franklin D. Roosevelt and his optimistic introduction of the policy of the New Deal, there was a slow but perceptible return to economic stability. Blacks found that they were still George Schuyler's "mudsill of America" and in the struggle for employment they had lost ground even in the hated "jobs." Accustomed to the fight for survival, many were like Walter Davis, and accepted the situation.

> 32   I woke this morning laughing, laid down last night a-crying, (*twice*)
> Lost all my money, broke and didn't have a dime.

When I had money, I had friends for miles around,
Hmmmmm–mmm I had friends for miles around,
Ain't got no money, my friends don't seem to know me now.

For all too many of them conditions were not markedly different from those that they had endured when the nation as a whole was enjoying a period of relative prosperity, and it was only half in humor that Lonnie Johnson declared that "hard times ain't gone nowhere."

33   People is ravin' 'bout hard times, tell me what it's all about,
      People is hollerin' 'bout hard times, tell me what's it all about,
      Hard times don't worry me, I was broke when they first started out.

      Friends, it could be worser, you don't seem to understand, (*twice*)
      Some is cryin' with a sack of coal under each arm and a loaf of bread in
        each hand.

      People ravin' 'bout hard times, I don't know why they should, (*twice*)
      If some people was like me, they didn't have no money when times was
        good.

The New Deal brought employment to hundreds of thousands of workless men and with the institution of the schemes of national relief by Roosevelt with Harry Hopkins at his side, black families were given a chance to resuscitate themselves. In the mid-thirties some fifty per cent of these families in the North were receiving national assistance, but in Atlanta sixty-five per cent were on relief and eighty per cent in Norfolk, Virginia. The optimism of earlier years had gone, to be replaced by more cautious hopes, but the North still afforded better chances for a man to obtain some form of employment and perhaps to save sufficient to bring his family to him. The migration North continued. Tommy McClennan moved up from Yazoo, Mississippi, to Chicago in the late thirties.

34   I left my babe in Mississippi, picking cotton down on her knees, (*twice*)
      She says, "If you get to Chicago, please write me a letter if you please."

      (All right . . .)
      I said, "Baby, that's all right, baby that's all right for you, (*twice*)
      You'll just keep picking cotton right there, – oh, babe until I get
        through"

> Baby, when I get to Chicago, I do swear I'm sure gonna take a change, (*twice*)
> If I don't never get back to Mississippi, I'm sure gonna change your name.

National relief gave him sufficient to live above starvation level, but it did nothing to give the unemployed man the self-respect that working for his living promoted. This the Public Works Administration, the Works Projects Administration, and other schemes provided, and the ambitious program of river dams, public highways, bridges and other municipal and federal construction undertakings gave direly needed employment. The fear of losing it remained a very real one, as Jimmy Gordon pleaded:

> 35   Lord, Mister President, listen to what I'm going to say, (*twice*)
> You can take away all of the alphabet but please leave that P.W.A.
>
> Now you are in Mister President, an' I hope you'se in to stay (*twice*)
> But whatever changes that you make, please keep that P.W.A.
>
> P.W.A. you the best ol' friend I ever seen, (*twice*)
> Since the job ain't hard, and the boss ain't mean.
>
> I went to the poll and I voted, I know I voted the right way, (*twice*)
> Now I'm praying to you Mister President, please keep the P.W.A.

Though the men were not driven as many of them had been on the southern plantations and the work was not by these standards hard, yet the road grading, the drilling, and manual labor involved in many of the construction schemes was heavy enough, and the work paid only moderately well. Faced with the high rents that were charged in black sectors, and the debts incurred by having goods on credit in lean times, a laborer still had good reason for anxiety. Peetie Wheatstraw recorded several blues about the W.P.A. projects.

> 36   Working on the project with holes all in my clothes, (*twice*)
> Trying to make me a dime, ooh well, well, to keep the rent man from putting me out doors.
>
> I am working on the project, trying to make both ends meet, (*twice*)
> But the pay-day is so long, ooh, well, well, until the grocery man won't let me eat.

> Working on the project with pay-day three or four weeks away, (*twice*)
> Now how can you make ends meet, ooh well, well, when you can't get
> no pay?

If he was married or had a woman living with him, he had little time for her unless she could help bring the money in, though opportunities for work for her were few, as W.P.A. employment for women was confined to indoor occupations and these were limited.

A percentage of the work to be undertaken for any particular project was reserved for Blacks, but the proportion was often grossly unrelated to the number of black unemployed, expecially in the South where discriminatory practices operated against them. A man was fortunate to be on the W.P.A. for generally the wages, though low, were still higher than the sums that he might earn on the farms, or obtain on relief – one reason for the discrimination against him: the southern farmers did not wish to see him obtain more on relief projects than he would in their employ. While they sought a job on a project thousands were thankful, like Charlie McCoy, who styled himself the "Mississippi Mudder," for charity relief.

37   I said charity, charity is my only friend, (*twice*)
      When I lost my job the Charity took me in.

  I said you ain't got no money and you got no place to stay, (*twice*)
  You got to get you a job on the P.W.A.

  I am going tomorrow out on Charity Street, (*twice*)
  And ask "Mister Charity Man, can I have some beef and meat?"

  The rent man keeps askin' "When is you goin-a pay?" (*twice*)
  I said "Just as soon as I get my money from the W.P.A."

  I said the Charity give me my groceries, even buy shoes and clothes,
      (*twice*)
  I said who'll give me my lovin', I swear nobody knows.

The majority of black project workers were unskilled with the result that their pay was in the lowest of categories. But the black worker looked at his fellows who were unable to obtain any form of employment and was thankful enough. By 1940 there were some 237,00 black workers on

3186—W.P.A. BLUES and SOMEBODY
        CHANGED THE LOCK ON THAT DOOR
        Vocal—Piano-Guitar-Bass Fiddle Acc.
        Sung by Bill Casey´ ....59¢

W.P.A. projects representing a slightly higher proportion of the total than their representation in unemployment figures. But outside the P.W.A., W.P.A., and the United States Housing Authority, there was little thought for unemployed Blacks and few attempts made by official forces to give them work.

In the meantime the unions had grown in power, and fierce disputes raged between them and the employers. The sheets were by no means clean on either side – gunmen and spies were hired by both union men and employers, and bitter battles were fought at the picket lines and the factory gates throughout the States. Appalling atrocities were committed by both factions, for in fighting for their livelihoods the men were literally fighting for their lives in this period of devastating national distress. Black workers were often taken on as strike breakers; labelled as "scabs" they were brutally man-handled by the striking workmen, though frequently they were unable to see that they were being exploited as tools for the employers. At this time many unions made emphatic legislative measures to ensure that Blacks were excluded from their number; others rejected them by tradition even though no clauses in their constitutions specifically demanded their exclusion. To their credit there were some unions that prohibited discrimination, though they were in the minority. Consequently when a strike occurred at the factory or mine many a black man provided willing non-union labor. His woman rejoiced when, like Merline Johnson, pay-day came and neither stopped to count the cost.

38   My man is down the mine, he's got a Cadillac Eight,
      And I have got the job to keep his business straight.

         I've got a ma-a-an in the 'Bama Mine,
         I can spend his dollars, like I can his dimes.

      (*Spoken*) Yes, I got a man in the mine. You women ought to try to get
      a man like me. He mighta look dirty when he comes out – but I
      swear he knows . . .

      You let your women fool you and give me the air,
      I tried to be in reason, now I don't even care.

Pressure was relieved for the white worker with the entry of the United States into World War II. Whilst hundreds of thousands of men were being drafted into the armed services it was estimated by the Bureau of Labor Statistics that close on one and a half million extra workers would be required between April 1941 and April 1942 to meet the demands of the defense industries. But in spite of this need for a vast army of civil workers, it was to be a white man's war. Grimly deliberate, the plants sought to exclude black workers from the factories even though there was an ever-increasing number of colored men on relief and insufficient workers to meet the demands of industry. Four hundred thousand Blacks lived in New York, but of over twenty-nine thousand employees in ten defense plants in the area, a meagre one hundred and forty were colored. Westinghouse, with Government contracts worth over $8,000,000, employed three Blacks out of its eight hundred workers in its Baltimore factory; there were only a dozen amongst the twelve thousand workers in the aircraft industries of southern California and the deplorable story could be illustrated indefinitely. So, in this time of national emergency there were many who felt, like "Doctor" Clayton, that they were "on the killing floor."

39   Please give me a match to light this short that I've found, (*twice*)
I know it looks bad for me, picking tobacco up off the ground.

Lord, it's zero weather an' I ain't got a lousy dime, (*twice*)
I'm walking from door to door an' I can't find a friend of mine.

I'm going back to the lowlands, and roll up my jumper sleeves, (*twice*)
Then I'll be sitting pretty baby – long as I kill grass and weeds.

Blacks who had gone North to find better employment became disillusioned; the South that they had left in bitterness now seemed less cruel. Cotton prices had risen to nine cents in 1940, to fourteen cents in 1941 and were to rise to twenty cents in the following year. Many were attracted southwards. Sang Roosevelt Sykes:

40   (*Spoken*) Well I'm going back down South, where men are men, and
women are glad of it.

Oooh – I've got those Southern blues, (*twice*)
Cotton prices going higher, an' I ain't got no time to lose.

Chicago and Detroit. Folks have you heard the news? (*twice*)
Old Dixieland is jumping – I've got those Southern blues . . .

Goin' back down South, saddle up my old grey mare, (*twice*)
Around Christmas time, folks is leavin' from everywhere.

Exasperated with the situation in the war and factories, "Race leader" A. Philip Randolph called for a march on Washington to be made by some fifty thousand Blacks on July 1, 1941. Four days before it was to take place President Roosevelt wrote his Executive Order 8802 which, in urging a policy of non-discrimination in industry, caused the cancellation of the march and the establishment of the Committee on Fair Employment Practice. Blacks were taken on in defense factories though they had good reason to fear the effects of the lay-off with the cessation of hostilities.

41   I had a little woman working on that National Defense, (*twice*)
That woman got to the place, I'm glad she did not have no sense.

Just because she was workin', makin' so much dough, (*twice*)
That woman got to the place she did not love me no mo'.

Every payday would come, her check was big as mine (*twice*)
That woman saw that Defense wouldn't gonna last all the time.

That Defense has gone, just listen to my song, (*twice*)
Since that Defense has gone, that woman done lost her home.

Much of the good that was done during the latter part of the war in obtaining good and equal employment for Blacks was spoiled when the companies retrenched with the end of the strife. Returning white servicemen claimed their previous posts, or better ones, whilst those Blacks who had been brought into the factories at a later stage were the first to be laid off. But there was no Depression parallel to that of the post-World War I years and by comparison black workers were economically somewhat better placed. In the West Coast cities there had been a phenomenal growth in the black populations owing to the opening of defense factories to them which presented many problems of post-war adjustment. The Fair Employment Practices Commission lost much of its effectiveness, and some of its branches actually acted as screens for discrimination. California voted against its continuation but consultants were appointed to take its place.

Though an analysis made in 1948 revealed that the average black family was still earning little more than half that of the medium white family, there had been over all a slow but undeniable improvement in the labor situation of the American Black. He still found his principal sources of employment in the non-skilled and semi-skilled categories, but he had made small yet significant inroads into the professional and technical fields. By the late 1950s integration was gradually taking place; perhaps most successfully when it was not the result of Supreme Court Decisions backed by armed intervention. Those who profited by the great advances in black education, by the experiences of the war and by those improvements in industrial and social relations that had taken place looked more astutely and with greater understanding at the problem than hitherto. Their philosophy was summed up by Charles (Crown Prince) Waterford when he sang of living in Los Angeles, a city where southern attitudes of mind still persisted; where overcrowding made an automobile into a front parlor; but where, if he was to meet conditions half-way and was prepared to give and to take, he was confident of ultimate concord.

42 Well, some call it the Land of Sunshine, some call it old Central
    Avenue, (*twice*)

I call it a big ole country town, yes, where the folks don't care what
they do.

Well, if a man can make it in Los Angeles, he can make it anywhere
(*twice*)
But you got to have one of those used Cadillac cars, yes boys, and you
can stay square.

Well, some like fried chicken, well, I'll take a pie, (*twice*)
You can't eat it too fast boys, or you'll get the gravy in your eye.
Yes, every wink don't mean I'm 'sleep, and every good-bye don't mean
I'm gone,
I'm gonna settle down on the West Side and make L.A. my home.

Slow though its acceptance of the inevitability of industrialization may
have been, the South had to develop for its own survival. Employment of
Blacks in industry ultimately came to the South in spite of the persistence of
the beliefs in their incapacity to undertake such work, and though the
majority of black workers in the 1950s were still employed in unskilled jobs,
the proportion of farm laborers dropped from thirty-six per cent in 1900 to a
mere six per cent a half-century later, whilst the total of black industrial
employees rose from a miserable one per cent to thirty per cent within the
same period. And in the Mississippi Delta regions, where progress was
slower and old traditions and modes of thought died hard, there were
already signs of change and the glimmerings of hope. Yet Louis Hayes and
Alex Seward expressed the fears and uncertainty of poor Blacks as they faced
the prospect of the 1950s.

43   We don't want no more war, and no Depression at all, (*twice*)
It would be too hard for a poor man to get a job, at all.

Lord I hope that no more hard times, Lord will ever be, (*twice*)
Now if they come – ooh well, Lord gonna help poor me.

We don't know the future lies, whether it's dark or light, (*twice*)
Each day brings something, whether it's wrong or right.

Well-a you people you better save a dollar and try to make other plans,
(*twice*)
Don't you know they windin' up the welfare; eatin' out of them
garbage cans.

2   *Railroad for my pillow*

In 1890 eight out of every ten Blacks lived in rural districts; during the course of the next thirty years fifteen per cent of this population moved towards the towns. Significant of a change in the pattern of living though this was, the ensuing decade witnessed a still more marked increase in the urban population: in 1930 nearly half of the black population was living in the towns. Between 1910 and the entry of the United States into World War II close on two million Blacks had migrated from the South to the northern urban centres. The war brought a further million, whilst large numbers moved to the West where hitherto they had been few in number. The process continued and though more than three-quarters of America's Blacks still lived in the South, the shift from the agricultural to the urban communities was remarkable; by 1950 less than a fifth lived in southern rural districts. Thus there has been a considerable movement of people within the South itself, and, though the Great Migration to the North was an extraordinary phenomenon, the effects of which were made outstandingly apparent by reason of the startling growth of the black sectors in the cities, this internal circulation within the South was no less spectacular.

The redistribution of the black population witnessed during some fifty years was largely dependent upon the changing conditions of employment and the new requirements of industry in the twentieth century. But this movement of workers lent support to the deliberately stimulated notions of black shiftlessness. Accusing fingers were pointed at the wandering workers and families and bitter tongues spoke of the work-shy, the unreliable, the undependable Black who had, in fact, only moved on through dissatisfaction and the desire to better his economic status. Even though the black worker could earn in 1960 approximately four times his wage of 1940, while he continued to earn little more than half the salary of the average white wage earner the circulation of labor was bound to continue.

During these years of migration the blues developed and it is no doubt largely as a result of this circulation of black people that it has spread in so remarkable a manner. A folk music reflects the environment of the people who create it, and when their background is a constantly varying one it is scarcely surprising that the images that are mirrored in the blues have much to do with the movement of the black worker. Not only does the blues illustrate his search for work compatible with his talents and appropriate to his needs; it also reveals the personal quarrels, the foibles, the weaknesses that have caused men to leave their homes in the hope of finding new and happier surroundings; it gives a glimpse of what it must mean to be one among the many rejected, homeless migrants – to be one single unit in the impersonal statistics that represent the millions of rootless men and women.

If the search for employment constituted the principal reason why large numbers of Blacks left their homes, there were nevertheless many other motivating factors which, for the individual, were no less compelling. Amongst the most significant of these must have been the reaction against segregational practices, when the frayed material of human endurance was worn through. For years a man might suffer the petty indignities that were as much the manifestations of racial discrimination as were lynchings. He or she was obliged to take his seat in the back of the bus; or to stand, herded with his fellows in the inadequate "Jim Crow" cars of the trains. He made his exit from the station by the door marked *Colored* – he drank from the water fountain marked *Colored*. He was accustomed to the policy of "separate but equal" educational facilities that could mean that he had been taught by an unqualified teacher in an unheated, ill-equipped shack. He entered by the back door, never by the front; he took his hat off when he spoke to a white man and noticed that no hand was lifted to the hat when a white man addressed his wife; he answered to "Uncle" or "Boy" but never heard himself addressed as "Mister," he stepped off the pavement when a white person approached and was careful not to look too hard at a white woman. He saw the white boys trying to "make" the young black girls and knew that he dare not protest. If he was a "good Nigger" and "knew his place," if he was not "uppity" and made no attempt to assert his rights as an American citizen, he lived in an uneasy peace. And with his personal pride hurt, his individuality suppressed, he wondered why he merited such discrimination, and what the future might bring. He listened to the teachings of the preacher that all men are children in the eyes of God and tried to equate the words with the facts of his own experience and the revelations of his own eyes.

> 44   They say we are the Lord's children, I don't say that ain't true, (*twice*)
>   But if we are the same like each other, ooh, well, well, why do they
>   treat me like they do?

I want to live on, children, children, I would just like to see, (*twice*)
What will become of us, ooh, well by nineteen and fifty-three.

Some of the Good Lord's children, some of them ain't no good, (*twice*)
Some of them are the devil, ooh, well, well, and wouldn't help you if
    they could.

Some of the Good Lord's children kneel upon their knees and pray,
    (*twice*)
You serve the devil in the night, ooh, well, and serve the Lord in the
    day.

Any analysis of blues lyrics reveals that verses which state the singer's intention to "leave" figure prominently. He is "going to leave this town," to "walk down the dirt road" or to "catch the next thing smokin'." Often the singer has "a mind to ramble" – but it *is* a mind, a dream of escape. "They call me the 'Bald Eagle' because I sail above the clouds" sang Willie "61" Blackwell, whose nickname incidentally was taken from the number of the highway that runs north–south through his native Mississippi.

45   My mind begins ramblin', won't be long before I stretch my wings,
      (*twice*)
    I'm goin' to sail away one morning and I won't be back till spring.

    I'll sail the Atlantic ocean, also the Chesapeake Bay, (*twice*)
    I was tryin' to spy the Pyrenees mountains, where the eagle pullets lay.

    You don't believe I'm leavin', just leave me the first sunshiny day,
      (*twice*)
    At the Statue of Liberty you will see your eagle just sail away.

A man who had seldom traveled further from home than he could walk in a day, who lived a few score miles from the nearest city and some five miles from the nearest village, whose whole horizon had been bounded by cotton-wood trees, but who had never seen a northern newspaper and had never possessed a radio, would find it hard to break away from the little world he knew; to leave his friends and his kinfolk in order to try his fortune in a country of which he knew nothing – such a man might never summon the nerve to make so bold a move. Instead he might content himself with the resolution that he would leave if "he still feels the same way, to-morrow," and in doing so channel the burning anger and frustration that might have prompted him to do so.

> 46   Good-bye Arkansas, Hello Missouri, Gal I'm going up North,
>   I declare it ain't no foolin' if I can just –
>   Feel tomorrow, ooh, like I feel today,
>   Lord, I'm gonna pack my suitcase,
>   Boy, I'm gonna make my getaway.

If the dream of escape from the South remained as a dream for the majority of Blacks, many thousands turned the dream into reality. Somehow they found the courage to leave familiar surroundings for an unknown future in a city a thousand miles or more away.

The threads that tied a man to his home might snap: the strain become greater, the tautening of racial tensions become too much. He would hear of better conditions in the distant North where discrimination was supposed not to exist and where employment was to be gained for the asking. Though Charles "Cow Cow" Davenport from Alabama appears to have treated the stories with a certain amount of skepticism, he resolved to move to the North, bearing in mind the thought that, if his hopes were not realized, he could return to the Jim Crow South again.

> 47   I'm tired of being Jim Crowed, gonna leave this Jim Crow town,
>   Doggone my black soul, I'm sweet Chicago bound,
>   Yes Sir, I'm leavin' here, from this ole Jim Crow town.
>
>   I'm going up North, where they think money grows on trees,
>   I don't give a doggone, if ma black soul should freeze,
>   I'm goin' where I don't need no B.V.D.s.
>
>   I'm goin' up North, baby, I can't carry you,
>   Ain't nothin' in that cold country, a green gal can do,
>   I'm goin' get me a Northern gal, baby, I'm through with you.
>
>   Lord but if I get up there, weather don't suit –
>   I don't find no brown. Go tell that bossman of mine,
>   Lord I'm ready to come back to my Jim Crow town.

Euphemistically, Blacks may call racial discrimination "bad luck" and sing of its effects, but sometimes it was a chain of misfortune rather than the effects of direct discrimination that led a man to migrate: trouble with his crops, with his domestic affairs, with the police, and with his friends, driving him to the point where he would rather leave the district than remain. For the future may have held nothing. "Kokomo" Arnold sang as one who chose not to remain where his family had lived and died in the cotton rows, or to stay where his own failure had made his wife hostile.

48 Trouble, trouble, I been havin' it all my days, (*twice*)
    Now it seems like trouble gonna put me in ma lonesome grave.

    I'm scared to stay here, scared to leave this ole Bad Luck town, (*twice*)
    So when I wake up every mornin', my head is goin' round and round.

    Now listen here, people, I don't want no one's advice, (*twice*)
    I done change ma way of living, gonna find some woman goin' to treat
       me right.

    I'm gonna tell everybody what bad luck I've had in ma life, (*twice*)
    I killed my sisters and my brothers; now that woman that wrecked my
       life.

When the pattern of racial discrimination became in its total effect almost unbearable, a man might consider making a break. It was not simple; sharecropping, work on the levee, or on the turpentine farm could keep him with a heavy debt to pay before he was free to leave. The house did not belong to him, the land was not his own; the peck of meal in the bin and the rusting plow beside the outhouse probably belonged to the company store; like Charley Jordan, he lived in fear of the visits of the "rent man."

49 The times are getting tighter, getting tighter day by day,
       (*twice*)
    But the rent man comes as usual, when he knows that we can't pay.

    I stood him off so long till I'm afraid to facin' him here now, (*twice*)
    Because I know when I do facin' him, there's goin' to be a row.

    Now my coal bin is empty, not a log there will you find, (*twice*)
    I would buy coal by the bushel – if I only had a dime.

    Now the times is so tight, they keep you walkin' up and down the
       street, (*twice*)
    With all these debts are coming in, not-a one of them can we meet.

"Times" were always tight for share-croppers and tenant-farmers, but if they earned enough to pay off their debts they frequently moved. There was no incentive to improve buildings or yards because they received no credit for doing so; instead, they sought a tenancy with better "furnishings." But in Mississippi in the early 1930s over a fourth of all black tenant-farmers' homes did not even have cooking facilities. "The times is so hard" sang Charlie Spand, that "the birds refuse to sing."

> 50   Lord I walked and I walked but I cannot find a job, (*twice*)
>   Lord I cain't talk about no money, and I sure don't want to rob.
>
>   Now my woman's hard to get along with, as I'm sittin' here, (*twice*)
>   I ain't cooked me a square meal, honey in God knows when.
>
>   Everybody cryin' "Depression," I just found out what it means, (*twice*)
>   It means a man ain't got no money, he can't buy no bacon and greens.

For the woman no less than for the man, the conditions of living and working under the share-cropping system could be so frustrating as to leave her with no will to work or to share his life. Bellies swollen with pellagra, his children would watch solemn-eyed, whilst a woman, cooking the grits in the skillet, "loudmouthed" her man for his laziness. She may not have understood why his work never seemed to get them out of debt, but she knew that she had to bear children, raise, clothe, and feed children and try to keep a home together. Children were capital in a community where freedom from virtual slavery could only be obtained by maximum output of work. A black man would therefore often be prepared to accept as his own the children of his wife by a former husband or lover and raise them along with his provided that they work in the fields and help to clear the cropper's debt. Only with the gradual rejection of the crop-lien system and better marital relations, resulting largely from improved educational facilities, did this loose form of family tend to decline to be replaced for a while in the 1950s by a socially more secure structure. The substitute parent was not necessarily resented by the man who left, who was frequently prepared to accept the situation philosophically; he would "make his getaway" to a new district, sometimes to better his fortunes in the process, as Big Maceo did.

> 51   She had a man, on her man; had a kid man on her kid, (*twice*)
>   She had so many men, until she could not keep it hid.

I left that woman, one mornin', jus' about the break of day *(twice)*
You know I packed my suitcase, made my getaway.

Here I am, in Chicago, and I'm doin' very well, *(twice)*
I don't find the woman I love, I'll just live all by myself.

Figures that illustrate the extent of the Migration are necessarily few, for the full import was not appreciated at the time nor were there reliable methods of measurement available. Nevertheless certain statistics do indicate the degree to which black men left their homes, and the numbers of desertions of their wives and families that had taken place. Of some two hundred thousand homeless men in Chicago in 1930 some ten per cent were black transients and a sample taken of these indicated that more than half had been married. Of those who had been married, nearly three-quarters had deserted their wives and families. A similar pattern was evident in New York, where of some seven thousand five hundred and sixty black arrivals, the same proportion of married men was to be found, and of these thirty-five per cent had deserted their families. These figures were echoed in the scores of cities to which the black men migrated during the twenties and thirties and caused serious social problems in the South, where many families were left with the mother alone to care for them. Not unexpectedly the black mother tended to be more admired – and more missed – by her offspring than was the father. St. Louis Jimmy remembered his mother with respect in later life.

52   What a sad old Sunday, people, this year in May, *(twice)*
     I think of my mother and I kneel down to pray.

     Mother was a woman sure to me, I really do know, *(twice)*
     I'll never have a friend like my dear old mother no more.

     Since we didn't have people to make a home like it should be, *(twice)*
     But although poor mother doin' the best she could for me.

In the ante-bellum years the black family was a true matriarchy. The importance of the father was deliberately reduced under the slavery system and the children often had less respect for their male parents, if indeed they knew who they were. At this time strong and well-developed Blacks were literally kept at stud on many plantations with the sole purpose of procreating children likely to be effective as workers or as saleable material.

The women were informed who their mates were to be and love played no part in their relations in all save the most humanitarian plantations – and slavery was not a humanitarian system. Furthermore, nubile black girls were reserved for the sexual excesses of the young white planters and the slave concubine was normal in the South. Some were well provided for, but the majority were cast back into the slave-quarters to bear their children and to continue to labor as soon as they had fulfiled their purpose. Consequently the mother was frequently the only parent that the child knew, and his affections were naturally centered upon her. With the conclusion of the Civil War there was a period of promiscuity amongst Blacks which was a manifestation of the new-found freedom. But there was also considerable evidence of an increasing sense of self-respect on the part of black males and, as the years passed, an assumption of family responsibilities. Nevertheless, the rule of the mother and of the grandmother persisted in a very large number of instances and black families continued to show a proportionately much higher rate of female "heads" than did white families.

Greater opportunities for escape and for evacuation, the promiscuous living attendant with overcrowding in slum areas, and many other factors combined to make the proportion of families with female heads greater in the urban than in the rural areas, and greater in the rural non-farm areas than in the farming districts. Thus the rural areas often show a figure of some fifteen per cent, whereas in the cities the numbers of such families may often be in excess of a third of the total. For example the black sociologist, Franklin Frazier, states that in 1930 nearly forty per cent of the sixteen hundred black and mixed race families in Nashville, Tennessee, had female heads – a term which covered mothers, married and single, foster-mothers, and elder sisters.

With the problems of maintaining a family and of securing an income, many women readily accepted another man in the home but, though such relations could be harmonious, they also stimulated much jealousy and disunion. The problems besetting a mother who had to cope with the combined passions and desire for freedom of the many children in a large family as the boys approached their maturity were great. Young men did not heed the warnings and entreaties of their parents, as Jimmy Gordon recalled with regret.

> 53 I've treated my dear old mother, I've been treatin' her so unkind, (*twice*)
> Without a mighty change I believe I'm gonna lose my mind.

So many men are in trouble and their mothers have been their slave,
  (*twice*)
So much grievin' and worryin' I've carried her to her grave.

If I had to go back home, I'm gonna fall down on my knees, (*twice*)
I will never leave my happy home no more because my poor old heart
  would bleed.

Not surprisingly, some would find the remonstrances of their parents
boring or unintelligible; they would ignore the advice given them, delight
in their reputations as irresponsible children, and take advantage of any
indulgence towards them. Young, and with voice still unbroken, the
"Mississippi Moaner," Isaiah Nettles, rebeled against the half-hearted
restraint of his parents.

54 Aaaah cryin', mama, papa said "Daddy do love, I do, a double do,
       double do love you."
     Cryin' – eeeh your daddy do love you,
     You'se a high-steppin' mama, an' I don't care what you do.

     I was a li'l boy, on ma way to school,
     Was a little boy – ooh – on ma way to school,
     Met a high-brown woman, an' she broke my mammy's rule.

     Mama said I'm reckless, daddy says I'm young and wild,
     Mama said I'm reckless oooh; daddy said I'm young and wild –
     Said, "He's so reckless, he's my baby chile."

Many parents would try to restrain their children and try to set an
example to them that might help to negate that which they often saw about
them. But the family structure was too loose, the problem too great and it
was not always possible to cope. Sons and daughters were lured away from
home by false and attractive promises against the advice of their parents. At
times of national or racial stress the number of children on the move greatly
increased. Such catastrophes as the East St. Louis riots of 1917 and other
social disturbances made little sense to the children who failed to realize their
seriousness. Memphis Minnie remembered the aftermath:

55 Lay down at night, trying to play my hand,
     Through my window, out stepped a man,
         I didn't know no better, oh boy, in my girlish days.

My mama cried, papa did too,
"Aw, daughter, look what a shame on you,"
　　　I didn't know no better, oh boy, in my girlish days.

I flagged a train, didn't have a dime,
Tryin' to run away from that home of mine,
　　　I didn't know no better, oh boy, in my girlish days.

I hit the highway, caught me a truck,
19 and 17, when the winter was tough,
　　　I didn't know no better, oh boy, in my girlish days.

Children wandering aimlessly on the roads presented a major problem in the twenties and thirties and the researches of the Children's Bureau conducted in 1932 by Dr. McMullen of Chicago University suggested that there were then some two hundred thousand child hoboes on the roads and railroads. Later examination revealed that the number was probably in excess of half a million. These vagrant children of all national and racial groups, but of whom a considerable proportion were Black, were tough and embittered, homeless and independent; they scorned the camps of the Civilian Conservation Corps – the C.C.C., subject of more than one blues – though the Corps drew more from children who were in unhappy homes than from those who had left them.

The achievements of the C.C.C. were considerable – over 200,000,000 trees were planted by boys in its camps as a defense against soil erosion. Two and a half million boys were enrolled in the seven years of its operation, of whom 300,000 were black. In some southern states the enrolment was almost entirely of young Whites and black youths did not benefit. Sometimes they were simply unaware of the existence of the Corps; sometimes they were considered to be ineligible to join. Washboard Sam sang of his frustrations when he attempted to sign on:

56　I told her my name and the place I stayed,
　　She said she'd give me a piece of paper, "Come back some other day."

　　　　I'm goin' down, I'm goin' down, to the C.C.C.,
　　　　I know that the W.P.A. won't do a thing for me.

　　I told her I had no peoples and the shape I was in,
　　She said she would help me – but she didn't say when.

I told her I need a job, and no Relief,
And on my rent day she sent me a can of beef.
  I'm goin' down, [etc.]

Rather than enroll for work in the camps many young Blacks preferred to join the growing army of homeless "drifters." A visible sign of the acuteness of the Depression, the droves of colored men, women, and children who were to be seen scuffling along the dirt roads were unwelcome to both white and colored communities. As the years wore on and money became scarce, when the poverty of those who wandered in the streets was almost equaled by that of the residents of homes for which they could not afford the rent, the begging cup of the hobo "bumming his chuck" and seeking a "handout" became more resented. Peetie Wheatstraw spoke for many when he recorded his *Road Tramp Blues*.

57 I have walked a lonesome road till my feet is too sore to walk, (*twice*)
  I beg scraps from the people, oh well, till my tongue is too stiff to talk.

  Everybody can tell you people, ooh well, that I ain't no lazy man,
   (*twice*)
  But I'll guess I'll have to go to the poorhouse, mmmm well, well, and
   do the best I can.

  I am what I am, and all I was born to be, (*twice*)
  Mmm, hard luck is in my family and it's rollin' down on me.

  When I get off my troubles I'm gonna bring my money down, (*twice*)
  And change my way of living, oh well, so I won't have to tramp
   aroun'.

In the blues songs of the homeless and workless there is certainly some evidence of the self-pity that Odum and Johnson declared was a characteristic of black song. Yet pride, philosophical acceptance of the present situation, and often a strong vein of hope are constantly recurrent features which mark the blues. The poverty and the unhappy conditions described were clear statements of fact and in no wise born of self-pity. So was the moral dilemma which Bill Gaither acknowledged:

58 Seem like I was born for bad luck, just a bad luck chile and everything
  goes all wrong, (*twice*)
  I came home this morning, my baby has packed up and gone.

I will always remember what my mother told me and every word she
    said was true, (*twice*)
I've had so much trouble, I didn't know what in this world to do.

I'm gonna quit worryin' and I'm gonna stop grievin' 'cause this bad
    luck will change some day, (*twice*)
It's hard to walk in that straight and narrow way.

The blues acted as a catalyst for the anger, humiliation, and frustration
that tended to demolish the moral codes and spirit of a man, and the act of
creating blues brought satisfaction and comfort both to him and to his
companions. Essentially the blues singer is a realist and often his statements
are accurate portrayals of his state of mind, uninhibited in their self-
expression. Singing of his condition can bring relief to his heart and order to
his disturbed thoughts, though many a blues indicates that the singer has
come close to despair. Buster Bennett sang as one whose stomach was "filled
with nothin', nothin' else but grief."

59   My friends don't see me, no, they just pass me by, (*twice*)
     I wouldn't mind it so much, but they hold their heads so high.

     Now I'm roamin' the highways and pickin' up cigarette butts and
       everything I can find, (*twice*)
     I mean I'm broken down and disgusted, I sure got evil on my mind.

     Now I'm eatin' wild berries and I'm sleepin' on the ground, (*twice*)
     I'm broken down and disgusted and I'm tired of trampin' around.

Much of the southern rural scene is still a broad and under-developed
landscape in which small, condensed communities exist in isolation connected only by ungraded tracks. Making their various ways towards the
cities, the black transients had little more than the sun to guide them and a
vague conception of the direction in which they had to go. For those who
had been confined hitherto to limited areas, penetration into the unknown
regions beyond held unsuspected terrors and the tedium of pacing the
winding, endless roads was shattering on the nerves.

60   Look down that long old lonesome road, (*twice*)
     My poor feet is tired but still I've got to go.

There's no train to my home town, there ain't but the one way to go,
(*twice*)
There's mile after mile, stepping down that long old muddy road.

There ain't but one thing that worries me both night and day, (*twice*)
That's the place they call Death Valley, and it's just half-way.

I've been tramping this lonely road, night after night and day after day,
(*twice*)
If your prayers don't help me, you know I'll die trying to make my
way.

A lift on the tail-board of a wagon going to town, of a cotton cart going to
the gin, might help to bring him a little nearer to his destination, and so, in
Bobby Grant's words, he went "down that dirt road, that long, long dirt
road, that lonesome old dirt road; I'm goin' down that ole dirt road till
somebody lets me ride . . ." His best hope was to reach one of the main
highways or turnpikes that seam the face of the United States, for once on
these his direction was clear and there was the chance of P.W.A. work on the
highway itself. To the homeless man the highway was as good an address as
any other, as Lee Brown, a thousand miles from his Tennessee home,
implied.

61   Yes I'm goin', yes I'm goin' away, (*twice*)
      I'm gonna leave here walkin' down on Jeff Davis Highway.

      When you get lonesome darling, write me some day, (*twice*)
      An' if I don't be in your town baby, I'll be on Jeff Davis Highway.

      The woman I was lovin', she's so far away, (*twice*)
      That's the reason I'm gonna leave here walkin', down on Jeff Davis
         Highway.

For the migrant with his eyes focused on the far horizon the long ribbons
of the "odd" numbered highways had a magnetic fascination. Harsh edges
unsoftened by wayside vegetation, their stark concrete whiteness causing
them to glare cruelly in the unrelenting sun, they guided his steps to the
North. He sang of Highway 49 which led him from Gulfport through
Jackson to Clarksdale, or of Highway 99 which took him up the Pacific
Coastal route from Los Angeles. Often he sang of Highway 61 which begins

3233   **FLORIDA BOUND BLUES** and **BLUE NIGHT BLUES**—Vocal-Piano and Guitar Acc. Leroy Carr ------- 59c

in New Orleans and by way of Natchez, Vicksburg, Memphis, and St. Louis, continues northward to St Paul and Port Arthur; or of its fellow, Highway 51, on whose hard causeway countless thousands of flapping soles and bare black feet have made no indentation. Highway 51 also runs from New Orleans and by way of Jackson, Mississippi, and Memphis, Cairo, and Decatur, Illinois, swings eastward of Chicago through Madison. These were the best-known routes to the southern Blacks: among them Tommy McClennan, who lived on the highway way out of Jackson, where he could watch the cheapest form of road transport available to the fare-paying migrant – the Greyhound bus.

62   Now if I do die, before my time should come,
     I said if I do die jus' before my time should come,
     I want you to please bury my body out on Highway 51.

     Now yon' come that Greyhound, with his tongue stickin' out on the
        side, (yes, yes)
     Now yon' come that Greyhound with his tongue stickin' out on the
        side,
     If you buy your ticket, swear 'fore God and they'll let you ride.

     My baby won five dollars and now, now she spend it – on a V-8 Ford,
        yes, yes,
     My baby have won five dollars, she spend it out on a V-8 Ford (yes,
        yes),
     So's I could meet that Greyhound bus on that Highway 51 road.

With money a man could make a speedy departure by way of the Greyhound bus, for, in the words of Lee Brown, "Baby, ain't you ever been to the Greyhound bus depot? Babe, that's the fastest bus running on Highway 51 . . ." But for those who had not got the fare there were certain hazards in walking the highways. Few truck drivers would pick up Blacks; there was always the chance of arrest for vagrancy or one of the other charges designed to keep them from migrating. The railroad tracks offered a less conspicuous, but at the same time, an equally certain indication of the route. Talking to himself to keep from falling between the lines through the hypnotic effect of walking the ties, the migrant would follow the hard iron road. In spite of his affliction, Blind Blake journeyed hundreds of miles this way.

63   Keep on walkin' and walkin', talkin' to myself, (*twice*)
      Gal I love's with somebody else.

      I got the hard road blues, walkin' on down the line, (*twice*)
      Maybe some day my gal will change her mind.

      It's a hard, hard road 'when your baby done throwed you down, (*twice*)
      Goin' keep on walkin' from town to town.

      I'm goin' find my baby, don't think she can be found, (*twice*)
      Goin' walk this hard road till my moustache drag the ground.

For southern Blacks the appeal of the railroads has always been both a real and a symbolic one. In the slavery periods when they were unable to travel between districts without written "bonds" from their owners, the snorting engines, with brilliant furnaces tracing their progress and clouds of black smoke that hung in the still air above the tracks long after the screaming whistles had died away, inspired in them an awe which their descendants still retain. For them the train that appeared from the horizon and roared towards the plantations to roll on into the unknown regions beyond was a symbol of power, of freedom, and of escape. When organized escape routes were planned for slaves to make for the free North they were known collectively as the "Underground Railroad," lending further significance to the railway system. But this time the hay-lofts and barns owned by friendly Whites were the "stations," and the "conductors" were the anti-slavery sympathizers, who risked imprisonment, even their lives, to guide the slaves to freedom. This symbolic importance of the railroad was imprinted on black religion and the spirituals told of the "Glorious Gospel Train;" even today the trains that take the Damned to Hell and the Righteous to Glory are still favored themes of sermons. As the blues developed in the post-bellum years the railroad figured prominently in the songs; the symbolic had become reality and now the trains bore northwards innumerable black males who were leaving the South, for as the old verse has it:

64   When a woman gets the blues, she goes to her room and hides, (*twice*)
      When a man gets the blues, he catches a freight train and rides.

There are grounds for criticizing the man who escapes from his problem rather than remaining to face it. But to a wretched, friendless, workless, and hopeless man these are arguments that are unlikely to make sense or reason,

and the temptation is great to make a rapid escape to another and remote
district where prospects may be better.

65 I'm standing here by this lamp-post with my mind in a different land,
    I ain't got no home, woman's got some other man.

    And some people just sing the blues just because they know the song,
    But when you hear me singin', I ain't gonna be here long.

    I dreamed last night, thought the whole round world was mine,
    I woke up this mornin' didn't have one lousy dime.

    I gambled, 'clare I gambled, but I can't win no more,
    Every once in a while rent-man knocks on my door.

    So I'm leavin' here to-night if I have to ride the blinds,
    Catch a freight train special – Engineer, lose no time.

    I'm stone bare-footed and my last pair of pants is tore,
    'Clare I've never been in this hard luck before.

As the long freight train took a curve, a figure might break from cover
and dash towards the track, taking advantage of the slowing of the train to
make boarding possible, and of the bend to hide his movements. Crooked
fingers would clutch the couplings as he swung perilously on the swaying
truck before getting a firmer grip. He might make for the "blinds" if he
could. These are the baggage cars next to the tender, which are "blind" or,
in other words, have no side door. Sitting on the step he would be safe and
out of reach of the "brake-man's" club, but to reach the blinds he had to
come close to the tender and risked being observed in doing so. More
dangerous, but out of sight and unapproachable, were the brake rods that
ran beneath the freight cars. Risking his life he might try to worm his way
across these, or if he was unusually adept he might carry a small board to
throw across the rods and then precipitate himself upon it in the narrow gap
between them and the underneath of the truck. Holding on to axle beams,
brake rods, or coupling links throughout the day and night, in icy winds, in
the choking poisonous fumes of the railroad tunnels, he could freeze to
numbness or succumb to exposure and drop to certain death on the track
below. To hobo a ride took the determination of the utterly desperate, and
cold, reckless nerve. It was not the escape for the fainthearted, as Bumble
Bee Slim admitted:

66   Well, I'm blue and evil, so many things to learn, (*twice*)
      So many days to worry, so many ways to turn.

      I had so much trouble, swear my nerves is weakenin' down, (*twice*)
      I would swing on a freight train, but I'm afraid to leave the ground.

      Whistle keeps on blowin' an' I got my debts to pay, (*twice*)
      I've got a mind to leave my baby, Lord I've got a mind to stay.

There was no room for mistakes; no second chance: the loss of a limb was
the least penalty for failing to "nail a rattler" successfully the first time, as
blues singers such as Furry Lewis and Peg Leg Sam discovered to their cost.
But the children learned from the older, more experienced hoboes who
generally liked to have a child with them to make their fires, to cook, and to
solicit for handouts when they reached the cities. Living promiscuously and
dangerously they continued to hop the flat-cars, swing on to the gondolas
until disablement of mind or body forced them to beg their rides from the
"mean old fireman" and the "cruel old enginner." "I decided I'd go down
South the last time and take it as it comes. I reckoned that mean old fireman
and engineer would too," commented King Solomon Hill:

67   There's so many people have gone down to-day,
      And this fast train north and southern, traveling light and clear.

      Mmm mm – I wanna ride your train,
      I said, "Looka hyah engineer, can I ride your train?"
      He said, "Look here you oughta know this train ain't mine an' you
          askin' me in vain."

      Said, "You go to the Western Union, you might get a chance."
      (*Spoken*) I didn't know the Western Union run no trains.
      Said, "You go to the Western Union and you might get a chance . . .
      You might wire to some of your people, and your fare will be sent
          right here."
      (*Spoken*) Hadn't thought of it that way before.

      I wanna go home, and that train is done gone dead,
      I wanna goooo and that train is done gone dead,

I done lost my wife and my three little children and my mother's sick
 in bed.

Mmmm -- please, help me win my fare,
Cause I'm a travelin' man, boys I can't stay here.

Appealing to the railroad men seldom had any effect, although the
engineers on some lines were Blacks. But they were anxious to retain their
jobs in days when jobs were scarce enough and when hoboes and "bums"
constituted a major problem to the railroad companies. The hoboes hated
the "snakes" -- the switchmen, whose lapel buttons with an "S" motif
earned them their names, and most of all the brakemen, the "stingers" -- so
named from the "B" that they wore on their buttons. Firemen would turn
their hoses on the hoboes who clung to the tops of the box-cars so that their
wet clothes would freeze to them and they would fall from their perches;
brakemen swung the clubs with which they tightened down the brakes in
defence against the tough and desperate hoboes. They were the traditional
enemies of the railroad bum and their ranks were supported by the railroad
"bulls" -- the company police who with "billy" and "nightstick" fought off
the tramps and wielded their clubs through the hobo encampments. To
protect themselves against the assaults of the railroad officials and police, the
hoboes frequently banded together to ride in groups upon the cars,
especially the Blacks, who also had to contend with racial prejudice. Out of a
racial clash between two such groups and a white gang with a couple of
white prostitutes arose the terrible Scottsboro affair.

Having reached a district in which they might hope to find work, or
where they intended to settle for a while the bums gained strength and
protection from the railroad police by living in the hobo "jungles."
"Sleepy" John Estes from Brownsville, Tennessee, warned his listeners of
the railroad police in his local area.

68   Now when I came in on that *Mae West*, I put it down at Chicago
         Heights, (*twice*)
      I eased over in the hobo jungle and that's where I stayed all|
         night.

      Now if you hobo to Brownsville you better not be peepin' out, (*twice*)
      Now Mister Wynn will get you and Mister Gallaher will wear you
         out.

Now out east of Brownsville, it's 'bout four miles from town, (*twice*)
Now if you ain't got your fare, that's where they will let you down.

Hidden deep in the wayside brush but known to the experienced tramps, the jungles were primitive shack towns made from scrap metal, wood, and cardboard, and the packing cases that hobos had tipped off the trains. On the bare earth the denizens of the jungles, some of whom having made the disease-ridden tips their permanent homes, cooked their coffee and beans. Son Bonds from Brownsville, Tennessee, sang in a dialect so marked and in tones so rough and deep that his indistinct words can only be detected with difficulty. Accompanying himself with delicacy and subtle originality on his one personal possession, the guitar with which he earned a few nickels and dimes, Son Bonds showed only a trace of bitterness of the ultimate frustrations and misery that a migrant life between the jungles could bring.

69   I'm a broken-hearted bachelor, travelin' through this wide world all
          alone, (*twice*)
       It's the railroad for my pillow, this jungle is my happy home.

       This ole jungle, this ole jungle, has me sleepin' by myself, (*twice*)
       Well, I'll believe I'll go, honey, find somebody else.

       Well jungle, this ole jungle, cinders blowin' back in my face, (*twice*)
       I'm gonna get me a little woman, gonna fin' some another place.

Of the vast army of "transients" who were "on the bum" during the thirties – estimates ranged from two to four million – a large proportion relative to their national percentage were Blacks and of these only a small number were true "boomers," or migrant workers. Far too many had no prospects whatsoever and toured aimlessly, with the police ready to arrest them for vagrancy or for failing to pay their fares. Living from day to day, skipping aboard the freight trains as they rattled slowly across high trestle bridges, clambering on to the passenger trains as they gathered speed on leaving the stations behind, they let the great locomotives carry them to distant cities. Monkey Joe Coleman made his way from New Orleans to Memphis, Chicago, and eventually, the East Coast.

70   They tell me that the New York Central train runs faster than any
          Greyhound bus can run, (*twice*)
       I'm gonna ride it this mornin', just to leave this bad luck town.

With her eyes full of tears Trixie Smith sobs—"I hate to hear that engine blow O-O-OO-OO. She can't ride on the freight train—mean cruel brakeman won't even let her ride the blind. So the whistle blows—the train goes—and Trixie goes to her room and hides. But when a man gets the Blues, he gets on a freight train and rides.

2211 { Freight Train Blues—   **Trixie Smith and Her Down Home Syncopators**
      { Don't Shake It No More

A New Record By Anna Lee Chisholm

12213 { Cool Kind Daddy Blues—Guitar Acc.   **Anna Lee Chisholm**
      { Georgia Sam Blues

Jelly Roll Morton—Popular Pianist

12216 { Thirty-Fifth Street Blues—Piano Solo—   **Jelly Roll Morton**
      { Mamanita

Have You Got These Popular Records

12201 { Red River Blues.—Guitar and Banjo Acc.—Pruett Twins—   **Lottie Beaman**
      { Honey Blues

12205 { You Ain't Foolin' Me—Piano Acc. James Blythe—   **Priscilla Stewart**
      { True Blues

20332 { Mr. Jelly Lord—Instrumental—   **Jelly Roll Morton's Steamboat Four**
      { Steady Roll

12202 { Chicago Monkey Man—   **Ida Cox and Her Blues Serenaders**
      { Worried Any How Blues

I ain't never seen a train I want to ride so bad before, (*twice*)
I'm gonna ride it this mornin', get off in Baltimore.

I could tell it could run when I seen it creepin up in the yard, (*twice*)
I'm gonna ride it this mornin', if I have to ride the rods.

Some were scared to pay for a ticket even though they might have the money: they were the Blacks who had been recruited to the northern labour forces in war periods and those with some form of criminal record or debt to pay who knew that their presence at the ticket box would be noticed and reported. For the man in trouble the railroad afforded the swiftest method of avoiding apprehension, and the long distances that the transcontinental trains covered could enable him to get outside the state where he could gain immunity from the local arms of the law. So in St. Louis the singer, Walter Davis, knew that the M. & O. Line – strictly speaking, the G.M. & O., or Gulf, Mobile, and Ohio, would take him South from the city more than five hundred miles to Mobile Bay, Alabama.

71   My baby got unruly, and she called the Chief of Police,
     My baby got unruly, called the police up to my door,
     An' I believe to my soul gonna have to ride that M. & O.

     I'm a railroad man and I love that M. & O. (*twice*)
     An' when I leave this town I ain't comin' back no mo'.

     I'm in a world of trouble an' I believe I got to go, (*twice*)
     I'm gonna leave here people, gonna catch that M. & O.

The train meant protection and with its fast-moving coaches he felt a close bond. To Blacks living in particular areas served by one railroad company or another, the trains became familiar friends and the field-hands welcomed their passing as they marked the progress of the day. They recognized the peculiarities of the whistles of certain trains and the "signature" of the firemen who operated them. On those lines where Blacks were employed the firemen arranged the steam whistles or "quills" so that a simple tune could be played, and on the Illinois Central, the famous I.C. which ran from Chicago to New Orleans, the firemen would send a rudimentary blues wailing across the Delta by "quilling" on the whistles.

72   Nobody knows that I.C. like I do. (*twice*)
     Now the reason I know it I ride it through and through.

That I.C. Special is the only train I choose, (*twice*)
That's the train I ride when I get these I.C. blues.

Mister I.C. Engineer make that whistle moan, (*twice*)
Got the I.C. Blues and I can't help but groan.

I got the I.C. Blues and box-cars on my mind, (*twice*)
I'm gonna pack my grip and beat it on down the line.

Numerous blues are sung about individual trains which appear to have their own peculiar personalities, especially the *Cannonball*, the *Redball*, and other famous express engines. Impressive in their speed and immense proportions, chilling the spine with their shrieking whistles in the night, thrilling the blood with the roar of their engines as they passed, even the more obscure trains had their significance for Blacks in the remoter districts. So the blues singer may tell of the *Flying Crow* which runs northward from the Texas Coast:

73 Flying Crow leavin' Port Arthur, why they come to Shreveport to
        change their crew, (*twice*)
    They'll take water in Texakarna, and for Ashdown they'll keep on
        through.

    Twenty-five minutes from evenin' – for a cup of coffee and a slice of
        cake, (*twice*)
    Flying Crow is headed for Kansas City, and boys she just can't wait.

    Yes she's gone, she's gone, with a red and green light behind, (*twice*)
    Well now the red means trouble, and the green means a ramblin' mind.

At times the trains themselves take on the stature of the folk hero that the railroad worker – John Henry, Joe Mica, Casey Jones – once provided in the black ballads, and the singer found in the character that he had made of the locomotive the qualities that he himself would have liked to possess, though such fancy was usually tempered with the flame of reality.

74 If I could holler like the *Bob Lee Junior* blows, (*twice*)
    Then I would call my baby, ooh, well, on the killing floor.

    If I had a head-light on some passenger train, (*twice*)
    Then I would shine my lights and call the red a sham.

Well, the *Bob Lee Junior* passed me with my baby all on the inside,
(*twice*)
And the conductor said, "I'm sorry, buddy, but your baby she got to
ride."

So marked was the imprint of its character that the singer often
personified the train, addressing his complaints and his comments to it and
thinking of its crew and the engine itself as one; a transference characteristic
among men who work and live in close contact with ships and vehicles the
world over, though not always found in their song. The machine became
the scapegoat for faults that might well have been laid at the door of the
singer himself, or the substitute for the blameworthy when events could not
be explained.

75   *Big Four, Big Four*, why would you be so mean? (*twice*)
Why, you the meanest ole train that I ever seen.

You taken my baby away and left me standin' here, (*twice*)
Well I ain't got no one to love, and I swear I cain't go nowhere.

Engineerman, I heard you when you blowed your whistle, fireman I
heard you when you rung your bell, (*twice*)
Well I hate to see my baby – my baby, fare you well.

Although the New York Central had taken it over in 1930, the *Big Four*, the
Cleveland, Cincinnati, Chicago, & St. Louis Railroad, was still known by
that name when Leroy Carr recorded his blues. Its main offices were in
Indianapolis, his home city, and he invested the train that he would hear
every day with a character that reflected his personal relationships. The *Big
80* or the *Dixie Flyer* could be a friend, as it thundered on to the South – but
the *Sunshine Special* or, for Georgia White, the *Panama Limited*, that took
away a loved one became the object of bitter resentment:

76   I've got the choo-choo blues, had 'em all night and day, (*twice*)
'Cause the *Panama Limited* carried my man away.

There goes that mean ole train, leavin' for New Orleans, (*twice*)
Lord I got the blues, I could almost scream.

In Black folksay there is a rich vein of railroad lore and this is strongly
represented in the blues. Known by their initials or words derived from·

them, the Chesapeake and Ohio (C. & O.), the Texas and Pacific (T. & P.), the Louisville and Nashville (L. & N.), the Missouri, Kansas, Texas line known more familiarly as the Katy, the lines known simply as the Southern, the Seaboard, the Wabash and a few score of others all figured prominently in the blues of the migrant. He sang of the Kaycee – the Kansas City Southern Line, or of the Yellow Dog, one of the most famous themes of the railroad blues. The Yazoo and Mississippi Valley Road, which was crossed by the Southern Line at Moorhead, Mississippi, was known widely as the Yellow Dog, some persons contending that it was named in humor or ignorance from the initials of the shorter term for the line Yazoo-Delta. But in Rome, Mississippi, they declared that it was named after a mongrel hound that noisily greeted every train as it passed through, whilst employees of the line said that it was the derisive term used by workers on a rival line – for railroaders called a small dummy-line train a "short dog." But it scarcely matters: another fragment was added to the great body of black folk-lore; a little more material for the blues was created, and every hobo understood when Big Bill Broonzy cried:

77   I was standin', lookin' an' listenin', watchin' the Southern cross the
      Dog, (*twice*)
    If ma baby didn't catch that Southern she must've caught that Yellow
      Dog.

    I'm goin' to Moorhead, get me a job on the Southern Line, (*twice*)
    So that I can make some money just to send for that brown of mine.

    The Southern cross the Dog at Moorhead, mama, Lord an' she keeps
      on through, (*twice*)
    I swear my baby's gone to Georgia, I believe I'll go to Georgia too.

To have "come from across the tracks" was to have been born in the lower-class section of a town, but the phrase had even more significance for Blacks, for the poorest sectors were those that back on to the railroad tracks, where the great locomotives as they gathered speed on leaving the immense railroad terminals of Chicago, Kansas City, or St. Louis caused the poor frame houses to shudder to their inadequate foundations, blackening their walls with grime and smoke, cracking the ceilings and killing the vegetation. When Jack Ranger sang of seeing his women pass his door as the Texas-Pacific train took her away, he was speaking literally, not metaphorically. Even though he addressed the engineer long after he was out of earshot, the train would have still been in sight.

78   I was laying in my window lookin' in ma baby's door, (*twice*)
     She packed her trunk this mornin', said now she was fixin' to go.

     Say, the T.P. is runnin', smoke settlin' on the ground, (*twice*)
     After the train was gone, couldn't find my easy rider around.

     I ain't got me no more lover, no more baby now, (*twice*)
     I said no more pretty mama to run me crazy now.

     Engineerman, engineerman, please turn your train around, (*twice*)
     I wanta speak one word to my baby, then she can let your window
         down.

     I was standin' in my door, peepin' at that T.P. when she blowed, (*twice*)
     Takin' my baby away, she ain't comin' here no more.

The railroad held few illusions for the the blues singer. Living beside the tracks in south-side slum or hobo jungle, walking the ties, riding the blinds, nailing the rattlers, firing the engines, greasing the bearings in the "round-houses" – he was too close to the ties, the tar, and the tallow for romantic notions. As transient, as tramp, as wanderer, or worker he sang from experience rather than sentiment.

3   *Pains in my heart*

In the 1950s there were ten, twelve, fourteen million Blacks in the United States, according to the conflicting figures given by various writers. This confusion is understandable for the identity of the individual Black is not easy to define. At the beginning of the century the state of West Virginia officially declared a Negro to be a person with one-sixteenth or more of his ancestral blood colored, but in 1930 they broadened this to include all persons with any "ascertainable Negro blood," which meant that there were in the U.S.A. many hundreds of thousands of persons technically "Black," though they may well have been unaware of the fact. Every year a few thousand Blacks "passed for White" and submerging themselves in the white world left their background behind them. They were the Blacks of whom the sole justification for so designating them was that they were perhaps seven-eighths white. Quite half of the Blacks in the United States were as much white as they were colored, but stigmatized by a fundamentally illogical system that measured only the degree of African blood in their veins. A man could live next door to a swarthy, dark-skinned American of Italian or Balkan extraction, and though his own eyes may have been blue and his hair blonde he was required to sit in the rear of the street-car marked *For Colored* whilst his neighbour sat in the section for Caucasians. For many years the African American had been officially termed "Non-Caucasian," a euphemism designed to show that he did not stem from the cradle of Indo-European stock. At the opposite extreme the pure-blood African American is as difficult to identify, for although George Cable was still able to distinguish nearly a score of African tribal groups in the 1880s it is doubtful whether, in the entire black population in the 1950s, more than ten per cent were pure African Americans, and some authorities would have disputed even this figure.

Between the extremes of color – from the black-skinned with tightly curled hair and marked prognathism to the light-complexioned with straight hair and aquiline nose – lies a multitude of types of skin pigmentation, skull structure and greater or lesser degrees of African and European characteristics. These have arisen from a multitude of causes in cross-racial

69

intermixing, but above all from the extensive miscegenation that was practiced during and after the slavery period. It was the custom for southern planters to keep one or even several concubines amongst the black women and to maintain a colored "second wife." The second wives, or black mistresses, were often well treated, well housed, even well provided for in the wills of their masters, though others fared less happily. Their progeny became slaves on the plantations as did the children who resulted from the casual and often brutal unions enforced by the younger southern white men, who sometimes marked their adolescence with the rape of a slave girl. The extreme brutality of these sexual excesses is staggering in a region that prided itself on the courtly manners and aristocratic bearing of the Southern Gentlemen. Slaves were powerless to intervene when their wives, sisters, and daughters were demanded, for any attempt at prevention would result in disfigurement, the severing of a limb – even death. In many states legislation was introduced forbidding mixed marriages and sometimes punishing adulterous unions between white and black, but the exercise of the legal powers was used with extreme caution, and the measures in almost every case were more rigorously applied against the black than the white offender. In the rural South such practices persisted into the 1960s, and in many areas black girls lived in fear of young white students and planters who followed the herd instinct and sought to prove their virility and "courage" before their fellows.

Curiously, in the "Big Houses" – the homes of the southern plantation owners – the house slaves and servants were privileged, even pampered and many were often looked after with affection. The black "mammies" who wet-nursed the children, who showered kisses and sympathy upon them and shared their secrets and love intrigues as they grew up, were the objects of devotion amongst the younger white children, whilst the stable-boys and black valets were often similarly respected. From this confusing pattern there developed in many white persons a pathological mixture of guilt, sex, and affection that found later expression in beatings, brandings, and burnings, and which eventually amounted to a regional sexual complex that was manifest over many years in the hideous lynchings, castrations, and mutilations of Blacks who were in numerous instances unquestionably guiltless.

For the Black, whether he was purple-hued or pink-skinned, his color was his problem, both within the black community and in the community as a whole. It was this which determined that his whole social life should be different from that of his fellow Americans, for his color and his cast of feature were the outward indications of his ancestry. Only the Filipinos, the Mexicans, and the Puerto Ricans suffered more than Blacks from the effects of their racial and national origins and their recognizable characteristics in hue or physique. Ethnocentricity is as evident in the black community as it is in most others whose cohesion is largely dependent on ethnic identity. Stereotypes of race are not necessarily based on color: the singer of the following blues was Blind Percy:

79   Let me tell you mama like the Dago told the Jew, (*twice*)
      If you don't want me, it's a cinch I don't want you.

      There's two kind of nations I sure can't understand, (*twice*)
      That's a Chinese woman and a Dago man.

These ethnic groups are generally to be found in ghettoes of their own, often identified by a patronizing diminutive: Little Mexico, Little Tokyo. Their distribution generally means that they are seldom contiguous with the black sectors, as was implicit in Willie Lane's bragging blues, *Too Many Women*:

80   Well I got so many women, I don't hardly know how to choose, (*twice*)
      Well I wake up in the morning, I got too many to lose.

      Some red, some yellow, some is black, some is teasin' brown, (*twice*)
      You can't tell much about 'em, 'cause they's scattered all over town.

      Five on the South Side, seven on the East Side,
      Nine on the West Side – North Side too;
      Ten out in Oakland, eleven on Sixth Avenue . . .

At times the characteristics of African racial features and color have an ominous significance in the blues, which may hint that they are indirectly related to social problems. So the state of being "blue" is associated with alienation, and is linked with an "evil mind" or an inclination to violence. Both are coupled with the inescapable condition of being black. "I believe to my soul, the Lord has put a curse on me," sang Alice Moore from St. Louis in more than one version of her *Black and Evil Blues*. That her hearers identified with her theme was evident in the popularity of the blues, which she made four times in different versions.

81   And I'm blue, black and evil, and I wished I had made myself, (*twice*)
      I would fix this man of mine, so he could have nobody else.

When I get so blue, black and evil, I get blood all in my eyes, (*twice*)
When I catch my man with his woman, he starts to tellin' lies.

I'm so blue, black and evil, until I can hardly see, (*twice*)
Caught my man with a girl last night, that was supposed to be a friend
of me.

The result of the inter-racial admixture, in which Blacks knew better than
to have any willing or active part as initiators, has been the creation of
complex caste system based not on economy but on color. Notwithstanding
the poor example before them, Blacks frequently aspired to the condition of
being white, as they saw the better jobs, the higher standard of living Whites
enjoyed. Men spent large sums of money on hair-straightening greases and
combs that were supposed to remove the kinks in African hair. Women
dyed their hair to a brick-red, powdered their faces and applied artificial
color in order to make their skins lighter and their complexions more
"white."

82   Wasn't for powder and the straightening comb,
      Wasn't for the powder and the straightening comb,
      The De Kalb women would not have no home.

Often the lighter-colored Blacks obtained employment more readily than those with a darker skin hue, for Whites who could accept the presence of a light-skinned man often felt a sense of unreasonable revulsion when in the company of a very black person. This primitive distinction by color was passed on to Blacks themselves and their population was many times divided by grades of skin pigmentation. In the caste system that evolved from this arbitrary means of discrimination, the lighter skinned tended to be on a higher plane, whilst the extremely black-skinned man was looked down upon, the lowest grade being the "blue-gummed nigger" in their own derogatory term, which identified the darkest and most African of their number. It is instructive that the term was also applied to mean and recalcitrant Blacks: the generations of children that have lived in fear that "a black man will eat you up" grew into adults who retained that fear and the belief that the black male is criminally-minded, and they have passed the belief across the color line. The dark-skinned Sonny Boy Williamson clearly felt the distinction and resented it.

83 Now I can hear my black name a-ringin' all up and down the line,
     (*twice*)
     Now I don't believe you love me, woman, I believe I'm just drivin'
     away my time.

     Well now, I had the blues before sunrise, oh, with tears standing in my
     eyes, (*twice*)
     Now that make me have such a funny feelin' man, a feelin' I do despise.

When conditions could not become worse they were, in black parlance, "too black bad," and the term "black is evil" become comprehensible when it is realized that the stigma of a dark skin precluded hundreds of thousands from any of the privileges that they legally and constitutionally deserved. Contemptuous terms that have long been used to identify dark-skinned persons – "shine," "snow-ball," "shade," "eight-ball" – are exceedingly offensive to Blacks, to whom the terms "coon," "darkie," and "nigger" are equally objectionable when used by Whites though they would use them in an endearing way amongst themselves. To differentiate between their many shades of color they evolved many words which are applicable to certain shades: "ashy black," "chocolate-brown," "coffee," "sealskin-brown," "brightskin," "high yaller," "lemon," and others, though some became offensive as the years passed, whilst others remained acceptable and even flattering. Blacks of one particular skin hue often kept together and may certainly have had a preference for that color, looking with contempt on those that were darker, but also with disapproval on those who had a high proportion of white blood.

84   So glad I'm brownskin, so glad I'm brownskin, chocolate to the bone,
  So glad I'm brownskin, chocolate to the bone,
  An' I got what it takes to make a monkey man leave his home.

  Black man is evil, yaller man so low-down, (*twice*)
  I walk into these houses just to see these black men frown.

  I'm just like Miss Lillian, like Miss Lillian, I mean Miss Glinn you see,
   (*twice*)
  She said, "A brownskin man is just all right with me."

And indeed the brown-skinned Lillian Glinn whom Barbecue Bob admired had expressed just this opinion, though she had been more careful or more generous where others were concerned:

85   Now all high yellers you ought to listen to me,
  A yellow man's sweet, a black man's neat,
  A brownskin man will take you clear off of your feet.

  And if you don't believe what I say,
  Just get him to shake the shivaree,
  That's why I say a brownskin man's all right with me.

To Barbecue Bob the black man was evil, and the yellow man low-down, but light skin was frequently admired, and envied. Louie Lasky had seen his ideal on the silent cinema screen and probably in the cheap prints displayed in the windows of store-front churches.

86   She got hair like Gloria Swanson and she walks just like Priscilla Dean,
   (*twice*)
  'Cause she's the prettiest woman, old Louie have ever seen.

  I'm gonna ask the Good Lord to send me an angel down (*twice*)
  But if she ain't not a good one, I'm gonna cling on to my teasin'
   brown.

In some sections of black society the lighter-skinned were mistrusted for it was assumed that they had less racial pride than those who could not hide their origins. Some grounds exist for this assumption since a light-skinned person could cross the color line and "pass for White," if he was able to make the necessary cultural and social adjustment. Whereas the practice of "day-time passing" in which Blacks obtained jobs normally reserved for Whites, but returned to their race at night was considered to be something of a joke at the expense of the Whites, permanent passing was considered to be "deserting the race." Among racially conscious groups the darker-skinned members were often considered more reliable and their more evident African ancestry met with approval. Sang Leola Wilson, who was very light of hue herself,

87 My mama told me before I left home,
   My mama told me before I left home,
   You better let them Jacksonville men alone.

   Some women want yeller men and some women want brown,
   Some women want yeller men and some women want brown,
   I know a black man will beat you but he sure won't throw you down.

To those attributes that seemed to have some justification were added others, which, true or imagined, helped to determine the Black's place in his own society and affected his choice of partner. The virtues of one group – distinguished as always by color – would be extoled to the detriment of others. Popular superstitions arose, such as the belief that among the lighter-skinned Negroes their color would eventually reveal its true self in a "stripe" of deeper pigment, a notion that was almost as widespread as the "black baby bugaboo," the fear that a light couple might produce a black child. In pointed metaphor Barbecue Bob, a very color-conscious blues singer, advised that his listener accept the situation:

88 High yeller she'll kick you, that ain't all,
   When you step out at night 'nother mule in your stall.

       A brownskin woman, best brownie after all
       They'll stick by you, winter, summer, spring, and fall,
       A brownskin woman, best brownie after all.

   Anybody tell you brownskin girls all right,
   High yellow gets twenty-five, they drives a black stripe.

   Ashes to ashes, and dust to dust,
   If you can't ride the train catch the ginger bus . . .

So the problem of color obtained not merely between the races but within the black race itself and there was not only one color bar, but in a sense, many. That this was also a bar to the progress of Blacks cannot be denied and racial integration was clearly retarded because of it. Love, of course, transcended these artificial barriers in many instances, but there was a tendency for darker-hued men to marry the darker-skinned women, adhering to the belief – anathema to many of lighter skin – that "the blacker the berry, the sweeter the juice." The lighter-colored prefer to marry lighter still, and over all there was probably a tendency to a preference, where possible, for a lighter partner, when a preference is, in fact, expressed. In the course of love, color may not play a very great part, but in the initial selection of the group with which they associated, and from which their partners might eventually be drawn, Blacks were undoubtedly influenced by skin hue, about which many were almost pathologically self-conscious by the very fact that they were perpetually reminded of its existence as a social barrier.

Physical attractiveness amongst Blacks did extend beyond skin color and "white" attributes were often much admired – "good" hair for example, which is long and straight and has no kinks. To improve their appearance some women bought "rats," "rats tails," or artificial hair, as Lightnin' Hopkins regretted:

89 Yes, you know I carried my wife to the hairdresser and this is what the
      hairdresser said:
    She said, "Sam, I can't treat your woman's hair, God knows, but I can
    treat her head."

> I told her, "No," if her hair ain't no longer than mine,
> Yes, you know she ain't no good for nothin' but trouble,
> Yes, keeps you buyin' rats all the time.

Yes, you know I woke up this morning, people, folks there even wake
up 'bout the break of day,
I even found a rat on her pillow where she usta lay,

> I don't want no woman if her hair ain't no longer than mine,
> Yes, you know she ain't no good for nothin' but trouble,
> Yes, keeps you be buyin' rats all the time.

There are some features which appeal to Blacks that do not come into the categories of beauty normally or expressly admired in white groups.

Contrast with dark skin accentuates the beauty of the teeth, and this is a feature to which attention is frequently given. Many are the blues that extoll the virtues of a woman whose "teeth shine like pearls." To draw attention to the teeth it was fashionable in the black southern cities in the early part of the century to have diamonds set between or within them, causing a brilliant and unexpected flash when the wearer smiled. The practice died out in later years being considered a mark of barbarity by educated Blacks, but in the *demi-monde* it persisted, in company with the wearing of red lipstick on the eyelids, and exaggerated or exciting modes of dress that might have been considered bad taste in more select society, but which were worn with *élan* by women with fine figures and poise. Washboard Sam sang about his "river hip" woman.

90   Now I've got a woman stream-lined from her feet to her head, (*twice*)
      If she should ever quit me she might as well be dead.

      Every time my woman smiles she shows the diamonds in her teeth,
         (*twice*)
      She wears fine clothes, and patent leather shoes on her feet.

      Men's all crazy about her, she makes them whine and cry, (*twice*)
      She's a river hip mama and they all wanna be baptized.

In spite of the appeal of pearl-white teeth, the treatment of decayed teeth in itself set its own peculiar standards and gold teeth were much admired, suggesting affluence and giving to the wearer a certain primitive splendor.

91   Now the woman I love got a mouth chock full of good gold,
      Now the woman I love got a mouth chock full of good gold,
      Every time she hug and kiss me it make my blood run cold.

The attractiveness of a "stream-lined woman" accords with the concepts of feminine beauty common among white males in America, and city Blacks were inclined to adopt similar standards. But among rural black males the measure was often very different. Instead of the slender, stream-lined woman, they sang of the "big, fat woman with the meat shaking on her bone" with obvious delight and admiration. The diminutive stature of a woman who was "li'l and low" was as much admired as the girl who was "tree-top tall," as "tall as a Georgia Pine," or in apparent paradox "long and tall like a cannon-ball." By this was meant the *Cannon-ball Express* on the

Illinois Central line. A number of venerable folk phrases are recalled in a blues by Willie Jackson from New Orleans:

92   And a long, tall woman will make a preacher lay his Bible down,
    I said a medium-sized woman will make a jack-rabbit move his family
      in town,
    But a big, fat mama will make a mule kick his stable down.

    My baby will make a man shake a court-house down,
    My long, tall mama, will make the judge shake that court-house down,
    And my long, tall baby will make the mayor turn the whole town
      round.

Long legs were considered attractive, but so, too, were "big bow-legs" though Blind Blake added sourly:

93   There's one thing in this world I cannot understand,
    One thing in this world I cannot understand,
    That's a bow-legged woman crazy 'bout a cross-eyed man.

"Doctor" Clayton gave eloquent expression to the features that he found beautiful in the woman that he loved, and his blues well summarizes some of the qualities that especially appealed:

94   Well, I feel all right and everything is okay,
    Yes, I feel all right, everything is okay,
    It's the love of my baby, oh, makes me feel this way.

    She's got ways like an angel, an' she's sweet like heaven above, (*twice*)
    She's got everything I want, everything I need and love.

    She's got great big legs, Lord and the cutest little feet, (*twice*)
    Says she's got a sweet disposition that worries every other man she
      meets.

    She's a copper-colored mama, Lord her shape is a solid dream, (*twice*)
    She's the loveliest woman I swear I've ever seen.

In the eyes of the lover the features of the partner are more beautiful than those of anyone else. Reflected in them is the passion that they share. Occupying every thought, giving color to every scene, the image of the lover remains. Sang Memphis Minnie to her husband, Ernest Lawler – Little Son Joe:

> 95   I see your face before me all through the night and day,
>   Oh – all through the night and day,
>   But I still love you in the same old way.
>
>   When you love me, Lord, I get such a thrill, (*twice*)
>   And when you put your arms around me, babe, I can't keep still.
>
>   When you love me, love me a great long time,
>   Joe I get everything else but you off my mind,
>   (*Spoken*) Play it, Son Joe
>   Keep your mind on it now . . . All right, Son, I'm looking at you.

In their volume *The Negro and His Songs* (1926), Odum and Johnson accounted for the "absence of the higher ideals of love and virtue" by telling the reader to bear in mind that these were the songs that represented only "what might be called the Negro lower class." Presumably the depressed classes were incapable of spiritual love – a Victorian concept that one would imagine would have failed to survive the turn of the century, but Iain Lang was to declare twenty years later that "among hundreds of blues" he had "come across only one celebrating loyalty based on affection rather than on physical attraction."

Song as a vehicle for the expression of the emotions and declarations of love is ageless and common to virtually all societies; with this tradition of song it is scarcely conceivable that black love songs did not exist in the nineteenth century; still less acceptable is the notion that they are non-existent in the present era.

During the slavery period free marriage amongst Blacks was far from common. If two slaves on neighboring plantations developed a love for each other they had little hope of being permitted to marry unless their respective owners were more than usually generous, but unions amongst couples on the same plantation were encouraged. Numerous instances of happy and faithful partnerships within the plantations have been perpetuated in the records, though the couples were never granted the blessing of the Church. Many well-authenticated tragic and moving stories have survived which tell of the hardships endured by devoted black couples, many of whom suffered death for their affections. Touching accounts exist of slaves who worked for pathetically long hours after sundown to buy themselves out of slavery, so that they could be free to work for the purchase of the freedom of their loved ones.

Though the post-bellum years were marked by a period of great unsettlement for the newly emancipated slaves, many settled down to married life or faithful unions with their partners when there was no one to "read the book over them." In subsequent years large numbers played their parts as responsible members of the community and, in so far as they were able in a segregated society, lived normal lives: falling in love, marrying, raising children, and enjoying the pleasures of family domesticity.

Imitations of black song are frequently overtly sentimental but the original is seldom mawkishly emotional. Blues has rarely acquired a polished veneer of decorative words or elaborately turned phrases, but within its compass there are innumerable examples of sincere and direct declarations of love and affection. When Odum and Johnson were publishing their works, a Dallas folk singer, Whistlin' Alex Moore, was singing with a simple, but valid, philosophy:

96   Like in a ragin' storm and the captain on the deck, (*twice*)
      My poor heart's bleedin' and my mind's all wrecked.

      I think it's unfair to love and not be loved, (*twice*)
      I think it means beware when you kiss and cannot hug.

      There's no heart in life unless you understand, (*twice*)
      There's no heart in marryin' someone, just because you can.

      Hatred is self-punishment, forgiveness is better than revenge, (*twice*)
      There's no heart in buying love, all to lose and none to win.

Through the history of recorded blues runs a persistent vein of contemplative verses, viewed from the personal angle of the singer, as is customary with the form, but having within them advice and counsel for others that stem from the singers' experience. Sometimes a series of general pronouncements is made, the conclusions resulting from knowledge that the singer has gained; sometimes they are directed to a particular individual, rather as the dedication of a book is addressed to one specific person though the contents have meaning for many.

97   You have to live and let live, you have to give and take.
      You have to make believe, you have to pardon me.

You have to think it over, you have to plan it out,
It's a proposition, worthwhile talking 'bout.

Those who make no mistakes, dear, don't do anything,
This broken heart needs a break, dear, whether or not you care.

Words of endearment and declarations of love are fundamentally private, shared and understood between the lovers themselves and having especial significance for them alone. This does not prevent the poet from expressing his emotions in verse, nor does it prevent the reader from sharing the sentiments, or from perceiving within them his own state of mind and feeling a bond of sympathy with the composer. In the blues a change from a statement addressed to the general listener to a more personal one intended for the lover alone is not uncommon, as in the blues by Bumble Bee Slim above, or in the following by Walter Davis:

98   The girl I love just as sweet as she can be, *(twice)*
     And every time I kiss her cold chills run over me.

     Listen here, little girl, my love for you is strong, *(twice)*
     And if you love me you won't do nothing wrong.

     So there ain't no need to worry 'bout me babe when I'm out of town
       (twice)
     Because my love is for you and it can't be turned around.

     I was just sittin' down thinkin' babe, just a minute ago, *(twice)*
     What in the world made you love me so?

For the newly-in-love the complexity of emotions felt is often greater and more confusing than any experienced before. The combination of happiness and despair, the hurt that is felt with the joy, the pain that is always so inextricably interwoven with the pleasure, has been for centuries the source of inspiration for songs, poems, books, and plays. In these the composer's self-conscious art is brought to bear upon the theme and strand by strand the threads of the lover's knots are untangled and examined. The blues singer brought a basic simplicity to the subject: he seldom attempted to unravel the problem but, like Curtis Jones, stated his condition of heart in uncomplicated terms which, in their sincerity, lost little.

99   Don't leave me, baby, 'cause I am so down and blue, (*twice*)
     Deep down in my heart, baby, my love is only for you.

     You are the only woman ever got into my heart, (*twice*)
     Lawsy, how would I live, baby, if we were to part?

     I'm down and blue an' I'm as blue as I can be, (*twice*)
     Because your love, baby, means all this world to me.

Psychologically, biologically, and anthropologically the belief that the black race is inferior to the white and incapable of the higher emotions is fallacious and insupportable. The capacity for love, for devotion, for courage, for selflessness is no less than that of any other group, even if conversely Blacks are as prone to similar weaknesses of rapacity, avarice, or hatred as are others. The patterns that have conditioned the growth of different societies and that have caused them to adopt varying attitudes to the importance of religion, of self-sacrifice, of romantic love, or the autocracy of grandparents, for example, are exceedingly complex and reach far back in time. But given equal social advantages and environmental influences the reactions of most races are very similar. The North American Black is culturally a part of the society of the United States and that which is owed to the African heritage, while still evident, has been reduced with the passage of time. In matters concerning the emotions Blacks do not react in a manner greatly different from that of any racial group amongst their fellow countrymen, though they may often express them in a less inhibited way. But often a black man feels the same distress when he falls in love with a woman who is not in love with him, the same misery when his advances are rejected, the same mixed feelings of desire and guilt when he finds himself in love with one whose age is much below his own. Sang Ollie Shepard:

100 I'm afraid I love you and I've tried so hard not to, (*twice*)
     You are young and lovely, what more can a poor man do?

     When I kiss you why do you tremble so? (*twice*)
     I realize this is your first affair, but I just can't let you go.

     There isn't any way in this world I can go on being without you,
         (*twice*)
     Your love is so true, that's all I ask of you.

The differences that exist between the behavior of black and white Americans was largely due to their relative positions in society as a whole; there were rich and cultivated Blacks, poor and uncouth Whites too, but in the main the former's social standing was substantially lower. His distress when left alone and in love was no different; Sonny Boy Williamson was sufficiently aware of his lack of privilege to realize the reason for his blunders.

101   Honey, my heart gets to beatin' like a hammer and my eyes get so full
          of tears, (*twice*)
       You only been gone twenty-four hours but it seems like a million
          years.

       Honey, if I ever mistreat you, God knows I don't mean no harm,
          (*twice*)
       Because I ain't nothin' but a little country boy, an' I'm right down off
          the cotton farm.

       Honey, I don't believe you think I'm nothin', you don't believe I think
          I'm nothin' but a little clown, (*twice*)
       Now when I was lookin' for you last night, and you was way out on
          the other side of town.

So the field-hand was left working in the vain hope that he might better the fortunes of his family and himself. For a share-cropper the desire to revolt against the virtual servitude became greater as he saw his woman bowed down by the work she too had to undertake, and many a man was driven to violent and unlawful acts as a result. Tommy McClennan gave voice to a conflict of emotions as he angrily sought to choose between the woman who could join him in a hopeless and unequal anti-social struggle, the woman who could make her own decision to assert herself – and the woman who could take the shafts of the plough, guide the mules, and work beside him on the land.

102   I don't want none of these funny women if they don't know how to
          rob and steal, (*twice*) (*spoken:* What you gonna do?)
       They workin' theyself to death, in some po' farmer's fiel'.

       What do you want with a woman if she don't know "Yes" from
          "No," (*twice*)

But what d'ya want with one of them good-lookin' women if she don't
know "Gee" from "Haw?"

Undoubtedly the strain of continual work "from sun to sun" in the
endeavor to gain freedom from debt and serfdom could kill the love in both
heart and body. Husband and wife labored side by side and the wife who had
spent her days in the fields and her nights at the wash-tub had little time for
the expression of love. Tommy McClennan's companion in Yazoo City,
Mississippi, was Robert Petway. He sang of a woman whose determination
to work had become obsessive.

103   She's a cotton-pickin' woman, Lawd, she do's it all the time, (*twice*)
    If you don't stop pickin' cotton now, baby, I believe you sho' gwan to
    lose your mind. Yes yes . . .

    She pick so much cotton, she even don't know where to go, (*twice*)
    She's leavin' in the mornin', sweet mama, honey she gwan' from do' to
    do'.

    How long, on my bended knee – yes I mean it,
    How long, on my bended knee,
    Pick so much cotton now, partner, will you forgive me if you please?

Bertha Henderson sang as one for whom the strain proved too much. The
day had come when all loyalties were severed, and trying to justify her
actions by asking her husband to consider her dead – "to pin *crêpe* on his
sleeve" – she left him before her sanity left her.

104   I've been dogged and mistreated till I done made up my mind, (*twice*)
    Gonna leave this old country, and all my troubles behind.

    Get my ticket at the junction and flag the 'fore-day train, (*twice*)
    I'm goin' to leave this country before I go insane.

    When I leave this morning, papa, pin *crêpe* on your sleeve, (*twice*)
    Ain't comin' here no more, you can love just who you please.

    When they all mistreat you, no need to think about me, (*twice*)
    'Cause I'm leavin' this country blue as I can be.

    If the blues kill me, tell everybody the news, (*twice*)
    Here lays a woman died with the leavin' gal blues.

Proportionately more black homes are broken than white, but the reasons are manifold: some homes are broken through the incompatability of the partners. A number of southern states permitted marriage at a very young age – in Mississippi it had been legal until the 1950s for girls to marry at the age of twelve. Owing to the pressure of economic stress upon their lives, black children apparently reached maturity early in life and assumed the physical responsibilities of adults – young girls nursed their younger sisters and brothers to relieve their mothers for heavier work, and young boys were soon "buck-jumping" in the cotton rows. Seldom did they remain at school after the age of eleven or twelve, and consequently many were free to marry when they were still emotionally and mentally immature and unable to bear the responsibilities of married life, with the almost inevitable result that many unions were broken. The girl would attack her husband for his seeming incompetence while he suffered from her failure to cope with the management of the home. In his bitter-sweet voice, Leroy Carr sang:

105   All of this schooling education didn't mean a thing to me, (*twice*)
       When I met a good-looking woman that was the end of me.

       This woman treated me mean, she's the cruellest I've ever seen, (*twice*)
       The house is always dirty and her cooking I swear ain't clean.

       Now rambling with this woman caused me to be down so low, (*twice*)
       And now my dear old mother won't allow me round her door.

Inadequate facilities and the perennial break in schooling during periods of considerable agricultural activity left many Blacks seriously lacking in education, and though some acquired a wise philosophy from their worldly experience, others whose lives had been circumscribed were limited also in their abilities to deal with the problems of ill-disciplined children and slatternly mothers. Many resorted to corporal means as the only method that they knew to correct the wrongs that occured, though this may well have aggravated rather than mitigated their troubles. Few problems have been solved by wild thrashings.

106   I'm gonna get me a picket off a graveyard fence, (*twice*)
       Gonna beat you brownskins till you learn good sense.

       Tell me, brownskin, what is on your mind? (*twice*)
       Reason I ask you, brownie, you 'bout to run me blind.

An excess of spirits, arising out of a slight success, a desire to "raise a little hell" when things go wrong, or to give vent to suppressed feelings when circumstances made it inadvisable to express opinions, the need to expend unused energies in lay-off periods and the need for an escape when times were bad – these could make a nervous man violent, a powerful man "mean." Gabriel Brown's woman was the inevitable butt of his feelings.

107   Ah, when I come home – think I'm doing well,
 Keep me from being in trouble, you just start to raisin' hell,
  That makes me evil, oh Lord, so evil,
  Yes I get evil, baby, when my love comes down.

 You better wake up pretty mama, 'cause you can never tell,
 Now I may start out-swinging, 'cause I ain't doing so well –
  You see I'm evil, oooh, Lord so evil,
  Well, I get evil, baby, when my love comes down.

To suffer violence from the man that she had loved and cherished for so many years was all the more distressing for a woman, no matter how his life may have conditioned his behavior. Words of love were forgotten and all that was left was the pain of "mistreatment" at his hands. Elzadie Robinson pleaded:

108   I'm down on my knees, cutie, now to you,
 I say I'm down, cain't stand the ways you do,
 I can't stand the misery I've gone through.

 Now you know you have made me cry, (*twice*)
 An' you say you could see me die.

 You'll regret the way you treated me,
 I'm begging you to cure my misery,
 Before I go and jump into the sea.

When her husband was out at work or when he was on night shift, she could leave a key for her "back-door man" to make his "'fore-day creep," Sara Martin offered a few words of wry wisdom.

109   I've got to have a daddy to tell my troubles to, (*twice*)
 One who knows how to love, and keep me from being blue.

Loving night and day is the thing I crave, (*twice*)
Give me lots of loving and I'll be your slave.

Little drops of water, only grains of sand, (*twice*)
Every sensible woman got a back-door man.

Last to know of the infidelity of his wife was usually the husband, who could
not believe that the woman that he had admired and on whom he had
depended had taken a "creeping man," and given her love to a "mean-
jumper." But it seems, the casual hints, the evasive answers, the slight
changes in behavior also sowed seeds of suspicion in Emery Glen's mind:

110 I went to bed last night with nothin' on my mind,
     I felt the good world – it was treatin' me kind.

     I dreamed I saw my mama tell me "Good-bye" (*twice*)
     Then around the back-door I saw her try another man's size.

     T'ain't no woman unback-door me, (*twice*)
     If I'm your one-an'-all or else your used-to-be.

     I got up this mornin', 'vestigatin' on my mind, (*twice*)
     I wanted to see if mama was the right kind.

     Sometimes these dreams just like bein' away, (*twice*)
     I saw another man eatin' of my chocolate cake.

The temptations cast before an attractive young woman with time on her
hands in the unrestrained environment of the "main stem" in the black
sector of a southern town were considerable. Pimps and gamblers in snap-
brim hats rubbed shoulders with muscular loggers in town with their
Saturday night "spending change." Saloons and barrelhouses rocked to the
live music of jug and juke bands while outside, the crap-shooters on the
sidewalks paused to admire the legs of the passing "good-lookin' brown-
skins" with their side-slit "Mary Jane" skirts. Hambone Willie Newbern
came into Memphis from Brownsville, Tennessee.

111 I've got a dreamy-eyed woman, lives down on Cherry Street, (*twice*)
     An' she laughs and talks with every brownskin ole man she meet.

Says I told her last night and all the night before,
And I told her last night and all the night before,
Said "If you don't quit some of your struttin', baby, you can't be mine
no more."

Put both hands on her hips and these is the words she said, (*twice*)
Said, "Big boy I couldn't miss you if the good Lord told me you was
dead."

A score of years later the joints rocked to the music of peacock-hued juke boxes, and the young women were fascinated by the styling of the Ford Mercurys, Pontiacs, and Cadillac Eights in which the sharp-clothed "cats" in their peg-top pants and "sky-bonnet" hats cruised round town. Lightnin' Hopkins watched his woman succumb and waited, with a laconic aside, for her return.

112   I saw you ridin' roun', you ridin' a bran' new automobile, (*twice*)
Yes, you was sittin' there happy with your handsome driver at the
wheel.

Your face was tint' with powder, your lips was all full of rouge,
Yes your face was tint' with powder an' your face was full of rouge,
Yes, but I know you was comin' home when you foun' out your driver
didn't mean you no good.
– In your bran' new automobile.

Lonnie Johnson sang the blues of a man who had struggled hard to try to secure for his wife a better home and standard of living, and in doing so had been forced to spend all his waking hours at work, "doubling" his jobs to secure extra pay; her unfaithfulness was especially bitter.

113   I work all day long for you, until the sun go down,
I work all day long for you, baby, from sun-up until the sun go down,
An' you take all my money and drink it up, and come home and want
to fuss and clown.

I worked for you so many times, when I really was too sick to go,
I worked for you, baby, when your man was slipping in my back-door,
I can see for myself so take your back-door man, I won't be your fool
no more.

I worked for you, baby, when snow was above my knees,
I worked for you, baby, when ice and snow was on the ground,
Trying to make you happy, an' you chasing every man in town.

It hurts to love a person that don't belong to you, (*twice*)
'Cause when they find out that you really love them and they don't
   care what they do,

They'll take your heart and they'll use it like a football on a football
   ground, (*twice*)
And when they git through playing with your heart, then they'll start
   blackin' your heart around.

None of these singers chose to identify their "two-timing" woman by
name, but Willie Blackwell was not so reticent. In a blues which combined
poetic simile and literal detail, narrative and hearsay, declared love and
veiled threat, he addressed his wayward Betty June.

114 Four o'clock flowers bloom in the evening, and close in the afternoon,
        (*twice*)
     They are only a summer beauty – so as my little Betty June.

     If you would only stop playing hookey and be a little more true, (*twice*)
     All the love I have to spare, Betty June would be for you.

     I'm a hard-workin' man, and I never gets my lovin' soon, (*twice*)
     And when I thinks about it in the mornin', it makes my heart ache in
        the afternoon.

     My job calls me at six p.m. and I don't gets home till day, (*twice*)
     My friends say she have done – Betty June don't make me feel that
        way.

     I'm not jealous but I'm superstitious, the most workin' men's that way,
        (*twice*)
     And if I catch you playin' hookey, Betty June – What a day, what a
        day . . .

The extremes of emotion seem closely allied: pain and pleasure are
inextricably interwoven; the deepest feelings of love may readily turn to

hate. Humiliation, frustration, bitterness, and selfishness are bound up in the complex emotions experienced by Bill Gaither over an unfaithful partner.

115   If I was cold and hungry, I wouldn't even ask you for bread, (*twice*)
       I don't want you no more, if I'm on my dying bed.

       At one time I loved you, but I sure do hate you now, (*twice*)
       Baby, you are the kind don't need a good man nohow.

       Ev'ry man in town knows about your ornery ways, (*twice*)
       Cain't nobody change you now, 'cause you've been a devil all of your days.

Marital unions were made and disengaged more freely among Blacks than among white persons from identical districts – particularly among the working class. This was partly due to the fact that there was virtually no black moneyed aristocracy in the majority of southern towns and in only a few was there a perceptible professional class. As a result, there was less need for conformity to conventional ideas of respectability and though the churches exerted a powerful influence upon their members, outside the church there was little stigma attached to a union that was not legally contracted. This has had the beneficial effect that illegitimacy was not considered a social barrier, but it also permitted a somewhat easy severance of family ties. Unions that were casually made, with couples "batching up" with little ceremony, were often as summarily broken.

116   My man left this morning, jest about half past four, (*twice*)
       He left a note on his pillow, sayin' he couldn't use me no more.

       Then I grabbed my pillow, turned over in my bed, (*twice*)
       I cried about my daddy, till my cheeks turned cherry red.

In more thoroughly urbanized communities and especially those in the North, there was more attention to the official registration and legalization of marriages, with the result that separations were taken less lightly. Without public assistance only a relatively small number of Blacks could obtain a divorce. For those who were estranged, but for whom divorce was not possible, there were many hardships, for the woman as much as for the man. In the lower-class communities women were often self-supporting and had a certain measure of independence, some even taking pleasure in supporting their men in idleness. But their distress was no less when they were deserted. Bessie Jackson:

117   I went to bed last night and these blues wouldn't let me rest, (*twice*)
     'Cause I ain't used to sleepin' by myself.

     Oh blues, oh blues, blues don't you see? (*twice*)
     You are carryin' me down, blues you tryin' to kill poor me.

     Now blues and trouble walk hand in hand – have mercy (*twice*)
     I never had these blues, until my best friend loved my man.

     He put his arms around me like a ring round the good Lord's sun,
       (*twice*)
     Said he ain't had no woman to love me, Lord, like I've done.

A woman who had been deserted suddenly, left without support and with the house rent to pay, children to clothe, and food to procure, was often left in desperate circumstances. When other families were clamoring to obtain rooms, no landlord would accept promises of eventual payment; the individual suffering of one colored woman did not swell the bank balance. Mary Johnson's solution was ironic.

118   My room rent is due this morning, I did not have a dime, (*twice*)
     The landlord told me he'd give me till half past nine.

     I said "Kind papa, will you please give me a chance? (*twice*)
     I'll get myself some money, and pay my room rent in advance."

     I'm just a poor girl, I have no place to go (*twice*)
     I have got no good man, and I'm drifting from door to door.

     I'm going to the radio station, put my voice on the air (*twice*)
     And maybe by broadcasting, I can save my room rent somewhere.

Separation sometimes clarifies the mind, and their dependence upon each other would become more evident to a couple when they were apart than when they were permanently in each other's company. For a single woman in a strange city, with heart and "mind a million miles away," anxiety was inevitable. But, as Georgia White's blues suggested, there was time to reflect and to prepare the way for a reunion.

119   Can't read, can't write, gonna buy me a telephone, (*twice*)
       I won't talk to my man, till he comes back home.

       I'm going away just to wear you off my mind, (*twice*)
       And I know, daddy, a good man's hard to find.

       Sitting on the kerbstone, worrying heart and soul, (*twice*)
       Just like a possum hiding in a ground-hog's hole.

       Now the rain is falling, falling down from above, (*twice*)
       Lord, I want to be with the man I love.

"Disheartened and disgusted," Tiny Mayberry was under no illusions about her friends and the help that they had failed to give her. She had swallowed her pride it seems, and turned to her former lover for assistance.

120   Watching and waiting, to hear a bit of news, (*twice*)
       Sighing and crying with these mailman blues.

       Run to the Western Union to send a telegram, (*twice*)
       Try to get a favor from your one-time man.

       Some folks are so deceiving, take friendship as a joke, (*twice*)
       They'll whip you when you're up and you can't find them when
           you're broke.

Friends and relatives are often willing to offer advice if not material aid. Sometimes, though, a temporary separation that may well have ended in a reunion and a relationship made closer in the realization of the need for the other partner, can be worsened and even made permanent by well-intended but misguided advice. That, at least, was the implication of a blues by J. B. Lenoir.

121   Lettie Mae wrote me a letter, these the last words she had to say, (*twice*)
       She said, "J.B. the way you done you will be sorry one old day."

       "Please don't call me or write me, I don't wanna hear from you, (*twice*)
       Darlin', I am my own boss, an' I know what I want to do."

       She weighs a hundred and five pounds, she got long black curly hair,
           (*twice*)
       Darlin', one thing I hate, people meddlin' with our affairs.

Many things may cause a man or woman to desert a partner – the awareness of having failed to provide an adequate home; the keen sense of frustrated ambition in a man who has no opportunity to improve his status or his family fortunes; the fear and humiliation of racial segregation; the lure of the cities and unknown districts where prospects promise to be better; the attractiveness of a lover and the deliberate shedding of responsibilities. These and many more: the outcome of personal tragedies and human failings. Material things are not all that matter in life and the desire for worldly gains that had seemed of such importance was secondary to the love that had been lost, as Lazy Slim Jim realized.

> 122 Money is the root of all evil, look what it have did for me, (*twice*)
> Caused me to leave my baby, now I'm living in misery.
>
> But I'm gonna find my baby, if it takes me until the day I die,
> Yes I'm gonna find my baby, if it takes me until the day I die,
> I should have never left my baby 'cause love is something money
> can't buy.

As in virtually every other genre of folk or popular song, personal relationships predominate in the blues: love, desire, longing, unfaithfulness, separation, desertion, regrets, reconciliation. While innumerable song types share these emotional concerns blues is frequently overlaid with an awareness of color, overtly stating the stratification within the the society based on skin pigmentation. That this had a literal meaning is not in question, but it seems likely that it was also expressive of the more profound division between the black and white communities that legal segregation enforced.

Similarly, in the hurt and humiliation expressed in a great many blues about unfaithful partners it is not difficult to see parallels with the black condition in relation to the white community. Both were, and are, mutually dependent, but the bitter disappointment felt by Blacks in the segregation era stemmed from lack of respect and opportunity. Though Robert Johnson's passionate and tormented blues were ostensibly about his relationships in love, it is possible that such a blues as *Stones in My Passway* was subconsciously expressive of a deeper frustration.

> 123 I got stones in my passway and my road seems dark at night, (*twice*)
> I have pains in my heart, they have taken my appetite.
>
> I have a bird to whistle, and I have a bird to sing, (*twice*)
> I've got a woman that I'm lovin', boy, but she don't mean a thing.

Now youse trying to take my body, and all my lovin' too,
You made a passway for me, now what are you trying to do?
I'm cryin' please, please let us be friends,
And when you hear me howlin' in my passway, rider please open the
    door and let me in.

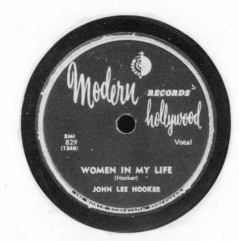

4   *I'm a rooster, baby*

Of all the stereotypes that have been fabricated concerning Blacks in the United States – laziness, stupidity, animal cunning, child-like emotions, perpetual good humor, and the others – there were none as persistent as the commonly held beliefs about love and sexual life. Many Whites believed implicitly that Blacks were sexually promiscuous, that their morals were loose or non-existent, that they cared little for family life and accepted no family responsibilities. They believed that black women were free with their favors, that the men were given to violent criminal assault and rape, and that they perpetually desired to violate the "sanctity of southern white womanhood." It was held that Blacks did not recognize the institution of marriage and that the higher emotions of love meant nothing. Corroborative evidence was found in black songs and particularly in the blues which were considered as pornographic and libidinous. It would be wrong to dismiss these beliefs as being fabrications without any basis in fact; they were a complex mixture of fallacies and truths of which the foundations were firmly laid in the shameful years of slavery and which were buttressed in the course of time by circumstances which were the outcome of the conditions in which Blacks had been forced to live.

Romantic love has had a turbulent and curious history, and the slave trade was a flourishing industry by the time the official legislations against the "filthy dalliance" of the Puritans were being relaxed in favor of a more natural relationship between the sexes. This in turn was replaced by the Victorian concept of the role of the woman in matrimonial matters, but whatever the prevailing notions of the time as to the merits of love between man and woman, they were applicable only to white persons. Blacks were slaves and, apart from their work, they were required to beget more slaves; as the men labored, the women were in labor. Love played little part in this: couples mated at the orders of the plantation owner if they had not made their own unions. Slaves were officially classified below the level of cattle, and when they were sold at the auction block they had to undergo the most humiliating and dehumanizing examinations which were primarily designed to ascertain their strength and potential procreativity. With the

95

"stud Negro" came the concept of the "big buck nigger" which inferred a distinctly subhuman status. Fecund mothers and fertile males were assets to the slaveholder who bred his slaves as he bred his livestock, the distinction of color helping to justify his actions to his conscience. Liberation did not bring a new attitude and the "animal concept" has persisted even to the present day; Blacks themselves came to accept such fictions as the supposed "Negro smell" which sustained the notion of animal, sexual scents.

After years of encouraged sexual freedom Blacks did not immediately and voluntarily self-impose a strict code of morals on attaining their freedom, and during those perplexing and unhappy years the white Southerners could point to the social behavior of many Blacks to find justification for their beliefs, never stopping to admit that these had been the root cause of the social disintegration. The strictures imposed by the religious denominations were probably the outcome of rudimentary attempts to strengthen the moral codes, sexual drives being canalized into religious passion. With the establishment of some form of stable society the desire to settle down and to assume the responsibilities of husband and parent was common to numberless colored men, and as they worked their "forty acres and a mule" they found, as had their previous owners, that children were a material asset. When the problems of living became too great for them to surmount and families broke up, Whites could point to the large numbers of fatherless children, the migrant workless men and the women who shared their lives without the blessing of the church, and saw ready support for their concept of the dissolute, debauched, immoral, feckless Black.

Deeply ingrained in the conscience of the nation and particularly of the South was a complex problem whose sexual and social implications had immediate bearing on the fundamental issues concerning race relations, manifest at the most superficial in the perennial question: "Would you like *your* daughter to marry a Negro?"; at the most violent and disgusting level in the mutilations and lynchings by the Ku Klux Klansmen; and at the most shameful in the mute acceptance of these attitudes on the part of a large proportion of the population. Diverting and important as the examination of this problem may be with its many strange aspects – the pride of the white man who has a strain of American Indian blood, for example – and its world-wide issues of race and nationality, it is relevant, but scarcely possible, to discuss the subject in the present work. Nevertheless, these were factors which influenced the prevalent attitude to Blacks; to their creative arts and to the blues, no less.

As the blues reflected the lives of many Blacks, and in particular those to whom the stereotypes were applied, both the truths and the falsehoods were to be found in them. Such were the conventions of American middle-class society that the blues often appeared to be shocking, and instead of being recognized as a genuine form of expression revealing its gaunt structure without a decorative façade, could be suspected of hiding even greater sins. To apply to the blues the standards, and to expect of the blues the conventions, of popular music is to use a false measure. In popular song and in particular, the concoctions of 52nd Street, euphemistic phrases are sung and winsome, sentimental, erotically evasive symbols are universally employed. As in the art of ballet, virile stories are emasculated by the use of conventional poses and movements, or in "polite" conversation the phrase "to sleep with" implies everything else in bed but sleep. Though sexual metaphors were extensively used in blues they were never evasive, but were used as figures of speech should be used: to amplify the meaning by analogy and comparison. "Riding" is probably the commonest metaphor for the sexual act in blues. Its frequent use did not deter Soldier Boy Houston, a singer recorded in Dallas, Texas, from employing it with gusto.

124 Well they tell me Fort Worth Texas is out where the West begins,
   (*twice*)
  Says I ain't no cowpuncher, but I'll challenge any man.

  Said I don't wear no ten-gallon hat, I don't wear no spurs on my heels,
   (*twice*)
  But when I get in the saddle and ride, all the women says I ride with a
  thrill.

  Says I don't know how to rope a cow, and I never branded a steer,
   (*twice*)
  But I leave my brand whenever I shift my gear.

  Don't know how to ride a bucking horse, never rode in a rodeo show,
   (*twice*)
  But when I start a-ridin', I ride just like a cowboy in a moving picture
  show.

  Well if you don't believe I can ride ask all the women on Batches Hill,
   (*twice*)
  Because when they see me coming they all holler "Here comes Ridin'
  Bill."

As with all other subjects the blues, when dealing with matters of love and sex, is forthright and uncompromising. There is no concealment and no use of oblique references. It was this open declaration of subjects that the conventions of polite society decreed should be kept hidden from view which caused so much offense and, incidentally, added the term "blue" to the English language as a word synonymous with "pornographic." During the twenties, when the blues was first appearing on record, there was much talk in sophisticated circles of "free love" and contraception, and the "flapper" enjoyed a new emancipation from the strict codes of the Edwardian era. But the fundamental Puritanical streak in American life persisted and the blues remained in disfavor for its open "flaunting" of matters kept secret. Blues is a singular folk song in the Western world in that it deals with all aspects of life and death, of disaster and war, in which a common man, a black American man, may find himself participating. Not even the white folk songs of the "Okies" during the Depression were as all-embracing in their themes. With the passing of the 1930s there was a certain return to a natural acceptance and understanding of sexual matters, though potted Freudian knowledge tended towards an over-intellectual, self-conscious awareness in which the impulses of adolescents and adults alike were interpreted in terms of psychological drives and complexes. With this came a new tolerance that had its most recent manifestation in an interest in the problems of the sexually deviant and in particular, the homosexual. More freely discussed in Great Britain than in America in the 1950s, this was a post-war development in freedom of thought on a subject hitherto considered taboo. Not so in the blues, where this aspect of human relationships with all its attendant difficulties has featured – not unduly prominently, but in proportion to its prevalence – since blues were first recorded.

Homosexuality is morally no crime, and deserving of understanding. But the hard shell of Puritanism was not easy to puncture and guidance for the black homosexual was slow in forthcoming. So he was left with his problem, puzzled and unable to resist the disturbing features in his being. In the 1920s when the homosexual was regarded with disgust and contempt if his existence was acknowledged at all, George Hannah sang in his high-pitched, feminine voice:

125   She call me a freakish man – What more was there to do? (*twice*)
       Just 'cause she said I was strange that did not make it true.

I say you mix ink with water, you bound to turn it black, (*twice*)
You run around with "funny" people, you'll get a streak of it running
up your back.

There was a time when I was alone, my freakish way to treat, (*twice*)
But they're so common now, you get one every day in the week.

Had a strange feeling this morning, where I've had it all day,
Had a strange feeling this morning, I've had it all day,
I wake up one of these mornings, that feeling will be here to stay.

Amongst uneducated Blacks there was as little sympathy or understanding for homosexuals as in any other group, though they were accepted. In
the nomenclature that was applied to male homosexuals there was ample
evidence of the misunderstanding that was rife; he was a "freak," a
"mellow," a "sissy," or a "drag." Especially vulnerable was the hermaphrodite who has the characteristics of both sexes – female breasts and male
genitals. With the characteristic combination of pithiness and pitilessness
that labeled a legless man a "Halfy," the hermaphrodite was known as
"Peaches" or "Peach Tree." This abnormality produces complex emotions
and passions that could not easily be controlled, and in the teeming
communities of the Black Belts it could not be kept private. Such a victim of
chance, "Peach Tree" Payne, sang of his troubles, imitating the voices with a
rare facility that his state had accorded him.

126 My home ain't here, it's down in Peach Tree land, (*twice*)
Everyone down home calls me that Brownskin Peach Tree man.

Why, even the li'l children says, "Mama, here comes that ole Peach
Tree man," (*twice*)
Your man says, "Where is he at? I thought you better get a bushel of
his peaches if you can."

You care 'em in the spring-time, you eat 'em in the fall, (*twice*)
The little girls say "Papa, mama, says you carry his peaches skins and
all."

You really oughta steal my peaches, slip in my doodla at night,
You wanta steal my peaches, tip in my bed late at night,
If I fix them bulldogs on you, be careful and don't let 'em bite.

Homosexuality is no more prevalent among Blacks than among Whites, taking the community as a whole, though the references to a subject so shunned elsewhere gave support to those who wished to contend that it was a common aberration. In the overcrowded northern ghettoes its incidence tended to increase as did all others, through the lack of privacy, the ease of soliciting, the difficulties inherent in maintaining social order when young and old, male and female, criminal and virtuous were thrown into close and unavoidable contact. Latent tendencies which might otherwise have remained dormant were activated in black youths who were enticed into homosexual practices by the unscrupulous attentions of undoubted perverts and male prostitutes. Much marital misery resulted from the seduction of young and vulnerable persons. Gertrude "Ma" Rainey, probably bi-sexual herself, sang:

127   I dreamed last night I was far from harm,
　　　Woke up and found my man in a sissy's arms.

　　　　　Hello, Central, it's 'bout to run me wild,
　　　　　Can I get that number, or will I have to wait a while?

　　　Some are young, some are old,
　　　My man says sissy's got good jelly roll.

　　　My man got a sissy, his name is "Miss Kate,"
　　　He shook that thing like jelly on a plate.

　　　Now all the people ask me why I'm all alone,
　　　A sissy shook that thing and took my man from home.

Not only the male homosexuals caused trouble in the homes; female homosexuals, though seldom castigated to the same extent, caused embarrassment to the other women with their aggressiveness and masculine tendencies. Lesbians were known as "bull-dykers" in black areas, a term which hinted at their bi-sexual characteristics, customarily abbreviated to "B.D. women," as in Lucille Bogan's blues.

128   Comin' a time, B.D. womens ain't gonna need no men, (*twice*)
　　　The way they treat us is a low-down and dirty sin.

　　　B.D. women, they all done learnt their plan, (*twice*)
　　　They can lay their jive just like a nach'l man.

B.D. women, B.D. women, you know they sure is rough, (*twice*)
They all drink up plenty o'whisky and they sure will strut their stuff.

B.D. women, you know they work and make their dough, (*twice*)
And when they get ready to spend it, they have no place to go.

Many young homosexuals of either sex live under great emotional strain
and mental conflict. He or she can either seek out the company of others in
similar straits and accept the social ostracism that this generally brings, or
attempt to supress their sexual instincts and live as heterosexual persons. In
spite of the difficulties involved some homosexuals did manage to achieve
the latter compromise and even settle down to married life. For black
homosexuals there was less guidance in taking this step, and the opportunities for conducting unrestricted social work into which white persons often
sublimate their inclinations were few. Instead, some put their energies into
Masonic or other secret organizations, or into the church. A close relationship exists between religious and sexual ecstasy, and the devotion to the
church of those who are sexually frustrated is a phenomenon familiar to the
psychologist, and implied in a blues by Bob White.

129   Say, you may not know my people, I will tell you who they are, (*twice*)
Say, four of them are mighty big devils, ooh well, my mama saw them
servin' God.

Say, my daddy was a preacher, and my brother done the same old
thing, (*twice*)
Say, if you don't believe I love chicken, baby, ooh, well, my babe let
me catch your wing.

Say, I love my pullet, cause that meat's so tender and sweet, (*twice*)
Say, I'm a rooster myself baby, ooh, well, I can't stand rooster meat.

Say, if you can't bring me four or five pullets, please try to bring me
only one, (*twice*)
If you can't grab me no pullets baby, ooh well mama, it's hens till the
waggon come.

Knowing the homosexual proclivities of some persons associated with the
church, which in black districts includes many unauthorized "sects"
meetings in "store-front" chapels at services conducted by unordained
"ministers," Bob White was anxious to make it clear that he was not himself

so inclined. But in his emphatic declaration of his own virility, "Leroy's Buddy" may have been making a wry joke.

> 130   She is a Louisville woman, lives up in old smoke town, (*twice*)
> But I'm too good a man, to let one woman worry me down.
>
> Now don't get me wrong, because I am a real he-man, (*twice*)
> I don't go in for no funny business, I want everyone to understand.

The phraseology that the blues singer employed was not that of popular song: he sang in the language that he used in everyday speech. To those only accustomed to the conventions of the printed and the recorded word, the blues sometimes seemed violent and coarse, but its expression was a natural and uninhibited one. The songs of the college campus, the baseball team, the barrack room, and the stag party were seldom less crude, and considerably less honest, than Springback James's words to his woman:

> 131   Woman, you don't do nothin' but lay around on your rusty can, (*twice*)
> But you got to get off it if you want me to be your man.
>
> Now I've told you woman so many times before, (*twice*)
> 'Bout these no-good men that is hangin' round your door.
>
> You want to show your D.B.A.; I'm a poor hard-workin' man, (*twice*)
> The last time I catch you mama, I'm gon' get on your rusty can.

"D.B.A." was black slang for "dirty black arse," incidentally. In like manner Mary Dixon rejected the advances of a would-be seducer in no uncertain terms:

> 132   What's the matter with you, stop your whining around, (*twice*)
> Find some other place to lay your lazy body down.
>
> You're too big to be cute and I don't think you are clean, (*twice*)
> You're the darndest-looking thing that I have ever seen.
>
> What you got in mind ain't gonna happen to-day, (*twice*)
> Get off of my bed, how in the world did you get that way?
>
> You'd better be gone when my man comes in, (*twice*)
> Stop shaking your tail, cause I don't know where you've been.

Now a dog like you must have too much bread, *(twice)*
Come out of my room, you can't sleep in my bed.

So the forthright, uninhibited language of the blues must be accepted
without apologies as a natural transposition of the everyday language of
both users and hearers. Nevertheless, it must be acknowledged that the blues
includes many sexual boasting songs that are apparently aggressive in their
use of phrases and images. It has been contended that these are a form of
protest song, and there is a reasonable argument that they are designed to
shock and thus assert the personality of the singer. But just as the blues
includes all aspects of the lives of its creators, expressing themes which are
seldom the subject of song, from vagrancy and begging, to sickness and
death by drowning, so too the blues singer brags of his sexual prowess. His
society was a simple one and he boasted in the manner of members of other
simple societies: Texas Alexander's words recalled those used by the keel-
boatmen of the Mississippi, the Texas cowboys or the Ohio backwoodsmen
who cried that they were "half-horse and half-alligator, a little touched with
the snapping turtle . . ."

133   I was raised on the desert, born in a lion's den, *(twice)*
      Says my chief occupation – taking "monkey men's" women,

      Says I never had a woman, couldn't get her back again, *(twice)*
      Says I traveled over this country every kind of man,

A man who took pride in his sexual prowess, real or imaginary, would
ridicule the "monkey men" – a derogatory term often applied to West
Indians and Africans by American Blacks, but also loosely applied to any
competitor. "I would be your monkey man, mama, just cain't climb no
coconut tree," sang Cripple Clarence Lofton, adding as an aside "My claws
ain't sharp enough." Asserting his own sexual superiority Blind Boy Fuller,
though handicapped, felt when he could not see.

134   I got a big fat woman, grease shakin' on her bone,
      I say, hey, hey, meat shakin' on her bone,
      An' every time she shakes some man done left his home.

      If when you boys see my woman you can't keep her long,
      I say hey, hey, you can't keep her long,
      I got a new way to keep her down, you "monkey men" can't catch on.

Baby, for my dinner, I want ham and eggs,
I say hey, hey, I want ham and eggs,
And for my supper, mama, I want to feel your legs.

Now you let me feel your legs, and they felt so strong,
I say hey, hey, and they felt so strong,
Baby, if you know what it's gonna be, baby, please don't let me know.

Though he despised the "monkey man" the blues singer frequently applied animal comparisons to himself: in all probability this was a legacy from slavery; an embittered acceptance of the lack of respect with which he was held causing him to take satisfaction from a violent assertion of those animal features of which he had been accused. So he became the "rootin' ground-hog who roots both night and day," the "rattlesnakin' daddy who wants to rattle all the time," or, in Bo Carter's blues, the wild boar – the "tush hog."

135   Mama, can't you hear this tush hog rootin' on your back door? (*twice*)
      But if you give him what you promised him, mama, he won't have to
      root no more.

      I rooted so long, mama, done rooted a hole through your door, (*twice*)
      But if you give me what you promised me, mama, I won't have to root
      no more.

      Mama, can't you hear this tush hog prattin' on your back door? (*twice*)
      But if you give him what you promised him, mama, you won't have to
      prat no more.

      Can't you hear this tush hog gruntin' all around your home? (*twice*)
      But if you give him what you promised him, mama, he will soon be
      gone.

But when Champion Jack Dupree sang that he was the "black wolf that hollers," he was using a metaphoric animal image that was common in Western society at the time.

136   When you hear this wolf howling, howling at every woman I see,
      (*twice*)
      Well, well, I'm only howling, ooh well, well, for what belongs to me.

So bye-bye, baby, this wolf going to take to the woods, (*twice*)
Well I had been wolfing at you, ooh well, well, but you don't mean me
   no good.

The images used in the blues are never based on tired and artificial,
sentimental associations; lilies – even magnolias – do not figure in the blues
of love-making; no blues singer has a "love like a red, red rose." He may be a
"prowling tom-cat," he may wish to hear his "panther squall," but he never
expects his kitten to purr. This is not to say that he has no sentiments, nor
that they are not genuinely felt: the distress of a man who knows that his
absence is causing grief, or that his woman is being unfaithful, is no less
because he uses strong images to express it, as did Big Joe Williams:

137   I went home last night babe, just about the break of day,
      I went and grabbed the pillow where my baby used to lay,
      I'm a rootin' ground-hog, you gonna need me some sweet day,
      Well look what Po' Joe done lost, eeh well, cause he's so far away.

      I'm a rootin' ground-hog babe, and I roots everywhere I go (*twice*)
      (*Spoken*) Lay it on me boy, it's bad!
      I'm tryin' to keep my woman takin' my lovin'; she ended up givin' it
         to Mr. So-and-So.

Bovine comparisons are resented in urban white society but those who
live close to the land make their comparisons with what they know best.
When a black country singer from Texas sang of his "wild cow" he
intended no conscious insult, the attractions of the girl being implied by the
use of hyperbole in his metaphoric descriptions. His was a tough poetry,
the natural poetry of a confessedly illiterate man. In a blues by Black Ace
the mixed metaphor "pigmeat heifer" underlines the extent to which the
language of the blues is the language of the black community, for the
paradoxical image would have been readily comprehensible.

138   I been a mighty good bull cow, Oh Lord, but I got to go (*twice*)
      I found me a pigmeat heifer, I can tell by the way she lows.

      She lows all night long, you can hear her for a solid mile (*twice*)
      I can't stand to hear her low, I cried just like a chile.

      Whoa babe, your bull cow got to go, (*twice*)
      I can't stay here no longer, she calls me when she lows.

3078—WHAT'S THE MATTER WITH MY MILK
COW (She Won't Stand Still) and RACE
HORSE BLUES—Vocal—Bill Weldon 59c

Mama, I'm gone, with a horn long as your right arm, *(twice)*
And when I get to hookin', I'll have me a brand new happy home.

Good-bye, Good-bye, an' I don't see you no mo',
Good-bye, mama, if I don't see you no mo',
Just remember me at night, when you hear mammy's heifer low.

Metaphors drawn from the rural South abound in the blues. The archetypal and influential singer from the Mississippi Delta, Charley Patton, was celebrated for his *Pony Blues*.

139   Hitch up my pony, saddle up my black mare, *(twice)*
      I'm goin' find a rider, baby in this world somewhere.

      Bought a brand new Shetland, man already trained,
      Brand new Shetland, baby, already trained,
      Just get in the saddle, tighten up on your reins.

      I've got something to tell you, when I gets a chance,
      Something to tell you, when I get a chance,
      I don't want to marry, just wanna be your man.

As noted previously, sexual intercourse in the blues is very often figuratively called "riding," and the male lover becomes the "rider," with "pony" and "mare" as natural extensions of the same image. Sometimes the female partner by transference of the figure of speech, herself becomes the "rider" or by the addition of a descriptive adjective, the "easy rider." It is indicative of the importance of his guitar to the blues singer that the term "easy rider" was widely applied by early blues men to their instruments. Whilst this undoubtedly derived in part from the fact that the guitar was carried by a strap slung across the singer's back, the use of a term which was widely applied to a lover, showed a close, if subconscious, psychological relationship between singer and instrument which is amply supported by the records made by the folk guitarists. In the towns characteristically, the image changed and Memphis Minnie, who lived largely in the city, put a new interpretation on the term "chauffeur."

140   Want to see my chauffeur, want to see my chauffeur,
      I want him to drive me, I want him to drive me down town,
      Says he drives so easy, I can't turn him down.

Well I must buy him, well I must buy him,
A brand new V-8, a brand new V-8 Ford,
Then he won't need no passengers, I will be his load.

Gwine t'let my chauffeur, gwine t'let my chauffeur,
Drive me around the, drive me around the world,
Then he can be my li'l boy, yes an' I can be his girl.

Not surprisingly the rhythms of love led to many effective parallels which were made with the lusty bawdiness of an Elizabethan playwright, but in terms that were of the present century: the work of the auto-mechanic, the oil driller, or the steamboat captain alike became the themes of songs, neither wholly innocent nor shamefacedly secretive, as in the Yas Yas Girl's *Easy Towing Mama*.

141   Well, let me be your towboat, I will tow you 'cross the pond, (*twice*)
      Well, I'll take you slow and easy, ooh well, well, it really won't take
      me long.

      When we reach th'Atlantic Ocean, the sea may be a little rough, (*twice*)
      But I will steady your boat, ooh well, well, 'cause I really knows my
      stuff.

      Now I've been a captain on this towboat for twenty-eight years or
      more, (*twice*)
      So just tell me how you want it, ooh well, well, I'll tow you fast or
      slow.

      Now blow your whistle, daddy, when you want a little more speed,
      (*twice*)
      Well, I am here to please you, ooh well, well, just tell me what you
      need.

In the rhythmic ebb and flow of water the psychologist recognizes a powerful sexual symbol; in the blues a sinuous girl may be termed a "river hip" woman. Many of the figures of speech used in such blues arise from the environmental or domestic circumstances in which the singer finds himself. The man who has few worldly goods can only offer these to the woman whom he admires, though in doing so, like Black Boy Shine, he may also attach to them a metaphoric significance.

142 When I went out hustlin', tryin' to do the best I could, (*twice*)
    I knowed you were broke and hungry and I tried to chop some wood.

    I got wood in my wood-house, and I've got coal in my bin (*twice*)
    'Cause my fire went out, Lord since God knows when.

    Now woman don't worry, 'cause my heater's always hot, (*twice*)
    'Cause good wood and coal is all I've got.

An exhaustive study of black sexual symbols is long overdue, indicative as they are of modes of thought and reactions to popularly held stereotypes. Among domestic metaphors culinary themes are especially common, which a brief examination of one stream of associations may illustrate. Arising simply from the motions of sexual intercourse the term "jelly roll" is a familiar one which has been in use for more than half a century. In black song it occurs frequently, as in a recording by Peg Leg Howell and his Gang,

143 Jelly-roll, jelly-roll, ain't so hard to find,
    Ain't a baker shop in town bake 'em brown like mine,
    I got a sweet jelly, a lovin' sweet jelly roll,
    If you taste my jelly it'll satisfy your worried soul.

    I never been to church and I never been to school,
    Come down to jelly I'm a jelly-rollin' fool,
    I got a sweet jelly to satisfy my worried soul,
    I likes my jelly and I like to have my fun.

The term was correctly applied to a jam (jelly)-rolled and lightly baked confection and in consequence the references to baking "nice and brown" had an added punning significance. So a lover admired his "jelly bean" and the way she could "jello" and prided himself on being a "good jelly-roll baker." But the baker made not only jelly roll but also other foods. Crisper than the jelly roll, the biscuit was well baked, and a desirable young girl was consequently called a "biscuit," whilst the good lover was a "biscuit-roller." Significant in both female and male applications the term was used by Lightnin' Hopkins.

144 I woke up this mornin', same thing on my mind, (*twice*)
    You know I thought about that woman have treated me so nice and
      kind.

    Don't your home look lonesome, biscuit roller gone? (*twice*)
    You know I ain't got no dog-gone feelin's baby even bein' alone.

Contrasted with these confections mere bread was a commonplace, and of breads, cornbread from maize flour was considered one of the poorest. Though "cornbread" might imply love-making that was coarse, whilst "jelly roll" suggested love-making that was sweet, some singers might refer to "cornbread rough" as a desirable quality, unconsciously accepting the idea of crude libidinous relations.

145　Some of these women I just can't understand,
　　　Some of you women I just can't understand,
　　　They cook cornbread for their husbands and biscuits for their man.

In order to make his confections, the good cook must have the necessary equipment and the singer would boast of having "a good range in my kitchen" and wanted no one to cool his ardor by "turning his damper down." Certain of the phrases that arose in this manner passed into black language. Thus the prostitute became the "kitchen mechanic." As Clara Smith complained,

146　Women talk about me, they lies on me, calls me out of my name,
　　　They talks about me, they lies on me, calls me out of my name,
　　　All their men comes to see me just the same.

　　　I'm just a workin' gal, poor workin' gal, "kitchen mechanic" is what
　　　　they say, (*twice*)
　　　But I'll have a honest dollar on that rainy day.

Many valid and pithy metaphors were thus derived from the process of cooking and other closely related culinary terms. Some had double, treble significance: "sugar" as a word of endearment had the added associations of wealth, for money is sweet to possess and is likewise called "shug" or "sugar." The "greenback" – the dollar bill – by virtue of its colour became known as a "leaf" and a wad of greenbacks became "cabbage." Further terms were added to the growing vocabulary of love-making, when such delights, as sweet to own as money, also became "cabbage" and the phrase "greasy greens" for much-handled dollar bills was aptly applied to the licentious lover. The colour of individual Blacks themselves inspired other related terms. A light-skinned person was "honey" hued, a shade deeper might be called "coffee" with the result that a lover would be a "bumble-bee," a "honey-dripper," a "coffee-grinder."

With a voice that sounded straight from the cotton-fields and alternating his vocal lines with his own harmonica accompaniment, Jaybird Coleman recorded a blues with repeat line couplets.

147   Gonna grind my coffee two or three dollars a pound
      And I grind my coffee two or three dollars a pound.

      Ain't a man in town can brown his coffee like mine (*twice*)

      It grind so good it'll make you bite your tongue (*twice*)

      I'm a coffee-grindin' fool, and let me grind you some (*twice*)

These are agreeable even slightly flattering terms but in the use of the term "pigmeat" a deliberate acknowledgement of the low status accorded to Blacks in the past may be detected. Most "unclean" of animals by Biblical standards, the pig was rated of more importance to the planter than the slave, who remained conscious of being "treated like a hog." So a blues singer may pride himself on being a "rooting ground-hog," even a "dirty ground-hog" in challenging self-abasement. At the same time bacon, chitterlings, hogs' maws, pig feet, pig ankles and pig ears, ham, and other meats were particular delicacies, sweet, appetizing, and cheaply obtained. Ardell Bragg sang of herself as "pigmeat."

148   Look heah, papa, you don't treat pigmeat the way you should,
      Ooh, don't treat pigmeat the way you should,
      If you don't believe that it's pigmeat ask in the neighbourhood.

      I ain't so good-lookin', I ain't got no great long hair,
      Ooh, I ain't got no great long hair,
      But I don't have to worry, I know it's pigmeat anywhere.

      You can carry me to the mountain, I mean and will be pigmeat there,
      Ooh, it will be pigmeat there,
      Raise a cold in China, stand to catch us anywhere.

It is not possible here to pursue further the many symbols used in the blues. As love is the most potent, the most profoundly moving of all human emotions, it is fitting and to be expected that blues on the themes of love should be richer in symbolic imagery than on any other subject as, in all probability, are love songs in every other folk music. Those terms that sprang spontaneously from the theme and which passed smoothly into the

Pig Meat Blues
by Ardell Shelley Bragg

*'Born and bred in the country,
But I'm raised in town,
And I'm pig-meat
From my head on down."*

ANOTHER new Paramount Blues singer — a real star from down Fort Worth way — is Ardell Shelley Bragg. She starts off with a bang with "Pig Meat Blues". "She has the kind of pig meat you won't regret", this out-of-the-ordinary Blues says, "Won't *regret* or *forget*", we say. There's a bear of a piano accompaniment to "Pig Meat Blues" by famous Tiny Parham, that's worth the price of the record alone. Ask for Paramount No. 12398 at your dealer's, or send us the coupon.

[12398—Pig Meat Blues and Cane Break Blues, Ardell]
Shelley Bragg, acc. by Tiny Parham at the Piano.

12404—Mama's Angel Child and All Birds Look Like Chicken To Me, Sweet Papa Stovepipe.

12401—Cotton Field Blues and Red River Blues, Dad Nelson and His Guitar.

12402—Jefferson County Blues and Biscuit Roller Blues, Priscilla Stewart; Piano Acc.

12395—Down In The Basement, and Trust No Man, "Ma" Rainey with Her Georgia Band.

Extra Good!
12403 — Dishrag Blues and Rollin' Mill Blues, by Leola B. Wilson.

12394—Old Rounder's Blues and Beggin' Back, Blind Lemon Jefferson.

12392—Ashley Street Blues and Crying Blues, Leola B. Wilson; Guitar Acc. by Blind Blake.

12354—Long Lonesome Blues and Got The Blues, Blind Lemon Jefferson.

Dance Hits—They're Red Hot!

12400—It's Tight, Jim and Harmony Blues, Preston Jackson and His Uptown Band.

12399—Stock Yards Strut and Salty Dog, Freddie Keppard's Jazz Cardenals; Vocal Chorus by "Papa" Charlie Jackson.

12391—In The Alley Blues and Merry Maker's Twine, Lovie Austin's Serenaders; Vocal Chorus by Henry Williams.

Inspiring Spirituals

12396—I Heard The Voice of Jesus and Fight On, Your Time Ain't Long, Biddleville Quintette.

12349—Oh Why Not Tonight and Wasn't That A Mighty Day, Biddleville Qua.

12073—When All The Saints Come Marching In and That Old-Time-Religion, Paramount Jubilee Singers.

12350—All I Want Is That Pure Religion and I Want To Be Like Jesus In My Heart, Deacon L. J. Bates.

SEND NO MONEY! If your dealer is out of the records you want, send us the coupon below. Pay postman 75c for each record, plus small C.O.D fee when he delivers records. We pay postage on shipments of two or more records.

Paramount
The Popular Race Record

The New York Recording Laboratories
Port Washington, Wis.

Send me the records checked ( ) below 75 cents each.

Name
Address
City   State

language were often used with scarcely a thought for their value as metaphors, but in the course of everyday speech. The man who wished "to pick her tomatoes," who was "wild about her yellow yams," and who complained that the "niggers run around her potato vine" wished to taste the fruits of love and expressed his desire in phrases that were readily understood. Yank Rachell's words were no more direct, and his images scarcely less poetic than those of the ancient Arab desert songs of love that were loosely bound together to become the Song of Solomon – though one doubts whether they would ever be the subject of interpretations as Christian symbolism.

> 149   Don't the peaches look mellow hanging way up in your tree, (*twice*)
> I like your peaches so well, they have taken effect on me.
>
> I'm gonna get my step-ladder, babe, I'm gonna climb up on your top limb, (*twice*)
> If I get among your yaller peaches, it's gonna be too bad, Jim.
>
> Every time I start to climb your tree, babe, I wonder what make you smile, (*twice*)
> You want me to climb up your tree ever since you was a chile.

But such terminology was prone to misinterpretation. To Odum and Johnson it was impossible to print a great mass of the material that they collected in the first quarter of the century because of its "vulgar and indecent content. These songs," they added, "tell of every phase of immorality . . . and filth; they represent the superlative of the repulsive." The principal theme was that of sexual relations and there was no restraint in expression. Admitting that they shortened many of the songs "by the omission of stanzas unfit for publication," the authors contended that no other form of folk song was as indecent as that of the Negro. It would seem, however, that most forms of folk song have their counterparts elsewhere, though the uncompromising declarations of the blues have been placed on record, whereas those of all but a few remote peoples have seldom been recorded, though their existence is not questioned today. There is no denying that many black songs are frankly pornographic and amongst the blues there are many that fall in this category, no more and no less meritorious than those in any other branch of song.

It is well established that slaves used their work songs to sing the insults and comments to their overseers that they could not say outright to their faces, and the practice continued to the 1950s on the State and County Farms and amongst the share-croppers on the larger holdings. Similar insulting songs are chanted by the Italian rice-workers and others have been noted in various countries. In the group song there is a certain anonymity, the individual offender being lost in the team, and punitive measures are seldom taken against the singers. Furthermore the overseers and straw bosses were well aware that anger or humiliation that gains an outlet in song is less likely to seek one in physical violence. Related to this habit has been that of singing blues and insulting songs apparently directed at inanimate objects, mules, farm animals, or other persons in the community, but as all concerned are well aware, referring obliquely to officials and white persons in authority. These often took a strong and offensive form, many being of an obscene nature, but they served to give vent to frustrated emotions. In turn this led to a similar type of song which was specifically directed against other members of black society – the "Dozens."

"Putting in the Dozens" developed as a folk game in the late nineteenth century. A number of persons would gather and endeavor to exceed each other in the insults that they invented with a view to goading someone present to lose his temper. In the process many obscene and scandalous inferences as to the ancestry of the individuals concerned would be made. Sometimes the anger of persons who had received unfair treatment or who were the victims of racial prejudice would be dissipated, but at other times the "Dozens" was sung with intent to hurt and to provoke. If a particular person was the subject of enmity in a black folk community the offended man would "put his foot up" – in other words, jam the door of his cabin with his foot and sing a blues that "put in the Dozens" at the expense of his enemy, "calling him out of his name." This was the "Dozens" with vengeful intent, but often youths would "play the Dozens" to work off their excesses of spirits in a harmless and cheerfully pornographic blues-singing competition.

150   I like your mama, I like your sister too,
      I did like your daddy, but your daddy wouldn't do,
      I met your daddy on the corner the other day,
      You know about that, that he was funny that way.

          So he's a funny mistreater, a robber and a cheater,
          Slip you in the "Dozens," your pappy is your cousin,
          And your mama do the Lordy – Lord . . .

> Now, now, boys say you ain't actin' fair,
> You know about that you got real bad hair,
> Your face is all hid now your back's all bare,
> If you ain't doin' the bobo, what's your head doin' down there?

> Now you're a dirty mistreater . . .

Frankly libidinous, the "Dozens" survives today in the "toasts"; it takes its name from the dice throw of twelve, the worst in crap-shooting. But though the "Dirty Dozens" is in part improvised, it is somewhat on the fringe of the blues. There is reason for the "Dozens" and some justification for it, as there is in the pornographic blues that occasionally appear. In theory the blues has no need for pornography for its candor of expression obviates any necessity for secretive and allusive songs. The greater the tendency towards the "point number" – the song with sexual hints and dig-in-the-rib suggestiveness – the closer to the sophisticated night-club song and the further from the folk form the blues becomes. But it has its measure of *double entendre* and ribaldry: there is good natured humour, and bland insolence, openly expressed desire, and swaggering bragging in the blues – Bumble Bee Slim's *Feather Bed* for instance.

> 151   If you want to live happy, go back home with me; (*twice*)
> I will sing you songs . . . such as "Nearer My God To Thee . . ."

> I got a brand new sofa and a great big feather bed, (*twice*)
> You won't have to worry about a place to rest your head.

> I've got nice clean linen, and easy ridin' springs, (*twice*)
> But it don't mean nothin' if you can't shake that thing.

> And they call me "jelly" 'cause I rolls all in my sleep, (*twice*)
> I will roll your jelly and also grind you deep.

> I got a jazz-playin' piano and a great big rockin' chair, (*twice*)
> You can rock in rhythm by the music that you hear.

5   *The jinx is on me*

For the most part the blues is strictly secular in content. The old-time religion of the southern churches did not permit the singing of "devil songs" and "jumped-up" songs as the blues were commonly termed, and it is not an expression that is natural to the church member. Music and song, he considers, must be for the purpose of praising the Lord, and though "holy dancing" is permitted by many black churches, "sinful dancing" is strictly forbidden. To the outsider the distinction may be a fine one, but within the church it is clear enough: spontaneous dancing which is the result of religious ecstasy and in which the legs are not crossed, is the only form acceptable. Often the black cultist churches are even more strict in the application of their codes of behavior than are the orthodox Baptist and other denominations, and the segregation of the sexes, even to the exclusion of conjugal union between married couples, was not uncommon. Going to the movies, smoking, alcohol, even wearing dresses above the ankle were innocuous forms of behavior that the strictures of the cult churches rigorously banned. Though "conversion" may come to blues singers, membership of such a church or cult was not for them if they continued to sing the blues. Some blues singers – "Georgia Tom" Dorsey, Sara Martin, Virginia Liston, Bertha Idaho, and later, Walter Davis and Little Richard, to mention a few, eventually gave up the blues and were embraced by the church to which they devoted their talents as singers and composers. A number of other blues singers worked also as singers of spirituals, amongst them Blind Boy Fuller – under the name of Brother George – Blind Gary Davis and Brother Son Bonds, but they were somewhat exceptional cases. They kept their blues and religion strictly apart and though the influence of blues phrasing and instrumental accompaniment is to be noted in the work of some gospel singers and, more recently, the passionate expression of the gospel singer has been detectable in developments of the secular form, blues that is performing a specifically religious function may scarcely be said to exist. A worldly blues singer, like "Funny Paper" Smith, did not use his song for hymns of praise, though an occasional reference to religion may be found in his blues.

152   Some people tells me that God takes care of old folks and fools, *(twice)*
    But since I've been born he must have changed his rule.

I used to ask God questions, then answer that question myself, *(twice)*
'Bout when I was born, wonder was there any mercy left?

Y'know until six months ago I hadn't prayed a prayer since God know
    when, *(twice)*
Now I'm asking God every day to please forgive me for my sins.

You know it must be the devil I'm servin', I know it can't be Jesus
    Christ, *(twice)*
'Cause I ask him to save me and look like he tryin' to take my life.

In its bare realism the blues is somewhat bereft of spiritual values. Lower-class Blacks often had to decide whether to accept with meekness the cross they had to bear in this world and to join the church with the promise of "Eternal Peace in the Promised Land" or whether to attempt to meet the present world on its own terms, come what may. The blues singer chose the latter course.

Victimized by circumstances over which he had no control, facing adverse conditions with no conception of the events that brought them about, witnessing friends and relatives falling sick and dying with no cause that he could comprehend, the uneducated man fell readily into super-stition. Observing a sequence of events or noting the coincidence of happenings strange or unexpected in themselves, he would satisfy his desire for understanding and seek to quieten his disturbed mind by drawing illogical but acceptable relationships between them. Frequently it was the lack of even a rudimentary education rather than inferior intelligence or intellectual capacity that caused a man to invent or to accept such superstitions as a substitute for knowledge. He may be well versed in "folk-lore," having a considerable fund of such beliefs on which he might draw and with which he advised others, and by intuitive rather than scientific or rational deduction he might, on occasion, draw conclusions that were largely accurate. Varying trends of the weather might be attributed to the behavior of a flock of birds and thus successfully forecast a climatic change: observations correct, but the deductions inaccurate though they led to the right conclusion. Such superstition would have had no basis in fact or fiction but the force of tradition and the desire to be safe when an element of doubt arose accounts for the persistence of unsound beliefs. Even in the most educated of Western societies horoscopes and astrologists' forecasts are followed avidly by the lonely and the nervous; touching wood, stepping aside from ladders and black cats, avoiding talk of the devil or a tally of unhatched eggs are "precautions" that are taken by a high proportion of the community. Few persons are without private superstitions though these may be simply born of reluctance to break established habits of behavior. Whatever the belief it arises principally from uncertainty about the future, and a desire to know the unknowable. Fear and anxiety were present in a blues by Willie Brown, an associate of Charley Patton and Son House in Mississippi.

153   Can't tell my future, I can't tell my past,
      Lord it seems like every minute sure gonna be my last.

      Well minutes seems like hours, hours seem like days, (*twice*)
      And it seems like my woman ought-a stop her low-down ways.

Superstitions flourish where standards of education are low. Blacks in the South seldom benefited from an education that in any way abided by the principle of "separate but equal" facilities and standards. Often the annual expenditure per black child in a county or state was but a tenth that of the expenditure *per capita* on white children. Compulsory attendance at schools was seldom enforced; it had been part of a policy which originated with slavery, that the black child should be very sketchily educated lest he became aware of the extent of the injustices he had suffered, or became "uppity" and exceeded his "station." Windowless, draughty, ill-heated and ill-equipped black schools stood within sight of white schools built at a hundred times their cost, in areas where the colored population was equivalent to that of the white. Even in an area such as Madison County, Mississippi, where Blacks owned some ninety per cent of the land and paid an equivalent proportion of the taxes, the county revenue was administered by Whites with the inevitable anomalies rife when the educational accounts were drawn up. There were opportunities for black teachers in the South, but they had to accept low standards of living and working conditions and had to be motivated by a strong sense of mission. Many teachers in black rural schools were therefore unqualified and often had scant education themselves. They had to be prepared to lose their classes when cotton picking or the demands of the parents on the labor of their charges drew their pupils from school. It was not until the late 1950s that marked strides were made towards non-segregated education with the resultant raising of standards. Under the system that had obtained for so long it was to be expected that black children in rural communities who had grown up in surroundings circumscribed by the superstitious beliefs of their fathers, would have accepted them in lieu of any better-informed instruction.

The social position of Blacks was as often reflected in their folk beliefs as in their fear of black articles; the black butterfly that heralded bad news and the dreams of black water that foretold evil happenings were indications of an awareness and resentment of their color. With punning reference to both animal and human being, Ma Rainey sang:

154   Black cat on my door-step, black cat on my window-sill, (*twice*)
        If one black cat don't cross me, another black cat will.

        Last night a hoot owl come and sit right over my door, (*twice*)
        A feelin' seems to tell me I'll never see my man no mo'.

        I feel my left side a-jumpin', my heart a-bumpin'. I'm mindin' my P's
            and Q's,
        I feel my brain a-thumpin', I've got no time to lose,
        Mama's superstitious, tryin' to overcome these blues.

Much significance was attached to the behavior of animals and birds which were looked upon as omens and portents of good or evil. The events anticipated by the hooting or screeching of owls may only be allayed, it was believed, by turning the pocket inside out or putting a shovel in the fire. The lowing of cattle in the "early dark" or the midnight call of the whip-poor-will forecast a death; a rabbit crossing the path would bring bad luck, a rat running towards one brought good luck; whilst a spider on the shoulder was a sign of fortune. Old beliefs died hard, as Ida Cox reminded her hearers.

155   Why do people believe in some old sign? (*twice*)
        You hear a hoot owl holler, someone is surely dying.

        Some will break a mirror, and cry bad luck for seven years, (*twice*)
        And if a black cat crosses them they'll break right down in tears.

        To dream of muddy water, trouble's knocking at your door, (*twice*)
        Your man is sure to leave you and never return no more.

More deeply seated in their implications were the strange relationships that were thought to exist between apparently unconnected actions: the pinning of a hair-grip to a tree which would bring a letter in the next post; the wearing of a hat backwards that counteracted evil; the insanity that results when a hair that has fallen from the head was used by a bird to build its nest. As old as history itself is the practice of interpreting dreams, and modern psychiatry has substantiated at least a small proportion of the conclusions drawn by the seers when they interpreted intentions or desires from dreams. Still, black or muddy water was a sign of trouble for the dreamer, but if he dreamt that the ill-omened water was running it was a sign that his bad times would eventually pass. The meanings of many dreams were interpreted as the direct opposites of their content – a belief which does have some psychological justification when it is concerned with conditions of the mind. Watching where he placed his feet, taking care not to break the spider's web that crossed his path, turning the pictures to the wall when there was a death, burning the sassafras wood only outside the house – Blacks of the older generation were bound by strictures and superstitions that governed everyday behavior. Amongst the more sophisticated Blacks such beliefs were partially discarded with improved education, but many who migrated from the Deep South to the northern cities took their beliefs with them: the permanent "blues what am." In his blues of this name Jazz Gillum repeated old folk beliefs: that a coffin will turn when peanuts are brought into the house; that someone must leave the home if the dogs howl or the lamp dims. He feared to be touched with a broom, he was alarmed lest his brother should put his bare feet in his own shoes, seeing bad omens in these seemingly harmless actions. Elizabeth Smith was resigned to the effects of the power of such superstitions over her life:

156   I stubbed my toe against the kitchen door (*twice*)
      And now my hens won't lay no eggs no more.

      I went to church, sat in the thirteenth row, (*twice*)
      Next day my landlord said I had to go.

      I suppose there ain't no use in shedding tears, (*twice*)
      I'm gwine to have bad luck for seven years.

It is tempting, but facile, to attribute the southern Black's beliefs exclusively to his African heritage. They have much in common with superstitions of peoples from Scandinavia to the Philippines: in other words, the growth of such ideas is a familiar phenomenon amongst simple and uneducated persons of all nations. Many clearly have Anglo-Saxon origins, absorbed from the culture of the plantation-owners, and the "poor Whites": the itching ear that meant that somewhere one was under discussion; the irritating foot that warned of a forthcoming trip; the smashed mirror and the umbrella opened under the roof that meant misfortune. Others had a symbolic significance: the corn grains that brought fertility and the hatchet that cut the pains of childbirth had their parallels in many cultures. Some black folk-lore has an indisputable similarity with beliefs current amongst West African tribesmen whose peoples were seriously depleted during the centuries of slave traffic. A definite connection seems likely in many instances, but others may have been born of the new conditions experienced in the New World.

Well established and documented is the survival of African magic in the Americas and particularly in the West Indies. Dahomean religion was brought over by slaves imported by the French to remain largely intact until the present day in the former French colonial possessions. It flourishes in Haiti where "*voudun*" or "voodoo" is the dominant magical-religious practice amongst the black Haitian Aradas. In Cuba, similarly, many African religions survived in modified forms with an ancestry traceable to the Congo and the Niger River regions and these flourished through the medium of cults and secret societies. Here the influences were from the Kimbisi and Abakwa tribes, as far as has been determined, though conections with smaller groups have been identified, whilst the influence of the great Yoruba tribe and its worship of Shango the thunder god is to be found extensively in Trinidad. Elsewhere in the West Indies and the coastal regions other clear influences from Africa may be traced with spirit worship, snake cults, and other manifestations of African magic readily discernible.

In Louisiana and related regions in the South of North America the French brought large numbers of slaves drawn from these areas and from Haiti following the revolution in 1803 of the Negro King Cristophe. George Cable's oft-quoted and discerning article in the *Century Magazine* of February 1886 identified Negroes from some eighteen tribal sources in Africa and singled out for special mention the "voudou-worshipping" Aradas. In North America the newly imported slaves were expected to adopt the Roman Catholic religion. Its mysticism appealed to them and many unexpected parallels between the stories of the saints and aspects of their own still-remembered religion were drawn in their minds. From this confusion of religious beliefs developed the southern magic arts of "voo-doo" – or as Blacks preferred to called it, "hoodoo" – with its practitioners centered in the French South; above all in Louisiana, where "Big Boy" Crudup planned to go:

157   Believe I'll drop down in Louisiana just to see a dear old friend of mine, (*twice*)
      You know maybe she can help me, darn my hard, hard time.

      You know they tell me in Louisiana there is hoodoos all over there, (*twice*)
      You know they'll do anything for the money, man in the world I declare.

      Now Miss Hoodoo Lady, please give me a hoodoo hand, (*twice*)
      I want to hoodoo this woman of mine, I believe she's got another man.

In Louisiana and Alabama there were undetermined numbers of men and women versed in the lore and beliefs of voodoo who practiced their arts for both good and evil in "white" and "black magic." These were the "conjures" or "conjure ladies," the "root doctors," the "hoodoos" and the "gipsies" whose occult powers were believed to be extensive and who were consulted by the crossed-in-love, by the bereaved and by the murderously inclined alike. The conjures who devoted their powers for good often prepared their spells and offered their services free; those whose abilities were put to more evil use exacted fees relative to the undertaking. Both were widely respected and feared. The faith that many Blacks had in the pronouncements of the gipsy women was frequently sufficient to ease troubled minds – Joshua Johnson's, for instance:

158   Well I went to the gipsy an' I laid my money on the line, (*twice*)
      I said, "Bring back my baby, or please take her off my mind."

      That gipsy said, "Don't worry, everything's gonna be all right some day, (*twice*)
      That girl she really loves you but she just can't stand your ways."

Conjures were called upon for a variety of purposes to work spells that involved careful preparation and selection of materials for the charms used, and the study of many portents for favorable signs indicative of the appropriate time and circumstances of their application. The "two-headed

Luck - Love - Romance - Success

HOLY OIL WITH MAGNETIC LODESTONE

Do you want to be happy, lucky in love, money—have success and power? Magnetic Lodestone attracts and is said to draw the things you desire. We make no such claims, but sell only as a curio. Can be removed from Holy Oil ...... **50¢**

Holy Oil With High John The Conqueror Root

Are you in love? Do you wish money? Do you want to hold the one you love? Would you like to have High John the Conqueror Root in Holy Oil?—Power, Love Success? We make no such claims and sell only as a curio. Price ...... **50¢**

Algier's GOOD LUCK Incense

Algier's Good Luck Incense contains John the Baptist Root, Passion Flowers and other known lucky ingredients. Some pieces have numbers said to be lucky. You will be thrilled by the magic spell of love of this Oriental odor as it burns. Price only ...... **35¢**

ALGIERS ROOT AND HERB BAG

Contains HIGH JOHN THE CONQUEROR, ADAM AND EVE ROOT AND DEVIL'S SHOE STRING

This is positive specially prepared bag contains High John the Conqueror Root, Adam and Eve Root and Devil's Shoestring dressed with Dragon's Blood Powder. We are told by many that carrying this bag with them helps drive away evil spirits, brings luck in love, games, etc. for we make no such claims and will reach for a bag of Herbs Carrying Bag is sent FREE with bag ...... **50¢**

Algiers Lucky Love Sachet Powder

Keeps You Sweet—Attracts. How To Use. Place in bag and carry around your neck—put it in your dresser drawer to perfume your underclothing. Rub it on your body to keep it sweet, fragrant and to attract the one you want. You can be irresistible—make it easy to hold your sweetheart. Some say this powder has brought them GOOD LUCK. But we make no such claim ...... **35¢**

MAGIC NIGHT OF LOVE PERFUME

Magic Lovable Enticing Perfume for Lovers. ...... **35¢**

Power

LODESTONE

Ancient peoples believed Lodestone would attract love, affections, riches when carried on one's person. But we make no such claims and sell only as Genuine Magnetic Lodestone. We give you the handy Carrying Bag FREE with your Lodestone. Price ...... **25¢**

ALGIER'S CANDLES

Red, anointed with Mystic Love Perfume — Green with Holy Oil. Some believe burning Red candles bring love, Blue drives evil spirits away. Green brings money. We make no such claims and sell only as good candles ...... **50¢**

VAN VAN OIL

Sprinkle a few drops on doorstep, clothes, pocketbook. An age-old superstition is that Voodoos and others used it to drive away the una and evil spirits being winnings and luck. We make no such claims and will only as curios ...... **50¢**

HIGH JOHN ROOT

Said to contain wonderful lucky properties when carried on one's person. Carry one with you all the time. We make no such claims and sell only as genuine High John the Conqueror Root. Handy Carrying Bag FREE with every Root. Price only ...... **25¢**

Good Luck

LODESTONE PERFUME

Good Luck Lodestone Perfume has that Sweet, Alluring Dreamy odor with the added quality to attract of the Genuine Magnetic Lodestone it contains. Do you want love — do you want to hold the one you love — would you like to attract people? Many claim a few drops works wonders. We make no such claims and sell only as good perfume. Price ...... **50¢**

ADAM AND EVE ROOTS

In mystic Love Oil are believed by many to make them attractive to those of the opposite sex, and to attract love. We make no such claims and sell only as Adam and Eve Roots in Oil. Price only ...... **50¢**

MYSTIC LOVE PERFUME

Has fragrant, captivating oriental odor that lingers about you like a fascinating dream. Attracts people. Makes you irresistible. You will like this delightful oriental odor. Price only ...... **50¢**

Algier's Good Luck ORDER BLANK

ALGIERS CO., PORT WASHINGTON, WIS.

Please send me the items checked below, I am sending ...... in stamps ...... money order ...... cash.

___ Algiers Good Luck Incense. Price ......35¢	___ Algiers Lucky Love Sachet Powder ......25¢
___ Good Luck Lodestone Perfume ......50¢	___ Algiers Mystic Love Perfume ......50¢
___ Van Van Wishing Oil. Price ......50¢	___ Algiers Root and Herb Bag ......50¢
___ High John Conqueror Root ......25¢	___ Adam and Eve Root in Love Oil ......50¢
___ Algiers Live Lodestone ......25¢	___ Algiers Lucky Candles ......50¢
___ Holy Oil with Live Lodestone ......50¢	___ Magic Night of Love Perfume ......36¢

___ Holy Oil with High John the Conqueror Root ......50¢

Send to (Write Plainly) Total Amt. of order $ ......

Name ......

Street and No. ......

Route ...... Box ......

City ...... State ......

Money Order, Cash or Stamps must accompany all orders for less than $1.00. Larger orders will be sent C. O. D. A deposit of 50c must accompany all C.O.D. orders. Above items may be ordered C.O.D. with any other merchandise on this circular.

doctors" were called in at childbirth to ease the labor and to prepare spells that would help to ensure a good life for the newcomer. Barren women sought their advice and purchased their charms so that they might also conceive, and when death came, the spells of the voodoo doctor smoothed the journey of the departed and safeguarded the lives of those who remained. On the doorsteps of the brothels they sprinkled Good Luck Dust and from roots and animal fur, ashes and hair they fabricated charms that would bring fortune to the gambler. Among the most potent weapons were High John the Conqueror Root which had to be gathered before September 21, and Goofer Dust, powdered earth gathered from a grave, preferably that of a child, which would bring death to the victim when it was sprinkled on his pillow.

159   Don't tell me no story, don't tell me no lie, (*twice*)
      Now youse a good-lookin' mama, but you was born to die.

      I'm gonna sprinkle a little goofer dust all around your nappy head,
        (*twice*)
      You'll wake up some of these mornings and find your own self dead.

As in English folk-lore the rabbit foot is a powerful charm for protection, but the strongest charm to bring back the wayward lover was the Black Cat's Bone. Costly and valued, its scarcity was largely due to the elaborate ceremony which attended its preparation. Zora Neale Hurston attended such a ceremony, having first starved for twenty-four hours, subsisting only on one glass of wine at four-hour intervals. A black cat was captured in the dark after a heavy fall of rain – not an easy task in itself – and hastily taken deep into the woods where, in a ring protected by nine horseshoes, a new vessel on which the sun had not been permitted to shine was filled with water and brought to the boil. Into the water was thrown the cat, three times cursed as it screamed in agony. At midnight the remains of the cat were drawn from the boiling water and its bones passed through the mouth until one was found whch tasted bitter – the Black Cat's Bone. The ceremony was attended by a state of tension and terror that Zora Hurston found almost indescribable, but in the morning she returned with the precious bone in her hand. A part of her training as a voodoo priestess, the ceremony took place in New Orleans, Louisiana, which was also the birthplace of the singer Lizzie Miles.

160   I done crossed my fingers and counted up to twenty-three, (*twice*)
      I seen a star fallin'; that means bad luck done fell on me.

      A black cat bone's a-boilin', I put it on at half past twelve, (*twice*)
      I'll tie it in a sack and walk off, talking to myself.

      I let a black cat cross me, I walked right through a funeral line, (*twice*)
      But when the stars are shootin', I know bad luck is in that sign.

This most prized of voodoo charms was sure to bring back home a lover
who had left, or to secure the love of the person against whom its power was
directed, as an Alabama singer, Barefoot Bill, believed:

161   I didn't know I loved my baby till she packed her trunk to leave, (*twice*)
      I telephoned the undertaker, "Just come and bury me, please."

      Might get a black cat's bone, going to bring my baby back home,
      (*twice*)
      Lord, and if that don't do it, might be one more rounder gone.

Amongst the Louisiana and Alabama Blacks the power of "gris-gris,"
"jujus," and "hands" was greatly respected. Such "mojo hands" – the
African terms "gris-gris" and "juju" were largely discarded – were made
with great care from personal fragments and from natural objects. Hair
from the armpits or pubic region, finger-nail parings, pieces of skin were
considered especially effective in love charms, as were fragments of
underclothing, of a menstrual cloth, and other closely personal effects.
Combined with parts of night creatures, bats or toads, and with ashes and
feathers from sources selected for a symbolic significance relative to the
purpose for which they had been prepared, they were tied into small
"conjure-bags" or put into an innocuous-looking receptacle and either
carried to exert their power upon the victim when contact was made with
him, or buried beneath his doorstep, hidden in his bed or hearth. Sang
Muddy Waters, newly up from Mississippi:

162   I'm going down in Louisiana, baby, behind the sun, (*twice*)
      Well, you know I just found out, my trouble just begun.

      I'm going down in New Orleans, hmmm – get me a mojo hand, (*twice*)
      I wan' show all you good-lookin' women just how to treat your man.

Traditional as a center of voodoo in the southern states was New Orleans where the fame of many of its conjure women and voodoo doctors spread far. Blacks who had strong faith in their abilities both for good and evil traveled long distances and parted with not inconsiderable sums of money in order to consult them, and to purchase their preparations and "hands." Among those famed for their supernatural powers were, in the words of "Funny Paper" Smith from Texas, "Seven Sisters in New Orleans, that can really fix a man up right."

163   I hear them say the oldest sister look like she's just 21, (*twice*)
     And she can look you right in your eyes and tell you exactly what you
       want done.

They tell me they've been hung, been bled and been crucified, (*twice*)
But I just want enough help to stand on the water and rule the tide.

Now it's Sara, Minnie, Bertha, Holly, Dolly, Betty, and Jane, (*twice*)
You can't know them sisters apart because they all looks just the same.

The Seven Sisters sent me away happy; round the corner I met another
   little girl, (*twice*)
She looked at me and smiled and said "Go devil and destroy the
   world." (*spoken:* I'm gonna destroy it too – I'm all right now).

Seven times a year the Seven Sisters will visit me in my sleep, (*twice*)
And they said I won't have no more trouble, and said I'll live twelve
   days in a week.

Most famous of the conjure women was the celebrated Marie Leveau, the daughter of Christophe Glapion, whose birth was registered in the St. Louis Cathedral, New Orleans, on February 2, 1827. A Creole quadroon, she studied under the earlier Doctor Alexandre and for more than half a century practiced her magic at her houses in St. Anne Street and Bayou St. Johns. Subsequently, her work was carried on by her reputed nephew, Luke Turner, and many other conjures with wide reputations in the mysterious underground world of voodoo. But though New Orleans and, to a lesser extent, Mobile were principal centers on the Gulf Coast, there were many other hoodoos and seers in other parts of the South. One of the most famous of these was Ida Carter, known as Seven Sisters, who practiced in Hogansville, Alabama. Her fame was almost as great as that of Aunt Caroline Dye, whose name appears in blues songs from the earliest days of

their recording. Aunt Caroline Dye lived in Newport News and continued
to spin her magic until her death in 1944. In 1937 Johnny Temple planned to
consult her.

> 164   Yes I went out on the mountain, looked over in Jerusalem, (*twice*)
> Well, I see them hoodoo women, ooh Lord, makin' up in their low-
> down tents.
>
> Well I'm going to Newport to see Aunt Caroline Dye, (*twice*)
> She's a fortune-teller, oh Lord, she sure don't tell no lie.
>
> And she tol' my fortune when I walked through her door, (*twice*)
> Says I'm sorry for you buddy, but your woman don't want you no
> more.

Apart from the more celebrated practitioners, there were many who
enjoyed strong local reputations and who eked out meagre livings with
"conjuration." Some rural Blacks were inclined to attribute to the conjures
all forms of misfortune, but they also called them in to cast their spells or
give advice. One attended the birth of the pianist Charlie Spand, who came
from rural Georgia.

> 165   A man born of a dark woman is bound to see dark days (*twice*)
> Lord a real dark woman is bound to have evil ways.
>
> I was born in Ell'jay at twelve o'clock at night (*twice*)
> The moon wasn't shinin', it was not a bit of light.
>
> A hoodoo woman came in, and sat by my mother's bed, (*twice*)
> She said, "Before he's over, this boy child'll wish he was dead."
>
> Lord, my poor mother cried, "How can I keep this trouble away from
> my child?"
> Lord, that hoodoo woman said, "Don't let him go while these women
> run wild."
>
> When I grew up I didn't listen to my mother's words, (*twice*)
> No good woman is the cause of me sleepin' outdoors with the birds.

Voodoo was illegal, even in New Orleans, and because it was an
undercover activity the extent of its practice was not easily determined

God

Sent

God's

Messenger

Guaranteed

To

Help

In

Three

Days

SISTER LOLA

The Religious Holy Woman healer, God's messenger who guarantees to heal the sick and the ailing, to remove all suffering and bad luck from your body. She is a religious and holy woman who will remove sorrow, sickness and pain, and all bad luck. The touch of her hand will heal you.

RID YOUR HOME OF HOO DOO!

She guarantees to cure you where others have failed, and take the sickness and pain away from you. One visit will convince you that she is God's messenger on earth. Sister Lola has helped thousands and thousands and guarantees to help you too. People come to see her from miles and miles away. If you suffer from alcoholism and cannot find a cure, don't fail to see this gifted woman who can help you. You can see results in three days. Donations only.

Remember the Bible says that God is the greatest healer and God gave me the power to help those who cannot help themselves. God wants you to be really happy. Are you facing difficult problems? Poor health? Money or job troubles? Unhappiness, drink? Love or family troubles? Do you ever get lonley; unhappy, discouraged? Would you like more happiness, success and good fortune in life?

If you have any of these problems, or others like them, dear friend, then here is wonderful news-new of a remarkable new way of prayer that is helping thousands to glorious new happiness and joy! And it will bring a whole new world of happiness and joy to you, and very quickly, too. So don't wait, dear friend, you will surely bless this day. So don't delay; consult Madame Lola:

CRIPPLED HAVE WALKED AND THE BLIND HAVE SEEN
All Prayers and Healing Free

OPEN EVERY DAY
8:00 A.M. to 10:00 P.M.
1012 ALABAMA - Phone JA 4-1036

Some indication may be gained from the black popular press which in the 1960s still carried in every edition advertisements for Easy Life Mixture, for Black Cat's Oil, Heifer Dust, Lovin' Powder (at twenty-five cents) and Extra Fast Lovin' Powder at a slightly higher price. With them came fantastic guarantees, and beguiling phrases which were designed to suggest to the police that the powders and philters sold were mere novelties, but which still gave to the intended market the assurance of success. Their sale was widespread and the advertisements appeared even on the backs of record lists intended purely for the black market. Nor was the belief in voodoo confined to the South; it was extensive in the North where "gipsies" plied a highly lucrative trade, claiming at the same time some connections with the South in their origins, and in the source of the roots and charms that they sold. Jazz Gillum went to one of them.

166 I went down to the hand-reader just to have my fortune told, (*twice*)
He said, "You need to catch policy – dog-gone your bad luck soul."

He give me some Good Luck Tea and said, "Drink it before it gets cold." (*twice*)
He said, "Drink it all day, dog-gone your bad luck soul."

Then he give me some pills just to drive my blues away, (*twice*)
He said, "You bad luckin' rascal, take them three times a day."

Bad luck is in my family, an' there ain't nobody home with me, (*twice*)
I was a fool for ever thinkin' that my happy days would ever be.

Amongst the more sophisticated Blacks belief in voodoo or related superstitions was considered to be a matter for some shame and a throwback to the days of servitude in the South. So it was with a ribald sense of humor and a studied disrespect for the beliefs of the older generation that Peter Clayton – calling himself "Doctor" Clayton – sang his *Root Doctor Blues*.

167 I'm a first-class root doctor and I don't bar no other doctor in his land, (*twice*)
My remedy is guaranteed to cure you, pills and pains ain't in my plan.

You claim your regular doctor makes you feel like a real young girl, (*twice*)

Doctor Clayton's root treatments make you feel like an angel flyin'
round in another world.

After you receive my special root treatment, woman please don't start
no signifyin', (*twice*)
Don't clown because some woman beat you to my office, Lord I'd love
to work overtime.

Amongst the voodoo doctors the principal book of magic was a reprint of
the *Book of Dream and Mystery* accredited to the medieval exponent of the
White and Black Arts, Albertus Magnus, which enjoyed a wide sale in
Harlem, though it was banned in Haiti. But the Black Arts have always
received much stimulation from Christianity and the Black Mass is an
inversion of the true Mass, with obscene substitutions for the symbolic wine
and bread, and lewd incantations for the Creed. The saints were proved to
be allies to voodoo and the Bible was given strange and unintended
interpretations. The Feast of St. John was almost as much voodoo as it was
Catholic and St. Anthony of Padua, St. Mary Magdalene, and many other
saints were incorporated into its ceremonies. Voodoo did not only appeal to
the superstitious: it also satisfied the need for protection, and acted as a form
of escape, particularly when coupled with spiritualism with which in the
cities it was often inextricably bound. Many Blacks sought the protection of
secret societies and cults, and the illegality of voodoo together with the air of
mysticism that surrounded its rites had great appeal. It has been loosely
linked with African cults and tribal societies, but to conclude that the
connection was a powerful one is somewhat superficial, for whilst there
existed half-forgotten echoes of Africa in voodoo ritual, the desire for the
comfort and intrigue of the cult is common to most societies. It has been
noted that in an ordinary American community of some seventeen
thousand, more than eight hundred independent organizations exist, a
pattern of behavior far from uncommon in the United States as elsewhere.

Charlatans and criminals who exploited the beliefs of uneducated Blacks
disillusioned many who put their faith in the voodoo cults. Whilst this effect
was not wholly bad, it often brought misery and insecurity to those who
were unable to turn to orthodox religion for comfort. Religious cults of a
non-voodoo, non-spiritualist nature that nevertheless have a high degree of
mystical content or, conversely, the strictest rules of conduct that have a
purgative effect upon the mind, have thrived as a result of this. The Peace
Mission of Father Divine; the Church of Bishop "Daddy" Grace – the

United House of Prayer for all People; Bishop Ida Robinson's Mount Sinai Holy Church of America Inc., and the Moorish Science Temple of Timothy Drew are among the more important and influential religious cults of this character. Sang Fat Hayden in 1939:

> 168   Since my gal went to New York, my how she's done changed, (*twice*)
> She don't like the boogie woogie, now you can't tell her a dog-gone thing.
>
> I bought me a voodoo, put it in the springs of my bed, (*twice*)
> Now if that voodoo could talk it would mark my woman stiff dead.
>
> I ain't no washfoot Baptist, and I can't do the Holy Roll, (*twice*)
> I joined Father Divine and he gave me peace that satisfies my soul.

Though some of the religious cults were very demanding, a large number channeled the savings of their members and the collections taken at services to the benefit of others. With congregations often numbering only a score the little "store-front" churches which had been adapted from converted shops, and the larger "temples" which were once theaters, picture-houses, or warehouses satisfied the spiritual needs of large numbers of the populace and provided protection for the socially insecure. Embracing the ritual and the rules of the church the new member renounced sinful pleasures – and with them the blues. There were, nevertheless, many groups which purported to be of a religious nature but which were, in fact, successful methods of turning the sincere convictions of innocent Blacks to the profit of a few unprincipled criminals. Accompanied by fake ceremony and ritual especially designed to appeal to those recently arrived from southern country communities, the services were conducted with a view to the extortion of sums of money in the form of bogus "collections" for the church. Baptismal waters and "holy" oils were sold by the bottle for twenty-five cents and higher grades for double the sum, both within the church and in the street from the perambulators of wandering vendors.

Black superstition was the subject of lucrative exploitation by the vendors of charms and love philters, and cheap pseudo-religious votive ornaments and accessories alike, but it was in the systematic organization of the Numbers Racket that the most relentless and deliberate exploitation took place.

The Numbers Racket or Policy Racket reputedly came from Cuba, where it was known as Bolito. A successful method of earning large sums of money for a small number of people, it was introduced into Harlem and subsequently into black urban districts throughout the States during the years of economic depression, when it was organized by "Dutch" Schultz. Bets were placed on combinations of numbers, generally in groups of three, and the winners received prizes of dazzling size in proportion to their modest bets. A return of fifty dollars might be received from a single cent played on a number, but the proportion of winners was exceptionally small – perhaps one in a thousand. Nevertheless, the large prizes possible from low stakes invited many players on the numbers game and hundreds of thousands of Blacks "played policy" every day. As a result of the successes that some who might otherwise be absolutely destitute had gained, the policy racket had wide support and the fact that it was illegal deterred very few from placing their stakes. Those who played and won remained in the mind whilst those, like Gabriel Brown, who played and lost were soon forgotten.

169   Me and my friends played a number, just as happy as happy could be,
      Everybody got paid for that number,
      Everybody got paid but me,
      (*Spoken*) I lost my stake.

           The jinx is on me, jinx is on me,
           I can't have no luck at all, the jinx is on me.

For many Blacks the Numbers became an obsession and they depended for their living entirely upon their winnings in the play. Inevitably they would put great store on possible combinations of numbers that would seem to be well omened, and on the numbers that occurred in dreams. So the Numbers Racket, called "Playing the Races" by some, including John Lee Hooker, continued to thrive.

170   I don't want no woman plays the races all the time, (*twice*)
      You know she ain't good for nothin' she do broke most all the time.

      Dreamed a number all the last night, yes, yes, yes, and my baby she did
        the same, (*twice*)
      My baby got up this morning and she played it the same.

      I come home every Friday, throw my check down on the bed, (*twice*)
      My baby takes all of my money, put it down on 5–6 and 2.

TABLE FOR FINDING LUCKY NUMBERS.

FIRST THROW	I	II	III	IV	V	VI	VII	VIII	IX	X	XI	XII
XII	14	0	27	0	4	0	75	0	11	0	26	28
IX	0	70	0	54	0	59	0	8	0	55	28	
X	57	0	10	0	89	0	41	0	63	5	18	
XI	0	17	0	77	0	16	0	45	15	51	0	
VIII	28	0	71	0	9	0	8	78	80	0	67	
VII	0	78	61	0	72	0	749	85	20	0	48	29 67
VI	68	0	61	0	56	7	64	0	38	52	62 67	
V	0	18	0	82	31	86	0	68	50	34	0	
IV	1	0	12	53	0	40	24	48	0	44		
III	0	87	60	21	0	58	86	76	0	42	65 44	
II	46	66	7 83	0	47	25	74	0	19	29	0	

SECOND THROW.

EXPLANATION.—Take two dice and throw; mark down the number of spots thrown; then throw again and mark as before; look at the top line of the table and find the number of your first throw; then follow the line straight down until you find on the opposite side of the table the number corresponding to your second throw. For instance, the number of spots in your first throw equals 6, which you will find on the top line of the table, marked in roman numerals, VI., your second throw gives 4 spots, which will be found on the outside column, marked IV. Place your finger on the VI. at the top of the table and follow the line down until it brings you to the IV. on the opposite side of the column, you will thus get the number 61, which will be the lucky number. In this manner you can get as many lucky numbers as you wish to play. In case you should come to a cypher (0), you must throw again.

NUMBERS FOR DREAMS OF THE MONTHS.

January	55	July	17
February	11	August	8
March	45	September	61
April	1	October	78
May	73	November	68
June	22	December	12

FOR THE DAYS OF THE WEEK,

Monday	4	Thursday	54
Tuesday	17	Friday	19
Wednesday	18	Saturday	35

To exploit this superstition the policy racketeers published "Dream Books" which gave lists of numbers which were supposed to have a mystic connection with aspects of human experience, with objects natural and man-made, and with every conceivable circumstance that might occur in dreams. Daggers and dogs, stars and strangers, Christian names and Christian symbols, connections obscure or obscene were all given their number codes, and the Policy player, upon experiencing a particular event, happening upon an unusual object, encountering a feature which he believed significant, or dreaming of any of these, consulted his book to guide him in playing. Blind Blake played typical combinations.

171   I dreamed last night the woman I love was dead, (*twice*)
      If I had played the "Dead Roll" I would-a come out ahead.

      I act like a fool and played 3–6–9, (*twice*)
      Lost my money, and that girl of mine.

      I begged my baby, let me in her door, (*twice*)
      Wanted to put my 25–50–75 in her 7–17–24.

Many omens of good luck were the reverse of the expected association and therefore accorded with popular superstition. Folk beliefs were carefully noted and commonly held notions perpetuated and employed to the ultimate benefit of the racketeers. To tread in excreta was commonly believed to be a sign of good luck and to dream of fecal matter likewise. The feces were assigned the combination 3–6–9 (or three, six, and nine) and this was considered a number of especial fortune, appearing on many records, including *Numbers Blues* by Ollie Shepard.

172   Going down to the office and get a numbers book, (*twice*)
      So I can catch a gang of clowns like a fish a fishing hook.

      I've got me a book, I got it from a numbers man, (*twice*)
      I can't play all the numbers but I'm sure gonna play my hand.

      I'm going down in Georgia and write some on the farm, (*twice*)
      If I ever hit on the book, I'm gonna bring that money home.

      I acted like a fool, I wouldn't play on 3–6–9, (*twice*)
      Just think of all that money in that numbers book of mine.

It is of interest to note that the most famous black regiment of World War I was the 369th, which had a distinguished record of service though it had suffered poor treatment. This particular number combination may have come from such a source. As the Numbers Racket was illegal the "office" has a euphemistic term: it may have been a drug store, a saloon or a beauty parlor that acted as a "drop" for the racketeer. Others operated from a street corner, but whatever the drop, its position was carefully and jealously protected by the racketeers. The numbers were usually "drawn" by spinning an enumerated wheel. Such "Policy Wheels" were known by colorful names: "Bootleg," "Red Devil," "Streamline," "Black and White," and the books issued from the particular drops contained slips of identifiable colors. Numbers could be backed in groups of three, or a succession of numbers, which operated both from left to right and in reverse order, might be bought for an additional sum by the customer who specified when purchasing that he was playing the numbers "saddled" instead of "straight." In the 1950s Policy grossed some twenty million dollars a year of which half at least went into the pockets of the racketeers and their four thousand minions, from the "big shot" down to the "numbers runner" who collected and issued the numbers in the street. He walked quickly, the numbers runner, keeping a wary eye for the police. By a code of winks and raised eyebrows, by flickering fingers and muttered words as he rapidly passed he collected the orders and indicated the winning numbers. Jimmy Gordon composed a wry blues song about the runners.

173   Got the number runner's, I got the number runner's, got the number
         runner's blues,
      Got the number runner's, I got the number runner's blues,
      And every time I see a policeman, I almost jump out of my shoes.

      Standin' on the corner, standin' on the corner, wasn't doing nothing
         wrong, wrong, wrong,
      Standin' on the corner, wasn't doing nothing wrong,
      Oooh, that policeman was looking, he grabbed me by my arm.

      When I got a hearing, when I got a hearing, the judge looked at me a
         short while, – while, while, while,
      When I got a hearing, the judge looked at me a short while,
      He said "I believe that you' guilty, six months on that hard rock-pile."

Working on that rock-pile, working on that rock-pile, like I done a
  terrible crime, crime, crime,
Working on that rock-pile, like I done a terrible crime,
And when I left that rock-pile, I didn't have a single dime.

Now I'm scared to run the numbers, scared to run the numbers, scared
  to run the numbers now, – now, now, now,
Scared to run the numbers, scared to run the numbers now,
But if I keep on getting broke, going to run those numbers anyhow.

For many who were criminally inclined the attractions of being a
numbers runner outweighed the risks involved, for the returns were
considerable and assured. The bigger racketeers would bank a hundred
thousand dollars a week and the sale of the pitches and drops when the agent
was temporarily put away by the police or squeezed out by "muscle men"
of a rival faction also brought in large sums. "Dutch" Schultz was
suppressed in Harlem for a while by Governor Dewey; Chicago's "Jones
Boys" were squeezed out of their holdings, but they did not mind: they had
made their millions and were able to open a silk factory in Mexico City on
the profits. In the 1950s the Numbers Racket in central Harlem was
controlled by a six-foot, two-hundred-pound black racketeer called "The
Lamb," one Bumpy Johnson. And whilst the Policy Racket flourished the
player in the street bought his numbers book from the "Big Train,"
consulted his dream book, burnt a phial of incense to find the three lucky
numbers in the ashes, and prayed for a hundred-to-one win on the phallic
"Big Dick" – fifteen–sixty–seventy-five.

6 *Let the deal go down*

In the black underworld the most important members were the numbers racketeers whose success, whilst partly due to the exploitation of superstition, was primarily dependent on the widespread fondness for gambling. Of indictable offenses for which Blacks were convicted, illegal gambling provided a large proportion. It is exceedingly doubtful whether any racial group has an inherent propensity to gamble, but the black worker's liking for betting was born of the culture which evolved from his place in the American social structure. Economic instability and low social status induced many a black man to gamble in the hope that he might better his financial position and be able to afford the clothes, the Cadillac Eight and, if possible, the home, that were marks of the position to which he aspired in a society where status was, and is, measured in terms of prosperity rather than culture. Lack of opportunities to achieve positions of responsibility prior to civil rights legislation denied him the right to take important decisions or to exercise his initiative, thus refusing him sources of mental stimulation. Playing his hand, staking his chips, rolling his dice, the gambler gained the thrills that his work did not afford him. Pitting his wits against other gamblers he exercised his intellect. From the turn of the cards he could experience the sweet delight of victory or the knife-thrust of failure when he lost: he gained pleasure from them both. He did not have to suffer the indignities of the Jim Crow "Nigger Heavens" (in those theaters where he was permitted to attend shows at all), in seeking this entertainment; the street corner, the backyard or the parlor were the scene of his play. And he had the time to play. Six days of labor, and the seventh a day of rest – but not for the man on relief, for the man who has been laid off from his work, nor for the man whose work was insufficient to keep him active throughout the year. Raising cotton provided less than two hundred working days in the year; for half the year the share-cropper was idle unless he could find some other employment or had been able to obtain for his own purposes a plot of land that he could cultivate. So the unemployed, the laid off and the temporarily idle had plenty of free time. The woman raised the children, stitched the clothes, washed and swept. The man repaired the tools, cut back the wood, fashioned staves, went shooting a little, fished, hunted. When there was nothing else to do he joined his fellows to tell "lies," put in the Dozens, sing the blues. Or, like Blind Blake, he gambled.

174 I love to gamble, gamblin's all I do, (*twice*)
And when I lose, it never makes me blue.

I gambled away my money, I gambled away my shack, (*twice*)
Same way I lost it, same way I get it back.

I won a woman in a poker game, (*twice*)
I lost her too, win another just the same.

Sometimes I'm rich, sometimes I ain't got a cent, (*twice*)
But I've had a good time, every way I went.

It was the excitement of gambling and the belief that a run of bad luck was bound to change sooner or later, that kept a man playing the games when it would have been wiser to leave off. Gambling acts as a drug on the senses, stimulates and intoxicates. Whilst mild games cause little distress, the inveterate gambler is apt to play for higher and higher stakes and to lay down all that he possesses in the hopes of winning a high return. For these reasons gambling can be demoralizing and add considerably to the suffering of a black family, for the man who stakes heavily and loses is causing damage not only to himself but to his dependants. Once in debt to a calculating player who has played a deceptive game of losing for a while until the stakes run high, he may be forced to borrow, beg, or steal money in order to pay off and is almost inevitably drawn into further games in the desperate attempt to recoup his losses. Red Nelson's excuses and vain hopes did not appease his woman, apparently.

175 I gets my money from an ole lady, she says, "Son, give it to the poor,"
(*twice*)
She says, "Make 'em shoot dice an' play Coon-Can, an' don't give my money away till I'm long gone."

Ain't no use of me playin', bad luck is on my hands, (*twice*)
I been playin' all night long, an' your daddy win that first game.

When you lose your money, please don' lose your mind, (*twice*)
Because the best of gamblers, mama, get busted down sometimes.

When I was runnin' aroun' tryin' to gamble, Lord, I caught myself a
   cold, (*twice*)
Stayin' out late at night losin' my money, sleepin' with women I slept
   with before.

I even down there playin' horse-races, no card game ain't no good
   (*twice*)
You give me so much trouble, that I had to move from your
   neighborhood.

A true gambler accepts the rough with the smooth, the losses with the
gains. His fortune might depend on the turn of a card, on a timely maneuver
or an outrageous deception. As he played his game he had to weigh carefully
the improvement percentage of his hand with the relative value which he
was to call or bet compared to the size of the actual or likely jack-pot.

Poker is a favored game amongst black gamblers, especially in various
modifications such as Florida Flip – Five Card Stud in which each new card
is served down so that the players may elect which card to turn up before
every interval. One of the oldest card games associated almost exclusively
with Blacks is Coon-Can, a form of gambling rummy in which the dice are
also employed. Because it needs only two hands to form a game it is widely
played and extremely popular. Peetie Wheatstraw boasted:

176   Well, now they call me Coon-Can Shorty, the man from Coon-Can
         Land, (*twice*)
      Well, I know I will play with any man, ooh well, well, the game they
         call Coon-Can.

      My dice won't pay – 'cause it's the only game you see, (*twice*)
      And every chump in town, ooh well, well seems to fall out on me.

      My babe give me money – Coon-Can Shorty is my name, (*twice*)
      But before I lose her money, ooh well, I must spread news in town
         again.

      But some day my dice gon' pay and my money gonna be on the wood.
      Ooooh well, my money gon' be on the wood.
      And every chump in town, ooh well, they ain't gonna be no good.

      Some say they will Coon together – if you chain 'em down, (*twice*)
      But now you know I got it there – ooh well, well if you come in this
         town.

But the favorite game is Georgia Skin, fast and open to innumerable methods of cheating by experienced players. Two players act as "principals" and take it in turns to deal, alternating when one or the other loses – or "falls" – on a card. Each "piker," as the player is called, is dealt a card and as a player "falls" a further deal is made. After the deal, the players sing, "Let the deal go down," as the principal flips the cards from the top of the deck. Bets are placed on the cards as they drop but a player may "scoop one in the rough" by selecting any card from the deck on payment of an additional sum to the principal. Some of the fortunes and the atmosphere of the game are recalled by the gravel-voiced Georgia singer Peg Leg Howell in his *Skin Game Blues*:

177 Better let the deal go down, skin game coming to a close,
   An' you better let the deal go down.
   (*Spoken*) Hold the cards, dollar more. Deuce beat a nine, put up more,
      Nigger!

When I came to the skin game last night, thought I'd have some fun,
Lost the money that I had, baby, had to pawn my special gun,
Had to pawn my special gun, had to pawn my special gun, loving
   baby,
Had to pawn my special gun.

         Said you better let the deal go down,
         Skin game coming to a close,
         And you better let the deal go down.

Gambled all over Missouri, gambled through Tennessee, babe,
Soon as I reached ol' Georgia, the niggers carried a handcuff to me.

         Said you better let the deal go down,
         Skin game coming to a close,
         And you better let the deal go down.

Much depends on the turn of a card and inevitably superstitions as to the nature of certain cards have developed, some being considered as lucky and others as ill-fated ones to have in the hand. Because Blacks were called "Spades" by some contemptuous Whites, the Spades suit is sometimes considered ill-favored. Adapting the word by a popular form of jive slang (in which the vowels are repeated with unrelated consonants separating them), to "Spagingy Spagade," certain Blacks took an inverted pleasure in this, or boasted that they were the "King of Spades." In similar fashion the

East Texas blues singer, B. K. Turner, called himself the "Black Ace" singing, "I am the Black Ace, I'm the boss card in your hand," with challenging pride. Spades, Clubs, and Hearts have various symbolic meanings. Most favored of the suits was Diamonds and of the cards, the Jack of Diamonds, with which players sometimes associated themselves.

> 178   Jack of Diamonds you appear to be my friend, (*twice*)
> But gamblin' gonna be our end.
>
> We have traveled the whole round world through, (*twice*)
> There is nothin' in this world I've found that pleases you.
>
> I love Jack of Diamonds but he was a cruel man, (*twice*)
> He would play dice and cards and his game was old Coon-Can.

Jack of Diamonds, as Sippie Wallace suggested, is a deceptive card that can be of great service if played correctly, but "Jack of Diamonds is a hard card to play." In Bob Campbell's words it can turn your "money green" – in other words it can make coins into "folding money," into paper dollar greenbacks.

> 179   I said dices are dices, please, don't you three on me. (*twice*)
> I'm just as broke and hungry as a gambler can be.
>
> My buddy played a Jack when he give me that hardluck Queen, (*twice*)
> It were one of the luckiest o' cards that a gambler has ever seen.
>
> Jack o' Diamonds, Jack o' Diamonds will turn your money green,
>   (*twice*)
> It' the luckiest card that a gambler have ever seen.

Apart from gambling with cards, the gambling black workers liked best to "Roll the Bones" – to shoot craps with the dice. The game is simple, and can be virtually interminable, and other names by which it is known – Memphis Dominoes or Mississippi Marbles – are evidence of its popularity in the South. The crap shooters "lay their money on the wood to make betting good," and "keep it in sight to save a fight" – staking their bets on the throw of the dice. Best numbers are seven and eleven, the worst throws are two, three, and twelve, when "up jumps the devil." Justifying himself for losing and reassuring himself that his bad luck was only temporary, Charles "Speck" Pertum sang the *Gambler's Blues*:

180 I lose all my money on a point like nine, (*twice*)
I set down a four spot and the trey comes flyin'.

I lose all my money – got all my clothes in pawn, (*twice*)
Know you gonna feel surprised when you see me with my good clo's
on.

When I was down why did you let me lay? (*twice*)
For every man's subject to a losing day.

My gal's a gambler, she plays both night and day, (*twice*)
She plays High-Low Jack in the game, with ace, deuce, jack, and trey.

I don't shoot dice, strictly don't play no pool, (*twice*)
Because I sell tamales – don't think I'm nobody's fool.

Gambling was illegal in most of the states – the only truly "wide-open state" was Nevada – but this does not mean that there were not gaming-houses in abundance, though they operated as a result of dubious manipulations of the law. In the "tonks" and gaming dens of the black sectors few of the casual workers from the tobacco factories or the oil refineries succeeded in making their fortunes, for here they met the professional gamblers. Against the fuzzed shuffles, the fixed decks, the crimped and pricked cards that were detected only by the extra-sensitive, sand-papered finger-tips of the professional, the logger who tried to triple his pay had little chance of winning. But though he – or she – may have preferred, like Roosevelt Sykes' woman, to shoot craps, the temptation to enter the bigger games was hard to resist.

181 My baby she found a brand new place to go, (*twice*)
She hangs across town at the Monte Carlo.

She likes my money, tells me she goin' to the picture-show, (*twice*)
But that girl's been throwin' ma money away at the Monte Carlo.

(*Spoken*) Monte Carlo is one of the biggest gambling-houses in town.
If you stick it's bound to carry you down.

I heard she had a boy friend and they called him Buddy Joe, (*twice*)
He's a big shot across town, runs a game at the Monte Carlo.

New BIG 80 BLUES

Bumble Bee Slim

NO. 3267

3267—New Big 80 Blues and Wet Clothes Blues—Guitar Acc. Played and sung by Bumble Bee Slim..................59c

Big-time gamblers kept to the cities for most of the year, playing amongst themselves for truly high stakes. Tens of thousands of dollars might pass amongst them in a single bet. But in the early fall the gamblers appeared from Memphis, St. Louis, and Chicago in Clarksdale or Jackson. They came up from New Orleans and Mobile and visited the cotton and rural areas of Mississippi, Georgia, and Alabama. For this was the time of the year when the black farmer was relatively flush with money; he was excited as the end of the season arrived and the fall-money paid out for his crops burned in his pockets. In districts where wages were paid on a day-to-day basis as crops were weighed in, the worker was happy enough to spend his income as it came; in those areas where the share-cropping system operated he was paid in a lump sum at the conclusion of the harvest. The big-time gamblers waited for him. This was the time of the "Skin-Ball" and the games of Skin were established in every roadside juke-joint. In their thousands the croppers and the field-hands appeared at the gaming centres and, hoping to turn their year's returns to a fortune, some might stake their entire earnings on a turn of the card. Others were more cautious, but it was a time of infectious excitement, when caution was cast aside. When the small-time players, the croppers and workers of field and factory had been cleaned up, the noted gamblers amongst the local Blacks moved in and the play was in earnest, with numbers and liquor concessions, property and heavy sums staked, lost and won. Meanwhile, the field-hand returned to his home, like Lucille Bogan's man, poorer but not necessarily wiser.

182   Good morning skin game, hollerin' skin game please last, *(twice)*
     I done staked my man to win and I hope my money will pass.

     He done pawned my house, he got my life at stake, *(twice)*
     And I got to get it back with that money he gamble and make.

     He never lost no money until he draw that black Queen of Spades,
     Ooh, lost his money on that black Queen of Spades
     And my man was in need of beggin', he was in hard luck that very day.

     When he come back to me – got a dollar or two, *(twice)*
     I want him to go back to that skin game, and see what he can do.

     If my man he could only win my money back, *(twice)*
     I would take a walk down town, buy me a brand new pair of shoes and
       hat.

The rattle of the dice on the wood and the chanting of the players lured the gambler to the game, which could soon change, with the addition of an extra die, to "chuck-a-luck." Whether he was trying to "buck the tiger" at poker, sweep the deck in the skin game, or shake off the jinx that had caused his run of bad luck in the past, the player prayed that the scales would tip in his favor and that his nickels and dimes would turn to dollars. The stakes were not always high in the terms of the professional gambler but a man's fortune is his total wealth and the loss of a few dollars when they are all that he possesses could be as great a tragedy as any enacted before the croupiers in a Riviera Casino. "Little Son" Jackson from Fort Worth Texas, gave up gambling and joined the church.

> 183   You know I once was a gambler boys but I bet my money wrong,
>   (*twice*)
>   Now I ain't got no money, and all I got is gone.
>
>   You know I'm through with gambling, some jackstrooper can have my
>   room,
>   Boys I'm through with gambling, some other hustler can have my
>   room,
>   Well now drinking may kill me, but gambling won't be my doom.
>
>   Well I gambled so long till I thought I would never change, (*twice*)
>   Well I ain't gonna gamble no more, I swear I'm gonna save my change.

It was not only the gamblers who appeared in the South in the early fall, at harvest time and immediately after. For this was the period, until the late 1950s, when the traveling entertainments toured with the circuses and tent shows – Silas Green from New Orleans, the Georgia Smart Set, the Rabbit Foot Minstrels, or Irvine Miller's Brownskin Models. Gaily decorated trucks drove slowly through the townships and laughing, dancing jugglers high-stepping on their "Tom Walkers" – or stilts – drew the children and their parents from the doorways, to follow in cheerful procession to the show-grounds.

A visit from a traveling show was a big event in the small southern communities. It brought a period of gaiety and abandon during which moral codes tended to be relaxed. Side-stalls and amusements commenced to operate as the tents were erected. In the bigger centers there were fairs and circuses and field-hands content for the time being with their earnings traveled comparatively long distances to attend them, camping out in the vicinity of the show until the season was over or their money expended. Some of their number with instrumental and vocal ability joined the shows in a temporary semi-professional capacity as blues singers, traveling from town to town and village to village, freely sharing the loose, unrestrained and riotous living that the brief stops afforded. So a singer such as Gus Cannon or Ben Covington would leave his home district during the cotton-picking, corn-husking, cane-cutting, tobacco-harvesting season to entertain with the shows as they toured through the South and mid-West – though in the case of Texas Alexander, to some disadvantage:

184 I carried my woman to the St. Louis Fair, (*twice*)
   She got stuck on every man that was in the fair.

   I brought her back to Dallas with a traveling show, (*twice*)
   She had men hanging around like a circus show . . .

At this time of the year the traveling vendors of cheap patent medicines also exploited the comparative affluence of their country cousins. Few of the medicine "doctors" sold creditable wares; usually they were concoctions of their own devising which acted as strong purgatives. They realized that the southern folk believed that "the more you're sick the more you needed it," and made sure that their brightly colored, foul-tasting "medicines" had the desired effect of causing their purchasers to retch violently. To advertise their arrival many medicine salesmen employed blues singers – Joe Lee Williams, Will Shade, or Sonny Terry for example – to perform on a "medicine show" which attracted a crowd to whom the concoctions could be sold. The appeal of such shows was immediate, for ready-made entertainments were few. In those districts that sported a theater of some form, Blacks were not generally admitted, but the majority of the townships were without such refinements.

A black worker in search of amusement went to the "juke" where he could carouse, dance, and join in the rough entertainment that the establishment afforded. A timber-framed shack, with a low veranda and brightly painted metal advertisements decorating the exterior, the juke was often closed during the week and came into rough and noisy activity on a Saturday night. But during the lay-off season, when there was little else to do, the juke was open every night and the pleasure-seekers would "barrel-house" in wild, sweating dances to the music of guitars or piano. It was "low-down" stuff and the participants were condemned by the "do-gooders" – the strict church-going folk. Singing the blues and "stomping 'em down, bedslats and all," the "sinners" did not care. They needed an outlet for their unspent energies and knew few others. In a deep, gritty voice, "Mr. Freddie" Spruell sang of the only life he either knew or wanted in the Delta:

> 185   In the low-lands of Mississippi, that's where I were born, (*twice*)
> Way down in the sunny South, low-lands of cotton and corn.
>
> I'm lookin' for a low-down woman who's lookin' for a low-down man, (*twice*)
> Ain't nobody in town get more low-down than I can.
>
> I like low-down music, I like to barrelhouse and get drunk too, (*twice*)
> I'm just a low-down man, always feelin' low-down and blue.

White square-dances and cotillions had been adapted in the slavery period to suit the less formal tastes of the slaves and from these the "breakdowns" of later years and spontaneous open-air dances, sometimes called "sukey-jumps," evolved. To mark the conclusion of corn-husking, the raising of a house, a wedding, or indeed any social event that merited some form of celebration, "play-parties" were held which lasted until the dancers and celebrants dropped from exhaustion and liquor. Banjo, fiddle, guitar, and piano rags provided the music, but when the early morning light was breaking over the hills and the energies of the dancers were beginning to flag, the musicians dropped into the slow, interminable blues, and the couples "slow-dragged" across the floor. Sang Lemon Jefferson:

> 186   My feets is so sore, cain't hardly wear ma shoes, (*twice*)
> Out last night with wild women and it left me with those big night blues.
>
> I grabbed ma sugar an' I danced sweet mama till the clock struck twelve, (*twice*)
> I had to rassle so hard with my good gal, an' I ain't feelin' so well.
>
> I'm going back to that wild party, get with the wild women again, (*twice*)
> Well I ain't goin' leave home, till I have me a quart of gin.

At the jukes and honky-tonks provided by the companies for the workers on the "jobs"; at the breakdowns held in the back-of-town taverns in the southern villages or in the rough dance halls of Shreveport and Memphis, Atlanta and Nashville, the dances were not characterized by their refinement, and any grace that might be observed in them was born of freedom of movement rather than studied dance figures. Yet new dances were constantly being evolved. From Florida came the Swamp Shimmy, in which vigorous undulations of body, hips, and limbs made up for lack of forward movement. From the desperate black quarter around 4th Avenue, Nashville, known as the Nashville Bottoms, came a new "twister" with hand-claps and hops – the Black Bottom, the punning significance of its name doubtless appealing to its inventors. In its original form it made few concessions to respectability, but when it entered the white dance halls in the 1920s, many of its frankly erotic features were modified. Other dances such as the Texas Twist and the Georgia Crawl also indicated their place of origin. Echoes of folk amusements were to be found in the many dances that mimicked animal movements early in the century: the Grizzly Bear and the Elephant Squat, the Buzzard Lope and the Turkey Trot, the Eagle Rock and the Turtle Twist, the Bunny Hug and the Fishtail. Holding the Mule, Walking the Dog – the Southerners brought their dances from the Mississippi jukes to the back parlors of Chicago's South Side and New York's Harlem. From the South they also brought the "Rolling Blues" – rapid, twelve-bar blues played on the piano with six or, more commonly, eight beats to the bar to which the pianist, "Speckled Red" or Romeo Nelson perhaps, half-sang, half-spoke his instructions to the dancers:

> 187 Say, you li'l girl over there with the black dress on,
> Come right over here, stand up by me..
> Let me show you how to do that Head Rag Hop!
> Turn round. That's it.
> Now let's git it! Shake it! Shake it fast!
> That's just what I'm talkin' about.
> Baby you strowin' yo' mess now!
> I thought you tol' me you didn't know how to do that Fishtail?
> Ah, you doin' that Head Rag Hop now!

It was the ill-fated Clarence "Pinetop" Smith, who was killed by a stray bullet in a fracas when he was twenty-three, who first used the term "boogie woogie" on record. Known as "Walking the Bassess" by southern Blacks, he re-christened the style after the "boogies" or parties on the South Side where the loud and rhythmic blues-based piano music was popular. Too Tight Parties and Too Terrible Parties, Chitterling Rags and Calico Hops, Juggles and Struggles, Skiffles and Scuffles, Breakdowns and Shake-medowns, Stomps and Boogies – essentially they were one and the same thing, informal, reckless gatherings and dances, as popular in Atlanta as they were in Detroit. The blues guitarists and pianists arriving from the South found that their music was ideally suited to the wild assemblies that were even more a part of black life in the immediate post-World War I years than they were among the Whites. In the confined space of a tenement parlor there was as little room for freedom of movement as there was on the congested, sand-strewn floor of the juke, and the dancers evolved their "shimmies," their "shakes," their bumps and grinds that recalled the *danse du ventre* of the Oul'd-Nail, in which the dancers shrugged their shoulder, fluttered their fingers, traced and retraced the seams of their trouser legs, twitched and rippled and did the belly-rub, "dancing on a dime." The blues pianist or guitarist may not have called the gathering, but he was the most important member of the throng, demanding his liquor and his women, "whipping" his guitar "to a plank" and his piano "to a jello." While Charles Avery played a fast and rolling boogie and Tampa Red picked a sleek guitar accompaniment, Lil Johnson sang the blues and encouraged the guests.

188   Play that thing, play that thing just right! (*twice*)
       We got to scuffle the house rent tonight.

       My house rent's due, my gas given up 'til ten, (*twice*)
       I wouldn't have no light, but the light man couldn't get in!

       (*Spoken*) Oh, play that thing boy! Everybody dance and have a good
           time . . . I got everything to drink from soda water to wine . . . I got
           fried chicken, even got red beans and rice. Now don't you hear me
           talkin' to you? This is Miss Lil Johnson, Lord. Somebody buy the
           piano player a drink. He's just too tight . . .

"Don't forget the landlady!" she concluded; she, after all, put on the "Scuffle" and was why the event took place.

Spirits were high and the spirit flowed; tempers would flare into burning quarrels on the instant, to be decided with chib and steel blade on the back stairs. To some Blacks the parties became notorious as "razor-drills" or, in cynical recognition of the insensibility of the dancers by the morning, "flop-wallies." But they continued, partly because the strain of living in the overcrowded ghettoes caused an overwelling of frustration that needed some form of release, partly because they solved at least one aspect of the housing problem. When rents could not be paid, a man would throw a party, providing jugs of liquor and platters of pig-ankles, and engaging a blues pianist to provide the music. By charging a levy on his friends of some fifteen or twenty-five cents he gathered enough to meet the demands of his landlord, and mutually assisted his friends when their own turn came. So the "house-rent party" became an established institution in Chicago, Harlem, and Washington in the Depression years and, to a lesser degree, survived post-war. Irony, or a desire to suppress the bad reputation of the parties, inspired the euphemism, Social Whist Parties, and in Harlem for many years a lonely man known as the "Wayside Printer" pushed through the streets a barrow mounted with a small printing machine. Its platen was small, but it was big enough to print invitation cards with such a legend as:

> Wear your dress above your knees
> And strut your stuff with who you please.
>
> SOCIAL WHIST PARTY
>
> at Slamfoot and Mama Jackson's. 3rd. Apt.

or bearing some other apt quotation from a favorite blues recording, that belied the dignity of the name by which the party was known. So successful were these functions that "good-time flats" which were informally run on semi-permanent lines became popular. A piano and a stool or two for the guitarists and mouth-harp players, who would drop in when their shifts were over, took care of the music. Competition among the musicians was keen, and as soon as one pianist left the stool another would take his place. They got no special treatment, playing for tips and, if they were lucky, free drinks from the "house lady." But, as Walter Roland complained, they were not guaranteed.

189   Says "Hey, house lady, seems like you hard to hear, (*twice*)
      Says, if you is got no whisky, bring me just a little of your beer."

      Says "Hey, house lady, please ma'am don't get mad, (*twice*)
      I just want another little drink of that stuff what I just now had."

      Says "Hey house lady," said "you sure do treat me mean, (*twice*)
      Says you treat me just like I is not no human being."

      Says "I been sittin' here playing mama, for you all night long,
      Says house lady I been sittin' here playing for you the whole night
        long,
      And I says you did not even give me just one drink of corn."

A table with favored southern dishes made the "buffet flat," while the "barrelhouse flat" had a row of barrels with a plank counter above them to turn the parlor into an illicit saloon. Good-time girls who were free with their favors for little material reward frequented the flats and back rooms were used both by them and by the gamblers. Operating outside the rackets controlled by the beer barons and big-time gangsters who had the police in their pay, unable to meet the sums required for "protection money" which ensured freedom from molestation for the more expensive "speakeasies," the owners of the flats were hard pressed to keep their premises open. But in the close-crowded tenements the domestic "front" afforded some protection and addresses could be changed without attracting too much attention. Mary Johnson sang of her flat, and dreamed of owning one on "Dago Hill," the Italian sector of St. Louis.

190   I've got a barrelhouse flat in Detroit and one in St. Louis too, (*twice*)
Но my barrelhouse flat in Detroit really just won't do.

I'm gonna build me a barrelhouse flat way on Dago Hill, (*twice*)
Where I can get my beer and whisky when it's fresh from the still.
(*Spoken*) Police sergeant just won't let me be, he finds my beer and
whisky everywhere I hide it.

I got a barrelhouse flat in Chicago, it's fifteen storey high, (*twice*)
I get all of these high-yellers and play these babies dry.

Those babies like my good whisky, and they drink my cherry wine,
(*twice*)
If you women want a good time, come and try this barrelhouse flat of
mine.

Precautions were taken to keep the flats from the knowledge of the enforcement agents and the police, whose raids were feared by the bell-hops and kitchen mechanics, truck drivers and domestic cleaners who frequented them and who could ill-afford to lose their jobs. If the demands for protection money could not be met, the police raided the flat and forced it to close. Boards would be nailed across the windows, a padlock placed on the door and police seal affixed, and for a time the proprietor was out of business until he – or, as often as not, she (as in the case of Maggie Jones) – opened again elsewhere.

191 Cain't sell no whisky, I cain't sell no gin,
   Cain't sell no whisky, I cain't sell no gin,
   Ain't got no money to buy my winter coal,
   Cain't save a dollar to save my dog-gone soul.

   I can't keep open, I'm gonna close the shack,
   I can't keep open, I'm gonna close the shack,
   The Chief of Police tore my playhouse down,
   No use in grievin' – I'm gonna leave this town.

Paradoxically, it was the introduction of Prohibition that caused the marked increase of alcoholism in the United States during the twenties and the many evils that were associated with it. Prohibition came early to some of the southern states where it was introduced as a measure intended to safeguard the white population from the danger of "liquor-crazed" Blacks. As early as 1881 Texas filed its first Prohibition referendum; in 1908 Georgia had voted to be a dry state and within the space of a year Alabama and Mississippi followed suit. Tennessee was almost a hundred per cent dry – but not surprisingly, Memphis, Nashville, and Chattanooga remained "wet." At this time there were more than two thousands saloons in New Orleans alone and liquor was freely available to Blacks. When Prohibition was introduced in Georgia the convictions for drunkenness dropped initially by half. Believing that the danger from drunken Blacks would be minimized by similar action, a further half-dozen southern states and three firmly Protestant states also voted to be dry. When, in 1920, the Eighteenth Amendment came into force, thirty-three states already had voluntary Prohibition laws – the unexpected reaction was a marked increase in the production of illicit liquor: when the fermented fruit was forbidden it bore an ever greater attraction. Early figures certainly showed a decrease in the number of incidents of drunkenness punished by the courts, but now drinking was carried on in greater secrecy and probably to greater excess. In stills hidden in the backwoods and in the mountains, raw alcohol was produced under conditions which were scarcely conducive to the production of pure spirit. The "bootlegger" – so named from the belief that he carried a flask of his wares in his boot – made substantial profits from his illegal produce and went to more pains to avoid detection and capture than he did over the preparation of his liquor. Bo Carter, accompanied by the Mississippi Sheiks, sang the *Bootlegger's Blues*:

192   Case of whisky on my back and the sheriff's on my track,
  I'm going to make it to the woods if I can.
    If you can, if you can,
    You better make it to the woods if you can.

  If you want to have to leave home, you just mess with a bottle of corn,
  You got to make it to the woods if you can.

  You may think they're doing you wrong, but they'll send you to the
    County Farm,
  You better make it to the woods if you can,

  When you go out for a load, the sheriff will stop you on the road,
  You'll have to make it to the woods if you can.

  It's a real surprising thing, just to hear those .44s ring,
  You'd better make it to the woods if you can.

Crudely distilled and prepared under unhygienic conditions in bath-tubs and zinc bowls, the liquor was often extremely dangerous. Raw wood alcohol with sufficient cheap sherry added to hide its true nature would be sold as whisky, and liquor purporting to be Bourbon or gin was made from any vegetable matter that would rot and ferment. Plugs of tobacco and shots of methylated spirits were added indiscriminately and raw alcohol was employed as a foundation for crude drinks. "Rot-gut" whisky, gin, and other drinks prepared in these ways have colorful names that adequately sum up their properties and their "kick." "White Mule," "Mamma," "White Lightning," "Splo," "Alki," "Red Horse." Many deaths have been caused by "moonshine" liquor of this type and the police made vigorous attempts to check the production. Some states made a compromise in permitting the consumption of beer but not of hard liquor, but the production of moonshine could only be checked by breaking up the stills and stores, as Curtis Jones ruefully described.

193   I have made every beer tavern, I done stopped at every liquor store,
    (*twice*)
  So I tried the alley and stopped by the bootlegger's door.

  The bootlegger told me, "Stop! These G-Men have been around,
    (*twice*)

And broke up all the moonshine and poured the mash out on the
   ground."

So I'll get plenty women see if my pal follows me around, (*twice*)
So we'll take it soft and easy, get it a little farther down.

We've got to run a new racket, people, we've gotta find a better rule,
An' if we can'' get decent whisky, we will take a drink of Mule.

During the twenties, when Prohibition was at its height, vast fortunes
were made by gangs of criminals who profited from the nation's aggravated
thirst by supplying immense quantities of bootleg liquor. Gangster Al
Capone was netting a hundred million dollars a year – of which thirty per
cent was spent on graft. The criminal fleets of Spike O'Donnell and Johnny
Torrio, Big Jim Colosimo and Al Capone floated upon spiritous seas.
Between them the gang wars raged for the control of the liquor trade. Even
the biggest of the black gangsters were very small craft among them, though
the black population consumed a considerable proportion of the liquor. The
depredations of the Chicago crime machine eventually came to an end with
the Depression, when money became scarce, and with the repeal of the
Eighteenth Amendment. An effective reduction to the extent of bootleg-
ging, if not of drinking habits, occurred with the abolition of Prohibition in
many states. The re-introduction of hard liquor at competitive prices made
it an uneconomic proposition, with the liquor companies giving maximum
support to the police in their drive against the illegal manufacturers. Blind
"Blues" Darby – Teddy Derby – who was a St. Louis bootlegger in the early
1930s, explained the impact of these measures.

194   Bootleggin', bootleggin', bootleggin' ain't no good no more, (*twice*)
      Bootleg whisky twenty-five cents and you can get good whisky for
         twenty-four.

      I'm a real good bootlegger but I done fell poor, (*twice*)
      Since good whisky been in, bootleggin' ain't no good no more.

      Now I been bootleggin', bootleggin' six years or more, (*twice*)
      But now I'm a real good bootlegger, a good bootlegger that done fell
         poor.

      (*Spoken*) Lord I gotta get me another racket when I do my time.

"GOOD WHISKEY" BLUES

No. 2978

I'm so glad good whiskey has come
back again

Don't have to drink no Mooch
No more of this Moonshine

Now I can drink good whiskey
Without being afraid of Dyin'.

I can walk up and down the street
Without dodging every cop I meet.

Sung by PEETIE WHEATSTRAW

2978—GOOD WHISKEY BLUES and LETTER WRIT-
ING BLUES—Vocal—Piano-Guit. Acc.
Sung by Peetie Wheatstraw 59c

I done lost my corn and I ain't got a dime, (*twice*)
I'm just a good bootlegger, that's got to go and do his time.

Liquor laws varied from state to state; restricted hours of consumption, limitations on the nature of the drinks dispensed, and discriminatory practices applied in some states, whereas others permitted the free sale of alcohol but exerted heavy penalties for drunkenness. In most black communities legal or illicit gin-mills, barrelhouses, and beer taverns continued to operate: in tent and shanty saloons serving the lumber camps of Tennessee and Arkansas or the turpentine camps of Florida, maintained by the very companies that employed the men who spent their money in them; in the all-black townships of Mound Bayou, Renova, and Wyandotte; on Davis Street in Mobile, Alabama, or Farish Street in Jackson, Mississippi, and in a multitude of Catfish Rows and Blackbird Hollows from the Gulf Coast to the Great Lakes. They afforded temporary escape, but they created problems rather than diminished them. The rough saloons where sweating, lurching, quick-tempered men from the jobs jostled to reach the bar made their contribution to family disintegration and were frequently the scene of violent crimes, as Peetie Wheatstraw had doubtless often witnessed.

195   When the sun was shining I did not stay,
       I went to the beer tavern, I throwed all my money away.

       I went to the beer tavern, ma baby tol' me not to go,
       Come back home, my clothes was thrown out doors.

       I took a gal to the beer tavern, things was lookin' hot,
       But my ole lady took her pocket knife and cut out my baby's heart.

It was the beer tavern which provided an opportunity for social contacts and a measure of self-made entertainment. In the South particularly, one of the principal sources of discontent and crime was the lack of entertainment or a profitable means of occupying the long lay-off periods. At these times, when the burden of the hours hung heavy, the tavern or juke joint became a meeting place where the young men laughed, gambled and jived each other and the old men reminisced over their drinks. Many who drank to excess consumed cheap alcohol by the wayside, staggering with the "limber leg" until they collapsed in a stupor. A Mississippi singer Willie Lofton seems to have been under the influence of "jake leg" when he sang a rather chaotic blues about it.

196   I said jake leg, jake leg, jake leg, jake leg – tell me what in the world
        you goin' to do? (*twice*)
    I said I drunk so much jake, ooh Lord till it done give him the limber
        leg.

    I say I know the jake leg, ooh Lord, just as far as I can hear the poor
        boy walk, mmmmm mmmmm,

    I said peoples drink this jake on the roadside, ooh Lord, they even
        throw their bottle away, (*twice*)
    But the jake left 'em with a present, ooh Lord, that keeps 'em company
        every day.

    Mmmmm mama mama mama, Lord, children keeps on cryin'
        "Wonder what in the world poor daddy gon' do?"

    I say drink so much jake, ooh Lord, till it done give 'em the limber leg,
    Mama, Mama cried out and said "Oh, Lord, ain't nothin' in the world
        poor daddy can do,
    'Cause he drink so much jake, ooh Lord, till he got the limber leg too."

For the disappointed and the frustrated, liquor brought temporary
escape. If bootleg and proprietary brands of whisky and gin proved too
expensive, they could turn to Sneaky Pete and the other cheap wines whose
names suggest their insidious attacks on the reason. Blacks are rarely suicidal;
the suicide rate amongst colored people is far below that of Whites, but the
percentage of Blacks convicted of liquor offences was some eight times that
of Whites *pro rata*, and accounted for nearly half of the total number of
arrests of this nature. These included violation of the various liquor laws
applying in the different states, and following the introduction of the so-
called "Jones Law," introduced in 1929 to combat breaches of the Volstead
Act, heavy fines were imposed. James "Stump" Johnson, who played piano
at Boot's, a notorious joint on the St. Louis levee, sang with irony,

197   All the world's cryin' "Mercy" babe, what does mercy mean? (*twice*)
    Old Mister Jones baby, didn't have no mercy on me.

    There was a time baby, you could get half a pint of gin,
    Oooh ooh babe: for half a pint of gin –
    Ten thousand dollar fine babe, five long years in the pen.

    Old Man Jones babe, sure don't worry me, (*twice*)
    Oh the present ain't so bad – but what will the future be?

Police cracked down on some of the violators, broke up the illegal stills and arrested the small-time bootleggers. "Big shot" racketeers were frequently above the law, had the police often in their pay, and evaded prosecution. By far the majority of arrests were for drunkenness among Blacks. A few nights in the "cooler," a period to "dry out," and the drunk who had a jail sentence had time to reflect, as Arthur Petties, a Mississippi guitarist who moved to Chicago in 1929, found out.

198   When you'se a good feller, the law will leave you 'lone, (*twice*)
     When you'se a bad feller, the jail will be your home.

     Canned heat ain't no good boy, keep you with a flyerin' mind (*twice*)
     Jailhouse doors open, and you got a ramblin' mind.

     You sad and you wonderin', you lookin' through your mind, (*twice*)
     You don't want no more canned heat when the judge give you your fine.

"Canned heat" was a particularly lethal drink which was obtained by extracting the alcohol from solidified methylated spirits which was sold as a fuel for cooking outdoors. A similar drink was obtained by drawing off contaminated alcohol from proprietory brands of boot polish. The recourse of hoboes in the jungles, canned heat could be obtained from street dealers who had made a business out of the process. Guitarist and jug band leader Will Shade lived all his life on Fourth Street, just off Beale Avenue in Memphis, and was well aware of the effects of canned heat.

199   People across the water, they're crying for meat and bread (*twice*)
     And the women down on Beale Street, crying for that old canned heat every day.

     I give my woman a dollar to get herself something to eat, (*twice*)
     She spent a dime for neckbones, and ninety cents on that old canned heat.

     If a woman says she don't drink corn liquor, don't think that's nice and sweet, (*twice*)
     If she don't drink that old corn liquor then your partner must drink that old canned heat.

Canned heat is like morphine, it crawls all through your bones, (*twice*)
And if you keep on using canned heat mama, you soon get to the place
    you just can't leave it alone.

When you catch your woman begging nickels and dimes all up and
    down the street, (*twice*)
She's only hustling them people to get that stuff they call that old
    canned heat.

Among women the proportion of drunkenness was relatively low in the
southern rural communities; greater in the cities, particularly in the North.
In the South the church exerted its influence upon the women members
who formed the bulk of the congregations, but the disrupting effects of the
migratory move to the North with its tearing of family roots, the hopes of a
newer and better environment and eventual disillusion, broke the spirit of
many women who no longer had the church on which to lean for
condolence and comfort. Insanitary living conditions, where one broken
toilet served a dozen families, and a number of women had to share the same
meager cooking facilities; the horrors of the hot-bed apartment and the
fruitless search for a better home could cause her to lose her self-respect and,
as in St. Louis Jimmy's account, seek oblivion in heavy drinking.

200   I don't want to discourage you, don't want to give you a bad name,
        (*twice*)
      The way you are drinking, mama, it's a dog-gone shame.

      You start to drinking at 29th Street, drink on down to 61st, (*twice*)
      You spend a thousand dollars trying to satisfy your thirst.

      You won't go to the hairdresser, mama you cain't keep clean no more,
        (*twice*)
      You ain't cooked a decent meal since you been in Chicago.

      I don't want to leave you, wants to give you one more break, (*twice*)
      Just to see, kind mama, what kind of a woman you'll make.

Habitual consumption of low-grade or bootleg liquor had a poisonous
effect and rapidly caused addiction to alcohol with ultimately fatal results.
The addict who "swilled the lush" soon became known as a liquorhead, a
wine-o, a whisky-headed man or woman. There are numerous terms, for

among the poor there were, and are, many addicted persons for whom life held few prospects. With minds less alert and faculties dulled, their resistance weakened. Clara Morris declaimed the excuses and underlined the misery of a whisky-headed woman.

> 201 I drank so much whisky I staggered in my sleep, (*twice*)
> Soon every morning, I'm staggering down the street.
>
> I can't get no whisky – dear me, I go home and whine, (*twice*)
> The way I keep from worryin' I stay drunk all the time.
>
> When I ain't got no liquor, look like everything I do go wrong, (*twice*)
> That's when I get evil, me and the devil cain't get along.
>
> It was so-bad whisky, made me lose my best friend, (*twice*)
> But I can't help it, I will drink until the end.

Up to the present there have been few satisfactory methods devised to bring about the cessation of this blight on the black community. Addicts tend to resent attempts on the part of the churches to break them of the habit, while the work of associations inaugurated with the specific intention of steering them back to normality was on too small a scale to cope with the extent of the problem. Operating with every bit as much vigor and on a far greater scale, the manufacturers of the cheap gins, wines, and alcoholic drinks purporting to be whiskies, ensured that the liquor was available and in large quantities. Every year tens of millions of moonshine gallons were distilled and the bulk of this illicit output went to those in the lowest income groups who could afford no better – amongst whom Blacks formed a disproportionately high percentage.

Less prevalent than might be supposed before the 1960s, was addiction to drugs, though evidence of drug traffic was frequently to be found in colored areas, and Blacks were often associated with it. White drug-peddling organizations prefered to have their headquarters in black districts where they could "lose" themselves more easily and where their traffic was less readily observed. But Blacks were employed in the traffic itself and a number of criminals made large incomes from it.

Few Blacks could afford to pay the sums demanded by the "dope" racketeers for shots of their drugs and narcotics, and the victims were more readily found among impressionable middle-class white youths and girls.

Easily influenced to partake of the drugs initially, they were more able to meet the heavy demands for money when forced by their growing dependency to continue to purchase them. Opium was popular amongst black addicts, and "junkers" – so named from the Oriental origin of the drug – indulged in "kicking the gong around." Unable to afford the fresh opium, called "mud" in the trade, they purchased Yen Shee, the opium equivalent to the butt end of a cigarette: the cinder left when the opium pill has been burned. A teaspoonful broken up and mixed with water made a pellet which the addict chewed. It caused festering sores, but it provided the desired relief. Drug-taking habits are difficult to break. Most despised of criminals, the dope peddlers knew this and for a while supplied the opium free, fully aware that once the habit had been formed they would reap dividends for a lifetime – the lifetime of the addict. Jack Dupree knew it too.

202 They call me, they call me a "junko" 'cause I'm loaded all the time,
   I don't use no reefers, I'd be knocked out with that angel wine.

   Six months, six months ain't no sento' and one year ain't no time,
   They got boys in penitentiary doin' from nine to ninety-nine.

   I was standin', I was standin' on the corner with my reefers in my hand,
   Up steps the sergeant, took my reefers out' my hand.

   "My brother, my brother used a needle, and my sister sniffed cocaine.
   I don't use no junk, I'm the nicest boy you ever seen."

   My mother, my mother she tol' me, an' my father tol' me too,
   "That junk is a bad habit, why don't you leave it too?"

   My sister she even tol' me, an' my grandma tol' me too,
   "That usin' junk, pardner, was goin' be the death of you."

Only a small number of Blacks were "snowbirds" going "on a sleigh-ride" by sniffing cocaine. The effects of the drug were terrible, causing acute physical distortions and inducing at least temporary insanity. The commonest drug used by Blacks was marijuana, the form of hashish which could be cultivated under backyard conditions and was consequently cheap. Known variously as "the mezzes," "muggles," "tea," or "weed," it was smoked in the form of cigarettes called "reefers" which were peddled in the streets, in clubs and dance halls. "Vipers" – as addicts of marijuana were called – could obtain brief spells of elation and dreamy forgetfulness without suffering markedly deleterious effects. The drug has the peculiar property of destroying a sense of the passage of time and a smoker may remain in a state of apparent consciousness whilst he experiences the illusion of limitless time. It was therefore favored by improvising jazz musicians and featured more prominently in their parlance and in the titles and content of their tunes than it did in the blues. Because of its cheapness many Blacks seeking "kicks" would "get high" through its use, but the pleasures were temporary and could leave the addict more depressed than before.

203 When my head starts achin', I grab my hat and go,
    'Cause cocaine and reefers, can't reach my case no more.

        I gotta find my baby, I declare I wouldn't lie,
        I ain't had no real good loving, since that girl said good-bye.

When they danced away the hours at the juke Blacks were seeking an entertainment that did not bring with it reminders of Jim Crow discrimination; when they spent long periods laughing and "lie-telling" at the barrelhouse they were hiding from periods of uselessness and inactivity in the endless days of the "lay-off;" when they frequented the "good-time flat" they forgot for a while the realities of the congested ghettoes of the city; when they went to the rent party they helped others whose plight was similar to their own and who would soon be called upon to perform the same service. They gambled in the hope that they might augment meager incomes; drank or fell victims to the dope habit in order to build a screen between themselves and their environment. But none of these measures solved any fundamental problems. They did not occupy their time to the profit of their minds or pockets. They did not relieve the internal pressure of the Black Belts nor minimize the exploitations of unscrupulous landowners. Ultimately Bill Gaither realized that as solutions to his problems they were of little value to him.

204 I used to live in New Orleans, it's been a good many years ago, (*twice*)
    But since I been up North I been sleepin' on the bar-room floor.

        I been on relief in Chicago and soup-lines in Kokomo, (*twice*)
        But I'm going right back down South where I won't be driven from
           door to door.

I don't shoot no more dice, I don't play no more Georgia Skin, (*twice*)
There's so many ways to lose and only one way to win.

All I want is some overalls and a job that fits just right, (*twice*)
My baby can cook me cornbread and cabbage, and I'm New Orleans
    bound tonight.

7 Evil and mean and funny

Social problems in depressed areas are the indirect result of numerous environmental deficiencies: insufficient work, low rates of pay, long periods of inactivity, lack of opportunities for advancement, lack of forms of entertainment, inadequate living conditions, and overcrowding. In black districts the external pressure of racial discrimination and the internal pressures of class and social group aggravated the situation. As the black population ratios in the South and North altered and as the urban areas grew, so these social problems increased. Better chances of obtaining rewarding work attracted Blacks to the cities, but their migration brought its own problems. The colored people who already lived in the cities resented the arrival of the newcomers and were often openly hostile to them. When Ramblin' Thomas arrived from the country he found few welcoming hands extended to him, and more competition than he had imagined:

205 And Dallas is hard, I don't care how you work, (*twice*)
  There will be somebody covering on your pay-day to collect.

  Man don't never make Dallas your home, (*twice*)
  When you look for your friends they will all be gone.

In the height of the black flood-tide to the southern cities and to the North, the housing situation arising from the influx was acute, and became even more extreme as the years passed. The white population resisted with determination, and often with arms and explosives, any inroads into their districts made by colored people. Black areas did not physically grow in a rate commensurate with the increases in population, and frequently did not expand at all. They only became more congested. White fears at the rapid increase in the colored population of the cities ignited terrible race riots that flared up in sudden bursts of violence. Many Blacks were massacred in July 1917 when such a riot occurred in East St. Louis, but although scores of Blacks were arrested there was not a single arrest of a white rioter. Two

165

years later a similar riot occurred in Chicago, remembered by Pinetop and Lindberg Sparks:

206   East Chicago is my native home, (*twice*)
     Goin' to Chicago, peoples, and it won't be long.

     I was in Chicago I had my good rags on, (*twice*)
     I'm in this town, got all my new suits in pawn.

     East Chicago is on fire, East St. Louis is burnin' down . . .

In Washington the same year a black man was brutally man-handled during a race riot in the very shadow of the White House without so much as a whisper of protest being raised. Though these districts, and others that had suffered similarly, eventually settled into uneasy silence, the strain between the incoming Blacks and those already resident continued to increase. As the numbers grew in districts which could only expand into the poorest white areas where the property had long been condemned, deplorable slums developed.

Chicago's black population in 1900 was a little more than thirty thousand. By 1925 this figure was quadrupled, and the numbers steadily increased between the wars with the result that some four hundred thousand Blacks lived there in 1950; only a score of cities in the United States had a higher *total* population. The residential area did not expand in proportion and more and more Blacks were crammed into the congested South Side. Restrictive covenants as to race controlled the tenancy of three-quarters of Chicago's residential areas. New York had its own particular problems. The area known as Harlem formerly housed some eighty thousand persons but by 1927 this population had increased by a further two hundred thousand – most of them black. The colored population more than doubled in the next two decades. Landlords made fortunes by purchasing old tenement buildings and letting them at exorbitant rents to black tenants, though they were bitterly fought by such organizations as the Hudson Realty Company which bought the property and evicted the colored tenants. Most remarkable was the instance of Detroit where eight thousand Blacks lived in 1915. In a decade the colored population had multiplied more than ten times. Most had come from the South hoping to escape the housing conditions that they had suffered there. In Mississippi and parts of Georgia eighty-five per cent of black families had homes without toilets or privies, and similar conditions prevailed in Texas and Louisiana. Those who had worked on the "jobs" and had lived in company-owned towns had lived often under terrible conditions. Of 423 towns comprising approximately fifty thousand dwellings examined at this time, nearly forty per cent had no bath, toilet, running water, gas, or electricity. Small wonder that they left these areas for the promised luxuries of Harlem, Chicago, and other northern cities.

Slums that were long reputed to be the worst in the world, worse even than those in contemporary Naples, were to be found in the black quarter of Philadelphia, the "City of Brotherly Love." The block on Lenox and 143rd was unique and the congestion without parallel. And still the numbers increased so that, by the mid-1950s, there were six hundred thousand Blacks in New York as a whole. Where did the people live in a district which had multiplied its population six times in a score of years? Ten thousand of them could be found in basements and converted cellars with virtually no light or ventilation. They divided and subdivided their rooms and partitioned them yet again, whilst they paid as much as twenty-five dollars for the use of a single room. Two dozen or more families might share a single toilet on Chicago's South Side and six families live in an apartment built for the use of one. Some there were in the South who, with good reason, distrusted the invitations of the enlistment agents and who preferred to stay in their home towns rather than risk the conditions that, it was rumored, existed in the North. New Orleans, for example, was a superficially glamorous French town whose beguiling architecture, wide-open disregard for the law, and colorful reputation closed the eyes of many to the squalor that existed "back of town." Even in the 1920s, New Orleans Willie Jackson could comment:

207   Have you ever been down South in dear old New Orleans? (*twice*)
     It's an antique town – got things there that you never seen.

     Canal Street's made of diamonds, and St. Charles Street's made for
       gold, (*twice*)
     But when you go "back of town" you're bound to see nothin' but
       old Creoles.

To go "back of town" in New Orleans led one eventually into the American District where, as a result of the color-caste system, the darker "American" Blacks lived in their tumble-down, tar-paper-roofed shacks. Roads so deep in mud as to be unnegotiable by a wheeled vehicle alone served them, and the entire population of a street relied upon a single pump for their disease-infested water. Yet there were some who were still prepared to endure these conditions rather than face those that they had heard obtained elsewhere. Genevieve Davis among them:

208   New York's a pretty city and the lights there shine so bright, (*twice*)
       But I'd rather be in New Orleans walkin' by candle-light.

       "The streets here are muddy" – that's what I'm told . . . (*twice*)
       When I'm with the man I love I think they're paved with gold.

       Did you ever dream lucky, wake up cold-in-hand, (*twice*)
       And you didn't have a dollar to pay your house-rent man?

Louis Dumaine and the members of his band who accompanied her remained in New Orleans, but other jazz musicians joined the migrating millions to spread their music in the North. Theirs was a move which, though numerically small, was far-reaching in effect. The emphasis that has been placed upon the closing of the Storyville red-light district, and the evacuation of its musicians, has tended to give an unbalanced impression of the total move at that time. Similarly, their arrival in Chicago and points East brought a new and exciting music, and for many of them considerable lucrative employment which was not shared by most migrants. Later, when the Depression set in, many were to live and die in miserable circumstances, but their interest as personalities and as creative musicians has drawn attention from the plight common to so many of their race. Even the rent parties have been chronicled more as colorful devices for overcoming a financial crisis, which had the fortunate effect of perpetuating boogie-woogie piano, than as manifestations of deplorable living conditions.

Through the thirties the congestion in the Black Belts was aggravated, and the occasional housing schemes, though very laudable, were on too small a scale to alleviate the acute distress to any marked degree. For the working-class Blacks who formed the majority of their population, living in the "Bronzevilles" was squalid, insanitary, and corrupting, but any attempts to move or to find better accommodation were met with open hostility, not only from the white populace, but also from any Blacks who were already living there. Huddie Ledbetter (Leadbelly) from Shreveport had his vocabulary enlarged by his white friends and sponsors when he came to Washington D.C., but there is no doubt that he experienced active discrimination there. His *Bourgeois Blues* summed up his anger.

209   Me and my wife run all over town,
       Everywhere we'd go the people would turn us down.

Lawd, in the bourgeois town, ooh the bourgeois town,
I got the bourgeois blues, gonna spread the news aroun'.

Me and Marthy we was standin' upstairs,
I heard a white man say, "I don't want no niggers up there."

Me and my wife we went all over town,
Everywhere we go the colored people would turn us down.

The white folks in Washington, they know how –
Chuck a colored man a nickel just to see him bow.

Tell all the colored folks t' listen to me,
Don't try to buy no home in Washington D.C.

Those who had a home, though it might only be a one-roomed
"kitchenette" apartment or even the corner of an apartment partitioned
with a sagging curtain, held on grimly to their quarters and paid the
avaricious landlords – of whom in Chicago some eighty-five percent were
white. Those who slept over the street gratings envied even the tenant of the
"hot-bed" apartment for his place to rest. The "hot-bed" was an apartment
which was rented to three separate groups of tenants, each of whom used the
flat for eight hours of the day or night. When their period of tenancy was up
for their part of the day they relinquished the bed and the gas ring to the next
tenant who climbed on to the still warm mattress and tried to make the best
of his rent. Meanwhile the streets teemed with the homeless, the rejected,
and the evicted, and the lines of cars gave a false air of prosperity to the
district. For many Blacks their car constituted their sitting-room, even their
bedroom. One could be purchased for a sum equal to a few months' rent,
but many were too poor to afford even this means of providing a "home."
In the flats the black man who had difficulty in meeting the rent feared the
notice telling him he had to quit: there was always another waiting on the
doorstep to take his place. Many moved back South, as Jazz Gillum intended
to do.

210 It's a sign on the building, yes I mean, you hear me sing,
     There's a sign on the building, we all got to move right away,
     I ain't got no money, no rent that I can pay.

     It soon will be cold, you hear me sing, yes I mean,
     It soon will be cold, I ain't got no place to go,
     I'm going back South, where the chilly winds don't blow.

Such overcrowded conditions of living meant that men and women, boys and girls of all ages were forced to spend their days and nights with little or no privacy. Absconding fathers, husbands, and family partners, low wages and high rents, the depredations of ruthless elements in the communities, together broke down moral standards. Clara Smith had her own defence.

> 211   Day's comin', days go, but my work is never done, (*twice*)
> I have to get up every morning with the rising sun.
>
> That road is narrow and it's crooked, leads to you don't know where, (*twice*)
> It's hard for an honest girl to make her way up there.
>
> All these so-called sweet and pretty men, please take 'em away, (*twice*)
> All they want to do, to lead some poor girl astray.
>
> Some are like jelly-beans, so cute and so sweet, (*twice*)
> I carry carbolic acid for every one of them I meet . . .

In the segregated areas it was often impossible to find a residential street that did not contain a brothel, and did not have its parade of street walkers both night and day. To bring up a child without immediate contact with prostitution was therefore difficult. There was sympathy for the prostitutes, for frequently they were girls who have been forced to resort to the only method left to them to obtain a living, but black families strived desperately to emulate the respectability of the white middle-class and their presence could be an embarrassment to the professional black person who resided in the same district. White land and property owners found that renting buildings for purposes of prostitution was lucrative and did not affect them personally. Recruits were drawn from the many young girls who found themselves homeless and workless in the city, and from those who, having come straight from the country, were attracted by the glamor and bright lights of urban life, beguiled by the smart clothes and smooth manners of the town-dwelling men. Such a girl was flattered by the attentions she received and looked with scorn on the simple manners of the country boys, as Smokey Hogg complained.

> 212   Yeah, a country gal, man, have wrecked my life to-day, (*twice*)
> For I didn't stint myself, my poor girl she throwed it away.
>
> You can buy a country gal in my home, man, she wanna sleep on a
> spring mattress every day, (*twice*)

When the poor thing ain't used to nothin', people, but sleepin' on
   cotton and hay.

Ooooh, a country gal think she smart when she lovin' every man in
   town, (*twice*)
When the poor thing ain't doin' nothin', people, but tearin' her
   reputation down.

One of the results of the all-pervading depression and the meager
opportunities for satisfying work with good opportunities of promotion
and responsibility was a deterioration in the attitude of many black men to
legitimate employment. They felt that they were being duped and exploited
and in many urban districts the man who obtained a good living without
working, who relied upon gambling or a "racket" for his income, was
admired, envied, even esteemed. The pimps – or "P.I.s" – with their
pointed, patent leather, two-toned shoes, their "sharp" clothes and diamond
pins, lived by their wits and their power over women and were grudgingly
or openly admired. Overcoming any initial resistance with "sweet talk,"
they plied the girls with brightly colored clothes and flashy jewelry, and
afforded them protection from the attentions of undesirable clients or other
procurers, their razors concealed in the lining of their lapels. It was the
ambition of many a black male to live on "Easy Street" and the earnings of a
woman who would support him by prostitution or by more legitimate
work. In the 1920s many black women worked as housemaids, domestic
servants, yard girls, and kitchen mechanics. They had better chances of
retaining their employment than had their menfolk, and many a woman
took pride in supporting a man. They were even prepared to share him with
other women for the protection that he afforded them and the love that he
could give.

   There were, of course, just as many Blacks who bitterly resented the "easy
lifers" who relied on women for their support: Lonnie Johnson spoke for
many who worked long hours at hard and ill-paid labor and felt keenly the
apparent injustice in so poor a reward for trying to earn an honest living,
whilst others existed in comfort and ease from such means.

213 What makes the rooster crow every morning 'fore day? (*twice*)
   To let the pimps know that the workin' man is on his way.

   We're up before sunrise slavin' sixteen hours a day, (*twice*)
   We pay a house rent and grocery bill and the pimps get the rest
      of our pay.

But the pimps remained untroubled for they were primarily concerned in obtaining and vetting the clients that their women served, protecting and, if necessary, fighting on behalf of their girls as the occasion arose; seeing that they were not double-crossed and keeping the police quiet. Attempts to keep the soliciting of prostitutes in check were perfunctory and the girl "on the turf" who was accused of stealing when entertaining a man, or who had been brought in on a similar charge, was given a "shakedown" – required to pay a sum to the police officer for protection, and then left free to carry on her trade, her "P.I." meeting the sum and her bond if necessary.

> 214   I was walking down Morgan, stopped on Maxwell Street, (*twice*)
> I asked the desk sergeant what police brought my gal offa the street.
>
> I stood an' talk to the desk sergeant, till he went fast asleep,
> Hey, hey, till he went fast asleep.
> 'Cause I knew my mama got arrested on Maxwell Street.
>
> Lawd I'm talkin' 'bout the wagon, talkin' 'bout the police car too,
> (*twice*)
> 'Cause Maxwell Street so crowded on Sunday, you can hardly press
> through.
>
> There's Maxwell Street Market, South Water Street Market too, (*twice*)
> If you ain't got no money, the women got nothing for you to do.

Papa Charlie Jackson sang about Maxwell Street on Chicago's South Side, but in the black sectors of every large town were infamous tenderloin districts – some of which have been romantically perpetuated in the public memory, in the titles and themes of jazz and popular song; Basin Street and Rampart Street in New Orleans (with the splendid mansions which excluded black clients) in the one and the miserable hole-in-the-wall cribs of the other); Nashville's Black Bottom and Fourth Avenue. In the language of its underworld Cecil Gant sang,

> 215   Have you ever been to Nashville, down on Fourth Avenue? (*twice*)
> They got something new there, they call it Owl Stew.
>
> Well I've been to Chicago, points East, North and West, (*twice*)
> But the stew in Nashville, it really is the best.
>
> It's not so very high, and the price is very low, (*twice*)
> If you get it once, you gonna want some more.

Memphis had its colorful and corrupt Beale Street, and its Gayoso too, less widely known but locally no less notorious; Chicago its Maxwell Street Market; Shreveport its Fannin' Street; Jackson its Farish Street; Detroit its Hastings Street; and Dallas its Elm Street, about which Texas Bill Day warned his friend, Billiken Johnson.

216   Ellum Street's paved with brass, Main Street paved with gold *(twice)*
        I've got a good girl lives on East Commerce, I wouldn't mistreat her to
        save nobody's soul.

        Ah Billiken, these Ellum Street women don't mean you no good,
        (twice)
        When your back is turned they're with every man in the
        neighborhood.

        These Ellum Street women, Billiken do not mean you no good, *(twice)*
        If you want to make a good woman, have to get on Haskell Avenue.

Leaning from low-silled windows, lounging in doorways or standing on street corners, dark-skinned girls, eyelids colored with lipstick and gold teeth flashing, seduced the passer-by. Pretty Beulah "Sippie" Wallace came to Detroit from Houston, Texas.

217   I come to you, sweet man, and I'm falling on my knees,
        I come to you, pretty papa, and I'm falling on my knees,
        Says if you ain't got nobody, kind daddy take me please.

        'Cause I'm a mighty tight woman, a real tight woman, I'm a real jack
        of all trades,
        I can be your sweet woman, also be your slave,
        I can do things so good till you swear that I won't hay.

        I hear everybody say that I'm tight in everything I do,
        I've got all the men cryin' that I'm a broad that never feels blue,
        All I want is a good man to make him happy too.

        If you're a married man you ain't got no business here,
        When you out with me, I might make your wife shed tears,
        'Cause I'm a mighty tight woman, there is nothin' that I fear.

Many of the women who made their living from prostition earned for themselves considerable reputations in their own districts, and men fought

to be their pimps. Half a century after they were active many of the more
notorious women who worked in the New Orleans brothels – Mary
Meathouse and Coke Eye Laura, Mary Jack the Bear and Bird Leg Nora, or
the strong-arm women who haunted Dearborn Street and Armour Avenue
in the "Levee" of Chicago, Lizzie Davenport, Florrie Moore, and the
twenty-five-cent "zooks" of Bed Bug Row – were still remembered. They
had a less distinguished clientele than Cora Pearl, Kate Cook, and Mabel
Grey of nineteenth-century London but their favors and their vitriolic
personalities have impressed themselves no less in a colorful but sordid
history. The women who sought to keep their menfolk feared the boastful
claims of the brazen "hustling gals."

> 218   Women cryin' "Danger," but I ain't raisin' my hand, (*twice*)
>   I got a way of lovin' they just can't understand.
>
>   I can strut my pudding, spread my grease with ease, (*twice*)
>   'Cause I know my onions – that's why I always please.
>
>   Wild about my coffee, but I'm crazy 'bout my China tea, (*twice*)
>   But a sugar daddy is sweet enough for me.
>
>   And they call me "oven," they say that I'm red-hot, (*twice*)
>   They say that I've got something the other gals ain't got.

boasted Nellie Florence from Atlanta, and as she sang the demoniacal
laughter of "Laughing Charlie Hicks" could be heard in the background.

Next to the gambling rackets the commercialization of prostitution
constituted the most lucrative form of crime in the United States and was
operated on a syndicated system that was nation-wide. Big-time racketeers
controlled the brothels and saw that the receipts were channeled to their
own pockets. The girl would receive relatively little, though her standard of
living was higher than if she were not so employed. Of her total earnings as
much as half might go to the landlord, a percentage to the mobster who
introduced her to the syndicate, protection money had to be paid to police
and politicians, and her final income was passed to her pimp who provided
for her. The racketeers exploited the belief that Blacks were basically sensual
and immoral and established a large number of the brothels in sectors where
white males seeking a "good time" would gravitate. Proportionately, the
number of colored prostitutes far exceeded that of white girls – more than a

quarter of all the women being black. In some districts the percentage was much higher and though statistics of arrests do not necessarily give an accurate impression, in New York some fifty-four per cent of all arrests of prostitutes were of colored girls, a rate that was ten times that of white women in proportion to the population figures.

Social workers tried to help the girls and advise the young men, but lonely, dissatisfied unhappy men, husbands of unfaithful wives, eager youths, provided an endless clientele for what "Hi" Henry Brown termed uncompromisingly, the *Nut Factory*. He was singing about "Deep Morgan" in St. Louis, later re-named Delmar Avenue in the hopes that its notoriety might be forgotten.

219   Well it's down on Deep Morgan just about Sixteenth Street, (*twice*)
      Well it's selling a business, where they women do meet.

      Well it's down in a basement, where they work so hard, (*twice*)
      Well it's all on account of their husbands ain't got no job.

      Some draw checks babe, some draw nothin' at all, (*twice*)
      When they don't draw nothin', they husbands bust them in the jaw.

      Down on Franklin Avenue, jellybeans standing to and fro, (*twice*)
      Well you hear one jellybean ask the other one, "Which a-way did the
         good girl go?"

Inevitably the prevalence of prostitution in black districts caused the spread of virulent social diseases, in particular syphilis and gonorrhea. How widespread these diseases were became apparent in 1940 when it was discovered that of the first hundred thousand men drafted into the armed services the number of black sufferers from syphilis was proportionately eight times that of the whites, the latter being 18.5 per thousand whilst the Negro syphilitics made the startling total of 241.2 per thousand men drafted (see page 250). Large numbers of these men had not contracted the disease through any fault of their own, but through hereditary passage of the virus and contacts with the disease caused by the deplorable, insanitary conditions in which so many lived. Nevertheless, reckless promiscuity in the cities and the lack of medical attention for prostitutes were the prime causes. As they grew older many Blacks were to regret, like Bumble Bee Slim, their youthful "fast living."

220   I wonder why fast life keeps on follerin' me, *(twice)*
Well it seems like ole fast life, ain't gonna never let me be.

Fast life is killin' me, stiff-dead on my knees, *(twice)*
Fast life is a living, that is awful hard to please.

It don't pay nobody to live this life so fast, *(twice)*
Just take it slow and easy as long as it will last.

More sinister perhaps than the prevalence of prostitution was the commercial exploitation of male sexual deviance, especially in the "freak show," once common in Harlem, where crude exhibitions and perverted stage displays were presented. Also common in the twenties were Drag Parties or transvestite dances. Such functions were illegal in many states as was open soliciting in the streets by homosexuals. For some the arrival of the police wagon, arrest, and ultimate imprisonment was welcome, for sexual perversion was rife in American prisons where extreme overcrowding in highly unsuitable premises created conditions conducive to it. Young offenders were expected to share cells with hardened "three-time losers" and vagrants; petty thieves and perverts were frequently forced into close association. Supervision was hindered, in many instances, by inadequate staffing and heavy, solid, cell doors, whilst minor prison officials, ill-paid and sometimes unprincipled, were apt to exploit the conditions to their own gain. A situation far from uncommon in the North was rampant in the southern county jails and on the prison farms, where prison society was sharply divided between the "wolves" – those who seduced and corrupted other prisoners – and the "gal-boys" or young prisoners who were forced to accept a female role. Such corruption was widespread and prevailed until reforms in the prison system were made, such as those implemented by the Texas Department of Corrections in the 1970s. Advances had been earlier in some prisons in the North and West which had enlightened governors with a sense of mission and a determination to institute penal reforms. Their work proved worth while in every instance though sometimes they were hindered by the ignorance of other, less progressive authorities and by the suspicions of the prisoners themselves. Humane treatment of sexual offenders has produced encouraging results and progress is being made in the extremely difficult task of correcting the antisocial tendencies of seasoned criminals, reflected in a blues by Peetie Wheatstraw.

221 I live on a young man to make my living the easy way, *(twice)*
     But since I have been locked up in jail, ooh well, well I found out it did
        not pay.

     I laid in jail all night long with my closed eyes to the wall,
     I laid in jail all night with my closed eyes to the wall,
     Thinking that cute little way, ooh well, well was the cause of it all.

     I had the easy way blues from my head down to my feet, *(twice)*
     I had to send for Mister Bud Mellow, ooh well, well to come and put
        my feet on the street.

     Do you know how I felt when the news come back? *(twice)*
     "Since you're not in town, ooh well, well now he's out on the old race
        track."

     He put my feet on the street, but this is what he said: *(twice)*
     "You go get yourself a good girl, oh well, well cut out that easy way."

Homosexuals who took the female part often affected the mannerisms of
women, paid particular care to their manicure and even attempted to use
smuggled make-up. Their "husbands" gave them presents to the best of
their meager resources, used feminine pronouns when referring to them,
and showed the same feelings of jealousy that they would display over
women in heterosexual relations. The jealousy that a man felt for his partner
frequently led to violence in the prisons, in the wire-fenced road camps, in
the shack towns on the "jobs," and in the stressful environment of the city
warrens.

Where Whites used fists and thus perpetrated no crime in the eyes of the
law, a dispassionate examination of cases revealed that Blacks more
frequently resorted to the use of knives with the result that indictable
offences were committed. Very often jealousy on the part of a man or
woman was at the root of impetuous crimes.

222 I've got a two-by-four, and it just fits my hand, *(twice)*
     I'm goin' to stop all you women from runnin' around with my man.

     I don't want to hurt that man, just goin' to kill him dead, *(twice)*
     I'll knock him to his knees, go back to the man I once have had.

     When I leave home, your other woman is knockin' on my door, *(twice)*
     I'm going to stop so much talkin' and raise heck with my two-by-four.

Double-bladed, and the width of the hand, the "two-by-four" about which the "Yas Yas Girl" (Merline Johnson) sang, was a clasp knife, much favored by the prostitute who could conceal it in her kimono without difficulty; broken and jagged edged, it became a "froe" and still had its lethal uses. Longer was the chib, keen-bladed and deadly when manipulated with the upward thrust that made disarmament far more difficult. It was the weapon of the "strong-arm woman" who seduced a man and when he was in her arms, robbed him and cut him "every way but loose." It was the weapon that killed blues singer Charlie Jordan on 9th Street, St. Louis, the home city of Edith Johnson.

223   Now if you get loaded baby, and think you want to go,
        Aaah if you get loaded and think you want to go,
        Remember baby, you ain't no better than the man I had before.

        When I get drunk I'm evil, I don't know what to do, (*twice*)
        Guess I'll get my good chib and get something good for you.

Less likely to cause death, the razor permanently scarred a victim and razor-slashing attacks and fights arose from the vicious determination to leave a recognizable signature of revenge. With the handle removed, the spur of the blade lay back along the hand and the blade projected a fraction between the fingers: a couple of swift slaps and the victim was unaware that he had been cut until he felt the blood upon his face. Bessie Tucker, apparently no stranger to prison, sang of its effect.

224   I got cut all to pieces, aah-aaah . . . about a man I love, (*twice*)
        I'm gonna get that a-woman, just as sho' as the sky's above.

        Now when my man left me, I was half-dead, lyin' in my do', (*twice*)
        I was sufferin' and a-groanin', "Oh, daddy, please don't go."

Tools of trade often make dangerous weapons: the cotton-hook with which the roustabout man-handles the cotton bales, the cleavers of the abattoir workers on "the killing floor," the knives of the cane-cutters. Amongst the railroad and telegraph men, the street cleaners and builders, the ice-picks became tools of murder, and the small size of some of these, coupled with their excellent balance and penetrating bills, made them a favored weapon, which, as Whistlin' Alex Moore suggested, could be easily concealed.

225 I thought my woman had the blues, she looked so worried and sick, (*twice*)
Come to find out in her bosom she's carrying an old ice-pick.

But she wasn't sick – I could see trouble in her eyes, (*twice*)
She wanted to stick me with that ice-pick, Lord, and I don't know why.

Half-a-pint in one hand, cigarette between her lips, (*twice*)
Trying to get that ice-pick out with her finger tips.

Why don't you go to bed, woman, and put that old ice-pick down? (*twice*)
From room to room squabbling, half the night in your gown.

Most victims of a razor-slashing attack survive; those who have been attacked with an ice-pick seldom do, for the sharp spike, designed to pierce rock-hard ice, penetrates the skull of the attacked person without difficulty. The blues singer Sonny Boy Williamson died as the result of such an attack, as he came home after singing at the "Flame Club" in Chicago on a bitter evening late in 1947. His week's wages were in his pocket and for this sum he lost his life at the hands of a street mugger. The mutilated body of a victim would be robbed and the "bloody carpet rags" – in the harsh vernacular of the black underworld – picked up by the all-night prowl cars, whilst the "roundheels" disappeared in the shadows of the slums. Muggings were originally aimed at white men who came into the black districts seeking colored women, but the desperate form of protest was soon directed at other Blacks in blind and futile antisocial acts. Sometimes such robbers worked with a girl as a decoy. Standing in a position from where they could see her every move as she went up the street, they waited until she had successfully solicited a man. As she brought him back past the alley or side entrance to a building where the robber was hiding, he sprang upon the unsuspecting man and "jumped" him, beating him senseless and swiftly robbing him.

226 I got a mind to ramble, I got a mind to rob and steal, (*twice*)
I got a mind to hijack people, you don't know how I feel.

Kidnappers Blues

No 3249

PEETIE WHEATSTRAW

3249

KIDNAPPERS BLUES and FROGGIE BLUES
—Vocal, Piano, Guitar Acc. Peetie Wheat-
straw 59c

I can stand right here, look over on to the avenue, *(twice)*
I can see everything my li'l ole baby do.

With the attacker lies the advantage of surprise and the odds that he will succeed in his intentions are vastly in his favor. Felonious assaults of this nature were frequently in the poorest black urban districts. Minor criminals who lived within the districts were known and to some degree protected by the codes of behavior that operated in the underworld; the girls who worked regular beats were able to pass unmolested, for their pimps had made working arrangements and safeguarded their interests. It was the girl who penetrated another's beat and the racketeer who attempted to "muscle in" on another's territory who were immediately marked as prospective victims. But above all the attacks were made upon those who were alien to that part of the Black Belt, or who were newly arrived from the country and unfamiliar with the ways of the city slums. George Hannah bragged:

227 I'm a man from the gutter, women go in your dive at night, *(twice)*
I'm evil and mean and funny, so don't let me come back with my line
of jive.

I met a woman from the Delta, grabbed her and I held her,
Squalled like a panther, still that didn't help her,
She was in the clutches of a drunkard, a man from the gutter,
Wriggled and she twisted, boy, real two-fisted,
But I was working the jive that evening, I let nothing slip by.

The woman I'm loving, got eyes just like a snake, *(twice)*
But I'm a man from the gutter – she'll really have to wait.

Underworld organization is complex and delicate; aspiring criminals do not "break in" easily. Crime is less organized in black sectors than elsewhere in the cities and violent incidents tend to be more spontaneous. Black gangs do operate effectively in the gambling and drug rackets though some are answerable to larger criminal organizations that control the underworld of a whole state. A special problem was raised by the black gangs led by youths in their very early teens. In clothes, in manner, they emulated the big-time racketeers, but the impetuousness of youth and the desire to be esteemed by their companions made them more desperate. Ten times as many black children as white, in proportion to their numbers, were slain in fights and disputes between gangs or individuals. The acute housing shortage forced them on to the streets and the large numbers of broken homes threw many on their own resources. They were joined by thousands of homeless children, vagrants who had hopped the trains, slept in the jungles and had become skilled in stealing, fighting, and fending for themselves. For these children there were few organizations providing aid, security, and guidance. Instruction, by way of example, came from the "ramblers," the criminals, whose way of life, authority, and swift vengeance attracted them by their glamor and their ruthlessness. To preserve his position as the sole, undisputed leader, the gangster had to be unrelenting, merciless, and unemotionally concerned with all that happened in his district. Those who attempted to oppose him had to do so with methods even stronger and more violent, or expect the inevitable, violent suppression. Calling himself "Peetie Wheatstraw, the Devil's Son-in-Law," William Bunch assumed the gangster's role.

228   I am gonna take you for an easy ride,
    Drop you off on the riverside.
        I've got the gangster's blues, I got the gangster's blues,
        I've got the gangster's blues, boys I am feelin' mean.

    I'm gonna bind your mouth so you can't talk,
    Tie your feet so you can't walk.

    You can start your screaming but must give in,
    I'm gonna tear you to pieces and put you back again.

During the Depression when men in their millions were without work, the crime rate rose alarmingly. Some two-fifths of all homicide and assault offenses in the United States were committed by Blacks, – a figure unquestionably related to their more severely distressed circumstances. The squalid, rat-infested shacks that made up the black section of Pine Bluff, Arkansas, between the old river bed and the railroad tracks; the homes of the roustabouts and stevedores who lived along Vicksburg's Catfish Row and its adjacent streets where twenty-three thousand Negroes were crammed together; the M. & O. Bottoms of Tuscaloosa lying in the lowland delta between the railroad and the Alabama River; the teeming ant's nest of Jackson, Mississippi, with its colored population of nearly fifty thousand of whom almost half did menial unskilled labor – these were inevitable centers of violent crime. Rock Town and Bush Bottom in Nashville; Buckeye Quarters and Ram-Cat Alley in Greenwood – the very names are suggestive of the conditions. Hopeless congestion, malnutrition and disease, rotting timber walls and unpaved roads littered with decaying vegetable matter numbed the senses, destroyed values and frustrated initiative. Some repressed their anger and adjusted to conditions that they could not improve; others expressed their revolt in violence; still others, like Violet Mills, fantasized instead.

229   Want to set this world on fire, that is my mad desire,
      I'm the devil in disguise, got murder in my eyes.

      Now if I could see blood runnin' through the streets, (*twice*)
      Could see everybody lying dead right at my feet.

      Give me gunpowder, give me dynamite, (*twice*)
      Yes, I'm gonna wreck the city, gonna blow it up tonight.

These were the conditions that made Memphis, Tennessee, the "murder capital of America." In the 1870s the town was a veritable pest-hole where yellow fever was rife. White landowners deserted the town but the Blacks and the "poor Whites", short of food, without money, and ignorant, were left behind. Of the mere twenty thousand persons who were left in the town some seventy per cent were black and for some years, until the cotton industry was re-established, the criminal element flourished. Its home was to remain in the black sector, in the "Underworld Block" from Hernando Street to Fourth Street. Its nerve center remained until the 1960s, the celebrated Beale Street, which extended for a mile from the De Soto Fish Dock on the Mississippi Waterfront. Here could be seen the gamblers and the gangsters, the pimps, the ponces, and the prostitutes, the crippled and the corrupt. Cuttings and shootings amongst the roustabouts, loggers and field-hands in town on a spree were a nightly occurrence in the early part of the century and the low premium on life caused others to take the law into their own hands in the black sector of the town, where the dictatorship of Boss Crump made little of official law enforcement. Sang a Memphis blues singer, Furry Lewis:

230   I believe I'll buy me a graveyard of my own, (*twice*)
      I'm goin' kill everybody that have done me wrong.

      If you want to go to Nashville, mens, ain't got no fare, (*twice*)
      Cut your good gal's throat and the judge will send you there.

I'm goin' git my pistol, forty round of ball, (*twice*)
I'm goin' shoot my woman just to see her fall.

I'd rather hear the screws on my coffin sound, (*twice*)
Than to hear my good gal, says, "I'm jumpin' down."

Many other cities have black sectors with reputations almost as notorious and it seems undeniable that these were the result of adverse environmental conditions. Second only to Memphis was Atlanta, Georgia, where the murders exceeded an average of a hundred a year in the 1940s. That Harlem and Chicago's South Side had similarly alarming figures should scarcely cause surprise. A survey made in 1939 showed that there were eighty-seven thousand more Blacks in Chicago's Bronzeville than the lowest acceptable living standards would permit. During the war the population increased by a further sixty thousand and the influx has continued during the subsequent years. But the South Side, though bulging at the seams, did not increase in area, and the crime rate showed little sign of decreasing.

Of the tens of thousands of slum-shocked persons living under these conditions, many were almost irrevocably lost to society: men and women who were feared by those who lived with them and revealed in their aggressiveness to outsiders a cold, open hostility. Sang Bumble Bee Slim:

231   You' a cold-blooded murder' an' I can't look in your face, (*twice*)
Now you got blood in your eyes, you got low-down dirty ways.

Now you got me in between the devil and the deep, blue sea, (*twice*)
When I try to love you I keep trembling in my knees.

You'se a cold-blooded murder' an' I'm still in love with you, (*twice*)
We cain't get together, no way I try to do.

Some of the homicides committed by Blacks were brutal slayings by "bad niggers" or "mean niggers" as Blacks, using a double-edged form of abuse, themselves called them. But the majority of attacks were probably *crimes passionels* committed, or attempted, in fits of jealousy over the infidelity of partners.

232   I looked out my window, just 'bout the break of day, (*twice*)
Just in time to see another man taking my best gal away.

An' I looked for my pistol but I found I had the safeter on, (*twice*)
But before I could shoot it, that man had my best gal and gone.

If he was a bit better prepared than was Jimmy Gordon he might waylay his
rival with his "hard-shootin' .45," or with a favorite among Blacks, the
more accurate and equally deadly weapon in close quarters, the "32.20 built
on a .45 frame." As mild perhaps in ordinary affairs as his hard life permitted,
Big Maceo Merriwether explained to his friend, Tampa Red.

233   I walked all night long with my 32.20 in my hand, (*twice*)
      Looking for my woman, well I found her with another man.

      When I found that woman they was walkin' hand in hand, (*twice*)
      Well she didn't surprise me when I found her with another man.

      She started screamin' "Murder!" an' I never raised my hand, (*twice*)
      Tampa, she knew I had them covered 'cause I had the stuff right there
          in my hand.

      I ain't no bully an' I don't go for the baddest man in town,
      I ain't no bully and I ain't the baddest man in town,
      When I catch a man with my woman I usually tear his play-house
          down.

It is probably indicative of one of the functions of blues – to bolster
confidence by emphasizing assertiveness and unwillingness to submit to
repression – that while aggressive positions are taken by many singers, blues
very seldom reflects a violent crime from the victim's point of view. But
there are exceptions, such as Bobbie Cadillac's *Carbolic Acid Blues*, recorded
in Dallas.

234   My right hand is itchin' and my left eye begin to burn, (*twice*)
      I know my man don't want me by the way he's doin'.

      I told her I loved her man, grave will be her restin' place (*twice*)
      She looked at me with burnin' eyes, threw carbolic acid in my face.

      Carbolic acid has poisoned me, Doc. Precious Wynn will tell you so,
          (*twice*)
      I got burned about the man I love, now I got to let him go.

Layin' in my bed, my face burned to the bone, (*twice*)
If carbolic acid don't kill me, penitentiary gonna be my home.

Statistics drawn from the Uniform Crime Reports of the U.S. Department of Justice in the 1930s reveal that Blacks accounted for a quarter of the total number of convictions for prostitution, some forty-four percent of the convictions for assault, more than thirty percent of those for robbery, and forty percent of the convictions for homicide. These figures give at least an approximate indication of the proportionate crime rates in these categories. They do not include the large numbers of gang crimes which remained unpunished through fear of further consequences or the hope that the gangs would eliminate each other by their own means. Nor do they account for the many crimes against Blacks committed by white persons which were never brought to court or which were deliberately hushed up. Numerous acquittals "for lack of evidence," or on the grounds of "self-protection," allowed trigger-happy armed bus drivers, and veritable lynching parties operating under a different guise, to go free. Nevertheless, between 1911 and 1935 the rate of homicides amongst Blacks was seven times that of white persons between the ages of twenty-five and thirty-four, and ten times that of Whites amongst adolescents. Substantially the same relative proportions continued through the 1950s.

In other fields the Blacks were held to be almost exclusively responsible for the violation of segregation laws, according to the numbers of arrests made, though in violently prejudiced areas a white person who showed sympathy to Blacks might be punished outside the law. Blacks were precluded from committing the crimes that go with the accumulation of wealth: tax evasion, financial exploitation of the public, embezzlement, fraud, counterfeiting, and others that required higher social and professional position for their success. The crimes for which they were indicted were less premeditated and, to the public, more sensational.

That black crimes were the immediate results of their environment was well demonstrated in Chicago where fifteen hundred families from the worst slums of the South Side were rehoused in a new, clean, and spacious district where modern but economical apartments known as the Ida B. Wells Homes were constructed. Living in a healthy community where trees lined the streets and children had room to play, the families became models of social behavior: in five years only one family gave rise to complaint and even the minor crimes were virtually unknown.

Though segregation and Jim Crow covenants were finally abolished, there was, and is, a long way to go before Blacks achieve equal status with other members of the community. When the slums are cleared and decent homes are available, when true equality in educational facilities and employment opportunities is available; when, in fact, Blacks are able to play their full part in American society, crime in black society will diminish until it is no better, perhaps, but certainly no worse, than that of the rest of the nation.

8   *Goin' to take a rap*

From the moment of their capture and incarceration in the floating hell of the slavers' ships Blacks have known violence. Shackled in the slave coffles, laid head to toe in the 'tween decks of the vessels in their hundreds to suffocate or survive in the fetid heat and the stench of their own fæces; jettisoned when storms broke or ships of the line appeared; sold at the block to the highest bidders, they suffered unspeakable privations. The history of slavery is a long and shameful one in which the succession of brandings and burnings, dismemberings and flayings is only brought into more stark relief by the infrequent contrast of occasional humanitarian treatment. In 1724 the Black Code laid down the punishments that could be meted to offending Negro slaves by their owners. Looking back to medieval times in their brutality, recalling the savagery and the cold-blooded nonchalance of the torturers in a panel by Gheerhardt David, or an oil painting by Pieter Brueghel of the treatment of the Flemish during the Spanish Domination, these punishments included the slitting of noses, the severing of limbs, and the hamstringing of legs for the most trivial of crimes. A third attempt at escape from slavery meant death – by breaking on the wheel. For a century and a half the Black Code persisted, to cease officially only with the Civil War.

> No more hundred lash for me, no more, no more,
> No more driver's lash for me,
> Many thousand gone . . .

sang the slaves freed from bondage. But the barbarism of the Code was ingrained in the soul of the South and could not cease with the stroke of the pen. Catholics and Blacks alike were terrorized by the Ku Klux Klan whose incantations, Kleagles, Grand Wizards, religious hypocrisy, and declarations of knightly behavior did not – and do not – hide the underlying brutality of a murder society; the hooded night-shirts echoing the garb of the Inquisition hide individual identities, but they have never concealed the iniquity of the masquerade. Ostensibly, the floggings, lynchings, and castrations perpetrated by the Knights of the Klan were punishments meted out to murderers, rapists, and other criminals. But they were punishments administered outside the law, crimes committed by Whites who judged and condemned without giving the accused a trial. That many of the Blacks who were lynched were innocent of the crimes that they were supposed to have committed is established beyond dispute; even if they were guilty, their guilt would not justify their murder at the hands of a blood-lusting lynch mob. The Klan was revived in 1915 by William Simmons, a Methodist preacher, and numbered amongst its members police officials, state governors, a Supreme Court judge, politicians, and professional men as well as a cross-section of the entire community, respectable and rabble. Four out of every five Southern politicians during the twenties and thirties had been members of the Klan and had added their money to its eighty million dollars capital. Since 1880 over four thousand men and women – three quarters of them Blacks – were burned to death in the kindling fires, swung as mutilated and violated corpses from cotton-wood limbs, were charred with blow-torches, or torn to pieces with corkscrews. The fingers of lynched men were displayed in butcher's shops and disgusting "mementoes" stood pickled in the Klan museums. The tentacles of the Klan stretched to every state and it is no surprise that, although its speeches were available on phonograph records, examples of recorded blues about Klan activities and the lynching mobs are not to be found. A singer could recall his experiences on the Georgia chain gang when he had escaped to the North and was safe from retribution; but he could not be sure that the Klan would not seek him out.

A seven-week filibuster in 1938 succeeded in ousting a proposed anti-lynching Bill and the several attempts at passing such a Bill through Congress subsequently have been quashed by Southern senators. Although the "protection of Southern womanhood" was frequently the excuse for a lynching, less than a quarter were, in fact, punishments for rape or even the suspicion, genuine or faked, of the crime. Many had been for attempting to vote, for trying to defend wife or daughter, for defiant talk, or for no reason whatever. Some white women found incitement to lynching a convenient method of disposing of an unwanted lover and some even claimed to have been violated by "looking."

Lynchings and floggings have often been committed on the most slender grounds. But "suspicion" also constituted grounds for legal arrest in most states: more than twenty-seven per cent of all arrests on grounds of suspicion were against Blacks, and these vague and unspecified "crimes" accounted for more arrests than any other category. Inevitably, many flagrant injustices could be committed as a result of this, though it did afford a slight measure of preventative action. Lack of visible means of support, begging, and vagrancy were all grounds for arrest in many states; many Blacks were punished for having "carnal knowledge by spying" – a charge open to the most serious abuse; in all but three states adultery was a criminal offence. Whereas the law was not always rigidly applied in these and other "offenses," an unwanted man could easily be victimized by unscrupulous application of the law and grounds of "suspicion" could terminate the freedom of an innocent person. Eddie Boyd was a blues singer who eventually chose to leave the United States for good, to settle in Sweden.

235   Got me accused of peepin' – I can't even see a thing,
Got me accused of beggin' – I can't even raise my hand.

Bad luck, bad luck is killin' me,
I just can't stand no more of this third degree.

Got me accused of taxes, I don't have a lousy dime,
Got me accused of children an' nary one of them is mine.

Got me accused of murder, I never harmed a man,
Got me accused of forgery, I can't even write my name.

Convict lease was a system which arose out of slavery whereby convicted prisoners were leased to contractors to provide labor in the cotton fields, the sugar plantations, or the coal mines. The system also provided a convenient method of adding to the state income by exploitation of the convicts. A man would be fined, for example, thirty dollars and ten dollars costs for a statutory offence, making a total of forty dollars which he had to pay off with his own labor. The value of his labor would be assessed at fifty cents per day and he would thus be obliged to work for nearly three months to pay off his fine. The contractor would hire his labor at seventy cents per day and be obliged to provide food and "board." This was cheap enough, but the standard of board provided can be imagined; provided the county received the money, it paid no attention to the welfare of its prisoners who were slaves to be disciplined and worked by the contractor at his will. Through the protests of humanitarians and labor unions against this legal slavery, the convict lease system was outlawed by Congress in 1887. This did not deter the majority of the southern states, who were anxious not to lose so useful a source of revenue; the ruling was flagrantly ignored. In Alabama the method was pursued with particular ruthlessness and prison officers were paid a fixed sum for making an arrest, another for writing the warrant, another for filing it, and so on. It paid to keep the prisons full. Barefoot Bill from Alabama recorded several blues about imprisonment.

236 Say, High Sheriff been here, got my girl and gone, (*twice*)
I say left me lonely, yes I'm all alone.

Oh, listen, Mister, what have my baby done? (*twice*)
I just want to know if she done anybody wrong.

You took your gun, made her raise her hand, (*twice*)
And you was wrong, 'cause she never harmed a man.

My baby in jail an' I can't get no news, (*twice*)
I don't get nothin' but these mean ole High Sheriff blues.

In 1928 the last convicts left the Flat Top coal mine of Alabama and this event marked the cessation of convict lease. It had been already superseded elsewhere by the contract system in which the contractors came to the prisons bringing with them the materials and instructions for the manufacture of certain articles, paying the prison according to the output rather than to the number of hours worked by the men. This had the predictable result that the men were overworked in order to increase output; the evil of one system was scarcely less than that of the other. It was still useful to have prisoners for employment in the prison workshops, to be engaged in the manufacture of boots, the trimming of tombstones, the making of automobile registration plates, and the many other items that contractors required. Sang Leroy Carr:

237 Thirty days in the workhouse, six long months in jail, (*twice*)
Yes, I'm in trouble, no one to go my bail.

"Please, Mister Jailer, please unlock this door for me, (*twice*)
This jail is full of blues, I know they'll come down on me."

I'm a hard-working prisoner, sent up without a trial, (*twice*)
My heart is almost breakin', must be that last long mile.

Though open to abuse the contract system did employ men usefully and, when they were not overworked, prevented the deterioration of morale that resulted from being idle. Until the Depression such internal employment worked satisfactorily enough, but when millions of men were without work in the free, outside world, the unions complained that the convicts were being engaged on labor that could be given to the unemployed. Subsequently, businessmen producing goods that were close or identical in kind to the goods made in the prisons complained of the low prices; they could not compete if they were to pay fair wages. As a result, prison-made articles were forced off the market by a succession of legal measures, and many of the prison workshops became redundant. While "sweatshop" methods were now abandoned, the prisons were blighted instead by idleness, the prisoners degenerating in long years of inactivity. A sentence that once seemed insufferable when spent in ceaseless toil in the workshop, now seemed as interminable and as hard to bear for the man who, like Lightnin' Hopkins, had nothing to do.

> 238   Well, I wouldn't mind stayin' in jail but I got to stay there so long,
>   (*twice*)
>   You know it seems like all my friends you know they done shook
>   hands and gone.
>
> Thirty days in jail with my back turned to the wall, (*twice*)
> Yes, you know some other skinner must be kicking in my stall.
>
> "Hey, Mister Jailer, will you please sir, bring me the key? (*twice*)
> I just want you to open the door, 'cause this ain't no place for me."

The forms of labor that persisted in the prison system were those that were classed as under "state use." Convicts were either self-supporting or provided amenities for the state. In theory the principle seemed logical and constructive; its practical applications were frequently far less so. The means and conditions of employment were often not greatly different from those of the convict lease system; whilst the methods of punishment had their origins in the basest iniquities of slavery.

When slavery was abolished it was believed that shackles and chains were at an end, but paradoxically, liberation coincided with changes of penal methods which were to find new uses for them. The ball and chain shackled to the ankle of a convict who was set to work in the market-place had been instituted in Pennsylvania as far back as the 1780s, but the building of the prisons in the ensuing years put the majority of convicts behind bars. During the nineteenth century the population of the prisons far exceeded the provisions made for them, and the insanitary cells in which they were incarcerated caused widespread disease. A sentence of ten years became a sentence of death. Prisoners fought the rats, tossed in fever, and rotted in filth until death released them. Convicted men were herded into prisons with cells as small as seven feet by three, and the overcrowding necessitated alternative methods of "correction," though one prison with five hundred cells of this size was still in use in the 1930s. A solution was found in the chain gang, a scheme simple to implement, and lucrative to the state, if frequently fatal to the prisoner. By leasing gangs of chained convicts under armed guard, and by using them on state projects, the prisons were relieved whilst railroads were built, the gravel quarries worked, swamps drained, and roads constructed. In 1902 there were 2,221 convicts employed in the chain gangs of Georgia alone, and of these 2,113 were black, amongst them 103 women. Children of twelve years of age were to be found working in chains with old and embittered men in the streets of Atlanta, and men and women were shackled together under inhumane conditions. In some states the system was abolished at the beginning of this century: when the camps in Louisiana were cleared in 1901 hundreds of forgotten men were found in conditions of appalling suffering; in one, every man was found to be dying of smallpox. Elsewhere the chain gangs continued, the convicts in bottomlands of the Brazos River in Texas died from disease, sunstroke, beatings and buckshot wounds, and women were forced to work alongside the men. Chain gangs made a profit of over $350,000 for the State of Georgia in 1907; thirty-five years later they were still operating. James "Kokomo" Arnold was a Georgia-born singer who found it safer to operate his bootlegging business in Chicago. His memory of Georgia chain gangs remained with him.

239   Says the judge he found me guilty, and the clerk he wrote it down,
     (twice)
    Sheriff said "Now I'm sorry buddy but, Lord, you' chain gang boun'."

    Says I didn't mean to kill her, but bloody murder was my crime, *(twice)*
    Now I'm out here on the chain gang, Lord, jus' servin' my time.

    Says I got chains round my body, chains all down round my shoes,
     (twice)
    Now that's the reason, Cap'n, hear me singing, Lord, these chain gang
    blues.

"No Job Blues"

by Ramblin' Thomas

HERE'S a new "find"—Ramblin' Thomas—now an exclusive Paramount artist. As he sings the clever words—they are really good—and you hear every note clear and sharp on his guitar, you'll stamp your approval on Ramblin' Thomas and on "No Job Blues." He spills the latest joy notes, no foolin', — hear for yourself, at your dealer's, or send us the coupon.

[**12609 — No Job Blues** and **Back Gnawing Blues,** Ramblin' Thomas and His Guitar.]

12587—Shake 'em Up and **Jingles** (For Dancing)—Clarence Williams and His Orchestra.

12607—Pullman Passenger Train and **Jug-A-Long Boys,** Pullman Porter's Quartette.

12608—New Bo Weavil Blues and **Moonshine Blues,** "Ma" Rainey and Her Georgia Band.

12604 — My Money Never Runs Out and **Jazz Gypsy Blues,** Banjo joy; Guitar Acc. by Blind Blake.

12597—Wabash Rag and **You Gonna Quit Me Blues,** Blind Blake and His Guitar.

12590—"Ma" Rainey's Black Bottom and **Georgia Cake Walk,** "Ma" Rainey and Her Georgia Band.

12605 — Molly Man and **Shrimp Man** (Red Hot) Mess.

12579 — Gone Dead On You Blues and **One Dime Blues,** Blind Lemon Jefferson and Guitar.

12565 — He's In The Jailhouse Now and **Southern Rag,** Blind Blake and His Guitar; Banjo accompaniment.

Sermons and Spirituals

12561—Judgment Day In The Morning and **Red Cross The Disciple of Christ,** Sermons with Singing by Moses Mason.

12599—I Have Anchored My Soul and **King Jesus, Stand By Me,** Norfolk Jubilee Quartette.

SEND NO MONEY! If your dealer is out of the records you want, send us the coupon below. Pay postman 75 cents for each record, plus small C. O. D. fee when he delivers records. We pay postage on shipments of two or more records.

Electrically Recorded!

Paramount Records are recorded by the latest new electric method. Greater volume, amazingly clear tone. Always the best music — first on Paramount!

New York Recording Laboratories,
                        , Wis.

Send me the records checked (✓) below at 75 cents each.

Name ....

Address ....

City .... State ....

Paramount

The Popular Race Record

Playing cards on a Texas train, being found in the street without proof of means of support, being under the influence of drink – these were sufficient grounds for committing a man for months to the chain gang to work in a forced-labor logging camp, to build a road or bridge while working waist-deep in swamp water, to break rocks under a broiling sun. A Texan, Ramblin' Willard Thomas, was a vagrant who described the experience of being pressed into the chain gang.

240   I been walking all day, and all night too, (*twice*)
      Because my meal-ticket woman have quit me and I can't find no work
         to do.

      I was picking up the newspapers and I looking in the ads. (*twice*)
      And the policeman came along and he arrested me for "vag."
      (*Spoken*) Boys you ought to see me in my black and white suit.

      I asked the judge "Judge what may be my fine?" (*twice*)
      He said "Get you a pick and shovel, and get deep down in the mine."

      I'm a poor black prisoner working in the ice and snow, (*twice*)
      I got to get me another meal-ticket woman, so I won't have to work
         no more.

Convicts in the "road gangs" rose with the sun and were bedded down with the sun. When they lay down for their rest on the hard earth their ankles were shackled to a long logging chain that ran the length of their rudimentary quarters. Those that had to travel a considerable distance to the place of work on the county roads were shipped in horse-drawn box cars. Five tiers of hardwood bunks were affixed on either side with only eighteen inches of headroom. The mobile cages that replaced them after World War II were little better equipped. When not working, the convicts – men and women – were heavily manacled, but when employed on their tasks their hands had to be free, and except when engaged in work requiring close order – ditch digging for example – it was found expedient to free them from the long chain. Instead, a step-chain, allowing a pace of only eight inches, was used, or a twenty-pound ball chained to the ankle. Gertrude "Ma" Rainey came from Georgia.

241   Many days of sorrow, many nights of woe, (*twice*)
      And a ball and chain, everywhere I go.

> Chains on my feet, padlocks on my hands, (*twice*)
> It's all on account of stealing a woman's man.
>
> It was early this mornin' that I had my trial, (*twice*)
> Ninety days on the county road, and the judge didn't even smile.

Boys and girls scarcely in their teens were worked side-by-side for sixteen or more hours a day and slept chained in line in the ditches. In the early part of the century as many as 250 prisoners, many of them first offenders, were shackled together on the "long chain" to work on the railroads, the wheat farms, and in the dreaded phosphate mines. When prisoners were punished they were brutalized with clubs and compelled to wear needle-sharp points affixed to their ankles which lacerated their legs as they walked. When Governor Arnall of Georgia instituted an investigation of the prison system in 1943 he discovered that such methods were still in use; leg irons with the heads of picks welded to them were being worn by many prisoners and some twenty-five men were suffering from open, festering wounds caused by the barbarous irons. To escape the horrors of the chain gang sixteen men had severed the tendons of their legs and were lying helpless. Women suffered privations and humiliation scarcely less brutal, being flogged naked before the eyes of male prisoners. The campus of Georgia State College was dug by aged black women working under the supervision of armed guards while young girls carried their picks to the road camps. Small wonder that Leroy Carr's "heart struck sorrow" when he saw his girl join the long chain for a sentence of "11.29" – a year, which under these conditions would seem an eternity.

242   Now I'm gonna see that judge and talk to him myself, (*twice*)
>   Tell him that he sent my gal to the county road and left me by myself.
>
>   Now never felt so sorry till the keeper walked down the lane, (*twice*)
>   And my heart struck sorrow when he called my good gal's name.
>
>   Then I heard the jailer say, "Hello! Prisoners all fall in line, (*twice*)
>   I'm also talkin' about that long-chain woman that got 11.29."
>
>   I've got the blues so bad that I just can't rest, (*twice*)
>   I'm gonna ask that jailer, "Can I do my good gal's time myself?"

The majority of workers in the camps and chain gangs built and maintained the state roads. North Carolina, still had nearly ninety road camps in the 1950s, its prison division being under the direction of the State Highway and Public Works Commission. More than seven thousand prisoners were employees in its camps. Alabama had only a third as many camps and Virginia's state convict road force employed a third the number of men. Elsewhere in the South convicts continued to be employed outside in the state prison and County Farms which covered many thousands of acres and were occupied by tens of thousands of men and women. Agricultural work on a considerable scale in the production of sugar and cotton, the clearing of timber and the growing of vegetable produce was undertaken, and meat and canning factories were usually associated with the farms. Alice Moore from Missouri sang about the County Farm.

243   Oh the judge he sentenced me, and the clerk he wrote it down, (*twice*)
My man said "I'm sorry for you babe, but you are county farm
   bound."

Oh six months in jail, seven months on the County Farm, (*twice*)
If my man he had've been any good he would have met my bond.

I worked hard on the county farm, tryin' to forget my babe, (*twice*)
Some day he's gonna be sorry he treated me this way.

I'm gonna build me a scaffold just to hang myself, (*twice*)
Because the man I'm lovin' 'bout to worry poor me to death.

Conditions on both the county and the state prison farms were hard, the work long, the punishments brutal; there had been little change since slavery times. For this reason the prison farms became storehouses of traditional work songs and group labor songs which may have varied little from those sung before the Civil War. Some long-term prisoners spent a lifetime within the bounds of the camps, men who had committed serious crimes and whose long confinement prevented their resettlement in the outside world. Many of those released from Sugarland, Clements, or Darrington State Farms in Texas soon returned to endure another sentence working on the plantation. One of them was Alger "Texas" Alexander, who was no stranger to the Texas prison farms. His blues were often derived directly from the collective work songs of the penitentiaries.

244   I was working on the section, 'cause I got a job to do,
I've got a dollar and a quarter, I won't have to work hard as you.

Back In Jail Again

NO. 3242

Sung by **BUMBLE BEE SLIM**

3242 BACK IN JAIL AGAIN and NEW POLICY
DREAM BLUES — Voc.-Guitar — Bumblee Bee
Slim 59c

Oh nigger lick molasses, and the white man licks 'em too,
I wonder what in the world is the Mexican gonna do?
Lord, nigger lick molasses and the white man licks 'em too.

"Oh captain, captain, what's the matter with you?
If you got any Battle-Ax, please sir, give me a chew,
Lord captain, captain, what's the matter with you?"

"Water boy, water boy, bring your water round,
If you ain't got no water, set your bucket down,
Water boy, water boy, bring your water round."

"Oh captain, captain, what time of day?"
Oh he looked at me, and he walked away . . .

It was to Sugarland that the great folk and blues singer, Leadbelly was
sent, until he obtained a pardon after singing a plea for his release to
Governor-Elect Pat Neff. A decade later in 1930 he was sent to the Angola
Penitentiary, Louisiana. As notorious as these were the Kilby and Atmore
Prison Farms of Alabama, the Cumins State Farm in Arkansas, Reid in
Boykin, South Carolina, and, perhaps best known of all, the Parchman
Prison Farm, Mississippi, where Bukka White spent several years:

245   Judge give me life this mornin' down on Parchman Farm, (*twice*)
     I wouldn't hate it so bad, but I left my wife in mourn.

     Oh, good-bye wife, all you have done gone, (*twice*)
     But I hope some day, you will hear my lonesome song.

     Oh listen you men, I don't mean no harm, (*twice*)
     If you wanna do good, you better stay off old Parchman Farm.

     We go to work in the mornin', just at dawn of day, (*twice*)
     Just at the settin' of the sun, that's when the work is done.

     I'm down on old Parchman Farm but I sho' wanna go back home,
       (*twice*)
     But I hope some day I will overcome.

There is no doubt that the prison farms were brutal and that many of the
guards were sadists who were recruited from those "poor Whites" who had

a hatred of Blacks and who were ignorant and incapable of getting employment elsewhere. Inhuman beatings with the "bat" – a fourteen-pound leather strap which could break a brick with a single blow – caused forty convicts in Angola to hamstring themselves in 1951, rather than submit to its torture. In 1957 more than a dozen men smashed their legs with sledge-hammers at Kilby because they could no longer cope with the ceaseless slave labor on the rock-pile. Yet black prisoners prefered to be in the state farms than in the jails. They could smell the earth, see the sky, sing, and work with their companions: in the jail they could at best, smell carbolic; the vista was one of stone walls and steel bars; they heard the sounds of the turnkey and communication was often restricted to furtive taps in code.

Prisoners particularly feared the coming of the transfer agents, also known as "long-chain men," who took rows of shackled convicts to the penitentiaries. Some became notorious and were the subject of prison songs, like Bud Russell in Texas or Joe Tunney (Joe Turner) in Tennessee. They took their dangerous charges to the stonewall prisons, Huntsville Walls, Texas, or the Nashville Walls, in Tennessee, subject of a blues by Robert Wilkins.

246   I looked out the window, saw the long-chain man (*twice*)
          Oh he's comin' to call us boys, name by name.

          He's goin' to take us from here to Nashville, Tennessee, (*twice*)
          He's goin' to take me right back boys to where I used to be.

          I got a letter from home, reckon how it read? (*twice*)
          It read "Son, come home to your mama, she's sick and nearly dead."

          I sat down and I cried, and I screamed and squalled, (*twice*)
          Said "How can I come home, mama, I'm behind these walls."

          Every morning 'bout four, or it might be half-past, (*twice*)
          You ought to see me down the foundry, trying to do my task.

          'Cause the judge he sentenced me boys from "Five to Ten" (*twice*)
          I get out I'm go to that woman, I'll be right back again.

The worst sore on the American prison system was the conduct and operation of its county jails. Every county had its jail which was theoretically the responsibility of the county authorities. In practice its maintenance was too often left in the hands of the sheriff who delegated his authority to a number of guards, some of whom were corrupt, dissolute, and indifferent. In spite of minor improvements after World War I most county jails were insanitary lock-ups. There was no system of inspection and no standards to be maintained. In 1930 Federal authorities visited a large number of county jails, applying a minimum standard to which it was agreed they should conform. The Report of the Director of the Bureau of Federal Prisons showed that of 650 prisons visited, only fifty reached this minimum standard. Though they deplored the filthy, immoral conditions that they uncovered, no significant improvements were to be made for many years. Small wonder that Blind Boy Fuller sang in 1938, "Lord, I never will forget the day they transferred me to the county jail . . ."

> 247 Then I sent for my friends: "Please spare the rod," (*twice*)
> Then my friends sent me word, "Lord the times was too dog-gone hard."
>
> I got friends 'as got money: "Please tell 'em to go my bail." (*twice*)
> And my friends sent me word, "Had no business in the county jail."
>
> Then I felt so right till the judge turned around and frowned, (*twice*)
> Says, "I'm sorry for you buddy, but you're on your last-go-round."

Arrested persons awaiting trial, young first offenders and old habitual criminals were thrown together in the county jails, where some attempts were made to keep the insane and the drug addicts apart from the others, but where cramped conditions sometimes made even such rudimentary measures impossible. At one time it was the practice to charge the prisoner a fee when he entered and to charge him a further sum when he left. With no chance to make any money, apart from gambling with newcomers, this encouraged corruption amongst the prisoners and the guards alike. In order to obtain his release a prisoner had to bribe a guard or get a visitor to induce somebody to go his bail; in Jack Dupree's case, his mother.

> 248 Well, here I am, locked up in this county jail, (*twice*)
> Well, well, it's on a Sunday, oh well, well, and no one to go my bail.
>
> Run, phone my mother, tell her the shape I'm in, (*twice*)
> Well, I'm locked up in the county jail oh well, well, and I haven't got no friends.

(*Spoken*) Yes, when you locked up in jail an' you ain't got no friends,
Way down here in this county jail . . . everything will be all right . . .
Just phone my mother, she'll take care for me.

When I got the news it was just about four o'clock, (*twice*)
When the judge discharge me, oh well, well, my heart begin to reel and
    rock.

Says I'm going back home, won't be bad no mo', (*twice*)
'Cause the county jail, oh well Lord, it ain't no place to go.

If he had committed an infraction of the law and was sent to the county
jail, a man who made his living by share-cropping was unlikely to have any
capital from which his wife or family might draw to pay his bond. For the
man without family connections or for whom there was no one prepared to
go bail, the outlook was bleak. Food was generally poor and cigarettes,
Coca-Cola, and other luxuries could only be purchased by bribing a guard,
unless the jail was one in which a small trolley of goods was trundled past the
cells so that prisoners could buy items whilst their two or three permitted
dollars lasted. As the prisoner was a drain on the resources of the county, a
system was rife which closely approximated that of the outlawed convict
lease. A local plantation owner who required temporary labor went bail for
the prisoners in the jail who were then indebted to him for this sum and had
to pay it in their labor, at a rate fixed by himself. Many Blacks in Mississippi,
where this was especially prevalent, found themselves unwittingly forced
into crop-lien slavery. When insufficient prisoners were in the jail county
sheriffs sometimes made "blanket arrests" of all vagrants in order to provide
the requisite number, and then quietly took their cut. Like all prisoners Big
Maceo resented the horizontally banded "black and white striped suit"
which convicts were obliged to wear.

  249   They picked me up, and put me in the county jail, (*twice*)
        They wouldn't even let my woman come and go my bail.

        Now I'm in prison, but I've almost did my time, (*twice*)
        They give me six months but I had to work out nine.

        Course I know my baby, she's goin' to jump and shout, (*twice*)
        When that train rolls up and I come walkin' out.

So take these stripes from round me, and these chains from round my
   legs, (*twice*)
Well these stripes don't hurt me, but these chains like to kill me dead.

Far better regulated than the county jails were the state prisons, though
they could vary widely in the quality of their administration. Some were
excessively severe on the prisoners, some dangerously lax, some markedly
progressive. The likelihood of violent riots was generally present and in
order that this was kept to a minimum the conduct of many state prisons was
very strict. There was only one panoptic prison in the United States, and in
general the cells were banked in tiers about a main hall like a hen battery. As
the prisons could not cope with the large numbers by affording each man
separate accommodation, two and even three men might be obliged to use
the same cell, causing unnecessary distress and inciting tyranny, hostility,
and homosexuality. The prisoner had his cell watched by ever-vigilant
guards, as Roosevelt Sykes cynically observed when he spoke of the wolves
that scratched on his cabin door. The blues singer's delight in layers of
meaning and pertinent metaphor was well demonstrated in his *.44 Blues* in
which the number of his cell is the number of a "train" whose "whistle" was
the shot from a .44 gun.

250   Lord, I walked all night long with my .44 in ma hand, (*twice*)
       I was lookin' for my woman an' I found her with another man.

       I wore my .44 so long, Lord, it made my shoulder sore, (*twice*)
       After I do what I want to ain't goin' to wear my .44 no more.

       Lord, and my baby said she heard that .44 whistle blow, (*twice*)
       Well it sounds just like ain't gonna blow that whistle no more.

       Lord, I got a little cabin, and my cabin is Number 44, (*twice*)
       When I wake up every morning the wolves scratches on my door.

For infringements of the rules prisoners could be punished severely,
losing opportunities for their cases to come before the parole boards, being
sent into solitary confinement or to the ill-ventilated, lightless cells known
in almost every prison as "the hole." In the early part of the century
prisoners in San Quentin would be punished by being forced to spend a day
up to their necks in water; tepid bath punishments were still widely

practiced in the 1950s. In the South the punishments were, in many instances, inhuman. Amongst them the "derrick," a form of *bastinado*, was used in Texas where beatings with "red heifer" whips were common. Throughout Georgia in the twenties and thirties black prisoners were tortured by being tied in a distorted position round a pick, were racked in medieval fashion, or were committed to the "sweat-box" and left to fry in the boiling sun. The "sweat-box" was still in use after World War II in Florida, and the doors of "the hole" in Jackson Prison still had a second, curved metal door hinged to them between which recalcitrant prisoners were confined, unable to move.

Some prisoners resisted these methods of subjugation with such spirit that their rebelliousness became intensified rather than broken, but for others the conditions sent them "stir-crazy." Small events assumed exaggerated importance, minor grievances became obsessions, and the prisoner with time on his hands and on his mind could sit and brood.

251   All last night I sit in my cell alone, (*twice*)
        I was thinking of my baby and my happy home.

        Sometimes I wonder, why don't you write to me? (*twice*)
        If I been a bad fellow, I did not intend to be.

        Baby, you may never see my smilin' face again,
        Whoa-oo, my smilin' face again,
        You can always remember, Frank Busby has been your friend.

There was little opportunity for self-expression within prison and consequently no preparation for integration within the free community. Rehabilitation programmes were instituted in few prisons, though some jails made notable advances towards penal reform – Sing Sing, for example, where during World War I, Thomas Osborne attempted to introduce revolutionary methods designed to give even the most dangerous of prisoners a valuable role in the closed community and which would prepare them for the part that they would eventually play outside. Osborne's scheme was viciously attacked and was destroyed by political pressure, but in the 1930s Warden Lewis E. Lawes applied an enlightened policy that helped considerably in the welfare of the prisoners in his charge. In Bill Gaither's blues it was still prison, nonetheless.

252 On my way to Sing Sing, there was only one thing I could say, (*twice*)
Stone walls will be my home for five years and a day.

Early one morning, long between nine and ten, (*twice*)
I thought about that woman and wished I could see her face again.

My mother told me, son, you've got to reap just what you sow, (*twice*)
Now I'm behind these hard stone walls, may never see the streets no
more.

Much of the misery of imprisonment is borne not by those inside but by
those that are left behind. Crimes that are committed as an indirect result of
the failure of society, by persons whose acts are fundamentally a revolt
against sub-human conditions of life, may have many far-reaching effects
upon innocent persons, quite apart from the victim and his dependants. Sara
Martin sang the blues of a woman whose anger was directed at the cause of
her misery, the prisoner himself.

253 I went to the jail-house crying, "Jailer please,
Please Mister Jailer, let me see my used-to-be," (*repeat verse*)

The jailer felt sorry, then looked at me and smiled,
Said, "I'm sorry, pretty lady, but your man's done patricide." (*repeat
verse*)

I turned to the cell, looked my daddy in the face,
"I'm sorry, pretty daddy, but I just can't take your place." (*repeat verse*)

Now girls you'd better buy yourself a padlock and key,
'Cause that's the only way you can keep your man from me. (*repeat
verse*)

And if the blues was whisky I'd be drunk all the time,
I had to go and leave my daddy behind. (*repeat verse*)

Fear of the disintegration of his home and of the loss of his loved ones is as
big an inducement as any for a man to escape from the confines of jail, prison
farm, or camp. The chances of escape from jail depend largely upon the
initiative of the prisoner in taking advantage of an opportunity when one
presented itself, and of seeing the possibility in an unusual situation. Under

suitable circumstances many a man has literally walked out of jail. More
frequently his escape has been facilitated by poor security measures or the
corruption of guards who were open to bribery. Such methods of escape are
therefore less available to Blacks against whom security measures are often
more strict and who are seldom in a position to buy their way out of prison.
Escape is facilitated at moments of disorder and convicts have set fire to
prisons and then escaped in the confusion. Nearly three hundred men died in
the Ohio State Penitentiary in 1930: convicts set fire to it in an abortive
escape attempt and the warders refused to open locked cells. Three years
before, Buddy Boy Hawkins had sung of an unsuccessful attempt at
effecting his woman's escape by simulating a prison conflagration.

254   (*Spoken*) "Hey, Mister Jailer, jail-house burnin' down!"

"Hey Mister Jailer, do not sleep so soun'."
I said, "Hey, Mister Jailer, I said do not sleep so soun'.
Jail-house on fi-yah, place is all burnin' down."

Because the woman I lo-ove, she is in the jail-house now, (*twice*)
So please, Mister Jailer, you gotta get her out' there somehow.

Mmmmmmmmm my woman's in trou-ble now,
I said mmmm-ah – my brown's in trouble now,
I said one o' these cool mawnin's I'm gonna get her outa jail.

When I get my li'l, fair brown-skin ou' I'll be country boun',
I said when I get my fair brown, buddy I'm goin' up the country
    boun',
And then, Mister Jailer, I hope your jail-house burn down.

There were far greater chances of escape from the county jails where the
guard tended to be more relaxed, and many instances were known of the
open connivance of the guards or the wardens in return for a bribe, or sex
with the prisoner. Escape was also possible from the road camps and farms
but, whatever the form of imprisonment, the prisoners ran the extreme risk
of being shot by agitated and nervously excited guards or trusties on whom
the blame for the escape might fall, or of being literally hounded to earth.
Alice Pearson sang of the mental agonies of a woman who had learned of her
man's escape.

255   When your man's in trouble you can't eat or sleep, *(twice)*
Your heart begins quiverin' and yo' flesh begins to creep.

And you run to the jail-house, cryin', "Sergeant, please, *(twice)*
Let me speak to my man, just to give my poor heart ease."

I got the greyhound blues and my heart begins to fail, *(twice)*
I know a long-tailed greyhound is on my rider's trail.

'Cause the sergeant has tol' me he isn't in that jail, *(twice)*
That's the reason why my heart begins to fail.

I'm going to the railroad, lay my head down on the rail, *(twice)*
Let that 2.19 take me from this lonesome jail.

Stumbling through the brush, struggling waist-deep through swamp water with salty tongue, pounding heart, and aching lungs, the prisoner who had broken free was terrorized by the baying of the bloodhounds that tracked his path. Almost unerring in their ability to run the escapee to the ground, the hounds were so reliable a method of capturing him that Southern warders have many times let prisoners go free so that the dependability of the animals could be demonstrated to interested visitors. The Central State Farm at Sugarland, Texas, is barely thirty miles from Houston and Victoria Spivey, like most black Houstonians of her generation, had heard the bloodhounds in pursuit of escaped prisoners and sympathized with them.

256   Well I broke out of my cell when the jailer turned his back, *(twice)*
But now I'm so sorry, bloodhounds is on my track.

Bloodhounds, bloodhounds, bloodhounds is on my trail, *(twice)*
They want to take me back to that cold, cold lonesome jail.

Well I know I done wrong, but he kicked me and blacked my –
   I done it in a passion, I thought it was the fashion –
I know I done wrong but he kicked me and blacked my eyes,
But if the bloodhounds ever catch me, in the electric chair I'll die.

Capital punishment has been abolished in a number of states, but there are still many that continue to apply the most atavistic of all punishments.

Sung by
Lil Johnson

3299—Murder In The First Degree and Scuffling
Woman Blues—Voc.-Piano and Guitar Acc
Lil Johnson ....59¢

Hanging was still practiced in some states in the 1950s and the sentenced men might wait a year in the condemned cell until the final, irrevocable punishment was carried out. They heard the gallows being assembled in the yard and were measured for height and weight by ruses that caused acute embarrassment and agony to all concerned. Then, at the appointed hour – dawn, or sometimes four p.m. – the prisoner, who had a day's notice of his imminent death, was taken to the place of execution to see perhaps a morbid group of pressmen and photographers awaiting the spectacle. Blind Lemon Jefferson projected himself in the predicament of the condemned man.

257   Hangman's rope sho' is tough and strong, (*twice*)
       They gonna hang me because I did something wrong.

I wanna tell you the gallis Lord's a fearful sight, (*twice*)
Hang me in the mornin', and cut me down at night.

Mean ole hangman is waitin' to tighten up that noose, (*twice*)
Lord, I'm so scared I'm trembling in my shoes.

Jury heard my case and they said my hands was red, (*twice*)
And judge he sentenced me be hanging till I'm dead.

Crowd round the court-house and the time is going fast, (*twice*)
Soon a good-for-nothin' killer is gonna breath his last.

Lord, I'm almost dyin', gasping for my breath, (*twice*)
And a triflin' woman waiting to celebrate my death.

Hanging was replaced by the electric chair in the majority of the states where capital punishment was employed. In theory it is the more humane method – if "humane" is the term – but the period of time between the moment when the condemned man leaves his cell and is executed by hanging may only be a matter of seconds, whereas a few minutes elapse whilst the straps, clamps, and electrical apparatus are adjusted when a man is committed to the "chair." Often the electric chair was situated only a matter of yards from Death Row and sometimes even in the same corridor so that other men awaiting execution over a period of months heard the sounds of the electrical apparatus in operation and saw the lights dim as one by one their companions were committed to their deaths. Again, seats were provided for spectators and as a refinement one or two institutions even permitted the condemned man to throw the switch that sent the burning charge through his body. Some "made their peace with God" and received the ministrations of the chaplain, but the minds of others were dulled to all reality but the chair itself. James Platt spoke for them.

258   I'm walkin' to the 'lectric chair, with a preacher by my side, (*twice*)
They got me for cold-blood murder and the truth can't be denied.

I wouldn't mind dyin' but I'm dying in such a cruel ole way, (*twice*)
Ain't got the heart to send a message, ain't even got the heart to pray.

Mmmmmmmmmmm – mmmmmmmmmmm,
Mmmmmmmmmmm – Lord, Lord,
Lord, Lordy, Lord, Lordy, Lord.

Lord, Lord, Lord, Lord all I can do is sit and cry, (*twice*)
My poor mother's at home, don't know I'm even goin' to die.

During the 1930s and 1940s the number of men executed exceeded 3,100; the number of women, mercifully, a bare two dozen. Of the total number of persons legally executed more than half were black, a proportion which represented a rate ten times that of white persons relative to the respective populations. Even when related to the respective incidences of culpable homicide the execution figures were excessively weighted against Blacks. Over 350 executions were for rape and these were almost exclusively Blacks; seldom is the white rapist of a black girl brought to trial and the victims knew better than to make any active protest. In spite of popular conceptions to the contrary black rapists were few in number; retribution was swift, certain and horrible. Murders where white persons are the victims are punished severely; the South takes a more compromising view of the murder of Blacks by Blacks. In some localities the law was rigidly applied, but in others the crime was dealt with leniently and violence within the race condoned. Generalizations on the attitude to crime can be misleading and conclusions are hard to draw, for the application of the law to offences by Blacks varied widely from state to state.

The prison population figures give no satisfactory impression of the incidence of crime, for Blacks generally received longer sentences for identical offenses than white criminals, especially – and somewhat surprisingly – in the North. Relative to their proportionate populations there were three times as many black males in Americans prisons and four times as many females. Judges were apt to award impossibly long sentences to ensure that no remission could be given from a life sentence, bringing a feeling of utter hopelessness for those whom they sent to jail. The lack of standardized sentences caused extraordinary anomalies in which a month in jail, a life term, or execution could be the range of legal punishment possible for the same offense. The law differed widely from state to state, and so did its application. There were scrupulous judges who exercised the law with impartiality to all who came before them, and some who even "leaned over backwards" to ensure fair hearings for Blacks.

But the scale of crime in many cities required drastic measures. By the 1920s Memphis Tennessee was known as "The Murder Capital of America" – a dubious title applied to other cities in later years, including Houston, Texas, and Washington, D.C. In 1924 there were 113 slayings in Memphis, 94 of the victims being black; with the backing of Mayor "Boss" Crump and the support of sixty black leaders and churches, Police Commissioner Clifford Davis cracked down on all crime in the city. Black criminals were arrested in large numbers, courts were firm, sentences long, and mitigating circumstances, or excuses, brushed aside. "First one come is the City of Memphis against Mister Crow" introduced "Papa" Charlie Jackson with wry humor.

259   The other afternoon, I'm sittin' in the courthouse soon, (*twice*)
      I were listenin' to what was going on.

      After their case was tried, the prisoners was hauled inside (*twice*)
      As they passed me by, I heard them holler and cry.

      I'm through with doing wrong, just listen to my song, (*twice*)
      I got the Judge Cliff Davis blues.

      I told the judge my tale of woe, he heard that very tale before,
      That's why you hear me wail, I'm on my way to jail,
      I've got the Judge Cliff Davis blues.

"Judge" Clifford Davis had some effect, but seventy-eight Blacks were killed in Memphis in 1934. Most arrests of black offenders were made by local police; only a few were of interest to the Federal agents. Known as G-Men – an abbreviation for Government Men reputedly first used by gangster "Machine Gun" Kelly – they entered popular folk-lore with the fight against organized crime. Curtis Henry made only a few titles at a session in North Carolina, and most of these were about his arrest and imprisonment.

260   "Looka-here Mr. G-Man, tell me what has I done?" (*twice*)
      Seems like as soon as my blues leave me, my troubles just begun.

      Says they walked and they talked me, down to the Federal jail (*twice*)
      I didn't have nobody to come and go my bail.

      When I went before the Commissioner, 5,000 was my bond (*twice*)
      I had start to wishin' for the man I had tried to con.

      When I went before the judge, everybody begin to laugh and grin,
        (*twice*)
      I were lookin' by my side for someone, but I didn't have a friend.

> If I ever get over my troubles, ain't goin' start no more, (*twice*)
> Because the G-Men is bound to get you Lordy anywhere you go.

Undoubtedly many Blacks would have received more favorable judicial treatment if their cases had been pleaded more sympathetically. The black lawyer was unusual in the South and in the small towns non-existent. Even in the bigger cities his color could prejudice his client, and no white persons in the South would employ a black lawyer no matter how good his qualifications were. Few Blacks understood the process of the law and fewer could afford expert legal advice. The lawyers who defended them were often failures who did not seek their clients from choice, but rather from necessity. A small number of humanitarian lawyers who were desirous of seeing justice for Blacks did operate on their behalf and showed, as in Sleepy John Estes's metaphor, that it was possible to reverse the stream of adverse opinion on occasion.

261   Now, got offices in town, resident out on Seventy Road,
         He got a nice little lake right inside the grove.

> Boys, y'know I like Mister Clark yes, he really is my friend,
> He says if I just stay out of my grave, he'll see that I won't go to
> the pen.

Now Mis' Clark is a lawyer, his youngest brother is too,
When the battles get hot, he'll tell 'im just what to do.

Now he lawyers for the rich, he lawyers for the poor,
He don't try to rob nobody, just bring along a little dough.

Now once I got in trouble, you know I was goin' to take a ride.
He didn't let it reach the courthouse, he kept it on the outside.

Now Mis' Clark is a good lawyer, he good as I have seen,
He's the first man that proved that water runs upstream.

Blacks who went "up the river," "down in the valley," "round the bend," or "to the well" – as they euphemistically referred to prison – received equal treatment with white persons only in the progressive penitentiaries; only the Mexicans and Puerto Ricans were likely to receive worse treatment. The problem of penal reform was not racial, however, but a serious one that concerned the whole nation. Improvements of prison facilities, higher standards of recruitment and pay for prison officials, the abolition of methods of torture and the death penalty, psychiatric treatment for the socially maladjusted and practicable methods of rehabilitation that would ensure that a larger proportion of convicted prisoners could become useful members of society: these were advances that were only slowly made. Prison officers and public alike must be better educated in the understanding of the delinquent mind. But fundamentally, the greatest reform must lie in the elimination of those aspects of society that make the criminals, and in this, too, the problem is not solely a racial one; if Blacks figured in the nation's crime in an exaggerated proportion in relation to their percentage of the population, it was because the "mudsill" still existed. Racial prejudice and segregation, inadequate education, poor housing, broken families – these were only some of the factors that collectively led to the making of criminals.

On the third day of June 1936, by some unexpected arrangement, a prisoner is reported to have been brought under guard into the Decca studios to record four blues. Only one record was issued, as by Jesse James. His voice was rough, and intensely moving, as he sang his only testament. There is no blues more poignant, none that reproaches more directly the indifference of those who hear and do not attempt to comprehend, or see and do not recognize, than this simple and beautiful creation of a Negro convict. But it was the blues of a man with spirit but with little hope, who had been so long severed from the outside world that Oklahoma was to him still the "Territory" of the Indian nations; and who had been paying a debt to a society that had given him nothing. "Yóu heah me talkin' to ya, buddy, what made ya stop by heah?" he demanded of the listener as a certain man might well have done of those who passed by on the other side of the Jericho road.

262 Now the day's been a long, lonesome day,
          – Ya heah me talkin' to ya, did ya heah what I say?
      Lord, the day has been a – long, old lonesome day,
      And tomorrow eeeh, Lord, will be the same old way.

      I been to the Nation, I been all through the Territo'
          – Ya heah me talkin' to ya, gotta reap what ya sow,
      I been all round the Nation, I been all through the Territo',
      But I found no heaven on earth, Lord, nowhere I go.

I'm goin' t'the Big House, and I don't even care,
     – Don't ya heah me talkin' to ya, scaldin' to ma death!
I'm goin' in the mawnin', an' I don't even care,
I might get four or five years, Lord, and I might get the chair.

Ah, stop an' listen, see what t'morrow bring,
     – You heah me talkin' to ya, start to prayin'!
You better stop'n' listen, an' see what t'morrow bring,
It might bring you sunshine, Lawd an' it may bring rain.

Some got six months, some got a solid year,
     – You heah me talkin' to ya, buddy, what made ya stop by
      heah?
Some of them got six months, pardner, and some got a solid year,
But I believe my pardner, Lawd, got lifetime heah.

9   *World black as midnight*

To Native Americans the great river that divided the continent was the "Father of the Waters" – the Mississippi. Appropriately enough, the name that they gave it remains today, for though the Indian has virtually disappeared from its reaches, the river forever continues to drain the waters of a score of states and to pour them into the Gulf of Mexico. In so doing, it shapes the lives and controls the destinies of millions of people who, through generation after generation, depend for their livelihoods upon the Mississippi and its thousands of miles of tributaries. The soil of the valley floor is very fertile, created by the river from the alluvial deposits carried in its flow. The plains which extend from the influx of the Ohio, south for some six hundred miles to the Mississippi outlet, are of rich black soil and they naturally became the sites for many great plantations. When, in 1811, Fulton's steamboat the *New Orleans* successfully navigated the length of the river – in spite of the New Madrid earthquake which temporarily reversed the current – a new era of river navigation was born and the shipping of produce became more practicable than by the poled "flat-boats" and "broad-horns" that had plied the waters until then. A few years later Henry Shreve's *Washington*, double-decked but shallow-hulled, set the pattern of future Mississippi steamboats on which, following the Civil War, thousands of free but uneducated Blacks found employment as roustabouts and deck-hands. Large numbers of their fellows were working on the developing plantations and the center of black population density shifted from the south east to the Mississippi Valley where in some states they outnumbered Whites. So concentrated did the black population become that only recently has the percentage of colored persons in Mississippi dropped below fifty per cent of the total population.

Black labor made the production of cotton and corn and the speedy handling of the river-boat cargoes possible. To catch the markets in New Orleans speed was imperative and the boats raced to reach the river ports and landing stages and, having loaded, to beat their competitors in arriving at the wharves of the Crescent City. Early steamboats took five and a half days to make the trip from Natchez; it took the *Robert E. Lee* only ten and a half *hours* in 1870, with boilers at full pressure and a black roustabout sitting on the safety-valve. Such racing was hazardous: boilers exploded and vessels were wrecked – the fate of Shreve's *Washington*. But an additional hazard was a feature of the Mississippi itself: its total unpredictability. Every steamboat captain knew that the river he negotiated on the return trip would be unlike that which he had navigated to the Gulf. For it sprawls and meanders, floods and abates, changes its course, carves channels, creates ox-bows and cut-offs in the broad spread of the valley where the land falls at a rate of only eight inches to the mile.

The unpredictability of the Mississippi is the price paid for the rich rewards of its lands. From the head-waters of the Missouri the river flows 3,872 miles to the outlet, and from Cape Giradeau, north of Cairo, to the Head of the Passes of the Mississippi delta, the meandering course of 1,125 miles is double the direct distance. Over this length the depth increases and the river curiously narrows from a mean of nearly a mile at Cairo to half that width at the Delta. There the discharge of water varies with the seasons, at times a million cubic feet a second, sometimes but a tenth of that. As the river flows it continues to leave alluvial deposits which make natural levees or banks at its sides and which contain the waters between definite limits though they also raise the water level when the river floods. Often the river is higher than the land adjacent to it, which gradually slopes away from these natural levees. When the river begins to flood the levees may be breached causing the inundation of the surrounding country, a danger which was early appreciated by the French who commenced building artificial levees in 1717 and who had a stretch of the river so protected to a height of three feet for some fifty miles in the vicinity of New Orleans by 1735. Plantation owners were legally obliged to maintain and protect the river walls then, but in later years they became remiss in this duty. The Civil War witnessed the destruction of many of the levees which were poorly repaired and a series of disastrous inundations prompted some Government action, though maintenance was still the responsibility of individuals or district levee boards early in the present century. The railroads had largely diminished the importance of the river transport, but the danger to the land remained a real one. Blacks supplied the labor to construct the levees when the plantation owners cared to spare them from the fields. The planters' homes were safe on the higher ground, but the field hands who worked in the River Bottoms and whose shacks were in sight of the water knew, as did Kansas Joe, the danger if the levee broke.

263   If it keeps on rainin', levee's goin' to break, (*twice*)
      And the water gonna come and have no place to stay.

      Well all last night, I sat on the levee and moaned, (*twice*)
      Thinkin' 'bout my baby an' my happy home.

      I works on the levee, mama, both night and day, (*twice*)
      I ain't got nobody to keep the water away.

      Oh, crying won't help you, praying won't do no good, (*twice*)
      When the levee breaks, mama, you got to move.

      I works on the levee, mama, both night and day, (*twice*)
      I work so hard to keep the water away.

There is no stopping the Mississippi floods: they can only be kept under control. In the fall and early winter the level of the river is at its lowest, for although there is a slight rise in November the freezing of the northern tributaries reduces the tendency to a larger flood. In January, early rains in the Ohio valley regions where the land is still frozen cause a quick flow of the water to the Ohio river and, as the snows on the mountains begin to melt, they add to the volume of water carried to the Mississippi. By April the eastern flood waters are ceasing and the Mississippi subsides. The Mississippi valley regions normally get their heaviest rainfall in May and the resultant rise in the water is augmented by flood waters from the Missouri, which enter the Mississippi in June. Seasonal flooding is anticipated but the levees are constructed to control it to some extent. As the height of the water is excessive, however, breaches in the levee walls are deliberately made at certain points to allow particular areas to flood and thus lessen the pressure of water. These are the "backwaters," which occur in the St. Francis Basin to the west of the river between Memphis and Helena, in the great Yazoo–Mississippi Delta north of Vicksburg, in the Tensas Basin west of Natchez, and at other selected points. When freak circumstances occur and the overflow periods clash through the delay of the Ohio floods or the early appearance of the Missouri flood water, even the backwaters cannot take all the excess. By extraordinary ill-fortune all these phenomena occurred together between April and June in 1927 causing the worst flood disaster ever recorded on the Mississippi when millions of tons of water burst through the levees after a period of heavy rainfall and drowned the land.

Flooding occurred not only along the Mississippi but in the bottomlands of the main rivers that flowed into it, and their tributaries, where the Tallahatchie joined the Yazoo for example, some thirty miles from the Mississippi. On her only record Mattie Delaney accompanied herself on guitar in Delta fashion.

> 264   Tallahatchie River risin', Lord it's mighty bad, (*twice*)
>   Some peoples on the Tallahatchie done lost everything they had.
>
>   The people in the Delta wonderin' what to do, (*twice*)
>   They don't build some levees, I don't know what became of you.
>
>   High water rising, got me troubled in mind, (*twice*)
>   I got to go and leave my daddy behind.
>
>   Lord this water risin' and I sure can't swim, (*twice*)
>   But if it keeps on risin' sure going to follow him.

No one had anticipated the full horror of the 1927 floods. Houses were washed away with their terrified occupants still clinging to the roof-tops; the carcases of cattle and mules floated in the swirling, deep brown water; isolated figures whom none could rescue were last seen crying for help as they hung in the gaunt branches of shattered trees. Dressers and table-tops, clothes and toys were caught in the driftwood and floating timbers, to twist madly in a sudden whirlpool, and then sweep out of sight in the surging, eddying, boiling waters which extended as far as eyes could see.

Because it is unaffected by breaches in the levees which lie to the south, the town of Cairo affords a good station for measuring the extent of the water flow. There, a rise in the water of more than fifty feet above the minimum recorded reading indicates that a severe flood is imminent. In 1927 the water had risen to 56.4 feet – nearly two feet above the previous highest reading. Further to the south at Vicksburg less than a hundred thousand cubic feet of water per second passed when the minimum depth of water had been recorded, but at the height of the 1927 flood an estimated two and a quarter million cubic feet per second would have passed if the waters had been confined to the levees, and an actual reading of 1,806,000 cubic feet per second of passing river water was attained. The level had risen some sixty-five feet and with such a tremendous volume of water that the devastation was on an immense scale. Breaches – or "crevassess" – in the levees were recorded in fifty places and twenty-eight thousand square miles of land were under water. Whole townships were engulfed and the frightened people – largely Blacks – made for the hills at Helena and Vicksburg. Many blues were recorded about the floods, but none with a greater sense of immediacy and the evidence of personal experience than the six-minute *High Water Everywhere* by the Mississippi Delta singer, Charley Patton. His words were indistinct but they conveyed the human drama of the cataclysmic event.

265   The backwater done rose around Sumner now, drove me down the
        line,
      Backwater done rose round Sumner, drove poor Charley down the
        line,
      Lord I tell the world the water done jumped through this town.

      Lord the whole round country, Lord, creek water has overflowed,
      Lord the whole round country, man is overflowed,
      I would go to the hill country but they got me barred.

      Now looka here now Leland, river was risin' high,
      Looka here boys round Leland tell me river is risin' high,
      I'm goin' move over to Greenville, fore I say "Goodbye"

      Looka here the water now, Lordy, done broke out, rolled most
        everywhere,
      The water at Greenville and Lula it done rose everywhere,
      I would go down to Rosedale but they tell me there's water there.

      Now the water now Mama, done struck Charley's town, (*twice*)
      Well I'm goin' to Vicksbourg for that higher mound.

      I am goin' above that water where the land don't never flow,
      Well I'm goin over the hill where water, oh don't never flow,
      Bolivar County was easin' over that Tallahatchie shore.

      Backwater at Blytheville, backed up all round,
      Backwater at Blytheville done took Joiner town,
      It was fifty families and children some of them sink and drown.

      The water was risin' up in my friend's door, (*twice*)
      The man said to his womenfolk, "Lord we'd better go."

HIGH WATER EVERYWHERE

by *Charley Patton*

Everyone who has heard this record says that "HIGH WATER EVERYWHERE" is Charley Patton's best and you know that means it has to be mighty good because he has made some knockouts. You're in for a real treat when you hear this record at your dealer or send us the coupon.

12909—**High Water Everywhere**, Part I and 2, Vocal, guitar acc., Charley Patton

12915—**Honey Dripper Blues No. 2** and **Nickels Worth of Liver Blues No. 2**, Vocal, piano acc., Edith North Johnson

12911—**Come Back Corrina** and **Farrell Blues**, Vocal, violin-guitar acc., Henry Sims.

12905—**Papa Do Do Do Blues** and **I'll Be Gone Babe**, Vocal, banjo acc., Papa Charlie Jackson.

12902—**Leaving This Morning** and **Runaway Blues**, Vocal, Ma Rainey.

12908—**Police Dog Blues** and **Diddie Wa Diddie**, Vocal, guitar acc., Blind Blake.

12860—**Forty-Four Blues** and **Frisco Bound**, Vocal, piano acc., James Wiggins.

12899—**Southern Woman Blues** and **Mosquito Moan**, Vocal, guitar acc., Blind Lemon Jefferson.

12872—**Bed Springs Blues** and **Yo Yo Blues**, Vocal, guitar acc., Blind Lemon Jefferson.

12877—**Pea Vine Blues** and **Tom Rushen Blues**, Vocal, guitar acc., Charley Patton.

SACRED

12903—**Judas and Jesus Walked Together** and **Handwriting on The Wall**, Biddieville Quintetta.

12910—**When The Moon Goes Down**, Vocal, Norfolk Jubilee Quartette and **Meanin' in The Land Will Soon Be Over**, Norfolk Jubilee Quartette.

SEND NO MONEY! If your dealer is out of the records you want, send us the coupon below. Pay postman 75 cents for each record, plus small C. O. D. fee when he delivers records. We pay postage on shipments of two or more records.

The New York Recording Laboratories
10 Paramount Bldg., Port Washington, Wis.

Send me the records checked (✓) below 75 cents each.

( ) 12909 ( ) 12902 ( ) 12877
( ) 12915 ( ) 12908 ( ) 12903
( ) 12911 ( ) 12899 ( ) 12910
( ) 12905 ( ) 12872

Paramount
The Popular Race Record
ELECTRICALLY RECORDED

Name
Address
City   State

Ooh water was risin', families sinkin' down
Say the water was risin', airplanes was all around,
It was fifty men and children, floods was sinkin' down.

Ooh Lord, women and grown men drown,
Ooh-uh, women and children sinkin' down,
I couldn't see nobody's home, and wasn't no one to be found.

Drastic measures were taken to try to keep the floods in check: the levees were dynamited in some places to bleed off the excess water. Severe flooding in New Orleans was only averted by this method when a short route to the Gulf diverting much of the water was hastily cut. But the levees had been poorly maintained, were of insufficient height and inadequate to withstand the immense pressure of the flood water, which still continued to pour over the walls. In all, the disaster lasted for six weeks; six weeks of horror and confusion for those who had hoped that the waters would soon subside, only to see them continue to rise. The homes of 750,000 people were flooded and every possible means of escape was used. Old and forgotten boats were once more pushed out on to the water, and leaking profusely, loaded to the gunwales with people and pathetic personal belongings, were rowed and poled to the higher ground. Families were herded into cattle trucks and hundreds evacuated by the trains. Marooned groups of shocked and numbed Blacks stood huddled together on small islands that still rose above the water and waited for the help that sometimes came. Others did all they could to save the homeless and the stranded. News of the flood and its victims spread rapidly. Blind Lemon Jefferson from Texas sang in sympathy,

266   Water all in Arkansas, people screamin' in Tennessee,
Oooh – people screamin' in Tennessee,
If I don't leave Memphis, backwater been all over po' me.

People say this rainin', it has been for nights and days, (*twice*)
Crowds of people stands on the hill lookin' down where they used to
    stay.

Children standin' screamin'. "Mama, we ain't got no home."
"Ooooh – we ain't got no home."
Papa says to the children, "Backwater left us all alone."

Backwater risin', come in ma windows and doors, (*twice*)
I leave with a prayer in ma heart, "Backwater won't rise no more."

Over six hundred thousand people were rendered completely destitute by the effects of the floods, presenting an immense problem for those who were trying to feed, clothe, and house them and who were struggling to ward off the imminent danger of cholera, typhoid, and outbreaks of other highly contagious diseases. In six weeks the Government spent five million dollars and the Red Cross stated its expenses to be some fourteen millions, figures that must be borne in mind when the record is considered. For without doubt Herbert Hoover's conduct of the relief was discreditable, and the American Red Cross, under whose auspices the operations were conducted, had much to answer for. Blacks were forced to pay in cash for the relief services and food that was officially provided free by the government. Needless to say the majority was unable to meet these demands: having lost all that they had they were unable to pay. Their debt was assumed by white landlords who had them transported to the plantations as soon as the emergency was over, there to be bonded in share-cropping peonage. Those refugees who had been share-croppers were ear-marked for return to the planters under whom they had worked. Lists of workers were submitted to the Red Cross who guaranteed their transportation. Blacks were herded into segregated concentration camps, surrounded by barbed wire, and prevented from leaving by National Guardsmen. As Charley Patton indicated, Blacks were "barred" from escaping to the "hill country" to the north and east by this measure. Many were suspicious that while in the camps they would be drafted into the Army. As it was, they received the last and most inferior issues of food and clothing, and in some instances Blacks who entered Red Cross food stations were seized and put to forced labor. By this method workers were conscripted for the construction, cleaning, and maintenance of white camps and for the use of employers needing men in the vicinity of the disaster. Under armed guards black refugees did the entire work on the Vicksburg levees and the treatment of the suffering, homeless people was inhuman. The conditions were immediately investigated by Walter White and certain independent bodies, and though Hoover denied the charges, the pressure of opinion was so great that he was obliged to set up the Moton Committee to investigate the situation under the direction of conservative Dr. Robert Moton of Tuskegee. By this time some of the worst offenses had been modified but the unpublished report still makes distressing reading. The black camps were closed by the end of June and the occupants not committed to planters were forced to return to homes still submerged, whilst the white camps continued until late in August. "We did not create the social conditions in the South and it is not our function to reform them," was the official Red Cross reply to the formal accusations. Small wonder that Blacks were reluctant to go to the Red Cross relief stations as Alabama Sam (Walter Roland under a pseudonym) was to put on record. The quantities that he cited were literally correct; often they were even less.

267   Says me and my good gal talked last night and y'know we talked for an
      hour,
      She wanted me to go to that Red Cross store and get a sack of that Red
      Cross flour,
            I told her "No-o, Great Lord, says woman I sure don't want to
            go,
            Do I have to go to hills, 'cause I got to go to the Red Cross
            store."

      Says you know them Red Cross folks said they sure don't treat you
      mean –
      Don't want to give you nothin' but two or three cans of beans.
            An' I told 'em "No, Great Lord girl, I says I don't want to go,"
            I said "Y'know I cannot go to hill,
            I got to go yonder to that Red Cross store."

      But you know the government are takin' in charge now, says they
      gonna treat everybody right,
      Says they give 'em two cans of beans now, and one little can of tripe,
            And I told 'em "No," etc.

      Says you get there early in the mornin', said he ask you "Boy, how you
      feel?"
      Get ready to get you a nickel's worth of rice and a bag of that boulted
      meal,
            And I told 'em "No," etc.

A final assessment of the damage put the total figure at more than three
hundred and fifty million dollars' worth and this prompted the government
to implement a plan prepared by the United States for the protection of the
country and the improvement of the levees, which involved an expenditure
almost as great as the sum lost by the flood damage. Work commenced on
the building of revetments made from vast mattresses of willow branches
laid side by side, with transverse lengths lashing them together. Supple-
mented by concrete slabs and asphalt layers these prevent the destruction of
the levees by underwater erosion. The levees themselves were heightened
and strengthened and sub-dykes built of sandbags constructed behind them
to hold the water that seeped through. Such schemes were conducted on a
large scale but at a heavy and uncredited expenditure of black lives. Under
the direction of white overseers and straw bosses of their own color, the
laborers in the levee camps were worked until they dropped; difficult men

were clubbed and beaten and their bodies buried in the levees. Paid only ten cents an hour they were forced to purchase their goods and food at the commissaries which kept them in debt. But by 1935 over two thousand miles of levee walls, averaging twenty-four feet in height, had been constructed. Above the Ohio the dams, roller gates, and locks controlled the flow of the Missouri waters and to the south dredging and the construction of emergency reservoirs afforded better protection in the Basin. When the heavy flood waters of 1937 poured down the Mississippi the floodways were opened and the strengthened levees held. Along the Allegheny and Ohio rivers, however, it was a different story, as Lonnie Johnson described.

268   It's been snowing forty days and nights, rivers and lakes begin to freeze, (*twice*)
    Some places through my home town, water's up to my knees.

    Storm begin rising and the sun begin sinking down, (*twice*)
    I says, "Mother and Dad, pack yo' trunk, we ain't safe here in this town."

    When it's lightning my mind gets frightened, my nerves begin weakening down, (*twice*)
    And the shack where we was living begin moving round.

    Women and children was screaming, saying, "Lord where must we go? (*twice*)
    The flood water has broke the levees and we ain't safe here no more."

    And it begin, cloud as dark as midnight, keep raining all the time,
    I says, "Oh, I wonder why the sun don't ever shine?
    And the way it keeps raining, it's driving me out of my mind."

Nine hundred people lost their lives in the Ohio floods which also took a heavy toll of property and, including the Mississippi regions, rendered a million white and black persons homeless. Only the previous year a grant of over $270,000,000 had been made by the Government for further flood prevention measures in the Mississippi Basin, and following the 1937 floods an additional grant of $40,000,000 to aid the new schemes along the Ohio was awarded. As a result of this considerable expenditure the protection of the land and the control of the rivers were very substantially improved, but the heavy flooding in 1943 when four million acres were under water, and the disasters in the post-war years are evidence enough that the river is still a source of danger to extensive areas of land and to large numbers of people whose homes lie within reach of the flood waters. In all probability the river may never be held in complete control though a considerable measure of restraint will have been effected. Along the tributaries and streams that empty their waters into the large rivers, the levee walls, the upkeep of the banks and the small wharves are still the responsibility of local landowners and authorities who have not the benefit of Government grants. There, minor disasters can and do occur which are tragic enough for those concerned though they may be purely local in effect. Underwater erosion may cause the collapse of the levee, rotting piles bring down the aged structure of the longshore, or excessive weight cause the collapse of a bridge already strained by flood water. Sleepy John Estes sang from personal experience of an accident when the car in which he was traveling skidded on a temporary bridge at Hickman, Kentucky.

269   Now I never will forget that floating bridge, (*three times*)
       Tell me: five minutes time under water I was hid.

       Now when I was goin' down, I throwed up my hands, (*three times*)
       Please take me on dry land.

       Now they carried me in the house and they laid me 'cross the bunk,
          (*three times*)
       'Bout a gallon, half of muddy water I had drunk.

       They dried me off and they laid me in the bed, (*three times*)
       Couldn't hear nothin' but muddy water runnin' through my head.

       Now people is standing on the bridge – was screamin' and cryin', (*three times*)
       "Lord have mercy – where's we gwine?"

North America is a continent of extremes – not only of landscape but of climate, where temperatures in one city may range from many degrees below zero in the height of winter, to excessive heat well above 100° in the summer. Mention has already been made of the severe drought which affected the South a couple of years after the rains, a foretaste of the Dust Bowl years, further west. Sang Spider Carter:

270   I woke up this morning just about half past four, (*twice*)
       All I could feel was hard luck knockin' on my door.

       It's so dry down home folks can't plant cotton and corn,
       It's so dry down here, folks can't plant taters and corn,
       Ain't done nothin', since the dry spell's been on.

       Everywhere that I went, was nothin' but bad news, (*twice*)
       That's why I'm singing these worst ole dry spell blues.

The north-east Atlantic Seaboard is noted for its severity of climate, but so, too, is the mid-West where the Great Plains experience vast differences of temperature and climatic conditions. Up the Mississippi Basin, along the Missouri and into Canada cyclones and whirlwinds are far from uncommon. Some may expend themselves within a distance of two or three miles, while others may travel much greater distances and be of a force that wrecks all but the most firmly built structures. The slum buildings that house the greater proportion of the city-dwelling Blacks, and almost all of those who live in rural districts, are small defense against the ferocity of these freak storms. Such a cyclone of more than usual severity struck St. Louis in the early afternoon of 29 September, 1927. Elzadie Robinson recounted the event, which in only five minutes took the lives of eighty-four people and did a hundred million dollars' worth of damage.

271   I was sittin' in my kitchen, lookin' out across the sky, (*twice*)
       I thought the world was ending, I started into cry.

       The wind was howling, the buildings begin to fall, (*twice*)
       I seen that mean old twister comin' just like a cannon-ball.

       The world was black as midnight, I never heard such a noise before,
          (*twice*)
       Like a million lions, if turned loose they all roar.

       The shack where we was livin', reeled and rocked but never fell, (*twice*)
       How the cyclone started, nobody but the Lord can tell.

Characterized by the heavy, black, storm clouds which foretell the imminence of the phenomenon, and the revolving column of dust, earth, and cloud which makes contact with the land, the cyclone presents a fearsome sight. Revolving counter-clockwise, it travels invariably in an easterly to north-easterly direction laying a path of destruction in its wake. Though people and animals, farm buildings and implements are sucked up and cast down by the whirling force of the wind, the destructive power lies primarily in the sudden drop in the barometric pressure that occurs with the advent of a cyclone. The air pressure within the buildings literally blows them apart and the wind takes up and throws down the pieces. On the "water coast" of Texas the whirlwinds produce dramatic waterspouts which pass rapidly across the sea and, traveling on over the land, wreak havoc as the soil is drawn up into the spiraling stem.

As a "twister" approached, the outer perimeter of the storm sent screens flapping, tore away loose fence rails and whipped the loose earth into choking eddies of dust. In the face of the twister's uncontrollable forces Lightnin' Hopkins regained his faith, for a while at any rate.

272 Yes, I was sittin' in my kitchen, I was lookin' way out across the waves, (*twice*)
 I see that mean old twister comin', I started in to pray.

 I fell down on my knees, these is the words I begin to say, (*twice*)
 I said, "Oh Lord, have mercy and help us in our wicked ways."

 Yeah, you know the wind was blowin', comin' in my windows and doors, (*twice*)
 Yeah, you know my house done fell down and I can't live there no more.

 I said, "Lord, Lord what shall we do? (*twice*)
 Yes, there ain't no other help I know, oh Lord, but you."

Just as the Japanese learned to adapt themselves to the havoc caused by earthquakes and made use of light-framed, thin screen structures that would not cause fatalities if they collapsed, so too the inhabitants of the islands of the West Indies and of the Florida coast adapted their building techniques to combat the effects of the hurricanes that sweep the Gulf of Mexico. Some employed heavy battens and beams to secure all loose fittings and doors, if their homes were sufficiently strong to withstand the force of the winds. Others prepared for the possible wreckage that might occur and, like St. Louis Jimmy, accepted philosophically the hazards of living in a warm, but far from equable, climate.

273 Some speak about tornadoes – the hurricane's the worst of all, (*twice*)
 They come and go through Florida, blow down fourteen feet of wall.

Hurricane is so powerful, blowed the house away where I live, (*twice*)
It make the hair rise on your head, give you fever with cold chills.

Winter clothes are not needed, you spend money rebuildin' your home,
    (*twice*)
When the ocean gets rough you're not in Florida all alone.

I really like Florida, if the wind don't blow me away, (*twice*)
But if that don't never happen, I'll be in Florida the rest of my days.

In the tinder-boxes of the rural "dog-trots" with their draught corridors separating their rooms, and the "shot-gun" shacks, wood-framed and with rooms built in line, that could be found on the outskirts of many a southern town, there was a greater danger of fire. Their structure encouraged strong draughts that fanned the flames; the dry timbers, the newspaper-covered walls ignited easily and were soon reduced to ashes. There was little that could be done: among the blues singers there was a favorite verse, recorded as early as 1926 by Gertrude "Ma" Rainey:

274   Your house catches on fire and ain't no water 'round,
      If your house catch on fire, ain't no water roun'
      Throw your trunk out the window let it burn on down.

On the local government of an "incorporated town" falls the responsibility of providing adequate drainage, mains water supply, and an efficient system of fire prevention. When the United States entered the war there were nearly 66,000 homes in Mississippi without a toilet or privy of any kind; nearly 78,500 in Alabama and 75,000 in North Carolina in which, needless to say, a disproportionately high percentage were tenanted by Blacks. Of these, the majority had no mains water supply nearby illustrating the perfunctory discharge of duties by local governments and indicating the inadequate facilities available for fire control. Many of these homes were in the black sectors of towns and not in rural areas, but even in New Orleans a single hydrant had to serve the water needs of a whole street. Similarly, the services offered for the protection and prevention of fire in these districts was frequently hopelessly inadequate. When the black smoke rose above a clutch of wooden homes in Brownsville, Tennessee, Sleepy John Estes could only pray that the Fire Department would come and that no one would hinder them on their way.

275 "Now, go call the Fire Department for my house is burnin' down,"
     (*twice*)
     You know that musta be at li'l Marthy Hardin, 'cause it's on the north
     side of town.

     I see the people is runnin' an' I wonder who could it be, (*twice*)
     You know that musta be li'l Marthy Hardin, I saw them turn down on
     Wilson Street.

     "When you see the Chief, boys, please clear the street," (*twice*)
     'Cause you know he's goin' down, save li'l Marthy Hardin's home for
     me.

     She's a hard-workin' woman, you know her salaries is very small,
     (*twice*)
     Then when she pay up her house-rent, that don't leave anything for
     insurance at all.

     Now I wrote li'l Marthy a letter, five days it returned back to me.
     (*twice*)
     "You know li'l Marthy's house done burned down; she done move
     over on Bradford Street."

Black homes – whether country shanties or tenement homes in the towns –
make a poor risk for the insurance companies. Premiums tend to be high and
insurance companies do not solicit the custom of those whose poverty may
make it difficult for them to keep up their instalments. So inflammable are
their homes and poor the property that some fire departments were
indifferent to the burning of rural shacks that were sufficiently apart not to
be a source of danger to other buildings.

    Openings for graft and corruption were many, and there was little redress
for inefficient work. Blacks had little faith in the persons appointed to
supervise fire prevention or control and the investigation of likely and actual
causes, especially when insurance claims were involved.

276 My house burning down, the firemen are taking their time, (*twice*)
     "Please, Mister Fire Detective, won't you save this old cabin of mine?"

     I spend my money looking to be happy some day, (*twice*)
     Now my house burned down, I ain't got no place to stay.

That fire detective, he don't mean me no good, (*twice*)
Let my house burn to ashes, didn't leave me one stick of wood.

My house burned down, didn't leave me a doggone thing, (*twice*)
Reason why it worried me to hear that fire-bell ring.

Dobby Bragg's tragedy was a private one, shared only by the members of his family and friends within his immediate neighborhood. But the burning down of a public place is a disaster which is shared by many, and the loss of a public personality who has perished is the concern of large numbers of people who have no immediate acquaintance with him. Black dancers, sportsmen, athletes, entertainers, and musicians were frequently termed "Race Heroes" or "Race Men" for they had challenged the alleged supremacy of the Whites on their own terms and had been successful in achieving equal esteem in their fields. As public figures their success was more spectacular than that of an academician, or a scientist perhaps, whose achievements, whilst of great importance in the national interest, had not the same popular appeal. Walter Barnes was a band leader of some distinction in jazz and swing music whose death, under especially tragic circumstances, shocked the black world. In spite of the lack of a railroad to the town some five hundred people had gathered in Natchez to attend a dance promoted by the Natchez Rhythm Club where Walter Barnes and his Orchestra were providing the music. To prevent curious outsiders from peering into the dance hall, a timber-framed, sheet-metal-clad building, the windows were securely battened across and boarded. When the dance was in full swing there was a sudden outbreak of fire. Panic-stricken dancers, unable to escape by the windows, jammed the single doorway, trampling scores to death as the dance hall became a holocaust. Two hundred people perished in the flames, including Walter Barnes and all but three members of his Orchestra. With the incident still burning in his memory Leonard Caston – Baby Doo – sang:

277   Lord I want everyone now to listen, listen to my lonesome song, (*twice*)
Lord I want to state what happened to po' old Walter Barnes.

Lord it was just about midnight, just about twelve o'clock, (*twice*)
Poor Walter played his theme song, the dancehall begin to rock.

Lord and the peoples all was dancin', enjoyin' their lives so hard, (*twice*)
Just in a short while – the dancehall was full of fire.

Sharing the sorrow of his friends and that of countless other Blacks on that April day in 1940, Gene Gilmore added his own epitaph and tried to offer a little comfort to the bereaved:

278   Lord, I know, I know – how you Natchez people feel today, *(twice)*
      Some of them thinking of the fire that took their children's life away.

      Lord, it was late one Tuesday night, people had come from miles
         around, *(twice)*
      They was enjoyin' their lives when that Rhythm Club went down.

      Lord, it was sad and misery when the hearses began to roll, *(twice)*
      There was over two hundred dead and gone, Lord, and they can't come
         here no more.

      I'm gonna tell all you people, to listen to what I have to say, *(twice)*
      Don't be uneasy 'bout your children, because they are all at rest today.

The Natchez Fire was a tragedy of great significance to Blacks; it was of little more than passing consequence to white persons – including those in Natchez itself, then a notorious center of racial discrimination. Not that Americans, white or black, were greatly interested in national issues that did not affect them personally. These were isolationist years, and international affairs impressed them even less. There is little indication in the blues of an awareness of what was happening in what was, to many Americans in the idiom of the time, a "cockeyed world." But there are occasional hints that Benito Mussolini's attack on Ethiopia, the epitome of white aggression against Blacks, was known about. In Jackson, Mississippi, in 1935, Minnie Wallace wrestled with what little she knew.

279   It's war in Ethiopia and mama's feeling blue, *(twice)*
      I tell the cockeyed world I don't know what to do.

      They say that Ethiopia is a long way from here, *(twice)*
      They trying to steal my man and hurry him over there.

      This cockeyed world will make your good man treat you mean, *(twice)*
      He will treat you just like a poor girl he never seen.

      It's war in Ethiopia and my man won't behave, *(twice)*
      I tell the cockeyed world I'll spit in my baby's face.

Even if her man did wish to fight in Ethiopia, Minnie Wallace had good reason to be suspicious of government intentions. In the depths of the Depression poor Blacks were bitter about the non-payment of bonus money to war veterans. Some joined the "Bonus Expeditionary Force" and marched, with their white ex-servicemen comrades, on Washington in July, 1932; they suffered the tear gas and the burning of their camps by Federal troops led by General MacArthur. Others, like Carl Martin, waited to see what would happen, singing in mock-patriotism,

> 280   Now listen all you veteran soldiers, who live in this town,
> Let's take off our hats, thanks to Uncle Sam.
>
> Lots of you are crippled, gassed, blind and cannot see,
> But we came back home with the Victory,
> > So when I get my bonus, I'm sure gonna have my fun,
> > I'm just sittin' here waitin', waitin' till my bonus come.
>
> Ain't gonna drink no more moonshine, nothing but "Bottled in
> Bond,"
> Cook up meals, pitch a boogie woogie, boys from sun to sun.
>
> Ain't had no good times since 19 and 29
> Times have been so tight, couldn't save a lousy dime,
> > So when I get my bonus, [etc.]

President Hoover made his position on the payment of the Bonus to Army veterans abundantly clear: "I am absolutely opposed to any such legislation," he announced. It was Hoover who had stated that there were "No hungry men in America." Not surprisingly he was voted out of office, and on the day that every bank in America closed, March 4, 1933, President Franklin Delano Roosevelt moved into the White House. In the "hundred days" that introduced so much new legislation many expected that the bonus money (still not due until 1945) would be paid out. It was a long time coming, as Joe Pullum indicated in a cautionary blues.

> 281   1935 is gone, 1935 is gone, in come 19 and 36, (*twice*)
> I'm going to get the rest of my bonus money, Lord and get my business
> fixed.
>
> Men be careful, men be careful, who you give your money to, (*twice*)
> Because as soon as you get broke, you know the whole round world is
> through with you.

Everywhere I turn, everywhere I turn, there's somebody there that
    wants to talk with me, (*twice*)
But it's all concerning nothing but my bonus money.

They are advising me, they are advising me, just like they did before,
    (*twice*)
But I'm going to put my money in the bank and be a fool no more.

War veterans had little reason to feel that their hardships in battle, and the sacrifices of their comrades, had brought them either benefit or gratitude. So there was little concern for the fears of war that were growing in Europe. Then, a fortnight after the Natchez fire, Hitler's army invaded Belgium and Holland, ignoring the latter's neutrality. Rotterdam was destroyed by the Luftwaffe and in a matter of days Panzer Divisions had bypassed the reputedly impregnable Maginot Line. The evacuation of the British troops at Dunkirk was followed on June 15, 1940 by the fall of Paris. Within a month Hitler had conquered mainland Europe. The news even reached the Florida Kid, Ernest Blunt, but his response was defeatist.

282 Woman I done told you, told you once or twice,
    Bring me plenty of lovin' before Hitler takes our lives,
        Because Hitler he's a bad man, tryin' to take every country now,
        Well, before he takes this country woman, please be my
        so-and-so.

Well ole Hitler says he's a man from his feet to his chest,
He don't bother with nobody but God and Death,

Hitler got his just-right tanks, his planes and his ships,
Get over your town he'll let his big boat slip.

Hitler says some of our people are white, says some are brown and
    black,
But Hitler say all that matters to him, they look just alike.

Well you better mind how you get drunk, be careful how you clown,
You wake up some of these mornings, Hitler be right in your town,
    Because Hitler he's a bad man [etc.]

Just a month to the day after the Florida Kid recorded his blues, an event occurred which had more far-reaching effects than those occasioned by any other disaster; a man-made catastrophe that ultimately exceeded any tragedies caused by natural forces; that embraced all colors, all races.

On December 7, 1941, in the midst of peace negotiations, Japanese dive-bombers, in an act of flagrant aggression, made a sudden surprise attack on the major United States Naval Base of Pearl Harbor in the Hawaiian Islands. Important military and naval installations were wrecked and a battleship, three destroyers, a target ship, and other craft were sunk. American naval strength in the Pacific was paralyzed by the blow which was timed to coincide with attacks on Guam, Midway, and Wake Islands and points in the Philippines, all made without declaration of war. The campaigns of the non-interventionists were of no avail for the United States was dramatically drawn into the war. Anger at the attack surged in the heart of the nation, and people of every social group living under the Stars and Stripes shared the fury and the pain.

283   December the seventh, nineteen and forty-one, (*twice*)
  The Japanese flew over Pearl Harbor and droppin' them bombs by the
   ton.

  The Japanese is so ungrateful, just like a stray dog in the street, (*twice*)
  Well he bites the hand that feeds him soon as he gets enough to eat.

  Some says the Japanese is hard fighters but any dummy ought to know,
   (*twice*)
  Even a rattlesnake won't bite you in the back, he will warn you before
   he strikes his blow.

  I turned on my radio and I heard Mr. Roosevelt say, (*twice*)
  "We wanted to stay out of Europe and Asia but now we all got a debt
   to pay."

  We even sold the Japanese brass and scrap-iron and it makes my blood
   boil in the vein, (*twice*)
  'Cause they made bombs and shells out of it and dropped them on Pearl
   Harbor just like rain.

In "Doctor" Clayton's blues there is evidence of a racial hatred justifiable under the circumstances and in time of war no doubt, though not when the recipients were loyal countrymen. For no reason apart from their color and their national origins Japanese Americans were poorly treated during the war and put in concentration camps largely for their own protection from fellow Americans. Race and nationality were being confused in the familiar manner by persons who saw no incongruity in accepting as the Supreme Commander of Allied Forces a man with German ancestry when they attacked others of their nation for their derivation. Blacks were guilty of such discrimination too, but they were spurred on by their frustration and humiliation when they found that this was to be a "White Man's War." Some Blacks were not surprised. They remembered that only ten per cent of the colored draftees in World War I saw combat service overseas; that the majority of black soldiers had been employed as stevedores, in the sanitary and labor corps; that the French had been issued with official "Secret Information Concerning Black American Troops" insisting on segregation; that the fact that black troops were the first of any Allied forces to set foot on enemy soil had been as swiftly forgotten as the gallant record of the 369th Cavalry; that within a year after the war many returning black servicemen were lynched.

When they received their registration papers, when they were "billed out and bound to go," when they sat and waited in perplexed helplessness for their medical examinations and their aptitude tests, there was a certain understandable lack of enthusiasm on the part of some Blacks to participate in the war. Others, like Big Bill Broonzy, took a more objective view.

284 I was sittin' here wonderin' with my number, in that old goldfish bowl, (*twice*)
    An' when I heard my number called, oooh Lord, I couldn't feel happy to save my soul.

    Everywhere I go I see that same ole "158," (*twice*)
    I knew I was billed up baby, ooh Lord, Uncle Sam say, "Bill don't be late."

    All you young men, I mean come and follow me, (*twice*)
    American soldiers went befo' – oooh Lord, well, why can't we?

There were only two black line officers in the regular United States Army in 1940 and the four black regiments – two infantry, two cavalry – were commanded by white officers. It was impossible for a black serviceman to enter the Marines, or for him to enter the Navy in any other capacity than as a mess attendant. Black troops in World War I had been primarily used for pioneer work with spade and pick even when they had been sent overseas for combat duties, and the prospect seemed little better in 1941. As Big Boy Crudup made clear, it was with some cynicism that many a colored draftee faced the prospect of going to war to die a hero in a segregated army, the struggle for survival in his segregated home district still in his mind.

285   I've got my questionairy and they need me in the war, (*twice*)
Now if I feel murder, don't have to break the county law.

All I want is a 32–20, made on a .45 frame, (*twice*)
Yes, and a red, white and blue flag waving in my right hand.

Now if I go down, with a red, white and blue flag in my hand, (*twice*)
Say, you can bet your life poor Crudup sent-a many man . . .

Mmmmm – "Hero" is all I crave, (*twice*)
Now when I'm dead and gone, write "Hero" on my grave.

Three million African Americans registered for service and a million were drafted, of whom half were to see service overseas; a considerable improvement on the situation in World War I. Though there were some who were inclined to let "the Whites fight their own war," the majority were eager to fight and the disappointment of those who were too old for service or who were not considered fit enough was real. Inevitably some vented their feelings on those who were departing or more good-naturedly goaded them as they left. When Brownie McGhee said he was going to "carry the coal" for the servicemen and "carry his business on" the soldier knew well enough that the reference was to the woman that he had left behind rather than to his neglected home.

286   Uncle Sam ain't no woman, but he sure can take your man, (*twice*)
Yes, gonna be many a young wife left back here cold in hand.

Uncle Sam will send you your questionnaire – what in the world you
    goin' to do? (*twice*)
Well you know you got to go – no need of feelin' blue.

Well, all you young men looks worried, blue as blue can be, (*twice*)
Well I've always got a smile on my face, Uncle Sam sure cain't bother
    me

Well, it's when you gone to the camp, no need to think about home,
    (*twice*)
I'll be back here carryin' your coal and kindlin' in, tryin' to carry your
    business on.

For any departing soldier the separation from his wife, his sweetheart, or his family is a sad and strained one. The tension as the time drew near, the fumbling for words that seemed so inadequate to express the mixed emotions of those who departed and those who were left behind, have been shared by millions of men and women as they have tried to comfort and reassure their partners. Walter Davis accurately captured the emotional conflict that they felt.

287   I was down at the platform with the tears standin' in my eyes, (*twice*)
Lord, my heart was goin' pitter-patter, because I hate to say good-bye.

The boys was standin' all around me dressed in that khaki uniform,
    (*twice*)
Lord, I heard that train whistle blowin' an' I know it won't be long.

"Baby will you please be a sweet girl now, baby, whilst I'm gone
    away, (*twice*)
Lord, I won't be back to you soon – but I'll be back, mama, some ole
    day."

"Lord, I hear that train whistle blowin', must-a be comin' after me,
    (*twice*)
Lord, mama, I'm just as unhappy, Lord as any po' man can be."

Black "rookies" were drafted to strictly segregated camps for training and commenced to prepare for war in earnest. The first extensions of the colored section of the Army had been the addition of a regiment of engineers, one of artillery, and a dozen truck companies, and further increases were slowly made. White officers still commanded the regiments, and in fact the advances that had been made by the end of World War I in the training of over six hundred black officers had been lost. Even at the end of World War II only four black officers had graduated from West Point and none from Anapolis. But though their chances of promotion were slender, trainees of all types prepared for combat. It is possible that a number of popular blues singers of the period, including Roosevelt Sykes, were prevailed upon to record patriotic stanzas in their blues and thus help counter the apathy to the war which many Blacks felt.

288   You may be mean as a lion, you may be humble as a lamb, (*twice*)
Just take your mind off your wife and put it on Uncle Sam.

I want all of you draftees to put your mind on your training camp,
    (*twice*)
So when you meet Hitler, your powder won't feel damp.

Just pack your suitcase, get ready to leave your mate, (*twice*)
You know you got to go and help save the United States.

When the day of embarkation leave came black soldiers were full of hope, returning to their homes for the last few days before crossing the U-boat infested waters for Europe, or commencing the hazardous voyage to the American bases in the Pacific. In those brief hours the reality of the imminent separation was inescapable. War is brutal and war is bloody; the soldier knows it. His training prepared him for its severity; he had learned to shoot and bayonet and he knew that his mission was to "kill the enemy." In the quiet moments of the embarkation leave he was likely to realize the truth of what he was fighting for. Like an experienced gambler, Lonnie Johnson stated the odds.

289   Please do the best you can, I'll be back to you some day, (*twice*)
    I will keep on fighting, with you in my heart I'll battle my way

    To keep you from suffering, baby, I don't mind dyin',
    Every Jap I kill, that'll be peace for you po' li'l mind.
    I know I can't kill them all, but I'll give them a heck of a time.

    You can watch the headlights shinin' as far as your poor li'l eyes can
        see, (*twice*)
    And you can tell the world that I'm fightin' for what really belongs to
        me.

The United States Navy and the Marines relaxed their restrictions and admitted Blacks into the services, but the majority who embarked for the theaters of war were destined for service in the Army. They were fighting fit and prepared for the front line, but when they arrived at their overseas bases many combat units found that they were to be employed as service troops, as stevedores and pioneers – a misuse of their training which had the gravest effects on their morale. Actual armed fighting broke out between colored and white servicemen at European and North American bases, and serious instances of Jim Crow discrimination occurred in the Pacific theater of war. When given their opportunity to fight, black troops engaged in battle with almost fanatical recklessness, determined to prove their worth. In spite of the effects of much racial trouble the famous 92nd Division which in Italy fought for twelve months against the crack German Panzer Divisions was covered in glory, though a quarter of its men were lost. Many of the men fought in the front line under the most hazardous conditions for five months without relief, and culminating its advance with the liberation of Genoa, the Division gained twelve thousand decorations. Equally outstanding were the black troops that acquitted themselves with such distinction and heroism at Anzio, whilst no white soldiers who fought beside them will forget the courage and tenacity of the Negro 761st Battalion in the Battle of the Bulge. In all, some twenty-two black combat units saw service in Europe, and earned the highest praise for their contributions. Equally distinguished was the work of the ordnance troops who unloaded over twenty million tons of cargo and, in the course of operating the famous *Red Ball Express*, performed the remarkable feat of moving 19,000 troops to the front line in a single night. But all this time the Red Cross maintained segregated camps and catering facilities, and contrary to every scrap of evidence available from anthropologists, insisted on segregating Negro blood in the blood banks for transfusion: an action all the more ironic because the blood bank in England was then under the charge of an African American, Dr. Charles Drew of Howard University. There was good reason for Blind Boy Fuller to wonder whether any sense could be made of the war by an ordinary G.I. in combat.

290   This war is ragin', what're you men goin' to do? (*twice*)
       If Uncle Sam calls you in the war, there's no use to feelin' blue.

       Eeeh, when you' fightin', blood runnin' in yo' face, (*twice*)
       There's no use to worryin' – this world is a funny old place . . .

In the United States Air Force the position was somewhat better, though General Marshall had declared in 1940 that "there is no such thing as colored aviation at this time," even after the training of black pilots had been urged by the Senate. Blacks were trained for flying duties when war broke out and, as Sonny Boy Williamson knew, the prospect of getting into the cockpit of a fighter was immensely attractive to men wishing to get into action.

291   Uncle Sam is gonna give me a Thunderbolt, he want me to fly away up
       above the clouds, (*twice*)
       He wants me to drop a bomb on the Japanese, I really got to make my
       baby proud.

I want a machine gun and I want to be hid out in the woods, *(twice)*
I want to show old man Hitler that Sonny Boy don't mean him no
  good.

I want to drop a bomb, and set the Japanese city on fire, *(twice)*
Now because they are so rotten, I just love to see them die.

I've got the Victory Blues because I know I've got to go, *(twice)*
Now to keep the dirty Japanese from slipping in through my baby's
  back door.

Justly celebrated were the pilots of the Fifteenth Air Force in the all-black
99th Pursuit Squadrons under Colonel B. O. Davis, Jnr., who were
continually praised by Field-Marshal Montgomery for their protection and
support of the Eighth Army. The 99th were known as the "Red Tails" and
their heroism in North Africa and in Italy will be forgotten neither by the
American and British troops who saw them in action, nor by the Germans
who so feared their low-level strafing attacks. In one outstanding raid the
Red Tails destroyed eighty-three German aircraft and many installations at
an airfield in Rumania; they gave strong support to Allied landings and
were warmly praised by Marshal Tito for their work in Yugoslavia.

Long before the end of the war, Blacks had proved that they could live
and fight and die as bravely, as well, and with as much honor, as any of their
countrymen. Some would never return to their country, and their remains
lay buried in countries far from their homeland. They died for the
preservation of liberty in a country that denied them much. Those who had
died were spared the pain that was shared by many of those who returned.
Bitter racialism was encountered by many who had anticipated that their
war service had cleared away the cruelties of segregation. Within the first
three post-war years more than forty Blacks were lynched and many more
were murdered or silently disappeared.

In July 1948 President Harry S. Truman signed Executive Order 9981
which required that "there shall be equality of treatment and opportunity
for all persons in the Armed Services without regard to race, color, religion,
or national origin." It was intended to lead to the desegregation of the
Army, but this was opposed by the Joint Chiefs of Staff.

A couple of years later there was a new call to arms. On June 25, 1950
troops from the Republic of North Korea crossed the 38th Parallel and
invaded South Korea. Though defending troops retreated before the
invading forces they were repulsed at the railhead of Yech'on, which was

regained by the all-black 24th Infantry Regiment newly arrived from the United States. Though the black troops fought courageously, back home there were many who wanted no part in another war. "This world is in a tangle," mused Mr. Honey,

292   This world is in a tangle baby now, everybody singin' a song,
      They're fightin 'cross the water baby, ain't gonna be here long,
            I'm gonna build myself a cave so I can move down on the
                ground,
            So when I go into the Army darlin', won't be no Reds around.

      I was layin' down in my bed, baby now, drunk as I could be,
      I was layin' there drunk, when Uncle Sam start in after me,
            I'm gonna build myself a cave, [etc.]

That the 24th Infantry was an entirely black regiment was a matter of pride on the one hand, but evidence of the segregation that still persisted in the Army on the other. Black troops continued to serve with distinction, even though the official history of the U.S. Army in the Korean War was heavily prejudiced against them. A number of blues were recorded about the war, but the eagerness to engage in the fighting which was a marked characteristic of blues in World War II was missing. Sunnyland Slim's blues was typical.

293   I was laying in my bed, turn on my radio, (*twice*)
      All I could hear was the news about the war.

      Way up in the sky, airplanes flyin' just like birds, (*twice*)
      Well I got my questionnaire this morning and you know I sure got to
          go.

      Well they're fightin' over in Korea and you know that ain't no fun,
          (*twice*)
      Every minute of the day I can hear nothin' but noisy guns.

      I got to go back to the old Army, but I hate to leave my little baby
          behind, (*twice*)
      'Cause duty has called me, you know I have got to go.

After the dismissal of General MacArthur by President Truman, whose authority he had attempted to subvert, General Ridgeway succeeded in securing an armistice in July 1951, after which prolonged negotiations for the exchange of prisoners commenced. The United States had suffered over 33,500 dead; the combined divisions of the other United Nations lost fewer than 3,200. Slowly the servicemen who were not holding the truce along the 38th Parallel came home.

> 294   Yeah you know the war is over, now I've got a chance to go back home, (*twice*)
> Yes, you know that woman spend all of my money, I'm gonna whip her for doin' me wrong.
>
> You know that mother been prayin', "Father send my poor child back home." (*twice*)
> Yes but you know it's a sin and a shame to come back, find every dime he has made is gone.
>
> Now the war is over, baby now ain't you glad, (*twice*)
> You know you can get back to your black used-to-be, have the good times that you used to had.

Disillusion, fear of the reality of the return, and a desire for future stability were symbolized in Lightnin' Hopkins's blues. But the war was not lost for Blacks. Those who died in the service of their country died for the freedom of all their countrymen, and the overwhelming majority of those who lived came back to continue to wage the war for the freedom of the individual at home: a war against prejudice and ignorance.

10   *Going down slow*

Some of their leaders contend that Blacks have never lost a race riot. In view of the tragic loss of life, the beatings, and oppression that have characterized the riots, this would seem a curious paradox. Blacks have been jailed for incitement to riot when they themselves have been the victims, whilst their aggressors have escaped punishment. But eventually the truth became known; in the long run, reforms followed the riots and each occurrence led thousands of people of all colors and classes to try and prevent any such event happening again. They have not always succeeded, but as in the case of lynching, the cumulative effect has resulted in social advancement for Blacks. Similarly, the great natural disasters of flood and fire and storm, and the manmade disaster of war, though bringing great misery and suffering for many at the time, have at least resulted in the betterment of conditions revealed by these calamities.

There are two sides to every argument, and though in their treatment of black refugees and soldiers the American Red Cross were culpable for much wrong, their actions were sometimes motivated by reasons not immediately apparent, which were ultimately designed for the Blacks' benefit. Blacks were put in "concentration camps" and their confinement was real, often occasioning much hardship, but it was occasionally a necessary expedient to prevent the spread of disease. When the Red Cross found that they had hundreds of thousands of Blacks and "poor Whites" in their immediate care they discovered sickness and disease rampant to an extent that had scarcely been suspected. The Mississippi floods brought thousands of Blacks whose necks and hands bore the hideous red rash of pellagra to the Red Cross camps. On the bodies of many, ulcers that refused to heal indicated that they were close to death. At least seven thousand people in the South died every year from pellagra and within the flood states alone some fifty thousand persons suffering from the malady were believed to be living. Knowing nothing of pellagra, the temporarily appointed Red Cross medical director William de Kline approached Dr. Joseph Goldberger of the Public Health Service, appealing to him to help those who were slowly dying.

295 Some people say that I'm dead, but it's all a big mistake, *(twice)*
Some say they were at my funeral, some say they was at my wake.

I'm in a bad condition, and I'm still going down slow, *(twice)*
The place I'm going, there's a thousand others to go.

The doctor he told me I would get well some day, *(twice)*
People, he may be right – then it may be the other way.

Now the time has come, I've got to take it real slow, *(twice)*
I'm in a bad condition, can't do as I did before.

Goldberger, who had devoted years to the study of pellagra, knew why the victims were, in St. Louis Jimmy's words, in a "bad condition," why they were "going down slow" and not dying from a sudden attack of a disease. His experiments had revealed that pellagra was not contagious; injecting himself, his wife, and assistants with discharges from the sores and with the excreta of pellagrins, he could not produce the symptoms of the illness. It was clear to him that pellagra was the disease of a class. Poor people suffered from it; rich persons did not. The difference he believed, and subsequently proved, was one of nutrition. Blacks and "poor Whites" lived on three staple items: cornbread, fat meat, and black molasses. Convict volunteers from Rankin Prison Farm, Mississippi, submitted themselves as subjects for his experiments in return for their freedom. Those that were kept on this limited diet, which was prevalent in the prison farms at the time, eventually contracted the illness, as did thousands of other people who were forced by poverty to live on the identical diet. "I don't want no cornbread, meat, black molasses," ran a song common in the chain gangs throughout the South, and noted by Odum and Johnson before blues appeared on record. Goldberger's cure was two cents' worth of yeast a day for every pellagrin.

His measures proved startlingly successful but when the treated persons became cured they were inclined to dispense with the yeast treatment without making any changes in their diet, and slowly succumbed to the disease once more. It became necessary to persuade southern Negroes to make up their dietary deficiency by growing greenstuffs which would avert the attacks of pellagra. Figures for the reduction of the disease fluctuated for many years, affected by ignorance, prejudice, famine, and drought. In turnip greens, a crop was found that strengthened the consumer's resistance to pellagra immeasurably. But whereas Pink Anderson sang that he was "crazy 'bout them greasy greens," Charlie Jackson moaned that "turnip greens, turnip greens: that's somethin' that I don't eat." The Federal State Department of Agriculture and the Red Cross together had to educate the croppers and landowners who were working the land to its ultimate sterility, to grow food that would provide the nourishment that they needed. In the similar fight against scurvy and other diseases resulting from serious vitamin deficiencies, medical practitioners had been constantly frustrated by the mistrust in which the farmers held them. Many a Black and "poor White" alike regarded the free supply of vitamin enriched drinks with suspicion. It took many years before they could be assured that they were not the victims of a commercial deception.

296 My grandma left this morning with her basket in her hand,
She's goin' down to the warehouse, to see the warehouse man.

She got down to the warehouse, them white folks say it ain't no use,
For the Government ain't givin' away nothin' but that canned
    grapefruit juice.

While pellagra could be related to poverty, silicosis was a disease of employment. Frequently fatal, it was a lung ailment that was caused by the inhalation of dust particles and was common among mine workers. Though Whites were almost exclusively employed in the anthracite industry and in much of bituminous coal mining, Blacks were taken on during World War I and were sometimes employed for strike-breaking. Black miners were mainly employed in the iron ore mines of Tennessee and Virginia, where the work was dangerous and unpleasant. They worked the sulphur mines of Texas and the phosphate rock mines of Florida and Tennessee. They were prominent in the granite quarries of the Carolinas and Georgia, and were extensively employed in tunneling for the railroads.

In most of these jobs they were "pick and shovel" workers, exposed to heavy concentrations of stone dust and other injurious particles, often in confined spaces. Scores suffered the consequences of inhaling them, graphically described by Pinewood Tom (Joshua White) who was still in his 'teens.

297 Now silicosis, you a dirty robber and a thief, (*twice*)
Rob me of my right to live, and all you brought poor me was grief.

I was there diggin' that tunnel for six bits a day, (*twice*)
Didn't know I was diggin' my own grave, silicosis eat my lungs away.

I says "Mama, Mama, Mama, cool my fevered head (*twice*)
And when I meet my Jesus, God knows I'll soon be dead."

Six bits I get for diggin', diggin' that tunnel hole, (*twice*)
Take me away from my baby, it sure done wrecked my soul.

Neither pellagra nor silicosis was contagious, but other diseases were transmitted by carriers, by rodents, by food, and above all by insanitary living conditions. In the South the lack of window screens in black homes meant that there was no prevention against the admission of malaria-carrying mosquitoes and disease-transmitting flies. Typhus and other diseases arising from poor storage facilities for water reserves raged unchecked, and the total lack of sanitation in many homes was the cause of untold illnesses and unnumbered deaths. Amongst the most virulent diseases in the 1930s was tuberculosis which attacked young and old, eating its way through the lungs of its victims. Generally it lay undetected until the sufferer had reached too advanced a stage in the disease for a cure to be effected. By that time the members of his family and his associates could have become infected, the coughing consumptive spraying the seeds of death. "Everybody spit in your face ain't friend to you," sang Jim Jackson, but his words had a deeper, more tragic significance. In the later stages the disease becomes apparent to all who see the sufferer and their elementary knowledge of the killing germs warns them to keep away.

For the relatives who, in all probability, had already breathed in the infection and were themselves in the early stages of the disease, it was acutely distressing to see the consumptive in the throes of tuberculosis.

298   Said "Lord, don't you go, baby, 'cause you sure really worryin' me,"
"Don't you go, now baby, 'cause you really is worryin' po' me,
I leave in the mornin' now, sweet mama, I'm goin' back to Jackson,
Tennessee."

She said, "Don't go, baby! Oh baby, I believe to my soul I'm dyin',
(*twice*) (yes, yes, yes)
If I ain't dyin' now, black man, I believe to all my soul I'm lyin'."

"Oh, don't go down, baby, cause I ain't gonna tell you even no lie,
Don't go down, baby, I ain't even tell you no lie,
Say you quit me now, little woman, and oh, that's the day you gonna
die."

"Wouldn't mind dyin' now, baby, but I gotta go by myself, (*twice*)
I don't mind dyin' now, little woman, I'm gwina carry me someone
else."

"Mmmmm, oh well dyin' is hard to me,"
Says "Oh, well, baby, dyin' sho is hard to me."
My baby told "You don't die easy baby, but you sho's gonna have the
doggone T.B."

Robert Petway came to Chicago from Mississippi to record this blues. Tuberculosis was rife in the northern cities where the overcrowding had created so much suffering. In the early thirties a single block in Harlem where four thousand Blacks were crammed together, had a tubercular death rate which was twice that of the whole of Manhattan. It was known grimly as the "lung block." Compared with the rate for New York City as a whole, the death rates from consumption in Harlem during the 1930s was four times higher. But at least Blacks in the North responded to campaigns designed to reduce consumption. When Detroit commenced its fight against the disease in 1936 under a panel led by Henry Vaughn, the Health Commissioner, Bruce Douglas, tuberculosis-controller, and other determined scientists and doctors, response was encouraging. The plague centers were systematically examined and in nine months three thousand unsuspected cases were under treatment. Before the visits commenced only two per cent of Blacks in these seriously depressed areas voluntarily presented themselves for examination even though dramatic warnings were being publicized and broadcast. Even so, the rate was eight times higher than the presentation among Whites. The visiting of health officers made a considerable difference. Nearly half the black population in Detroit's plague centers had gone to the city's physicians as a result of the drive, though less than twenty per cent of white persons from these areas had submitted themselves for examination and care. Instead of the bare thirteen per cent of "minimals" – persons in preliminary stages of tuberculosis – amongst those who were treated for the disease before the campaign, it was now possible to anticipate the ravages of the disease in nearly half the cases diagnosed, bringing a cure in less than nine months. For the remainder their disease was too far advanced and a cure could only be effected for a proportion of those in hospital, whilst the others in the sanatoria succumbed to the "white death."

299   Here I lay a-cryin', something is on my mind,
      It's midnight, wonder where the nurse can be?

      I feel down, not a friend in this town, I'm blue and all alone,
      Sisters are gone, brothers are too, no one to call my own.

I can't keep from cryin'; left alone while I'm dyin',
Yes it may look crazy for me to plead on my knee,
But if the Lord's indifferent, he means to break the T.B. – oh Lord.

Yes, he railroaded me to the sanit-orium,
It's too late, too late, but I have finished my run,
This is the way all good women are done when they got the dirty T.B.

Yes I run around for months and months,
From gin-mill to gin-mill to honky-tonk,
Now it's too late, just look what I've done done,
Now I've got the dirty T.B.

Diseases of the chest and lungs accounted for a high proportion of deaths among Blacks, largely caused by exposure and insufficient protection against the weather in both housing and clothing, and inadequate attention during illness. In the late 1920s, the peak years of the pellagra outbreaks, seven times as many Blacks died from pneumonia as from pellagra, and the deaths were proportionately three and a half times as many as the rate for white persons. The resistance of the southern Black recently arrived in the North, ill-clad and ill-housed, and unaccustomed to the bitter climate, was insufficient to withstand the onslaught of winter. Blind Lemon Jefferson died in a snowstorm in Chicago just a year after recording his *Pneumonia Blues*.

> 300 I'm achin' all over, baby, b'lieve I got the pneumonia this time, (*twice*)
> An' it's all on account of that low-down gal of mine.
>
> Slippin' round the corners, running up alleys too, (*twice*)
> Watching my woman trying to see what she goin' do.
>
> Sat out in the streets one cold, dark, stormy night, (*twice*)
> Trying to see if my good gal going to make it home all right.
>
> Wearin' B.V.D.'s in the winter, prowling round in the rain, (*twice*)
> Runnin' down baby, give me this pneumonia pain.

Even more devastating and more tragic in its effects was syphilis. The social diseases of syphilis and gonorrhea destroyed the lives of innocent and guilty alike, and blighted the health of new-born children. Conditions of living in crowded districts promoted promiscuous relationships that caused the rapid spread of venereal diseases. Many Blacks were totally unaware of the dangers of the disease and how readily it might be transmitted. The high prevalence of prostitution in black areas, for reasons already outlined, further promoted the appalling incidence of these diseases.

At the end of the 1920s the mortality rate among Blacks from deaths caused by syphilis was more than eight times higher than that among white persons, and the lack of proper treatment, of elementary precautions and education aggravated the problem. In buildings where a single unhygienic and leaking toilet fixture was shared by a dozen families the spread of syphilitic infection was all too possible. Syphilis could be passed on to the offspring of infected parents. The high incidence of blindness amongst Blacks was largely due to this, some being born without vision, others blind through accident, but many others lost their sight as the effects of the disease spread through the system. At the railroad depots, on the street pavements, and in the gutters blind men begged for help from those little better off than themselves. Yet few blind blues singers gave so much as a hint of their perpetual darkness, while others, like Blind Boy Fuller, only betrayed the fact by a passing but meaningful reference.

> 301   I can tell my dog, anywhere I hear him bark,
> I can tell my rider if I feel her in the dark.
>
> You's a cold-blooded murder' when you wants me out yo' way.
> Say, that's all right, mama, you gwine-a need my help some day.

In many districts the number of blind Blacks was as much as five times as great as the respective proportion among the Whites. While often due to the hazardous nature of their work, this was primarily the result of syphilitic infection. Though some attempts to check the spread of the disease were made during the 1930s the full extent was not appreciated until the commencement in 1940 of the Draft Board reports. Only then was it realized that a quarter of the nation's adult black males were suffering from some form of the disease. A vigorous campaign to test and treat was instituted and to entice Blacks to submit themselves to Wasserman tests, free ice-cream and drinks were offered to every male who presented himself for examination, and mobile units visited the outlying districts where infection was rife and unchecked. As a result many thousands of persons were saved, the parasitic blight that was sapping their energy and health brought to an end. But with others the disease had advanced too far and no measures to end its effects were possible. Jane Lucas was realistic enough to accept the situation with terse regret, but without self-pity.

> 302   Tell all my good friends, 'cause I know I can't last long, (*twice*)
> "Please don't you wait, for I'll be dead and gone."
>
> Yes I'm sinking, sinking, sinking down below my grave, (*twice*)
> Done had a good time but, Lord, how I done paid.

That venereal diseases flourished in depressed areas was substantiated by a great deal of evidence which indicated that not only the prevalence of prostitution, but the insanitary and unhygienic standards of living were prime causes of infection. It was often economically impossible for Blacks to better themselves materially and thus reduce the risk of disease; they were exposed to illnesses of many forms because they were insufficiently equipped to oppose them. Appalling ignorance through the lack of even elementary education for Blacks in the South resulted, in many instances, in the failure to take the most fundamental precautions in the care of the invalid.

Medical facilities were often pitifully inadequate, Jim Crow hospitals refused to take black patients and the few black hospitals had no spare beds to cope with additional cases. There were only 110 black hospitals in the entire United States in the 1950s and of these less than a quarter were registered. The Julius Rosenwald Fund spent more than a million and a half dollars in fifteen years on improved health facilities, but at the end of World War II there were still only ten thousand hospital beds available for thirteen million Blacks. As the average over the nation was ten beds available for a thousand of the population, the ratio for Whites was appreciably higher; in some depressed areas only seventy-five beds were available for a million black persons. That the figures should never have been drawn in terms of color is obvious – but necessary when discrimination by color played so important a part of the medical service. So the sick Black lay in his fever upon his own bed or pallet – not only by choice but by necessity. He knew what his chances of survival might be.

"Bring me flowers whilst I'm living," sang Peetie Wheatstraw sardonically. His blues was tragically prophetic for he died in a road accident only a month after the recording was made.

303 "Bring me flowers whilst I'm living, please don't bring them when I'm dead, (*twice*)
And bring ice bags to my bedside, ooh well, to cool my achin' head."

When a man is sick in bed, please come to my rescue, (*twice*)
When a man is dead and gone, honey, oh well, well, how in the world he know what you do.

Bring me water to my bed, a drink will keep me cool, (*twice*)
And just say after I have gone – ooh well, "I sure tried to help that fool."

I'll stay here long as I can, sleep when I cain't help myself, (*twice*)
We has all got to die, ooh well, well, an' I ain't no better than no one else.

Don't bring me flowers after I'm dead, a dead man sure can't smell, (*twice*)

And if I don't go to heaven, ooh, well, I sure won't need no flowers in
hell.

Black doctors had no hope of treating white patients and white doctors
would often refuse to treat Blacks. Consequently, black doctors were
overworked and had to serve families that were unable to meet their bills.
The medical profession held little attraction for doctors in the South. People
turned instead to the "White Magic" voodoo doctors, the conjures, and the
itinerant pill-vendors for aid. The fees that they charged for their dubious
services were much less, and the sick person was reassured by the foul-tasting
purgative. Sang Bumble Bee Slim between his coughs:

304   Doctor, please give me something just to ease these awful pains, (*twice*)
I done caught my death of cold and it's settling on my brain.

I cain't hardly breathe, I got a wheezing in my chest, (*twice*)
Well I'm having bronchitis, doctor – you should know the rest.

(*Spoken*) Give me Oil of Ninety-Nine, Three-Six – anything!
I done caught my death of cold – Lord have mercy.

I done caught my death of cold, well my friends cannot be found,
(*twice*)
Well I been wading in deep water an' I been sleeping on the ground.

Unable to give the sick the proper attention that they needed, their kin
often depended on folk remedies. Potions were mixed from roots and herbs,
a poultice would be made from cow-dung and hog-lard to off-set
pneumonia. Old superstitions were recalled: a bush hung over the head of
the bed would ensure that death was kept at bay whilst the thorns remained
sharp. No broom would be used to sweep beneath the bed, and the tables –
so reminiscent of the mortuary "cooling-board" – were treated with
respect. Living and dying alike awaited in dread the heralds of death: the
warning of the hoot owl, the tapping of the woodpecker on the door, the
cry of the whip-poor-will. These omens were more emphatic, more
inexorable to the folk Blacks than the onslaught of fever, as Dolly Ross
confirmed.

305   It was midnight on a Sunday, the clock struck thirteen times, (*twice*)
I was scared and I was frightened 'cause I sure believe this sign.

Lord, I heard the owl a-hootin', I knowed somebody was bound to die,
   (*twice*)
Put my head beneath the pillows, started in to moan and cry.

Then early in the morning the picture on the wall fell down, (*twice*)
And it ain't no use in talkin', somebody is graveyard boun'.

Hound dog started howlin', somebody's sure to leave this land, (*twice*)
Take who you want, Lordy, but please don't take my man.

Lord, I knows I'm black and ugly, but he's so good and kind, (*twice*)
Lord, take most anybody but please don't take this man of mine.

Cemeteries are fearsome places to superstitious people, where "haints"
and "plat-eyes" – disembodied, troubled spirits – may be encountered.
Often the blues singer arrogantly laughs at the superstitions, and calls the
cemetery the "bone-yard," the "ape-yard," the "bone orchard." He does
not wish to be reminded of death and he does not go there. But the day
comes when he has lost all that he has cherished and, like Bukka White, he
finds himself a stranger by an unmarked grave.

306   I'm a stranger at this place and I'm lookin' for my mother's grave,
      (*twice*)
   Well it seems like to me, ooh well, well, some of us goin' to wail.

   I was at mother's grave, when they put my mother away, (*twice*)
   An' I can't find no one ooh, well, to take her place.

   After my mother was put away, I thought my wife would take her
      place, (*twice*)
   I'll show you the difference 'tween a mother and a wife, well, my wife
      done throw me away.

   I wished I could find someone to take my mother's place, (*twice*)
   An' if I can't find no one ooh, well, well, you'll find me at her grave.

   I'm standin' on my mother's grave and I wished I could seen her face,
      (*twice*)
   I'll be glad when that day comes, ooh well, well, when it be to drive
      me away.

The inevitability of death and preparation in this world for the "here-after" were fundamental to the teachings of the black churches. "Where will you spend Eternity? Heaven or Hell awaits you," were familiar legends in the windows of the store-front churches. When he heard the chiming of the "Death bells" the sinner would be borne away to meet his "fatal doom," as Lightnin' Hopkins reflected.

> 307   Sounds like I can hear this mornin', baby, death bells ringin' all in my
> ears, (*twice*)
> Yes I know I'm gonna leave on a chariot; wonder what kind gonna
> carry me from here?
>
> You know every living creeper man was born to die, (*twice*)
> Yes, but when that chariot comes for you, they gonna break, run an'
> try to hide.
>
> Yes, you know my mother tol' me, my papa tol' me too: "Some
> day son that chariot gonna comin' after you."
> I been wonderin' what kind of chariot Lord, goin' to carry me from
> here?
> Yes, you know this life I'm livin', I been livin' oh Lord, for great many
> years.

The heaven and hell of his parents' belief meant nothing to Red Nelson who cynically observed that he was unlikely to meet them in the after-life unless he changed his way of living, and this he had little intention of doing. He exploited the superstitious fear of the graveyard, using the cemetery as a place in which to sleep in at night, safe in the knowledge that no one would dream of robbing a man who slept with the dead. Death, Nelson declared, came to the members of his family because their time had come.

> 308   If your mother's dead and gone to glory, my old dad done strayed
> away, (*twice*)
> Only way to meet my mother, I will have to change my low-down
> ways.
>
> Nobody knows my trouble, but myself any good? – No! (*twice*)
> I used to have a sweet woman to love me, now she treats me like a low-
> down dog.

Tombstones my pillow, graveyard gonna be ma bed, (*twice*)
Blue skies gonna be my blanket, and 'e pale moon gonna be my spread.

Black cat crawls late hours at midnight, nightmares ride till the break of
day, (*twice*)
What's the use of loving some woman, some man done stole your love
away.

Stop your crying, do away with all your tears, (*twice*)
If you can't stay with me, mother, it must've been your time to leave
from here.

The blues is still primarily the song of those who turned their backs upon
religion, and though some singers may have been brought closer to their
God with the closeness of death, the singer who had "rambled" – who had
led a sinful life in the eyes of the church – was more than likely to maintain in
his last hours the attitude that he had borne in the past, without an eleventh-
hour repentance. To the church member, the blues were "devil songs" and
Robert Johnson, a singer who walked hand-in-hand with the devil in life,
sardonically greeted him as a friend. He seems to have had some premon-
ition of his own death in the following year at the age of twenty-three,
poisoned, it is said, by a jealous lover.

309   Early this mornin' when you knocked upon my door, (*twice*)
And I said, "Hello Satan, I b'lieve it's time to go."

Me and the devil was walkin' side by side, (*twice*)
An' I'm goin' to beat my woman until I get satisfied.

You may bury my body down by the highway side –
(*spoken*) Baby I don't care where you bury my body when I'm dead
and gone.
You may bury my body, ooh, down by the highway side,
So my old evil spirit can get a Greyhound bus and ride.

Burial practices varied greatly, from the rich and sumptuous funerals
afforded by the black Masonic Lodges to the sad, humble interment in a
"shallow grave just six by three," on which a crude wooden cross was the
only marker and a bunch of wild flowers the only wreath. Many a rural
Black would rather be buried in the surroundings in which he had lived and

in accordance with the folk traditions of his community, than with all the splendor of a Harlem or New Orleans funeral parade. The women turned the pictures to the wall, hung *crêpe* on the doors and affixed it to their sleeves. Then they "re-ragged in red" – donned their bright red mourning gowns and their leather slippers, and followed the coffin to the burying ground, as "Big Boy" Crudup requested

> 310   I went down in Death Valley, nothin' but tombstones and dry bones,
>   (*twice*)
>   That's where poor me'll be, Lord, when I'm dead and gone.
>
>   Now if I should die – and die before my time, (*twice*)
>   I want you to bury my body down by that Frisco Line.
>
>   Aah, bye-bye, baby, I said "Good-bye," (*twice*)
>   Death Valley is my home, mama, when I die.
>
>   Tell all the women, please come dressed in red, (*twice*)
>   They goin' on 61 Highway, that's where the poor boy he fell dead.
>
>   Wear your patent leather slippers, put on your mourning gown, (*twice*)
>   You gonna follow poor Crudup down to his buryin' ground.

Some Blacks derived little pleasure from the preparations for a brave funeral; they implored their companions to "raise hell as we march along" and asked for six whores to be their pall-bearers. They were often tough, embittered characters who died as hard as they had lived, who did not care where their bodies were to be interred and who had no faith.

After a life of hard toil with little at the end of it to show for all the years of manual labor, of sweat and tears, death came as a welcome release for many of the poorest Blacks. "It's a bad wind that never changes," they said fatalistically, and looked forward to an after-life that was a rest from suffering. Many cherished the prospect of a splendid funeral which they believed would give them an appropriate send-off to a world more rewarding than the one that they would leave. For years they would contribute to burial societies, select their caskets, plush-lined and glass-topped, paying for them on instalment plans with hard-earned cash, and plan the details of a funeral in which every sign of affluence and expense was evident. Blind Lemon Jefferson sang of a hearse drawn by "white horses standing in line," and a coffin lowered on a chain of gold.

311 It's a long lane that's got no end, *(three times)*
     It's a bad wind that never change.

     Lord, it's two white horses in a line, *(three times)*
     Will take me to my burying ground.

     Oh, dig my grave with a silver spade, *(three times)*
     You may lead me down with a golden chain.

     Have you ever heard a church bell tone? *(three times)*
     Then you know that a poor boy's dead and gone.

Before the burial it was customary in rural areas for the body to be "laid out" in the open coffin. Women church members would preserve their baptismal gowns so that they could be used as a shroud, ensuring that they were properly attired when they "met their Maker." On their heads would be placed the "laying-out rag." During the wakes which sometimes lasted for two or three days and nights, the women would moan the blues through the long hours much as the Irish sang the "keen."

312 Daddy, oh daddy, won't you answer me please? *(twice)*
     All day I stood by your coffin trying to give my poor heart ease.

     I rubbed my hands over your head and whispered in your ear, *(twice)*
     And I wonder if you know that your mama is near.

     You told me that you loved me and I believe what you said, *(twice)*
     And I wish that I could fall here across your coffin dead.

     When I left the undertaker's I couldn't help but cry,
     And it hurt me so bad to tell the man I love, "Goodbye."

Most recently bereaved persons met the great tragedy in their lives with unsuspected resources of courage and fortitude. At first the enormity of the personal loss weighed heavily on the thoughts of the bereaved: every object, every scrap of clothing had associations. A calm acceptance of the inevitability of death eventually eased the pain and settled the disquieted mind. There was sadness but no bitterness in his voice when Buddy Moss sang of the death of his woman.

313 I'm goin' down to the undertaker and look down in my baby's face
     (twice)

I'm sorry she had to leave me, but I just can't take her place.

The hearse backed up to the undertaker and he rolled my babe away,
(*twice*)
And now I can't do nothin' but grieve my time away.

When a man feel bad when his babe on a coolin' board, (*twice*)
And know she's dead and gone, and see her smilin' face no more.

Lord, Lord, Lord, took the woman I love so well, (*twice*)
She may be in heaven above, or down below in hell.

Says and now she's dead and never more to roam, (*twice*)
She was a kind black woman and she'll make heaven her happy home.

Bereavement is a lonely state, seldom shared by any but the closest friends
and relatives. Mourning a well-loved person did at least bring the comfort
and condolences of those who also shared the sorrow. In the black world
there were perhaps only a few persons who were known and loved outside a
small and close community. For this reason it seems, there are few blues on
record which are about the death of a specifically named friend. Slim Green
appears to have been something of a bon viveur in North Carolina,
remembered for being a "viper," a smoker of "tea" or marijuana. His friend
Shorty Bob Parker played piano and sang a blues about his death,
accompanied by another member of his group in Charlotte, the guitarist
Kid Prince Moore.

314   Now I believe I'm gonna tell you people, well the very best I can,
(*twice*)
'Bout the death of Slim Green, he was a "viper" man.

It was one old day, one old lonesome day, (*twice*)
Well we begin' cryin', as he was passin' away.

He loved his smokin', how he craved his gin, (*twice*)
Well he had his "tea" until the very end.

He was known in Cincinnata and around the world back home, (*twice*)
Well our friend Slim Green, he is dead and gone.

Can you all remember what he used to do? (*twice*)
You would hear him say, "Cocky, cocky tails for two."

The death of a great blues singer probably touched more Blacks personally than that of almost any other member of African American society. Admittedly the direct effect upon their lives of a militant race leader in achieving, for example, the relaxations of segregational practices may have been greater, but the feeling of personal association with such persons was far less. A closer bond was felt with the colored sportsman or entertainer whose achievements, family lives, homes and opinions were featured in detail in the race periodicals and were followed avidly by the black masses. But the blues singer entered their own homes; his voice was known to all, his experiences were their own and his blues were the mirror to their own lives. Whether it was Blind Lemon Jefferson in the twenties, Bessie Smith in the thirties, Sonny Boy Williamson in the forties or Johnny Ace in the fifties, the death of a blues singer has been a tragedy recorded in grief by his closest friends and shared by a multitude. No singer was more loved than Leroy Carr, over a hundred of whose blues were issued. On February 25, 1935 he recorded eight titles, including *Six Cold Feet in the Ground*. It was to be his last title; two months later he was dead from nephritis brought on by acute alcoholic poisoning.

315   Just remember me, baby, when I'm in six feet of cold, cold ground,
          (*twice*)
      Always think of me, mama, just say, "There's a good man gone
          down."

      Don't cry, baby, baby, after I'm gone,
      Don't cry, baby, don't cry after I'm gone,
      I'm just a good man loves you, and I ain't done nothing wrong.

Only thirty years of age, he was greatly missed by his friends and mourned by the black community. Many posthumous blues were composed in his honor. His friend Bumble Bee Slim sang a blues dedicated to his memory:

316   Now people I'm gonna tell you, as long as I can, (*twice*)
      'Bout the death of Leroy Carr, well he was my closest friend.

      On one Sunday morning, just about nine o'clock, (*twice*)
      Death came an' struck him, an' he began to reel and rock.

      He said, "Lawd have mercy, I'm in so much misery, (*twice*)
      He's my friend, you all got to do [what] you can for me."

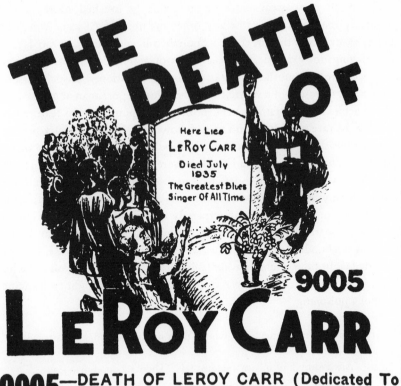

9005—DEATH OF LEROY CARR (Dedicated To His Memory) and BLUES BLUES. Voc.—Guit. By Leroy Carr's Buddy......65c

So on Monday mornin' just about the break of day, (*twice*)
He began cryin' and he was passin' away.

I then called the doctor on the telephone, (*twice*)
When the doctor came Leroy was dead and gone.

A few years later, in February 1941, another celebrated blues singer and one of the most recorded in the 1930s, Blind Boy Fuller, died in North Carolina. He had been ill for some time, a medical examination in 1938 revealing arrested syphilis and damaged kidneys and bladder. At times he sang in the streets, at times he was on welfare, but he continued to make recordings and to perform with his friends. Among them was the youthful

Walter Brownie McGhee, who sang a tribute to him when Fuller discharged himself from hospital and died at his home from blood poisoning at the age of 44.

317   He's gone, Blind Boy Fuller's gone away, (*twice*)
Well he heard a voice callin', and he knew he could not stay.

Well he called me to his bedside one mornin', and the clock was strikin'
   four, (*twice*)
"Brownie, take my guitar, carry my business on, I won't stay here no
   more."

Blind Boy Fuller had a million friends, north, east, south and west,
   (*twice*)
Well you know it's hard to tell which place he was loved the best.

Well all you women of Blind Boy, how do you want your lovin' done
   (*twice*)
I'll do my best, I'll do my best, to carry Blind Boy Fuller's business on.

In his playing blues and recording Brownie McGhee did indeed carry on Fuller's work, though he rather resented having his first records issued as by "Blind Boy Fuller #2."

If the death of a blues singer was a tragedy to Blacks, its repercussions were little felt by other Americans. Similarly the loss of a national figure was seldom recorded in the blues, for many blues singers did not feel sufficiently a part of the nation to share in its joys and sorrows. But the death of Franklin D. Roosevelt at his winter home in Warm Springs, Georgia, in April, 1945 left a more profound impression. As the instigator of the New Deal and the signatory of Executive Order 8802 he had seemed to African Americans to have been a savior on whom they could depend and to whom they could appeal for help.

318   Well you know that President Roosevelt he was awful fine,
He helped the crippled boys and he almost healed the blind,
      Oh yes, gonna miss President Roosevelt.
      Well he's gone, he's gone, but his spirit always 'll live on.

He traveled out East, he traveled to the West,
But of all the Presidents, President Roosevelt was the best,
      Oh yes, gonna miss [etc.]

Well now he traveled by land and he traveled by sea,
He helped the United States boys, and he also helped Chinese,
Oh yes, gonna miss [etc.]

President Roosevelt went to Georgia boy, and he ride around and
round, (*twice*)
I guess he imagined he seen that Pale Horse when they was trailin' him
down.
Oh yes, gonna miss [etc.]

Well now the rooster told the hen "I want to crow,
You know President Roosevelt has gone, can't live in this shack no
more,"
Oh yes, we're gonna miss President Roosevelt,
Well he's gone, he's gone, but his spirit always 'll live on.

Not untypically, Joe Williams stated the implications of the loss of the
president by using a simple rural analogy.

It seems that Roosevelt had attained almost mythical status in the eyes of
many Blacks, who, like Big Joe Williams, had relatively little knowledge of
the specifics of his tenure, but who were well aware that the New Deal had
considerably benefited them. "Gonna call up Headquarters I'm gonna write
to Roosevelt" sang Red Nelson in one blues, and many regarded the
president in a personal way. When he died at the commencement of his
fourth term in office they felt that they had lost a true friend.

319   I sure feel bad with tears runnin' down my face, (*twice*)
I lost a good friend, was a credit to our race.

F.D.R. was everybody's friend, (*twice*)
Well he helped everybody, right up to the end.

May God in heaven, have mercy on his soul, (*twice*)
And may the angels, ooh well, well, "take him right unto the fold."

I know I can speak for my friends if I choose, (*twice*)
'Cause he went away and left me and I got the F.D.R. blues.

That Roosevelt had good intentions and that he did much to improve the
lot of Blacks is undeniable, but it is also true that he was often evasive,
equivocal, and apathetic, and that many of the principal measures that he

took to improve race relations were the result of the painstaking diplomacy and firm pressure of honorable, if often little-known, race leaders. To Roosevelt went all the credit but they believed it right that it should be so, for it was essential that such moves should emanate from the head of state. So the race leaders sat quietly back and the common black people often felt far removed from them. When Walter White, the secretary of the National Association for the Advancement of Colored People, died in 1957 after a lifetime of service to the members of his race whose color, ironically, he did not even share, no one sang a blues to his memory.

Only occasionally, therefore, was the death of someone famous of sufficient concern to be the subject of a blues. Blues singers sang principally of their own impending demise, or of the death of a wife, lover, parent or, more rarely, a child.

Though the conditions under which many have lived may seem to have offered little hope of happiness, a certain philosophical detachment enabled them to wait to "see what tomorrow bring." The despairing intention to "lay his head on some lonesome railroad line" to let the passing train "pacify his mind," was often sublimated in singing the blues. For some life was indeed hard and death was not unwelcome, and they were, like Joe McCoy, reconciled to it. In spite of his soubriquet of "The Georgia Pine Boy" he was from Mississippi and died in Chicago in 1950 at the age of forty-five.

320   Now when I'm dead, baby, don't you cry over me,
     I'm trying to get back to my old used-to-be,
          Because this world's a hard place to live before you go,
          When you ain't got nobody that you can call your own.

     Yes I'm going up to heaven, gonna talk to the good Lord above,
     If I can't get me no angel, give me back the one I love,
          Because this world's a hard place to live before you go,
          When you ain't got nobody that you can call your own.

Being in no position to shape their destinies, and far removed from the social and political activities of those Blacks who were trying to negotiate for better living and working conditions, the majority concentrated on "getting along." In one of the very few blues that makes any reference to happiness, which the obscure singer R. T. Hanen recorded in Louisville, Kentucky during the depths of the Depression, he appealed to young people to make the best of life while they could enjoy it.

321   Life is short, that you know for truth,
       We better have the happy time, that's what to do,
              Boys and girls let's have a happy time before we go,
              Because life is so short, we can't tell where we goin' to go.

       When I'm in my moonshine, I'm drinkin' my gin,
       I'm having a happy time with the girls and boys again,
              Boys and girls let's have a happy time again,
              Because life is so short, you really can't tell just when.

       When I'm using whiskey, using me a half of gin,
       Oh the blues leave me, they don't never come back again,
              Now boys and girls, let's have a happy time before we go,
              Because life is so short we can't tell where we might go.

       Happy days, happy days, among my best friends
       When I got no money, have a happy time just the same,
              Now girls and boys, have a happy time before we go.

11   *Blues like showers of rain*

An appreciation of the part that African Americans have played in United States society and of the rights and other aspects of living that were denied them, is of major assistance in understanding meaning in the blues. But there are barriers to appreciation presented by the manner of delivery, of speech, and of form, and when these are overcome the full significance of the blues to the black audience still remains elusive. One has yet to learn why Blacks have the blues, sing the blues, and listen to the blues. For those unaccustomed to blues singing the words are frequently incomprehensible, presenting difficulties which were seldom a problem to the black audience for whom the recordings were primarily intended. To the European ear and even to that of the New Englander the soft burr of southern speech, whether white or black, is as difficult to understand as the "Geordie" of the Tynesider to the Londoner. Even among Blacks the characteristics of local dialects cause some perplexity and amusement, the speech of the rural South being mimicked and ridiculed in the North – most frequently by those who desired to forget their own southern origins.

There are a few examples on record of blues singers who employ such distinct and localized dialects as Gullah – or Geechee – the speech of the Georgia Coast and the Sea Islands. Words such as "juke" and "buckra" which stem from Gullah have entered the speech of the blues singer. In the omission of the article of the noun and the employment of the present tense only, some blues singers show that vestiges of "Flat Talk" – the compromise between African and European usages by which the slaves learned to speak English – still remain. Within recent years many recordings have been made employing "Gumbo" – the Louisiana dialect which is an admixture of Negro and French idiom, incorrectly but not infrequently confused with the Louisiana Acadian speech "Cajun."

Singers who had been tied by economic circumstances to one county or urban district, or who had chosen to remain there, naturally retained the characteristic speech patterns of their milieu, and the blues are subject to many dialectal variations which have not been eliminated entirely by the redistribution of the black population. Some singers have voices so thick and

265

accented that their speech is quite alien to European ears, whilst others, especially those living in areas where the density of the colored population is not great, have a diction closely related to that of their white neighbors. The voices of Lulu Jackson, for example, and even the Tennessee-born Leroy Carr are almost indistinguishable from those of white persons from the same territories, while at the opposite extreme the strong, megaphonic voice of Charlie Patton or the half-uttered end syllables and rough intonation of Son Bonds are indistinct. There is evidence to suggest that the physiological structure of the mouths of Blacks coming from nearly pure African stock favors certain dental and labial consonant forms. But this is easily modified by training or by changes of social environment and the fact that southern "poor Whites" speak in a similar manner suggests that these characteristics are largely acculturated.

Much of the obscuration of meaning in the blues arises through the peculiarities of phrasing, the imposed rhythms, the qualities of timing and enunciation in which lie a great deal of the unique beauty and fascination of the music. But they do not assist in the clarification of the content. Enjambments, elisions, and glottal stops are features common in the blues which add greatly to the dramatic intensity of the verses though they sometimes cloud the meaning. Blues singers now, as in the past, use their voices instrumentally, introducing extended syllables that follow through successions of rising and falling notes, permitting their vocal lines to ululate in order to heighten the expressiveness of their singing. For many blues singers this was only partially a conscious process; rather it was one governed and even necessitated by the purpose of their song. They declaimed and hollered the words in anger or protest, moaned them soft and low in sadness and sorrow. Sometimes the words assumed their shape as they emerged from seemingly formless murmurings; sometimes they were nailed with vocal hammer-blows half-shouted, half-sung to the beat of the music. There were times when words were dispensed with altogether: when they were supplanted by long-drawn groans and hummed phrases or by the utterance of joyous if unrecognizable syllables – "scat vocals" that were eloquent with abstract meaning. A singer's words might be brutally stabbed home; then punctuated with shrill falsetto cries; then uttered softly and scarcely audibly.

Within the blues were to be heard the compelling rhythms of work song and spiritual that embraced the listener and drew him into inevitable participation, much as the exhortations of the gang-leader or the preacher exerted their influence on workers or congregation. Here too were the overtones of meaning and expressive content that were to be found in the hollers of the "yard and field Negro," the calls of the section-hand and the joyous exclamations of the member of the camp-meeting. The spontaneous utterances, the unexpected asides, the canonical overlapping of lines and phrases, whether made instrumentally or vocally by companions or created by the singer on his instrument, linked the blues singer to his musical heritage. When he played his guitar he made it "talk" and "sing," he exhorted his piano to "tell 'em ivories"; he caused his harmonica to wail and cry as a complementary voice, speaking for and with him. He made of his instrument a second voice, though he did not try to make it a human voice. Imitative passages traceable to vocal origins occurred in almost all instrumental blues but they amplified and extended the vocal, to express what the voice was unable to say. This was the part played by the guitar or the piano of the blues singer and it is the part played by accompanying instrumentalists, whether jug band, Fletcher Henderson group, Chicago washboard band, or Rhythm and Blues combination.

Their comparative isolation has caused many southern Blacks to devise their own idiomatic phrases and to invent their own terms, many of which have been illustrated in the foregoing pages. Without a knowledge of the more common of these the listener cannot be expected to understand the content of the blues. In numerous instances such phrases were traditional, their origins forgotten by their users and often lost to the etymologist. Some undoubtedly arose through misapplication or misunderstanding of the meaning of white words. Fondness for alliteration, pleasure in the creation of rhyme, and delight in the coining of neologisms account for the invention of many such idiomatic phrases.

Many black terms arose through the deliberate intention to conceal meaning. In the South some would resort to "Pig Latin" (called "Dog Latin" in the North), in which a type of backslang was employed. Syllables were reversed and the vowels sounded first followed by the consonants with the addition of the vowel sound "Ay." A slang form as useful when referring to persons outside the social or racial group as it was for declarations of love, its effect was to scramble the sentence so completely that only the practiced could comprehend the meaning.

322   Oomanway, oomanway, oomanway; ouway urshay eesay oodgay
      ooshay eemay, (*twice*)
  Eemay oingay ooshay akeshay ooway ackbay, ightray ackbay ooshay
  Ennessee-esstay.

(Woman, woman, woman; you sure is good to me, (*twice*)
I'm goin' to take you back, right back to Tennessee.)

Ouway ontday alkshay oosay ainplay, outbay ouway urshay ancay
     allcay aemay amenay, (*twice*)
Eemay oosay adglay, oosay adglay atshay aemay ouryay eetsway,
     eetsway anmay.

(You don't talk so plain but you sure can call my name, (*twice*)
I'm so glad, so glad, that I'm your sweet, sweet man.)

Ollie Shepard hardly needed to obscure his meaning in Pig Latin. But innocuous words were often given secondary meanings which were closed to all but the initiated and by their use the singer could be more outspoken in the blues than might otherwise be prudent. Some of these became traditional terms recognized and used throughout the states by Blacks, for whom the colored man was the "monkey," the white man the "baboon." With comparative immunity Dirty Red could sing:

323   Monkey and the baboon playing Seven-Up,
          Monkey win the money, scared to pick it up.

          The monkey stumbled, the baboon fell,
          Monkey grabbed the money an' he run like hell!

But the monkey is also a traditional character in black folk tales; the "monkey man" could be a homosexual and he could also be a "bumbole," a West Indian Negro. For reasons that are readily apparent Blacks delighted in such mixed terminology since early slavery. As a singer placed layer upon layer of meaning on a phrase he protected himself with a cloak of obscurities.

Although Harlem Blacks will look contemptuously on the country idioms of their southern cousins, their own speech was liberally interlarded with phrases and words whose meanings were singularly elusive. A Harlem "cat" would "shoot the jive," using slick, witty, racy terms that enjoyed a brief vogue before they were replaced by others as ephemeral. "Jive talk" was a part of black culture; the telling, cruel metaphors and spontaneous slang being the creation of a poetic form of language of the most uncompromising kind. With his *Jive Blues* Peter Chatman used long, rolling words that gave cynical recognition to the advantages of education rather than a false impression that he had been well educated.

324 Mama meant me to twist it to the slammer and let me cut my throat,
    (*twice*)
I been throwed in the hole, black baby, ain't been able to dig no gold.

Baby, I'm beat to my socks, do you dig just what I mean, (*twice*)
I've got a terrible financial embarrassment and I'm sticking with Jim
    Clean.

I'm gonna dig me some jive and try to knock myself out, (*twice*)
Then everything will be foxy, I won't know what it's all about.

I'm gonna buy me a short and get on the old Riverside Drive, (*twice*)
I've got to buy from this bin, everybody's getting hip to the jive.

Much jive was invented on the spur of the moment by those gifted in the art and versed in its use, but the process of creation is also a conscious one. Black magazines and periodicals encouraged their writers to use jive phraseology and invited their readers to take part in the invention of new words in an ever-growing and perplexing language. Fundamentally, the reasons for its creation were still those that caused the southern Black to invent his own country expressions; there was genuine pleasure in being "hip to the jive" – in being well informed in the use of "sharp" terms, and there was a feeling of protection and security within the racial group afforded by their application. A sense of racial solidarity was generated by the use of these "in-group" expressions, but they also provided a screen for the expression of feelings of protest and frustration. Though blues that were sung in jive were by no means all on protest themes they did demonstrate a form of passive revolt; an assertion of identity. But in the withdrawal that the use of such terminology also implied they demonstrated the unfortunate result of his exclusion from society. He was drawing attention to himself and indirectly to his predicament, but he was also voluntarily forcing still wider the schism between himself and white America.

Blues sung in jive and Pig Latin were blues sung, to a certain extent, in a spirit of protest: protest that found in this form of expression a means both of defence and defiance. It has been frequently stated that the whole of blues is created in the spirit of protest. The inference is that the blues is a form of expression against racial discrimination, though there are whole categories of blues in which this belief is demonstrably insupportable.

There are blues that are sung in the spirit of remorse, or in distress or with the warmth of affection, and in these the measure of protest is negligible. In a very general sense, however, the argument may be upheld, for the blues is usually sung as an unburdening of emotions, and it is therefore giving voice to protest, directly or symbolically, against the circumstances that have brought about such a condition. Often, the circumstances of segregation and color discrimination were the root causes of these troubles, but in many instances the singer was the victim of the frailties of human nature irrespective of class or color.

When an exhaustive examination is made of recorded blues it becomes apparent that the number of items that are directly concerned with protest themes is exceedingly small. It is scarcely conceivable that the singers, commenting broadly on the multitudinous facets of black life, would deliberately ignore or reject those that were the result of racial prejudice and intolerance. The segregated waiting-rooms, the Jim Crow cars, the forbidden beaches, bathing pools, and theaters, the short measure, the cropper's "share," the stale goods, the race riot, the hooded Klansmen, the lynch mob, the hit-and-run killer – the countless manifestations of ignorance, brutality, race hatred, and violence, of discrimination and segregation must have been the raw material for innumerable blues created by a legion of singers both recorded and unknown.

That many of these sad and ugly scars upon the ageing face of the nation are now slowly healing does not entirely hide the fact that during more than three-score years of recorded blues many of them were sore and open wounds. But the periods when they were most rife and when they would have been uppermost in the minds of the singers that recorded would also have been the times when reference to them on disc would have been the most potentially dangerous. Amongst other Blacks their effect might well have been inflammatory with results that would have been disastrous, whilst those white persons that came across them in troubled areas would have been incensed. At periods when inter-racial disturbances were at a minimum blues singers would tend to ignore the subject, for their concern was with the present or the immediate past. Further, the personal character of the blues would require the singer to have experienced such effects of racial prejudice; but one who had so suffered would be rather less likely to bring further attention and trouble to himself. Among the record companies precautions were generally taken to ensure that material likely to cause embarrassment was rejected; a practice of censorship that may be criticized with some justice, but which is understandable.

A small number of blues have been recorded on themes of protest, however, in spite of these restrictions. Some were the work of socially conscious singers such as Josh White who intentionally sought and found an outlet for just such material and deliberately composed "protest blues." Others, such as Leadbelly in the 1940s, or Big Bill Broonzy in the 1950s, have been incited by small recording companies motivated by humanitarian or ideological principles. When the incitement or the sublimation of the social or racial sentiments of others is deliberate, the blues usually becomes self-conscious. It is seldom that the blues becomes an electioneer's soap-box, a politician's stand from which declamations are made and the sentiments of the listeners aroused.

By 1954 there were signs that a more political consciousness was awakening in the blues, prompted by the success of Dwight D. Eisenhower in the 1952 presidential election. Though Blacks had formerly voted Republican – the party of Abraham Lincoln – they switched their allegiance to Franklin Roosevelt and the Democrats with the implementation of the New Deal and the institution of welfare programs. After a couple of years of the Eisenhower administration, during which the President attacked "socialized medicine" and regarded any further expansion of the Tennessee Valley Authority as "creeping socialism," many Blacks were alarmed, among them Bobo Jenkins in Detroit.

325 Well, do you remember baby, 19 and 31?
That's when the Depression baby, just begun,
  Yes darlin', if you know what I'm talkin' about,
  The Democrats put you on your feet baby, well,
  You had the nerve to throw them out.

You didn't have to plant no more cotton baby, you didn't have to
 plow no more corn,
If a mule was runnin' away with the world, baby you'd tell him to "Go
 head on,"
  Yes darlin', if you know [etc.]

Well do you remember baby, when the steel mill shut down?
You had to go to the country, thought you couldn't live in town,
  Yes darlin', if you know [etc.]

Well do you remember baby when your stomach was all full o' slack?
Somebody help me get them Democrats back,
  Yes darlin', if you know [etc.]

In fact the heavily black Ward 3 in Detroit voted 90 percent for the Democrats, and in the southern states Blacks voted solidly for Adlai

Stevenson. In Houston, Texas, only 10 per cent voted for Eisenhower; the largest proportion was 40 per cent in Atlanta. Blacks were not responsible for the Republican "victory" which was actually marginal. However, they were feeling the pinch. Blues singer J. B. Lenoir, who also used the verse or couplet and refrain form of blues popular at the time, made no bones about it.

326   Hey everybody, I'm just talkin' to you,
         I'm just tellin' you the nach'al truh, mmm–mmm–mmm.
                 I got the Eisenhower blues
                 Thinkin' about me and you, what on earth are we gon' do?

         My money's gone, my phone is gone,
         Way things look – how can I be here long?
                 Mmm–mmm–mmm, I got the Eisenhower blues [etc.]

         Taken all my money to pay the tax,
         I'm only givin' you people, the nach'al facts,
         I'm only tellin' you people my belief,
         Because I'm headin' straight for Relief.
                 Mmm–mmm–mmm, I got [etc.]

         Ain't got a dime, ain't even got a cent,
         I have no money to pay my rent,
         My baby needs clothes, she needs some shoes,
         Peoples, I don't know what I'm gonna do,
                 Mmmm–mmm–mmm I got the Eisenhower Blues [etc.]

Soon after it was released J. B. Lenoir's record was withdrawn, in a blatant example of censorship. Later that year the Supreme Court's decision on school desegregation put the Eisenhower administration in a favorable light and in the 1956 elections the President trebled his vote among Blacks in many southern cities. There were no blues about it.

Though a very few examples of protest blues may have slipped through the net by virtue of the use of inter-racial terminology or oblique references whose obscurity has permitted their inclusion in the record lists, in fact, only a handful were recorded.

That the number was small is in part the result of black acceptance of stereotypes. In rural areas where education levels were low and the people knew no better environment, there was little with which to compare their mode of life. They were primarily concerned with the business of living from day to day, of conforming and making the best of their circumstances. As surely as the southern Whites intended them to "keep their place" the majority of Blacks were prepared to accept it. They knew that they could not change the world but that they had to live in it. An apathy developed which the racial leaders found exasperatingly hard to break, and even when aggravation reached the point where the spirit of revolt against the system arose, this was often soon dissolved in minor personal disruptions and eventual disregard.

In this manner the blues acted as an emotional safety-valve, canalizing feelings of anger and resentment. The music was enriched whilst the disappointment and frustration that had been experienced were diverted from more violent forms of expression. There were militant blues though; blues that are uncompromisingly aggressive in their outlook, though in a familiar psychological transference the aggression was often directed through bitterness and disillusion against the singer's own group rather than against a hostile system. This was most evident in the many blues which had as their theme some aspect of violent crime, including those which expressed the intention to commit one. Blues which displayed a marked tendency to sexual aggressiveness also channeled the desire for power to less potentially dangerous ends. According to the altering circumstances under which the singer lived, his blues might change, for his song was frequently a direct expression of his immediate experience. From this his listener took heart for he shared his predicaments and his fortunes and was reassured by his statements of reactions that were common to them both.

Here then, until the 1960s, was one of the functions of the blues. Though they may lie deeply hidden, there are functional purposes for every form of folk song: they are seldom if ever created whimsically, though in the course of time their original meaning and function may be lost, leaving "fractured" verses and seemingly irrelevant nonsense choruses. For the simple community – Scottish, rural English, Scandinavian, Balkan, African, Polynesian – folk song has its functions which may vary in kind according to the nature of other aspects of the culture. Song is a vehicle for speaking with God; for placating the gods. Song plays a major part in tribal custom; in ritual, in witchcraft, in the understanding of mysteries, and in the preparation of initiates to secret societies. Through folk song the elders teach the uneducated, pass on the traditions of the social group, and record its history. It provides a vehicle for courting and disowning alike; for evoking some emotions and suppressing others; for declaring passions and for easing pain. Speculations on the after-life, comments on the present social scene figure prominently in folk song; it is a means for enticement, for amusement, for incitement and appeasement. These and many others in varying degree are its functions the world over; they were the functions of the spirituals, the ballads, and the work songs of the American Negro and, with important differences of emphasis again, they were the functions of the blues in the era of 78 rpm records.

Work songs had a profound formative influence on blues both in structure and in mode of expression, but they were the creations of men engaged in work. Blues, on the other hand, may be said to be primarily the creations of men at leisure. Such an arbitrary distinction does not take into account that a working man may pass his time singing the blues to himself, nor that, for some, singing the blues is itself a form of work, but it does indicate the fundamental difference between the immediate pre-blues form of the field holler and the blues as a definite category of folk song. As the blues resolved into a largely extemporized song performed with improvised instrumental accompaniment, its practical function as an aid to work virtually ceased. On commercial records the blues was not sung in the process of work, and labor figures in the blues in retrospect, the singer reflects upon employment and, still more, on the lack of it. Blues serves as a projection of the sufferings, the aspirations, the thoughts of the singer and in this respect the ballad is closer to the blues, putting similar emotional and mental states into symbolic form. Many ballads are concerned with the exploits of folk heroes, characters larger than life, such as John Henry, the "steel drivin' man," or the desperadoes Stack O' Lee and Railroad Bill, whose abilities were prodigious and whose feats were those which could not be challenged by ordinary men. They defeated the machinery of their overlords and of the state, they cunningly avoided or overcame their enemies, they outwitted prison guards, murdered ruthlessly, but gave generously and died nobly against incalculable odds.

In an era of social advancement there would seem to be excellent opportunities for this symbolic ballad conception within the blues, the "race man" and "race hero" being admirable material. Amongst the most admired of all Blacks of his day, Joe Louis was the idol of the colored masses who saw a symbol of the New Negro in his invincibility within the ring. A number of blues were composed about him; Bill Gaither's *Champ Joe Louis* for instance.

> 327   I came all the way from Chicago to see Joe Louis and Max Schmelling
> fight, (*twice*)

Schmelling went down like the *Titanic* when Joe gave him just one
 hard right.

Well, you've heard of the King of Swing, well Joe is the King of
 Gloves, (*twice*)
Now he's the World Heavyweight Champion, a man that this whole
 world loves.

It was only two minutes and four seconds poor Schmelling was down
 on his knees, (*twice*)
He looked like he was praying to the Good Lord to "Have mercy on
 me, please!"

If I'd had a million dollars would have bet every dime on Joe, (*twice*)
I'd've been a rich man this very day and I wouldn't have to worry no
 more.

More than any other character, Joe Louis approached the stature of a folk
hero whose exploits were celebrated in the blues as they might have been in
the ballads of an earlier era. But even so the singer, whilst admiring him,
spoke of him as one seen rather than as one worshiped, and by the end of the
blues had turned from Louis the hero to his own personal predicament. He
was concerned more with the material gain that he might have made than
with adulation. A ballad symbolized the suppressed desires of the singer
when he could see no way of overcoming his oppression. It is a vocal dream
of wish-fulfillment. In the indomitable boll-weevil he saw himself as small,
crushable, but unsuppressed: the unbeatable "Stewball" ran a race for the
Race. The maturity of the blues came with the dawning realization that an
equal place on earth was a basic right and perhaps within the bounds of
possibility. While the ballad singer projected on his heroes the successes that
he could not believe could be his own, the blues singer considered his own
ability to achieve them. The ballad hero of noble proportions had little
relevance to modern life, but the blues was realistic enough for the singer to
declare his successes and failures with equal impartiality. Far from extoling
the virtues of the folk hero, the blues singer was so determined to deny them
as to be markedly ungenerous towards the achievements of others, even of
his own race. He did not identify himself with others; his listeners were more
inclined to identify themselves with him. The blues singer was himself the
race hero, and in this lay his popularity and the phenomenal success of the
blues as a musical form.

Here are four great records dedicated to Joe Louis, the Brown Bomber, still our bet for the championship. Be sure to get these records.

6071—Joe Louis Is The Man and Peters' Blue—Voc.-
Piano Acc. Joe Pullum 59c

7114—Joe Louis Blues and Let's Have A New Deal—
Vocal-Guit. Acc. Carl Martin 59c

7115—Joe Louis Chant and Baby O' Mine—Voc. Orch.
Acc. George Dewey Washington 59c

3046—Joe Louis Strutt and He's In The Ring Doing
The Same Old Thing—Vocal with Orch. Acc.
Sung by Memphis Minnie 59c

Blues is, above all, the expression of the individual singer. Declaring his loves, his hates, his disappointments, his experiences, the blues singer speaks for himself, and only indirectly, for others. The highly personal nature of the content of his songs makes them appear exceedingly remote from the world of the European listener, though the sentiments expressed in them may be fundamentally universal ones. A blues singer seldom considered his themes apart from himself, seldom narrated incidents in which he had not actively participated, or projected himself. He did not view his subject as an objective outsider but rather from within. Statements and reported accounts that are concerned solely with the lives and experiences of others with whom he had no direct contact were, therefore, rare, for the blues singer did not comment on a world as seen through a window but as a member circulating within it.

It is a peculiar feature of the blues that its subjective approach did not manifest itself in over-romanticism. Above all the blues singer was a realist, intimately concerned with his subjects but having no illusions about them: neither carried away with sentiment nor totally insensible and devoid of feeling; he was not repulsed by the uglier side of the world in which he lived but accepted the bad with the good.

In the sharply defined images of life that the blues reflects are mirrored the minutiae of experience of the ordinary black person. The words that the blues singer uttered, the thoughts, passions, and reactions to which he gave voice were those that were shared by countless thousands of others. An unemployed laborer found comfort in the blues of a man who had suffered the despair of the penniless, the "cold-in-hand"; the forsaken lover shared the bitterness of one who has been "mistreated" and the would-be philanderer swaggered along the sidewalk with the bragging blues of the "high-brown sheik." When the blues singer told of his escape from disaster, when he addressed the absent woman that he loved, when he sang of the train that would take him to a "better land," he sang to himself, but he was aware that others whom he did not know would sing the blues in like circumstances.

328   Did you ever wake up lonesome – all by yourself? (*twice*)
     And the one you love, off loving someone else?

     I wrote these blues I'm gonna sing them as I please, (*twice*)
     I'm the only one liking the way I'm singing them, I'll swear to
       goodness there's no one else pleased.

     I tell you people, I don't know your name, (*twice*)
     But takin' other men's women – I'll swear to God it is a shame.

The blues of an Atlanta street singer, Henry Williams, was echoed in the hearts of his unknown listeners. The appeal of the blues and the love and warmth of affection in which the blues singers were held by so many of their fellow African Americans lay in this feeling of kinship. It is not that the singers were racial spokesmen from the militant gestures of whom the blues singer often felt far removed; it was simply that in singing for himself the blues artist sang also for them.

In singing about himself and for himself the blues singer may be considered egocentric, selfish, and self-pitying, but though there are examples of such attitudes the blues has a wider significance. The blues singer, like the poet, turned his eyes on the inner soul within and recorded his impressions and reactions to the world without. His art was introverted and only when the blues became a part of entertainment and of jazz did it become extrovert. As if aware of the dangers implicit in these declarations of his inner self, the blues singer was as brutally self-examining as the true philosopher, recounting his desires, acknowledging his faults, stating his thoughts with almost frightening honesty. His hard realism, his lack of sentimentality, his harsh reporting make grim listening to the outsider.

In spite of popular belief to the contrary, there is comparatively little humor in the blues. There are good times and amusement in the making of the music, but humor appears most frequently in the non-blues songs that most blues singers know. When humor is employed it usually has a dry, if not callous, character. So Barbecue Bob, following the lead of a number of singers, made a blues about the Mississippi floods, but as a Georgia singer he was less involved, and instead, made a joke about it.

329   I'm sitting here looking at all of this mud,
        And my gal got washed away in that Mississippi flood,
              That's why I'm cryin', Mississippi heavy water blues.

        Got plenty of mud and water, don't need no wood or coal,
        All I need is some sweet mama to spin my jelly roll,
              That's why I'm cryin', [etc.]

        Listen here you men, one more thing I'd like to say,
        Ain't no women out here, for they all got washed away,
              That's why I'm cryin' [etc.]

It is more comforting, and assuages our guilt, to believe that blues *is* humorous, that blues singers are "crying to keep from laughing," rather than "laughing to keep from crying." For those who seek the comfortable escapism and the good humor of the commercial popular singer the blues has no appeal. But for countless Blacks over several decades there was assurance in these forthright and unequivocal statements made by a person from within their own group. When setbacks and disappointments threatened to shake confidence and destroy morale they turned for support to the blues singer – or sang the blues themselves.

Because the blues is self-orientated the singer was seldom interested in things exterior to him, and unless they had a direct impact upon his or her life was not concerned with them. Even the simplest, the most obvious features of natural beauty have little importance for the blues singer. There are no blues that tell of the beauties of a landscape, of the splendor of magnificent scenery or of a glorious sunset – experiences which seldom fail to move even the most sterile mind and cause even the mediocre thinker to wish that he had a paint-brush with which to express the scene, if not the gift of poetry. The artist tends to eschew such subject-matter because the appreciation of the beauties of the arc of a rainbow, the colors of a butterfly wing or of a flower in a hedgerow is too commonplace though it ennobles the spirit. But it is not for this reason that the blues singer ignored such themes: it was not these that gave him the blues. That he was aware of such beauties and was moved by them is evident in many passing references, but a singer such as Roosevelt Sykes, employed them for their metaphoric or comparative value and did not use them as themes.

330   The sun begin sinkin' down behind the western horiz-zone, (*twice*)
      The evenin' dew began to fall and I'm here all alone.

      I would go and sit down under the old oak tree, (*twice*)
      But I ain't got nobody to talk baby-talk to me.

Though it can be said with truth that the themes of the blues are to a large extent universal ones which have stimulated artists in all fields to create, it cannot be denied that many of the virtues and emotions that have inspired great art are absent. There are shortcomings to the blues. The spiritual values that are to be found in the gospel songs are seldom to be found in the "devil songs" of those who have turned away from the church. Blues are a worldly form of song and its values tend to be worldly also. The church promises a life after death and the spirituals looked forward to "crossing Jordan" into the Hereafter, the "Promised Land." Blues offers no such reward, though half-hearted references stemming from the singer's background sometimes appear. Yet the blues are much concerned with death and is little concerned with birth. This could be an emphasis that has lasted over from the spirituals. But it may also be symbolic of a hopelessness that sees little future for the black child. Childbirth itself would never seem to be the theme of the blues and the woman blues singers on record did not sing of the pains of labor or the joys of parenthood. There are few blues that show pleasure in children or even express concern for them, but when they do, as in Blind Lemon Jefferson's *That Crawling Baby Blues*, it is often as victims of circumstances:

331   Heard a baby crying, what do his mama mean? (*twice*)
       He's crying 'bout his sweet milk, and she won't feed him Jersey cream.

       Well, he crawled from the fireplace, stopped in the middle of the floor, (*twice*)
       Says, "Mama, ain't that your second daddy standing back there in the door?"

       Well she grabbed my baby, spanked him, and I tried to make her leave him alone, (*twice*)
       I tried my best to stop her an' she said: "The babe ain't none of mine."

       The woman rocks the cradle, I declare she rules the home, (*twice*)
       Married man rocks some other man's babe, fool thinks he's rockin' his own.

Looking back on his past life the blues singer usually brushed quickly over his childhood with but a passing, perfunctory reference to where he was born and raised. He neither yearned for the idle days of his childhood with the sentimental nostalgia of a fictitious Stephen Foster plantation Negro, nor did he reminisce with self-pity on childhood unhappiness. The acquisition of education and knowledge except by experience was also generally absent from the blues, though the singer might sometimes dwell upon his own illiteracy as a cause of his present plight. In his development as an adult personality the blues singer showed little inclination to build a home and little pleasure in home-making – but these were eloquent omissions. When he sang of prosperity and comfort it was usually with wry humor; a racial joke rather than an outright cynicism, as was the case with Peetie Wheatstraw's *Mr. Livingood*.

332   I could just phone, anywhere in town, (*twice*)
       Mr. Livingood wanted it o–ooh well, well, and they rush it on down.

       I had a butler just to fetch me gin, (*twice*)
       Living seven days a week, ooh well, now but I'm living ten.

On big parties, I throw money on the floor, *(twice)*
And leave it for the sweeper, and walk on out the door.

I buy my baby a silk dress every day, *(twice)*
She wear it one time, ooh well, well, then she throw it away.

As a rule he is not jealous of those who live in "Striver's Row," the successful Blacks who resided in the exclusive Sugar Hill district of Harlem. They had successfully competed with Whites and were now well removed from the singer's experience or from that of his customary listeners. As for the professional Blacks, they neither wished nor needed to sing the blues, a fact which imposed further limitations on its content. There were no blues by black teachers and professors; no blues that spoke for the attorney, the doctor, dentist, news editor ... But there were many blues that were sung by the recipients – and, in some instances, the victims – of their services, for they had reason to sing them. And it is in this that part of the explanation lies to the complex problem of the decline in popularity of blues in the black community by the 1960s.

Blues had not died by the end of the 1950s, but they had changed. There were technological changes, such as the demise of the 78 rpm record and the advent of the 45 rpm single and the long-play disc, both of which necessitated the purchase of expensive new equipment. There was change too, in the juke joints, as the juke-boxes became a means of purveying music without the need to employ live musicians. The juke boxes played their part in disseminating the more sophisticated urban styles to the rural areas.

Again, there were changes in the music itself. Rhythm and Blues singers with a witty line in lyrics, R. and B. vocal groups and brassy jug bands brought a new life to the music but reduced its content. The rapid increase in the availability of electric instruments – not only guitars but basses, harmonicas, even pianos as well – led to a louder, hard driving form of city blues, urgent and vital but forcing a less contemplative approach to blues singing. In fact, many of the themes that were the subject of vocal blues in the past disappeared; the medium had become the message.

A further aspect was the growing appeal of blues to white audiences, and the forming of white blues bands. Blues lost its exclusivity for Blacks, many of whom were turning to Soul, an amalgam of blues, R. & B., and gospel song, instead. When black militants needed a music which would express the upsurge of feeling in the Civil Rights campaign years, Gospel and Soul were to provide it. In spite of the ferocity of the Chicago bands, blues was beginning to look old-fashioned.

To the "New Negro" and most of all to the Black recently arrived from the South who was earnestly seeking to acquire the worldly Northerner's veneer of sophistication, there were overtones of the "Uncle Tom" element in the blues. Southern blues, folk music and talk, jive speech, and other creative forms that reinforce the morale of the under-privileged signified an acceptance of segregation and may even have appeared as devices that gave it support. By being essentially "Negro" arts they stressed the division between colored and white. Many black intellectuals looked upon the blues as retrograde and as a sort of corollary, even resenting the increased interest in African "primitive" arts, which they considered condescending, at a time when black status was improving. Though it would seem undeniable that black culture had developed great gifts in music, dance, the stage, and in other arts where poetry, rhythm, and grace of movement were outstanding virtues, emphasis upon them provoked anger. To speak of Blacks as "born entertainers" was to invoke associations of black-face minstrel shows, plantation, and "jungle" cabaret scenes. In the recesses of the racial memory the shadows of slavery still fall, and the arts that arose as a means of escape from the miseries of that era still bear for some the traces of lick-spittle servility. Thus, the unsophisticated arts of the uneducated blacks offended the cultivated colored persons who were striving for complete integration in which all were absorbed into the culture of the nation as a whole.

In contrast with this attitude, there existed a section of the colored intelligentsia, drawn primarily from the literati rather than from the members of the white-collar professions, who took pride in the black folk traditions; writers and poets like Arna Bontemps, J. Mason Brewer, Sterling Brown, Langston Hughes, Ulysses Lee, and Richard Wright among them. They recognized the beauty of such a blues metaphor as:

333   Mama, I love to look in your face, I like the way you spread your
          wings.
       Mama, I love to look in your face, I like the way you spread your
          wings,
       I'm crazy 'bout your way of lovin', mama, I love to hear you call my
          name.

– the evocativeness of a blues simile:

334   If you use my key, well you bound to love me some,
       Throw your arms around me like a circle around the sun.

– or the poetic imagery of such a blues stanza as:

335   In the wee midnight hour, not quite the break of day, (*twice*)
      When the blues creep upon you and carry your mind away . . .

Such writers did not look upon blues verses as trends of thought and modes of speech that let down the race and helped to add further stones to the barriers that obstructed its progress; they were proud of this special song form that, as a part of the whole field of African American music, may well be considered the one indigenous gift of the modern Americas to the world's art. This pride at times stimulated attempts to create a new black poetry in the blues idiom but the blues curiously defied imitation, however sincere the desire to use its form. Essentially a folk form of expression, it was at its best when least self-conscious, when least sophisticated; an art created by and for, the black working classes.

In spite of the advances made during the post-war years, Blacks in the 1950s were still predominately employed on unskilled or semi-skilled labor, and the educated intelligentsia represented a very small minority. For the latter, the blues may have had little significance, but the great majority of African Americans the blues as music was still a vital part of their lives, for the blues as a condition was still all around them.

336   Well it's blues in my house, from the roof to the ground, (*twice*)
      And it's blues everywhere since my good man left town.

      Blues in my mail-box, 'cause I cain't get no mail, (*twice*)
      Says blues in my bread-box, 'cause my bread got stale.

      Blues in my meal-barrel and there's blues upon my shelf, (*twice*)
      And there's blues in my bed, 'cause I'm sleepin' by myself.

For those who had the blues, for those who lived the blues, for those who lived *with* the blues, the blues had meaning. But for those who lived outside the blues the meaning of the blues was elusive. For the blues was more than a form of folk song, and though its meaning became clearer with an understanding of the content of the verses, the reason why Blacks sang the blues and listened to the blues is still not wholly explained. But though the blues may frequently be associated with a state of depression, of lethargy, or despair, it was not solely a physical, nor a mental, state. It was not solely the endurance of suffering or a declaration of hopelessness; nor was it solely a means of ridding oneself of a mood. It was all of these, and more: it was an essential part of the black experience of living.

Implicit in the term "blues" was the whole tragedy of black servitude since Black Anthony Johnson, the first of the "twenty and odd Negers" to set foot on American soil, landed from a Dutch "man of warre" at Jamestown in 1619. At that time to "looke blue" had been current for well over half a century as phrase to describe low spirits, and by the end of the eighteenth century "the blue devils" was a familiar condition of mind. As early as 1807 Washington Irving referred to "a fit of the blues" and colloquial use of the phrase was not uncommon after that date. At some indeterminate time Blacks embraced the term into their own vocabulary and invested it with a meaning of far deeper significance.

For the black folk the blues was an Immanence whose existence was never in question; an abstract presence which brought with it the "blues" as a state of mind. The blues was Mister Blues – Mister Blues who came before daybreak and who was never busier than when others are in need. Otis Harris knew the blues and recognized the blues.

337   Did you ever wake up with the blues and didn't have no place to go,
          (*twice*)
       An' you couldn't do nothin' but just walk from door to door?

       Good morning, Mister Blues, Mister Blues I come to talk with you,
          (*twice*)
       Mister Blues, I ain't doin' nothin' an' I would like to get a job with
          you.

The blues was seldom far away, even when lying dormant, half-forgotten like an inactive cancer. When times were good the blues disappeared, but when trouble came the Blues came too. Lucius Hardy realized that they had never been far away.

338   Howdy, Mister Blues, where have you been so long? (*twice*)
       I've been telling everybody that you were long gone.

       Tell me, Mister Blues, how long did you come to stay? (*twice*)
       Please go right now, you gonna drive my baby away.

       Oh Mister Blues, as soon as you got in town, (*twice*)
       My baby told me she would leave, she was Texas bound.

Now look here, Mister Blues, I want you to leave my door, (*twice*)
And when you go this time, I don't want you back no more.

The blues came unexpected, unheralded, trapping the unwary, as Tommy McClennan recounted,

339 Now the blues got on both legs soon this morning, they trip me,
    t'rowed me down.
    The blues grabbed my both legs this mornin' they trip me, t'rowed me
    down,
    Lord I wouldn't hate it so bad, but the news done got all over town.

    I had the blues 'bout that baby on one Sunday morn, (*twice*)
    Lord I hate to hear my baby wailin' when she gone.

For Ora Brown the blues took possession of her whole being:

340 Got the blues so bad, I can hardly sleep at night, (*twice*)
    Tried to eat my meal, my teeth refuse to bite.

    Did you ever feel lonesome, just to hear your good man's name? (*twice*)
    If the jinx is upon you, the blues fall like showers of rain.

For Kokomo Arnold, a score of years later, the blues continued to fall.

341 I cannot do right, baby, when you won't do right yourself, (*twice*)
    Lord, if my good gal quits me, well, I don't want nobody else.

    Now you can read out your hymn-book, preach out your Bible,
    Fall down on your knees and pray the Good Lord will help you.

    'Cause you gonna need, you gonna need, my help some day,
    Mama, if you can't quit your sinnin' please quit your low-down ways.

    My blues fell this morning and my love come falling down,
    Says my blues fell this morning and my love come falling down,
    Says I'll be your low-down dog, mama, but please don't dog me
    aroun'.

There was no escape, not, at least, for the agonized spirit of Robert Johnson.

342 I got to keep movinnnn', I got to keep movinnnn',
    Blues fallin' down like hail, blues fallin' down like hail,

"Blues Ain't Nothin' Else But"

"Oh, the Blues ain't nothin' but a good woman feeling bad"—a slow, aching heart disease—like consumption, it kills you by degrees. Ida Cox, at last, tells what the Blues are! Every verse is a picture. Hear it and discover how many kinds of Blues you've got. A 2-Hit Record! On the other side Last Time Blues has a sobbing, throbbing clarinet solo.

12212 { Blues Ain't Nothing Else But—
        Last Time Blues—Acc. Lovie Austin and Her Blues Serenaders   Ida Cox

This supplement describes the latest race records by Famous Race Artists
The New York Recording Laboratories
Port Washington   Wisconsin

Paramount
[Combined with Black Swan]   REG. U.S. PAT. OFF.
The Popular Race Record

Mmmmm-mm-mm-mm, blues fallin' down like hail, blues fallin'
    down like hail,
And the day keeps on worryin' me, there's a hell-hound on my trail,
Hell-hound on my trail, hell-hound on my trail.

The invincibility of the blues was seldom held in question:

343   The first time I met the Blues mama, they came walking through the
    wood, (*twice*)
    They stopped at my house first mama, and done me all the harm they
    could.

       Now the Blues got at me, Lord, and run me from tree to tree, (*twice*)
    You should have heard me begging, "Mister Blues, don't murder me!"

For some it was easier to surrender to the blues:

344   I'm going to the river, take me a rocking chair,
    Let the blues overtake me, I'll rock away from here.

Others felt, as Francis "Scrapper" Blackwell did, that the blues were
unpredictable, but always present.

345   Blues is funny, upon you they will sneak, (*twice*)
    They will come on Monday, stay with you all the week.

       Sometimes blues makes me happy, and then again they makes me cry,
    (*twice*)
    What makes me get that way? I can't tell the reason why.

       I do believe I was born with blues in my right hand, (*twice*)
    Why it takes the blues so long I just can't understand.

       Yes, if I've had these blues one time, had 'em a thousand times, (*twice*)
    And I can always feel them liftin' on my mind.

In *Conversation With The Blues* Big Bill Broonzy reasoned with the blues:
"Now look-a here, Blues, I want to talk with you, you been making me
drink and gamble and stay out all night too. Now you got me to the place I
don't care what I do; yeah, now, Blues, I wanna have a little talk with you.

Now I believe you been drinkin' moonshine, Blues, 'cause you don't care what you do."

> 346   Yeah now, blues, why don't you give poor Bill a break?
> Yeah now, blues, why don't you give poor Bill a break?
> Now why don't you try to help me to live instead of tryin' to break
>   my neck?

But the blues remained enigmatic and did not explain why they came:

> 347   Early this morning, the blues came walking in my room, (*twice*)
> I said, "Blues, please tell me what you are doing here so soon?"
>
> They looked at me and smiled but yet, they refused to say, (*twice*)
> Asked them again, then they turned and walked away.
>
> "Blues oh, Blues, you know you've been here before. (*twice*)
> The last time you were here you made me cry and walk the floor."

The blues is not trouble or hardship, it's not loneliness or misery, but, in Will Day's image, it's a companion to them all.

> 348   My blues and trouble both running hand in hand, (*twice*)
> These old women nowadays, they running from man to man.
>
> My heart's in trouble, mind's in misery, (*twice*)
> Got the blues so bad, I really can't hardly see.

Though he may know that for some there is a life without the company of the blues, many a colored man sees little prospect of freedom in his own lifetime from his unwanted companion.

> 349   Now the stars really are shinin' – clouds look awful grey,
> Now the stars really are shinin' – clouds look awful grey,
> I believe to my soul my blues and trouble are goin' to carry me to my
>   grave.

When lives were upset, families broken, love lost, the blues came falling down. The blues dogged the footsteps of the migrant, walked in the shadow of the destitute, sat at table with the hungry, shared the bed of the forsaken. It was the comrade-in-arms of those whose work was strenuous, monotonous, and ill-paid; it was the partner of the share-cropper, the section-hand, and the road-sweeper.

An argument might be advanced that the belief in the blues as an entity which influences the lives of men was a survival of African totemism. It could be reasoned that it was a substitute for a godhead made by those who had no faith in the church; that "devil songs" was an accurate enough term. Justification could be found for considering the blues to be a symbol of white domination: it seems likely that the belief grew from the persistent condition of repression that Blacks in the United States endured for long centuries. It is not possible to comprehend the reasons why Blacks sing the blues unless this dual conception of the nature of blues as an ever-present power and as a condition of mind is appreciated, for it is in this that the key to understanding lies. In the blues as folk song the African American gave form to the blues of his or her experience. The blues was the utterance of innermost feelings, the outpourings of the heart. When Walter Davis sang the blues he sang to drive away the blues and to relieve his mind of the blues.

350   People, if you hear me humming on this song both night and day,
      People, if you hear me humming on this song both night and day,
      I'm just a poor boy in trouble, trying to drive the blues away.

By the 1960s there were signs that the blues as a truly creative folk song were already on the wane, for the tragic themes of suffering and misery that had arisen from poverty and destitution, from disease and disaster, violence and brutality, from bad living conditions and aimless migration, were less frequently heard than in former years. The improved status of black people during the previous decade, the gradual but definite moves towards integration, the slow but perceptible advances towards equality of opportunity may have been reflected in the blues on record, for the blues by then was primarily concerned with personal relationships of love and desertion. On these subjects the blues, as all forms of song, has been more than eloquent and probably has little new to add. But if the more significant, though more disturbing, themes disappeared with the passing shades of an old and ignominious era, and if the blues as a virile form of folk song was to pass with them, the loss would be a small enough price to pay. The true and complete integration of Blacks into American society may eventually mean the death of a folk art form of great simplicity, beauty, and meaning.

But the blues still fell this morning.

Bibliographical references

A vast literature exists on Blacks in the United States and a great many works were consulted in the writing of this book. Principal references, which generally expand on the details given here, are cited below. In order to keep the list to a reasonable length several hundred articles have not been included. Bibliographical details of the works consulted are given, but where a book has been referred to before they are not repeated; the notes to the Preface, Introduction, or the chapter where the information first appears are indicated by (Intro), or a numeral, e.g. (6). Many references cited were contemporaneous, or written shortly after the events described, and black authors are prominent. Though the majority of references were consulted for the original edition, details of more recent studies are included where they augment the information.

PREFACE AND INTRODUCTION

More than a hundred books have been published on blues since 1960. General studies of black music which place blues in a larger context include Eileen Southern, *The Music of Black Americans* (New York, Norton, 1971, revised 1983) and Lawrence Levine, *Black Culture and Black Consciousness* (New York, Oxford University Press, 1977). Histories include Paul Oliver, *The Story of the Blues* (London, Barrie & Jenkins, 1969) and Giles Oakley, *The Devil's Music* (London, British Broadcasting Corporation, 1976). My other books referred to in the Introduction include two investigations of the musical and lyric sources of blues, *Savannah Syncopators: African Retentions in the Blues* (London, Studio Vista, 1970), and *Songsters and Saints: Vocal Traditions on Race Records* (Cambridge University Press, 1984). A collection of interviews with blues singers, Paul Oliver, *Conversation with the Blues* (London, Cassell, 1965) illustrates their lives, while Paul Oliver, *Screening the Blues: Aspects of the Blues Tradition* (London, Cassell, 1968; New York, Da Capo, 1989) develops some of the themes arising from this book. Theoretical works include a sociological study by Charles Keil, *Urban Blues* (Chicago University Press, 1967) and a Freudian analysis of lyrics by Paul Garon, *Blues and the Poetic Spirit* (London, Eddison, 1975; New York, Da Capo, 1979). Jeff Todd Titon's *Early Downhome Blues* is *A Musical and Cultural Analysis* (Urbana, University of Illinois Press, 1977) while a local style is examined in David Evans, *Big Road Blues: Tradition and Creativity in the Folk Blues* (Berkeley, University of California Press, 1982). Essential discographies include R. M. W. Dixon and J. Godrich, *Blues and Gospel Records 1902–1943* (Chigwell, Essex, Storyville, 3rd revised ed. 1982) and Mike Leadbitter and Neil Slaven, *Blues Records 1943–1970* (London, Record Information Services, 1987). *The Blackwell Guide to Blues Records*, ed. Paul Oliver, (Oxford, Blackwell, 1989) advises collectors on available issues. For additional references on black folkways see the extensive annotated bibliography by John F. Szwed and Roger D. Abrahams, *Afro-American Folk Culture, Part 1, North America* (Philadelphia, ISHI, 1978) and for blues in particular, the classified bibliography in Paul Oliver, Max Harrison, and William Balcom, *The New Grove Gospel, Blues and Jazz* (London, Macmillan; New York, W. W. Norton, 1986), pp. 177–88.

1   GOT TO WORK OR LEAVE

Black experiences in the period after the Civil War are described in Leon F. Witack, *Been In the Storm So Long: The Aftermath of Slavery* (New York, Alfred A. Knopf, 1979). The classic work on Reconstruction is W. E. B. Du Bois, *Black Reconstruction in America 1860–1880* (New York, Harcourt, Brace, 1935); Robert Cruden, *The Negro in Reconstruction* (New Jersey, Prentice-Hall, 1969) is briefer. An afterview is *The Era of Reconstruction 1865–1877* by Kenneth Stampp (New York, Alfred A. Knopf, 1965). Subsequent decades are discussed by C. Vann Woodward in *Origins of the New South 1877–1913* (Baton Rouge, Louisiana State University Press, 1951). A "composite picture" of the South is given in Howard W. Odum, *Southern Regions of the United States* (Chapel Hill, University of North Carolina Press, 1936 , hereafter abbreviated as Chapel Hill). For attitudes and values see W. J. Cash, *The Mind of the South* (New York, Alfred A. Knopf, 1941). Labor and living conditions are described in Carter G. Woodson *The Rural Negro* (New York, Russell & Russell, 1930) and given a closer focus by Arthur F. Raper, *Preface to Peasantry* (Chapel Hill, 1936). The southern monoculture is the subject of David Cohn's *The Life and Times of King Cotton* (New York, Oxford University Press, 1956). Interviews with black sharecroppers illumine Charles S. Johnson, *The Shadow of the Plantation* (University of Chicago Press, 1934). Anonymous workers speak to members of the Federal Writers' Project in *These Are Our Lives* (Chapel Hill, 1939). Conditions in the logging industry are revealed by Charlotte Todes in her *Labor and Lumber* (New York, International Publishers, 1931). Other "jobs" are exposed in Norman Thomas, *Human Exploitation in the United States* (New York, Frederick A. Stokes, 1934), and documented by A. Davis, B. Gardner, and M. Gardner in their study of caste and class, *Deep South* (University of Chicago Press, 1941). The persistence of the exploitation of Blacks is the subject of Pete Daniel, *The Shadow of Slavery: Peonage in the South 1901–1969* (New York, Oxford University Press, 1973). Decline in the plantation culture is described by Charles S. Johnson, E. Embree, and W. W. Alexander in their influential *The Collapse of the Cotton Tenancy* (Chapel Hill, 1935). The slow progress towards industrialization is examined in Calvin Hoover and B. U. Ratchford, *Economic Resources and Policies of the South* (New York, Macmillan, 1951) and further scrutinized by Gavin Wright in *Old South, New South* (New York, Basic Books, 1986). Migration from the South is analyzed by Rupert B. Vance and Nadia Danilevsky in *All These People* (Chapel Hill, 1945), while Henry Ford, the automobile industry, and black labor are the subject of August Meier and Elliott Rudwick's *Black Detroit and the Rise of the U.A.W.* (New York, Oxford University Press, 1979). Labor relations in the steel, meat-packing, and railroad car industries are the subject of Horace R. Cayton and George S. Mitchell, *Black Workers and the New Unions* (Chapel Hill, 1939). The collapse of Wall Street is recounted by the economist John Kenneth Galbraith in *The Great Crash* (Boston, Houghton Mifflin, 1954) and its human effects are described in Caroline Bird, *The Invisible Scar* (New York, David McKay, 1966). Arthur M. Schlesinger Jr.'s *The Coming of the New Deal* (vol. 2 of *The Age of Roosevelt*) (London, Heinemann, 1959) is a masterly study, but long; *The New Deal: Revolution or Evolution?*, ed. Edwin C. Rozwenc (Boston, D. C. Heath, 1959) is a useful collection of papers. A careful appraisal of such subjects as Relief and the employment of Blacks by the W.P.A. is found in *The Negro's Share*, ed. Robert Sterner (New York, Harper & Brothers, 1943). For Executive Order 8802 see Roi Ottley, *New World A-Comin': Inside Black America* (Boston, Houghton Mifflin, 1943), chapter 20.

2   RAILROAD FOR MY PILLOW

Though not always reliable for the South, statistics on the employment of Blacks, the numbers who remained in the states of their birth, or who migrated elsewhere (and much else), can be obtained, laboriously, from the reports for the Decennial Census of the Population. They are usefully synthesized in *Historical Statistics of the United States: Colonial Times to 1957* (Washington, D.C., U.S. Department of Commerce, Bureau of the Census, 1960). See also the *Statistical Abstract of the United States*, annually published by the Bureau of the Census since 1878. Especially relevant is Harold I. Ickes, Chairman, *The Problems of a Changing Population* (Washington D.C., Report to the National Resources Committee, 1938). Probably the best single source is Henry S. Shryock Jr., *Population Mobility Within the United States* (University of Chicago Press, 1964). The complex nature of racial discrimination was brilliantly demonstrated by Charles S. Johnson in *Patterns of Negro Segregation* (London, Victor Gollancz, 1944); post-war conditions are condensed from the Report of the U.S. Commission on Civil Rights by Wallace Mendelson in *Discrimination* (New Jersey, Prentice-Hall, 1962). Edward E. Lewis, *The Mobility of the Negro* (New York, Columbia University Press, 1931) is an important study for the earlier periods; chapter 8 of Gunnar Myrdal's classic work, *An American Dilemma* (New York, Harper & Row, 1944, 1962) summarizes the later statistics and the problems of interpretation. Encouraging letters and inducements to migrate appeared in the pages of the *Chicago Defender*. Some extracts are quoted in Robert B. Grant, *The Black Man Comes to the City* (Chicago, Nelson-Hall, 1972). Figures of young migrants calculated by the Children's Bureau of the Department of Labor are given in Gilbert Seldes, *The Year of the Locust: America, 1929–32* (1933; New York, Da Capo, 1973). The impact of the Depression on black children was reported by Charles S. Johnson, *Growing Up in the Black Belt: Negro Youth in the Rural South*, (American Council on Education, 1941). Extensive details of homelessness and the migration of adults and children are given by E. Franklin Frazier, *The Negro Family in the United States* (University of Chicago Press, 1939). Young hoboes were interviewed by Thomas Minehan as he traveled with them. His *Boy and Girl Tramps of America* (New York, Farrar and Rinehart, 1934) shocked the nation. Left-Wing Gordon, an unrecorded hobo blues singer, tells his life-story to Howard W. Odum in *Rainbow Round My Shoulder: The Blue Trail of Black Ulysses* (Indianapolis, Bobbs-Merrill, 1928.) His travels are traced in Howard W. Odum and Guy B. Johnson, *Negro Workaday Songs* (Chapel Hill, 1926). Many fragments of hobo reminiscences are given in B. A. Botkin and Alvin F. Harlow, *A Treasury of Railroad Folklore* (New York, Bonanza Books, 1953). See also Stewart Holbrook, *The Story of American Railroads* (New York, Crown, 1947). Many works on American folksong, white and black, include railroad songs. The most comprehensive is Norm Cohen, *Long Steel Rail: The Railroad in American Folksong* (Urbana, University of Illinois Press, 1981). For the recollections of blues singers as hoboes see Paul Oliver, *Conversation With The Blues* (Intro).

3   SWEET HONEY FOR ME

The classic work on the black family is E. Franklin Frazier, *The Negro Family in the United States* (2). That the black family was shattered by slavery and its aftermath has been challenged by Eugene D. Genovese, *Roll Jordan Roll: The World the Slaves Made*, (New York, Pantheon Books, 1972), and at great length by Herbert G. Gutman, *The Black Family in Slavery and Freedom, 1750–1925*, (Oxford, Basil Blackwell, 1976). Color and caste in black communities is examined by Gunnar Myrdal, *An American Dilemma* (2), chapter 30, and by St. Clair Drake and Horace R. Cayton, *Black Metropolis* (1), chapter 18. "Passing for white" is examined by Louis Wirth, in *Characteristics of the American Negro*, ed. Otto Klineberg (New York, Harper & Brothers, 1944), chapter 5. For the psychological implications of skin color see Abram Kardiner and Lionel Ovesey, *The Mark of Oppression: Explorations in the Personality of the American Negro* (Cleveland, World Publishing Company, 1951). Color preferences in partners are discussed by Jessie Barnard in *Marriage and Family Among Negroes* (New Jersey, Prentice-hall, 1966). *The Negro Family: The Case for National Action* (Washington D.C., U.S. Department of Labor, 1965) or "The Moynihan Report," argues that black social problems arise from deterioration of the family. This view supports E. Franklin Frazier, *The Negro Family* (2), and is contested by Gutman (above). E. Earl Braughman, *Black Americans* (New York, Academic Press, 1971), chapter 7, summarizes the debate. Howard W. Odum and Guy B. Johnson, *The Negro and His Songs* (Chapel Hill, 1925) complains of the "lack of higher ideals." Iain Lang's comment is made in *Jazz in Perspective: The Background of the Blues* (London, Hutchinson, 1947). Insights into personal relationships in working-class black communities may be gained from books by early black novelists, including Jean Toomer, *Cane* (New York, Boni & Liveright, 1923); Claude McKay, *Home to Harlem* (New York, Harper & Brothers, 1928), Richard Wright, *Native Son* (London, Victor Gollancz, 1940) and *Black Boy* (London, Victor Gollancz, 1945). Richard Wright's "folk history of the Negro," *Twelve Million Black Voices* (London, Lindsay Drummond, 1947) places them in context.

4   I'M A ROOSTER, BABY

Sexual exploitation of black women in slavery is summarized in Paul A. David *et al.*, *Reckoning with Slavery* (New York, Oxford University Press, 1976), chapter 4. John Dollard, *Caste and Class in a Southern Town* (New Haven, Yale University Press, 1937), concludes that sexual fears, preoccupations, and stereotypes were the basis of the South's justification for Segregation. Though widely believed to be so, rape was not the main reason for lynchings, see Arthur F. Raper, *The Tragedy of Lynching* (Chapel Hill, 1933), and Mary Ellison, *The Black Experience: American Blacks Since 1865* (London, Batsford, 1974). Hypersensitivity concerning black sexuality meant that very little was published on it until the 1960s. Among the rare exceptions are Charles S. Johnson, *Growing Up in the Black Belt* (2), chapter 8, and David Cohn, *Where I Was Born and Raised* (South Bend, University of Notre Dame Press, 1935), chapter 4. Guy B. Johnson's 1927 paper "Double Meaning in the Popular Negro Blues," published in the *Journal of Abnormal and Social Psychology*, is reprinted in Alan Dundes, *Mother Wit From the Laughing Barrel* (New Jersey, Prentice-Hall, 1973), as are Mimi Clar Melnick "Boasts in the Blues" (1967), and papers by John Dollard (1939) and Roger D. Abrahams (1962) on "The Dozens." "Rules for ritual insults" are identified by William Labov in *Rappin' and Stylin' Out: Communication in Urban Black America*, ed. Thomas Kochman (Urbana, University of Illinois Press, 1972) with other, later studies of "signifying." Odum and Johnson's reluctance to quote sexual songs was shared by other folksong collectors, for example Dorothy Scarborough, *On the Trail of Negro Folk Songs* (Cambridge, Mass., Harvard University Press, 1925), chapter 10, or Newman I. White, *American Negro Folk-Songs* (Cambridge, Mass., Harvard University, 1928), chapter 10. The long chapter 9, "The Blue Blues" in Paul Oliver, *Screening the Blues* (Intro) is intended to remedy the omissions. "Playing the Dozens" is analyzed in Roger D. Abrahams, *Deep Down in the Jungle* (Hatboro, Folklore Associates, 1964), chapter 2.

5   THE JINX IS ON ME

In "Preaching the Blues," chapter 2 of my book, *Screening the Blues* (Intro), I discuss the attitudes in the blues to the church, and the relationship of "jackleg" preachers and street evangelists to blues singers in "Honey in the Rock," *Songsters and Saints* (Intro), chapter 7. Inequalities in black education are documented in detail in chapters 17 and 18 of E. Franklin Frazier,

The Negro in the United States (New York, Macmillan, 1949), and in chapter 41 of Gunnar Myrdal, *An American Dilemma* (2). The evidence of intelligence testing is described in Thomas F. Pettigrew, *A Profile of the Negro American* (Princeton, Van Nostrand, 1964). Newbell Niles Puckett, *Folk Beliefs of the Southern Negro* (Chapel Hill, 1926) is the standard work. Africanisms in black beliefs and religious life are identified in chapter 7 of Melville Herskovits, *The Myth of the Negro Past* (New York, Harper & Brothers, 1958). Africanisms in Brazil, Cuba, Jamaica, Trinidad, and Haiti are collected in Harold Courlander, *A Treasury of Afro-American Folklore* (New York, Crown, 1976). Alfred Metraux, *Voodoo in Haiti* (London, André Deutsch, 1959) and Maya Deren, *The Voodoo Gods* (London, Thames & Hudson, 1953) are just two of the many works on Voudun. George W. Cable's much quoted article "The Dance in the Place Congo" is reprinted in George W. Cable, *Creoles and Cajuns*, ed. Arlin Turner (New York, Doubleday, 1959). Several papers on "Conjuration," including the "mojo," are reprinted in Alan Dundes, *Mother Wit From the Laughing Barrel* (4). Zora Neale Hurston in *Mules and Men* (Philadelphia, Lippincott, 1935) describes her experiences in training to be a voodoo priestess, and the finding of the "Black Cat's Bone." Marie Laveau and witchcraft practices are described in Robert Tallant, *Voodoo in New Orleans* (New York, Macmillan, 1946). Carl Carmer in *Stars Fell On Alabama* (London, Lovat Dickson & Thompson, 1935) recounts a visit to Seven Sisters and cites several supersititions. My copy of Albertus Magnus, *Book of Dreams and Mystery*, had no publishing details. All you ever need to know about black witchcraft is in the four-volume compilation by Harry Middleton Hyatt, *Hoodoo – Conjuration – Witchcraft – Rootwork* (Hannibal, Western Publishing, 1970). The strict codes of behavior in black cults are compared in chapter 7 of Arthur Huff Fauset, *Black Gods of the Metropolis* (Philadelphia, University of Pennsylvania Press, 1944). See also Sara Harris, *The Incredible Father Divine* (London, W. H. Allen, 1954). Store-front churches are discussed in chapters 17, 21, and 22 of St. Clair Drake and Horace R. Cayton, *Black Metropolis: A Study of Negro Life in a Northern City* (New York, Harcourt, Brace, 1945); see chapter 17 for details of the "Policy Racket." Policy in New Orleans is described in *Gumbo Ya-Ya*, ed. Lyle Saxon (Boston, Houghton Mifflin, 1945), and in New York by Roi Ottley in *New World A-Comin': Inside Black America* (1). For a full discussion of the Numbers Game in blues, see Paul Oliver, *Screening the Blues* (Intro), chapter 4, which also illustrates "Dream Book" entries (Da Capo edition only).

6 LET THE DEAL GO DOWN

Zora Neale Hurston, *Mules and Men* (5) describes games of Florida Flip, craps (chapter 9), and gives details of the Georgia Skin Game (Glossary). For craps, see *Gumbo Ya-Ya*, ed. Saxon (5) chapter 7, and for loggers and craps see Shields McIlwaine, *Memphis Down in Dixie* (New York, E. P. Dutton, 1948). "Hustling" pool and craps are discussed by Julius Hudson in *Rappin' and Stylin' Out*, ed. Kochman (4). A gambler and con-man who followed the carnival shows confesses in *Men of the Underworld: The Professional Criminal's Own Story*, ed. Charles Hamilton (New York, Macmillan, 1954). Malcolm Webber describes "grifters" in *Medicine Show* (Caldwell, Idaho, Caxton Printers, 1941). Blues singers on road shows and medicine shows are dealt with at length in Paul Oliver, *Songsters and Saints* (Intro), chapter 3, and dance songs and routines in chapter 1. Sukey-jumps and reels are featured in John A. and Alan Lomax, *Negro Folk Songs as Sung By Lead Belly* (New York, Macmillan, 1936). For many references to shows and dances see Marshall Stearns, *Jazz Dance: The Story of American Vernacular Dance* (New York, Macmillan, 1968). House rent parties are described by Langston Hughes in *The Book of Negro Folklore* (New York, Dodd, Mead, 1958), ed. Langston Hughes and Arna Bontemps, and "buffet flats" in Roi Ottley, *New World A-Comin'* (1), chapter 5. See also Gilbert Osofsky, *Harlem: The Making of a Ghetto*, (New York, Harper & Row, 1963). For early stages of Prohibition in the South and its effects on Blacks, refer to William Archer, *Through Afro-America* (London, Chapman & Hall, 1910), chapter 10. The Volstead Act was supported by Herbert Hoover; see Edwin Emerson, *Hoover and His Times* (New York, Garden City Publishing, 1932). The gang wars as graphically described at the time, feature in Edward D. Sullivan, *Look at Chicago* (London, Geoffrey Bles, 1930). For a history of the illicit liquor trade see Kenneth Alsopp, *The Bootleggers* (London, Hodder & Stoughton, 1964). Housing conditions in Chicago are detailed in Otis D. Duncan and Beverly Duncan, *The Negro Population in Chicago* (University of Chicago, 1957). Drugs and the addict's vocabulary are described by a musician–pusher, Milton "Mezz" Mezzrow, with Bernard Wolfe, *Really the Blues* (New York, Random House, 1946).

7 EVIL AND MEAN AND FUNNY

Chapters on "Urbanism and Race Relations" by Henry Allen Bullock and "Crime in Southern Cities" by Austin L. Porterfield and Robert H. Talbert are among relevant studies in *The Urban South*, ed. Rupert B. Vance and Nicholas J. Demerath (Chapel Hill, 1954). Elliott M. Rudwick's *Race Riot at East St. Louis, July 2, 1917* (Carbondale, Southern Illinois University Press, 1964) also discusses the Chicago 1919, and Detroit 1943 race riots. Attitudes to urban migration (1915–30) are documented in Robert B. Grant, *The Black Man Comes to the City* (2) and by Ira Katznelson in *Black Men, White Cities* (London, Oxford University Press, 1972), parts 1 and 2. Detailed studies of living conditions in the black ghettos include Charles Abrams, *Forbidden Neighbors: A Study of Prejudice in Housing* (New York, Harper & Bros. 1955) and part 6 of Robert C. Weaver, *The Urban Complex: Human Values in Urban Life* (Garden City, N.Y., Doubleday, 1964). The tenderloin areas as hosts to jazz and blues are summarized in Leroy Ostransky, *Jazz City: The Impact of Our Cities on the Development of Jazz*) (New Jersey, Prentice-Hall, 1978). Herbert Asbury's studies of urban criminality and syndicated prostitution include New Orleans in *The French Quarter* (Garden City, Garden City Publishing, 1938), and Chicago in *The Underworld of Chicago* (London, Robert Hale, 1951). Much quoted, they are sensationalized accounts. The problems of prostitution in black areas are examined in chapter 8 of E. Franklin Frazier, *The Negro Family* (2), and specifically for Chicago in Drake and Cayton's *Black Metropolis* (1), chapter 20. The sexual exploitation of male prisoners is described by Haywood Patterson (with Earl Conrad) in *Scottsboro Boy* (London, Victor Gollancz, 1950). Capital crime rates are reported in H. C. Brearly, *Homicide in the United States* (Chapel Hill, 1932). Social attitudes are discussed by Ira DeA. Reid in *Report on the Causes of Crime* (Washington, D.C., National Commission on Law Observance and Enforcement, 1931), vol. 1, part 3. Statistics of crimes committed by Blacks are included in the annually printed *Uniform Crime Reports*, formerly issued under the directorship of J. Edgar Hoover of the F.B.I. (Washington D.C., U.S. Department of Justice). It should be noted that the accuracy of these compilations has been frequently questioned, for example by Leonard D. Savitz in "Black Crime," *Comparative Studies of Blacks and Whites in the United States*, ed. Kent S. Miller and Ralph Mason Dreger (New York, Seminar Press, 1973), chapter 16.

8   GOIN' TO TAKE A RAP

In their revisionist work, *Time on the Cross: The Economics of American Negro Slavery* (New York, Little, Brown, 1974), Robert William Fogel and

Stanley L. Engerman argue that cruelty to slaves has been exaggerated. This view is vigorously contested by Paul A. David, Herbert A. Gutman *et al.* in *Reckoning with Slavery* (New York, Oxford University Press, 1976). Histories of the Ku Klux Klan include David M. Chalmers, *Hooded Americans: The First Century of the Ku Klux Klan*, (Garden City N.Y., Doubleday, 1965), and William Pierce Randel, *The Ku Klux Klan: A Century of Infamy* (London, Hamish Hamilton, 1965). Studies of lynching include Walter White, *Rope and Faggot* (New York, Alfred A. Knopf, 1929), and Arthur F. Raper, *The Tragedy of Lynching* (Chapel Hill, 1933). Statistics of arrests are carefully analyzed in Charles S. Johnson, *The Negro in American Civilization* (New York, Henry Holt, 1930), chapters 22 and 23. Figures in the dubious category of "Suspicion" are given by Savitz in Miller and Dreger's *Comparative Studies of Blacks and Whites* (7). The "convict lease" system is discussed by F. M. Green in *Essays in Southern History* (Chapel Hill, 1949) and Archie Green, *Only a Miner*, (Urbana, University of Illinois Press, 1972). Jesse F. Steiner and Roy M. Brown's *The North Carolina Chain Gang* (Chapel Hill, 1927) is a sober indictment; John L. Spivak's "Flashes from Georgia Chain Gangs" and "Negro Songs of Protest" by Lawrence Gellert, both in *Negro: An Anthology*, ed. Nancy Cunard (London, Wishart, 1933) contain vivid observations. See also Lawrence Gellert's *Negro Songs of Protest* (New York, Carl Fisher, 1936) and his *Me and My Captain* (New York, Hours Press, 1939). Black prisoners are described in David L. Cohn, *Where I was Born and Raised* (4). County courts and legal representation in Georgia are discussed by Arthur F. Raper, *Preface to Peasantry* (Chapel Hill, 1936), chapter 15. Punishments in Georgia prisons are documented, with photographs, in John L. Spivak, *Georgia Nigger* (New York, Brewer, Warren & Putnam, 1932). An even-handed report by Alexander Paterson, H.M. Commissioner of Prisons for England and Wales, *The Prison Problem in America* (London, Prison Commission, *c.* 1934) noted both failures and advances in the system. Other perceptions include Hayward Patterson, *Scottsboro Boy* (7), (inmate); Theodore Rosengarten, *All God's Dangers: The Life of Nate Shaw* (New York, Alfred A. Knopf, 1975), (inmate); Clinton T. Duffy and Dean Jennings, *The San Quentin Story* (New York, 1950), (warden); John A. Lomax, *Adventures of a Ballad Hunter* (New York, Macmillan, 1947), (song collector); John A. Lomax and Alan Lomax, *Negro Folk Songs as Sung by Lead Belly*, (6), (songster–recidivist); John Bartlow Martin, *Break Down the Walls* (London, Gollancz, 1950), (reform advocate); Stetson Kennedy, *Jim Crow Guide to the U.S.A.* (London, Lawrence & Wishart, 1959), (journalist).

9 WORLD BLACK AS MIDNIGHT

The Mississippi river has been the subject of many books. Ray Samuel, Leonard V. Huber, and Warren C. Ogden, *Tales of the Mississippi* (New York, Hastings House, 1955) is extensively illustrated. The river in relation to the land in the 1930s is recorded in Federal Writers' Project, *Mississippi: A Guide to the Magnolia State* (New York, Viking Press, 1938). The construction of the levees is summarized in Hodding Carter, *Lower Mississippi* (New York, Farrar & Rinehart, 1942), chapter 23. *The Mississippi Valley Flood Disaster of 1927* (Washington D.C. The Red Cross, 1928) has considerable statistics of the flood and flood relief, but is biased – Blacks are scarcely mentioned. Pete Daniel, *Deep'n As It Come: The 1927 Mississippi River Flood* (New York, Oxford University Press, 1927), is the most reliable account. Walter White of the N.A.A.C.P. refers to his conflict with President Hoover in *A Man Called White* (London, Victor Gollancz, 1949). An apologia for Herbert Hoover's conduct appears in chapter 8 of Edwin Emerson, *Hoover and His Times* (New York, Garden City Publishing, 1932), and by the chairman of the Flood Relief Committee himself, William Alexander Percy in *Lanterns on the Levee: Recollections of a Planter's Son* (New York, Alfred A. Knopf, 1946). The Moton Committee Report was *not* published (the Red Cross Report claims that it was). The papers can be seen in Box G.C. 48, Tuskegee Institute Archives, Alabama. The frequency and distribution of tornadoes and hurricanes are indicated in the state reports in *Climate and Man*, ed. Gove Hambridge *et al.* (Washington D.C., U.S. Department of Agriculture, Yearbook no. 6, 1941). For details of housing conditions and facilities see Bureau of Home Economics, *The Farm-Housing Survey* (Washington D.C., U.S. Department of Agriculture, 1939). "Race heroes" and "Race men" are discussed in Drake and Cayton, *Black Metropolis* (5), and typologies of leadership are listed in M. Elaine Burgess, *Negro Leadership in a Southern City* (Chapel Hill, 1960). A full acount of the Natchez Rhythm Club fire appears in Albert McCarthy, *Big Band Jazz* (London, Barrie & Jenkins, 1974), chapter 2. Black servicemen and songsters in World War I are observed in John J. Niles, *Singing Soldiers* (New York, Scribner's, 1927). Discrimination in the armed services is detailed in Charles S. Johnson, *Patterns of Negro Segregation* (2). The "Secret Information Concerning Black American Troops" is cited by Ottley in *New World A-Comin'* (1). War-time frustrations are expressed by Adam Clayton Powell, Jr, in *Marching Blacks* (New York, Dial Press, 1945). Black achievements in both World Wars are illustrated in Langston Hughes and

Milton Meltzer, *A Pictorial History of the American Negro* (New York, Crown, 1956), reported in William L. Katz, *Eyewitness: The Negro in American History* (New York, Pitman, 1967) and documented in John Hope Franklin, *From Slavery to Freedom* (New York, Alfred A. Knopf, 1956), chapters 18 and 24. See also chapter 8 of Eli Ginzberg, *The Negro Potential* (New York, Columbia University Press, 1956). For an overview, see "The Negro in the Armed Forces of America" by John P. Davis, in *The American Negro Reference Book*, ed. John P. Davis (New Jersey, Prentice-Hall, 1966), chapter 15.

10   GOING DOWN SLOW

Dr Joseph Goldberger's work on pellagra is documented in Kenneth Carpenter, *The History of Pellagra* (London, Hutchinson, 1981). A number of diseases arise from nutritional deficiencies; the relations between low income, family expenditure, and the nutritional value of food consumed is extensively debated in *The Negro's Share*, ed. Sterner (1), chapters 5–8. That malaria, typhus, and other insect- or water-borne diseases arise from poor sanitation and inadequate protection is a conclusion of *The National Health Survey, 1935–36* (Washington D.C., U.S. Health Service, 1938). The prevalance of tuberculosis is documented in Thomas F. Pettigrew, *A Profile of the Negro American* (Princeton, Van Nostrand, 1964), chapter 4. Details from numerous health reports are given by E. Franklin Frazier in *The Negro in the United States* (2), chapter 22. Segregation in hospitals is discussed in Charles S. Johnson, *Patterns of Negro Segregation* (2), chapter 2. Warnings concerning the rates of sexually transmitted diseases were given by Thomas Parran of the U.S. Public Health Service, in *Shadow on the Land – Syphilis* (New York, Reynal & Hitchcock, 1937). Rates for syphilis and gonorrhea were reported in *Physical Examinations of Selective Service Registrants During Wartime* (Washington D.C., Medical Statistics Bulletin no. 3, 1944). Ignorance of the relationship between "bad blood" and sexual relations, and the use of folk remedies, are reported by Charles S. Johnson, *Shadow of the Plantation* (1), chapter 7. Chapter 11 of Maurice R. Davie, *Negroes in American Society* (New York, McGraw-Hill, 1949 includes folk remedies, and extensive references on health. For remedies see also Newbell Niles Puckett, *Folk Beliefs of the Southern Negro* (5), chapter 5, and R. Emmet Kennedy, *Mellows: A Chronicle of Unknown Singers* (New York, A. & C. Boni, 1925), which also contains a note on burial. African retentions in funeral customs are compiled in Melville J. Herskovits, *The Myth of the*

Negro Past (5), chapter 6. Accounts of burials and wakes, cemetaries and ghosts in New Orleans appear in *Gumbo Ya-Ya*, ed. Saxon (5). Death and burial (and much else) in a rural community are sensitively depicted in Julia Peterkin and Doris Ulmann, *Roll, Jordan, Roll* (New York, Robert O. Ballou, 1933).

11   BLUES LIKE SHOWERS OF RAIN

Transcription of black idioms has always presented problems; see for instance, Reed Smith, *Gullah* (Columbia, University of South Carolina Bulletin 190, 1926). The analysis of speech patterns, sentence structure, and pronunciation have received considerable attention since the early 1970s. William Labov, *Language in the Inner City: Studies in the Black English Vernacular* (University of Pennsylvania Press, 1972), is a standard work on the subject of "B.E.V." For analysis of blues tradition, expression, and music in performance, see David Evans, *Big Road Blues* (Intro), and for the use of formulas in stanzas and analysis of blues tune families, Jeff Todd Titon, *Early Downhome Blues* (Intro). Titon has used ethnopoetic transcription to convey singers' timing in *Downhome Blues Lyrics: An Anthology from the Post-War II Era* (Boston, Twayne, 1981), though the system lacks both punctuation and rigor. Pig Latin and jive are discussed in Milton Mezzrow, *Really the Blues* (6), which also contains a glossary. See also *The New Cab Calloway's Hepsters Dictionary: Language of Jive* (New York, Cab Calloway, 1944). Slang is volatile and many terms are no longer in use or have changed their meaning; for later usage see, for instance, Roger D. Abrahams, *Positively Black* (New Jersey, Prentice-Hall, 1970). John Greenaway, *American Folksongs of Protest* (University of Pennsylvania Press, 1953) contains almost no blues. Some were collected by Lawrence Gellert and quoted in *Negro Songs of Protest* (8), but these were not commercially issued on 78s. I considered sexual blues as symbols of protest in "The Blue Blues," chapter 9 of *Screening the Blues* (Intro); chapter 5 also contains a comparison of "John Henry and Joe Louis." A "Pantheon of Heroes" is in Lawrence Levine, *Black Culture and Black Consciousness* (Intro), chapter 6. I have discussed the changing role of ballad heroes on Race records in chapter 8 of *Songsters and Saints* (Intro). For examples of black writers' recognition of blues see the collections and essays in *The Negro Caravan*, ed. Sterling A. Brown, Arthur P. Davis, and Ulysses Lee (New York, Dryden Press, 1941); and Hughes and Bontemps, *The Book of Negro Folklore* (6). Few black authors have written extensively on blues, but LeRoi Jones (Imamu Amiri Baraka), *Blues People: Negro Music in White America* (New York, Morrow, 1963), and Albert Murray, *Stomping the Blues* (New York, McGraw-Hill, 1976) are broad studies. Singers' attitudes to blues are expressed in Paul Oliver, *Conversation with the Blues* (Intro), and in that rarest of genres, the blues autobiography, William Broonzy and Yannick Bruynoghe, *Big Bill Blues* (London, Cassell, 1955) and Pleasant Joseph and Harriet J. Ottenheimer, *Cousin Joe: Blues From New Orleans* (University of Chicago Press, 1987).

PRINCIPAL JOURNALS CONSULTED

Though jazz and blues magazines are generally more concerned with biography and criticism than with content, all the following have carried articles which have been useful.

Black Perspective in Music (U.S.A.)
Blues and Rhythm (U.K.)
Blues Unlimited (U.K.)
Blues World★ (U.K.)
Jazz and Blues★ (U.K.)
Jazz Hot (France)
Jazz Journal (U.K.)
Jazz Monthly★ (U.K.)
J.E.M.F. Quarterly (U.S.A.)
Journal of American Folklore (U.S.A.)
Juke Blues (U.K.)
Living Blues (U.S.A.)
Old Time Music (U.K.)
Popular Music (U.K.)
78 Quarterly (U.S.A.)
Storyville (U.K.)
Talking Blues★ (U.K.)
Music Mirror★ (U.K.)
Record Research (U.S.A.)
St. Louis Jazz Report★ (U.S.A.)
Whiskey, Women, And . . (U.S.A.)

★Denotes journal has ceased publication.

Discography of quoted blues

All blues quoted in the preceding chapters have been transcribed from 78 rpm gramophone recordings, a Discography of which follows, the items being listed in the order in which they occur in the book. Beside each quotation a number is to be found and this is entered in the left-hand column. Record details are given as fully as possible and the matrix number allocated by the issuing company, where known, is noted in the second column and followed by the title of the blues. Next is given the name of the singer or pseudonym where this applies, together with any instrument played by the artist on the record. Pseudonyms are identified where possible in the following index of quoted blues singers. Where supporting instrumentalists appear on the disc, their names and the instruments played are listed where known, but instruments alone are entered when the identities of the musicians have not been ascertained (see Abbreviations: instrumental, below). The issuing company (see Abbreviations: labels, below) and the serial number allocated to the record are given in the fifth column. In the final column, the recording date in the order day/month/year is supplied in full, if available; otherwise according to information at hand. The recording venue is noted below.

Reissues of 78 rpm recordings on LP discs have not been listed. Many of the examples cited, or of blues on similar themes, are to be found on the following labels, among others: Agram (Holland); Blue Classics (U.S.A.); Blues Documents (Austria); Charly (U.K.); Chess (Italy); Krazy Kat (U.K.); Magpie (U.K.); Mamlish (U.S.A.); Matchbox Bluesmasters (U.K.); Old Tramp (Austria); Origin (U.S.A.); Rosetta (U.S.A.); Swaggie (Australia); Travelin' Man (U.K.); Wolf (Austria); Yazoo (U.S.A.).

ABBREVIATIONS

Instruments

bjo	banjo	sax	saxophone (all types)
bs	bass, imitation bass	tmb	trombone

304

clt	clarinet		tpt	trumpet
cnt	cornet		vln	violin
dms	drums		vo	vocal
gtr	guitar		wbd	washboard
hca	harmonica			
jug	jug		other instruments listed in full
pno	piano			

Record labels

Ald	Aladdin		J.O.B.	J.O.B.
Ap	Apollo		K.J.	King Jazz
A.R.C.	American Record		Mlt	Melotone
	Company		Mod	Modern
Arst	Artistocrat		Mu	Musicraft
Atl	Atlantic		O.K.	Okeh
Bb	Bluebird		Or	Oriole
Br	Brunswick		Par	Parrott
Cap	Capitol		Pe	Perfect
Ch	Champion		Pm	Paramount
Chess	Chess/Checker		Sav	Savoy
Chic	Chicago		Stp	Stovepipe
Co	Columbia		Su	Sunny
Cq	Conqueror		Tal	Talent
De	Decca		Tru	Tru-Blue
Disc	Disc		Vic	Victor
Dom	Domino		Vo	Vocalion
G.S.	Gold Star		Vrs	Varsity
J.D.	Joe Davis			

Recording locations

Atlanta	Georgia		Jackson	Mississippi
Aurora	Illinois		L.A.	Los Angeles, California
Charlotte	North Carolina		Louis	Louisville, Kentucky
Chicago	Illinois		Memphis	Tennessee
Columbia	South Carolina		N.O.	New Orleans, Louisiana
Dallas	Texas		N.Y.C.	New York City, New
Detroit	Michigan			York
Fort Worth	Texas		Richmond	Indiana
Grafton	Wisconsin		S.A.	San Antonio, Texas
Houston	Texas		St. L.	St. Louis, Missouri

ITEM	MATRIX	ARTIST AND ACCOMPANIMENT	TITLE	CAT. NO.	DATE LOCATION
1	S-7275-E	Mamie Smith (vo) acc. Rega Orchestra: Ed Cox (cnt); Dope Andrews (tmb) Ernest Elliot (clt); Leroy Parker (vln); Willie 'the Lion' Smith (pno); bas sax.	*That Thing Called Love*	OK 4113	14/2/20 N.Y.C.
2	56406	Bessie Tucker (vo) acc. K. D. Johnson (pno); Jesse Thomas (gtr)	*Mean Old Master Blues*	Vic 23392	17/10/29 Dallas
3	21020-4	Ramblin' Thomas (vo, gtr)	*Poor Boy Blues*	Pm 12722	–/11/28 Chicago
4	93008	Sleepy John Estes (vo, gtr) acc. Noah Lewis (hca); wbd	*Tell Me How's About It*	De 7766B	4/6/40 Chicago
5	C 3904	Big Bill Broonzy (vo, gtr) acc. Washboard Sam (wbd); pno; bs	*Going Back To My Plow*	OK 6484	17/7/41 Chicago
6	C 9922	Kokomo Arnold (vo, gtr)	*Bo-Weavil Blues*	De 7191	18/4/35 Chicago
7	L 425/6	Son House (vo, gtr)	*Dry Spell Blues, Parts I & II*	Pm 12990	28/5/30 Gratton
8	JD 5015	Gabriel Brown (vo, gtr)	*I'm Gonna Take It Easy*	JD 5015	13/9/44 N.Y.C.
9	049451	Florida Kid (Ernest Blunt) (vo) acc. Bob White (pno)	*Lazy Mule Blues*	Bb 8625	7/11/40 Chicago
10	91531	Jimmy Gordon and his Vip Vop Band (vo) acc. pno; gtr; dms	*Bleeding Heart Blues*	De 7536	18/10/38 Chicago
11	40520	Walter Davis (vo, pno)	*Cotton Farm Blues*	Bb B-8393	21/7/39 Chicago

12	149105	*On Our Turpentine Farm*	Pigmeat Pete and Catjuice Charlie (vo duet, gtr) Wesley Wilson (vo), Harry McDaniels (vo, gtr)	Co 14485-D	7/10/29 N.Y.C.
13	15666	*Mosquito Moan*	Blind Lemon Jefferson (vo, gtr)	Pm 12899	–/10/29 Richmond,
14/15	16685	*Honey, I'm All Out and Down*	Huddie Ledbetter (vo, gtr)	Mlt 13326	23/1/35 N.Y.C
16	C-5767	*Levee Camp Man Blues*	Gene Campbell (vo, gtr)	Br 7154	–/5/30
17	145366	*Gravel Camp Blues*	Lewis Black (vo, gtr)	Co 14291	10/12/27 Memphis
18	401488	*Spike Driver Blues*	Mississippi John Hurt (vo, gtr)	OK 8692	28/12/28 Memphis
19	K.J.-20	*Saw Mill Man Blues*	Pleasant Joe (vo) acc. Sydney Bechet (sax); Hot Lips Page (tpt); Sam Price (pno); Pops Foster (bs); Danny Barker (gtr); Sid Catlett (dms); Mezz Mezzrow (clt)	KJ 144 ·	30/7/45 N.Y.C
20	399:3054-2	*Sawmill Blues*	Elzadie Robinson (vo) acc. Will Ezell (pno)	Pm 12417	c./11/26 Chicago
21	C 4678	*Harvest Moon Blues*	Charles "Speck" Pertum (vo, pno)	Br 7146	1/11/29 Chicago
22	L-214	*Pennsylvania Woman Blues*	Six Cylinder Smith (vo, gtr) acc. hca	Pm 12968	–/12/29 Grafton
23	67483	*Chicago Mill Blues*	Peetie Wheatstraw (vo) acc. Lil Armstrong (pno); Sid Catlett (dms); Jonah Jones (tpt)	De 7788	4/4/40 N.Y.C.
24	20567-2	*Detroit Bound Blues*	Blind Blake (vo, gtr)	Pm 12657	c./5/28 Chicago
25	C 15503-2	*Starvation Farm Blues*	Bob Campbell (vo, gtr)	Vo 02798	1/7/34 N.Y.C

ITEM	MATRIX	TITLE	ARTIST AND ACCOMPANIMENT	CAT. NO.	DATE LOCATION
26	62480	Poor Man's Friend (T. Model)	"Sleepy" John Estes (vo, gtr) acc. Hammie Nixon (hca); Charlie Pickett (gtr)	De 7442	3/8/37 N.Y.C
27	028817-1	Warehouse Blues	Frank Tannehill (vo, pno) acc. gtr; tpt	Bb B-7945	30/10/38 S.A.
28	148237	Rolling Mill Blues	"Peg Leg" Howell (vo, gtr) acc. vln	Co 14438-D	10/4/29 Atlanta
29	76838	It's Hard Time	Joe Stone (J. D. Short?) (vo, gtr)	Bb B-5169	2/8/33 Chicago
30	403305-B	Broke Man Blues	Sylvester Palmer (vo, pno)	Co 14524-D	15/11/29 Chicago
31	147307	Cold Wave Blues	Barbecue Bob (vo, gtr)	Co 147307-D	26/10/28 Atlanta
32	D6AB-1808	My Friends Don't Know Me	Walter Davis (vo, pno) acc. Jump Jackson (dms)	Vic 20-2156	12/2/46 Chicago
33	C 91340	Hard Times Ain't Gone Nowhere	Lonnie Johnson (vo, gtr)	De 7388	8/11/37 Chicago
34	BS 044244	Cotton Patch Blues	Tommy McClennan (vo, gtr) acc. bs cano	Bb B-8408-B	22/11/39 Chicago
35	C 90917	Don't Take Away My P.W.A.	Jimmy Gordon (vo) acc. pno; gtr; bs	De 7207	–/10/36 Chicago
36	C 91164	Working On The Project	Peetie Wheatstraw (vo, pno) acc. gtr, Kokomo Arnold	De 7311	30/3/37 Chicago
37	C 9292	Charity Blues	The Mississippi Mudder (Charlie McCoy) (vo, gtr) acc. Charles Segar (pno); wbd	De 7046	13/8/34 Chicago

38	C 1976	*Got a Man in the 'Bama Mine*	Merline Johnson (vo) acc. Blind John Davis (pno); dms; gtr	Cq 8924	22/6/37 Chicago
39	BS 074168	*On the Killing Floor*	"Doctor" Clayton (vo) acc. Blind John Davis (pno); Alfred Elkins (bs); Ransom Knowling (tuba)	Bb 34-0702	27/3/42 Chicago
40	D8-VB-3267	*Southern Blues*	Roosevelt Sykes (vo, pno) acc. and his Original Honeydippers	Vic 22-0056	30/12/48 Chicago
41	C 386	*Defense Blues*	Huddie Ledbetter (vo, gtr) acc. Willie Smith (pno); Brownie McGhee (gtr); Pops Foster (bs); Sonny Terry (hca)	Disc 5085	–/6/46 N.Y.C.
42	25631	*L.A. Blues*	Charles Waterford (vo) acc. pno; sax; gtr; dms	Cap 40132	–/11/47 L.A.
43		*Keep Straight Blues*	Guitar Slim and Jelly Belly (Alex Seward and Louis Hayes) (vo, gtrs)	Tru 102	–/–/47 N.Y.C.
44	93588	*The Good Lawd's Children*	Peetie Wheatstraw (vo) acc. pno; hca	De 7879	12/3/41 Chicago
45	064633	*Bald Eagle Blues*	Willie "61" Blackwell (vo, gtr) acc. Alfred Elkins (tmb)	Bb B-8845	30/7/41 Chicago
46	WC2899	*Make My Get Away*	Big Bill Broonzy (vo, gtr)	Vo 05514	26/1/40 Chicago
47	4085-3	*Jim Crow Blues*	Cow Cow Davenport (vo, pno) acc. B. T. Wingfield (cnt)	Pm 12439	–/1/29 Chicago
48	63553	*Bad Luck Blues*	Kokomo Arnold (vo, gtr) acc pno	De 7540	11/5/38 N.Y.C.
49	C-9341	*Tight Time Blues*	Charley Jordan (vo, gtr) acc. (pno)	De 7065	10/9/34 Chicago

ITEM	MATRIX	TITLE	ARTIST AND ACCOMPANIMENT	CAT. NO.	DATE LOCATION
50	L-1038-1	*Hard Time Blues*	Charlie Spand (vo, pno)	Pm 33112	–/9/31 Grafton, Wi
51	D5-AB-316-1	*Kid Man Blues*	Big Maceo (vo, pno) acc. Tampa Red (gtr); Melvin Draper (dms)	Vic 20-2687-B	26/2/45 Chicago
52	R1379	*Mother's Day*	St. Louis Jimmy (vo) acc. Sunnyland Slim (pno); Sam Casimir (gtr)	Ap 420	26/8/49 Chicago
53	C 90960	*Mother Blues*	Jimmy Gordon (vo) acc. pno; gtr; bs	De 7250	26/10/36 Chicago
54	JAX 202	*So Cold In China*	Mississippi Moaner (Isaiah Nettles) (vo, gtr)	Vo 03166	–/10/35 Jackson
55	C 3761-1	*In My Girlish Days*	Memphis Minnie (vo, gtr) acc. Little Son Joe (gtr, bs)	OK 06410	21/5/41 Chicago
56	030821	*C.C.C. Blues*	Washboard Sam (vo, wbd) acc. Big Bill Broonzy (gtr); Josh Altheimer (pno); Bill Settles (bs)	Bb B-7993	16/12/38 Chicago
57	63540-B	*Road Tramp Blues*	Peetie Wheatstraw (vo pno) acc. Lonnie Johnson (gtr); bs	De 7589	1/4/38 N.Y.C.
58	C 97008	*Bad Luck Child*	Bill Gaither (vo) acc. Honey Hill (pno); gtr	De 7202	4/5/36 Chicago
59	C 4413	*Broken Down Man*	Buster Bennett (vo) acc. trio	Co 37560	24/2/45 Chicago
60	074069	*Lonesome Road*	Lonnie Johnson (vo, gtr) acc. Blind John Davis (pno); bs	Bb 34-0714	13/2/42 N.Y.C.
61	65272	*Jeff Davis Highway*	Lee Brown (vo) acc. Sam Price (pno); and his Fly Cats (bs, dms)	De 7587	24/3/39 N.Y.C.

No.	Matrix	Title	Personnel	Catalog	Date	Location
62	BS-044-986	*New Highway No. 51*	Tommy McClennan (vo, gtr) acc. bs	Bb B-8499	10/5/40	Chicago
63	20107-2	*Hard Road Blues*	Blind Blake (vo, gtr)	Pm 12583	late/27	Chicago
64	1767-1	*Freight Train Blues*	Trixie Smith (vo) acc. her Down Home Syncopators: Howard Scott (cnt); Don Redman (clt); Fletcher Henderson (pno); tmb; bjo	Pm 12211	–/5/24	N.Y.C.
65	C.90814A	*Standing By a Lamp Post*	David Alexander (vo, pno)	De 7211	1/7/36	Chicago
66	C 1780	*If I Make It Over*	Bumble Bee Slim (vo) acc. pno	Vo 04042	27/1/37	Chicago
67	L-1254-2	*The Gone Dead Train*	King Solomon Hill (vo, gtr)	Pm 13129	–/1/32	Grafton
68	6248A	*Hobo Jungle Blues*	Sleepy John Estes (vo, gtr) acc. Hammie Nixon (hca); Charlie Pickett (gtr)	De 7354	3/8/37	N.Y.C.
69	63661	*Old Bachelor Blues*	Son Bonds (vo, gtr) acc. Sleepy John Estes (gtr); bs	De 7558	–/4/38	N.Y.C.
70	C-2302	*New York Central*	Monkey Joe (Jesse Coleman); (vo, pno) acc. Willie B. James (gtr)	Vo 04618	8/9/38	Chicago
71	BVE-70676	*M. & O. Blues No. 3*	Walter Davis (vo) acc. Willie Kelly (Roosevelt Sykes) (pno)	Bb B-5129	12/6/32	Dallas
72	C 5857	*I.C. Moan*	Tampa Red (vo, gtr) acc. Georgia Tom Dorsey (pno)	Mlt 7-03-73	–/6/30	Chicago
73	61795	*The Flying Crow*	Black Ivory King (Dave Alexander) (vo, pno)	De 7307	15/2/37	Dallas
74	65208B	*If I Could Holler*	Johnny Temple (vo) acc. Sam Price (pno); Teddy Bunn (gtr); bs	De 7599	6/3/39	N.Y.C.

ITEM	MATRIX	TITLE	ARTIST AND ACCOMPANIMENT	CAT. NO.	DATE LOCATION
75	85498	*Big Four Blues*	Leroy Carr (vo, pno) acc. Scrapper Blackwell (gtr)	Bb B-5916	25/2/35 Chicago
76	67577	*Panama Limited*	Georgia White (vo) acc. Fess Williams (clt); Jonah Jones (tpt)	De 7783	18/4/40 N.Y.C.
77	85517	*Southern Blues*	Big Bill Broonzy (vo, gtr) acc. pno	Bb B-5998	26/2/35 Chicago
78	402768	*T.P. Window Blues*	Jack Ranger (vo, gtr); acc. pno	OK 8795	28/6/29 Dallas
79	20180–2	*Fourteenth Street Blues*	Blind Percy (vo, kazoos, gtr) acc. and his Blind Band (vln, gtr)	Pm 12584	–/11/27 Chicago
80	168	*Too Many Women Blues*	Willie Lane (Little Brother) (vo, gtr)	Tal. 805	–/–/49 Dallas
81	90183	*Blue Black and Evil Blues*	Alice Moore (vo) acc. (prob.) Jimmy Gordon (pno); Peetie Wheatstraw (gtr)	De 7132	19/7/35 Chicago
82	GM 501	*De Kalb Blues*	Leadbelly (vo, gtr)	Mus 226	1/4/39 N.Y.C.
83	BS-070147	*My Black Name Blues*	Sonny Boy Williamson (vo, hca) acc. Blind John Davis (pno); Charlie McCoy (gtr); Washboard Sam (wbd); Alfred Elkins (bs)	Bb B-8992	11/12/41 Chicago
84	146054	*Chocolate To The Bone*	Barbecue Bob (vo, gtr)	Co 14331-D	13/4/28
85	145315	*Brownskin Blues*	Lillian Glinn (vo) acc. Willie Tyson (pno); Octave Gaspard (tuba)	Co 14275-D	2/12/27 N.O.
86	C-915-C	*How You Want Your Rollin' Done*	Louie Lasky (vo, gtr)	Vo 02955	2/4/35 Chicago

87	26562	*Ashley St. Blues*	Leola B. Wilson (vo)	Pm 12392	–/9/26
			acc. Blind Blake (gtr)		Chicago
88	144279	*Brownskin Woman*	Barbecue Bob (vo, gtr)	Co 14257-D	15/6/27
89		*Short Haired Woman*	Lightnin' Hopkins (vo, gtr)	G.S. 3131	–/–/46
					Houston
90	BS 074060	*River Hip Woman*	Washboard Sam (vo, wbd)	Bb B-9039	10/2/42
			acc. Frank Owen (sax); Big Bill Broonzy (gtr); Roosevelt Sykes (pno)		Chicago
91	BVE40309	*Stole Rider Blues*	Blind Willie McTell (vo, gtr)	Vic 21124A	18/10/27
92	W142025	*Willie Jackson's Blues*	Willie Jackson (vo)	Co 14136-D	14/4/26
			acc. Steve Lewis (pno)		N.O.
93	3060-2	*Blake's Worried Blues*	Blind Blake (vo, gtr)	Pm 12442	–/10/26
94	D6VB-1925	*Copper-Colored Mama*	Doctor Clayton (vo)	Vic 20-2323	7/8/46
			acc. Blind John Davis (pno); Willie Lacey (gtr); bs		Chicago
95	C 4303	*When You Love Me*	Memphis Minnie (vo, gtr)	OK 6733	19/12/44
			acc. Little Son Joe (gtr); dms		Chicago
96	149534-1	*Heart Wrecked*	Whistlin' Alex Moore (vo, gtr)	Co 14518-D	5/12/29
			acc. pno		Dallas
97	C 1228	*You Got To Live And Let Live*	Bumble Bee Slim (vo)	Vo 03929	6/2/36
			acc. pno; bs; dms		Chicago
98	BVE-69417-1	*What Made You Love Me So?*	Walter Davis (vo, pno)	Vic 23282	10/6/31
					Louis
99	C 3961	*Don't Leave Me Baby*	Curtis Jones (vo)	OK 06428	18/8/41
			acc. pno; bs		Chicago
100	63796	*Little Pigmeat*	Ollie Shepard (vo)	De 7508	c./6/38
			acc. and his Kentucky Boys: tpt; ten; clt; pno; dms		N.Y.C.

ITEM	MATRIX	TITLE	ARTIST AND ACCOMPANIMENT	CAT. NO.	DATE LOCATION
101	064491	*Million Years Blues*	Sonny Boy Williamson (vo, hca) acc. Blind John Davis (pno); Ransom Knowling (bs)	Bb B-8866-B	2/7/41 Chicago
102	044990	*It's Hard To Be Lonesome*	Tommy McClennan (vo, gtr) acc. bs cano	Bb B-8669	10/5/40 Chicago
103	074118-1	*Cotton Pickin' Blues.*	Robert Petway (vo, gtr)	Bb B-9036	20/2/42 Chicago
104	20558-1	*Leavin' Gal Blues*	Bertha Henderson (vo) acc. Blind Blake (gtr)	Pm 12697	–/5/28 Chicago
105	15635-1	*Cruel Woman Blues*	Leroy Carr (vo, pno) acc. Scrapper Blackwell (gtr)	Vo 02893	15/8/34 N.Y.C.
106	80749-1	*Court Street Blues*	Stovepipe No. 1 (vo, stp) and David Crockett (gtr)	OK 8514	25/4/27 St.L.
107		*I Get Evil When My Love Comes Down*	Gabriel Brown (vo, gtr)	J.D 5003	c.–/–/48 N.Y.C.
108	2064-2	*Pleading Misery Blues*	Elzadie Robinson (vo) acc. possibly Will Ezell (pno)	Pm 12676	28/8/28 Chicago
109	9029	*Strange Lovin' Blues*	Sara Martin (vo) acc. possibly Sylvester Weaver (gtr); Charles Washington (bjo); E. L. Coleman (vln)	OK 8214	c.–/3/25 St.L.
110	145154	*Backdoor Blues*	Emery Glen (vo, gtr)	Co 1447ᴢ-D	7/11/27 Atlanta
111	402305B	*Hambone Willie's Dreamy-Eyed Woman's Blues*	Hambone Willie Newbern (vo, gtr)	OK 8693	14/3/29 Atlanta
112		*Automobile*	Lightnin' Hopkins (vo, gtr)	G.S. 666	–/–/46 Houston

113	63519A	*I Ain't Gonna Be Your Fool*	Lonnie Johnson (vo, gtr)	De 7509A	31/3/38	N.Y.C
114	064634	*Four O'clock Flower Blues*	acc. possibly Roosevelt Sykes (pno); bs; dms Willie "61" Blackwell (vo, gtr)	Bb B-8921	30/8/41	Chicago
115	C 91855	*Triflin' Woman Blues*	Leroy's Buddy (vo)	De 7826	22/10/39	Chicago
116	20667	*Victim Of The Blues*	acc. Honey Hill (pno); gtr; bs "Ma" Rainey (vo) acc. Tub, Jug, Washboard Band. Unknown tub; jug, wb, kazoos, bjo	Para 12687	–/6/29	Chicago
117	16997	*Man Stealer Blues*	Bessie Jackson (Lucille Bogan) (vo) acc. Walter Roland (pno); gtr.	Cq 8559	6/3/35	N.Y.C.
118	C-3452	*Room Rent Blues*	Mary Johnson (vo) acc. Ike Rodgers (tmb); Henry Brown (pno)	Br 7093	7/5/29	Chicago
119	06346	*Can't Read, Can't Write*	Georgia White (vo)	De 7166	16/1/36	N.Y.C.
120	64328	*Mailman Blues*	Tiny Mayberry (vo) acc. Charlie Shavers (tpt); Buster Bailey (clt); Lil Armstrong (pno); Wellman Braud (bs); Sid Cattett (dms)	De 7593	20/7/38	N.Y.C.
121	42344	*People Are Meddlin' In Our Affairs*	J. B. Lenoir (vo, gtr) acc. Sunnyland Slim (pno); Alfred Wallace (dms)	J.O.B.112	c./–/53	Chicago
122	AC-3655	*Money Blues*	Lazy Slim Jim (Ed. Harris) (vo, gtr) acc. gtr	Sav 854	–/–/52	N.Y.C.
123	DAL 377	*Stones In My Passway*	Robert Johnson (vo, gtr)	Vo 03723	19/6/37	Dallas
124	A452	*Western Rider Blues*	Soldier Boy Houston (vo, gtr)	AH971	–/–/50	Dallas

ITEM	MATRIX	TITLE	ARTIST AND ACCOMPANIMENT	CAT. NO.	DATE LOCATION
125	562	Freakish Man Blues	George Hannah (vo) acc. Meade Lux Lewis (pno)	Pm 13024	–/–/30 Richmond
126	8483	Peach Tree Man Blues	Guilford "Peach Tree" Payne (vo) acc. Ed Heywood (pno)	OK 8103	25/10/23 Atlanta?
127	2628	Sissy Blues	Gertrude "Ma" Rainey (vo) acc. tpt; tmb; sax; pno; bjo; dms; swanee whistle	Pm 12384	–/9/26 Chicago
128	16991	B.D. Womans' Blues	Bessie Jackson (Lucille Bogan) (vo) acc. Walter Roland (pno)	ARC 5-12-58	7/3/35 Chicago
129	049456	Pullet and Hen Blues	Bob White (The Woogie Man) (vo, pno)	Bb B-8595	7/11/40 Chicago
130	C 91855	Sweet Woman Blues	Leroy's Buddy (vo) acc. Honey Hill (pno); bs	De 7826	22/10/39 Chicago
131	90012	Rusty Can Blues	Springback James (vo, pno) acc. Willie Bee James (gtr)	De 7091	15/5/35 Chicago
132	148109	You Can't Sleep In My Bed	Mary Dixon (vo) acc. Ed Allen (cnt); J. C. Johnson (pno)	Co 14415-D	20/3/29 N.Y.C.
133	402642	Water Bound Blues	Texas Alexander (vo) acc. Little Hat Jones (gtr)	OK 8785	15/6/29 S.A.
134	22690	Meat Shakin' Woman	Blind Boy Fuller (vo, gtr)	Vo 04137	6/4/38 N.Y.C.
135	047654-1	Tush Hog Blues	Bo Carter (vo, gtr)	Bb B-8514	12/2/40 Atlanta
136	DA-3-6	Black Wolf	Champion Jack Dupree (vo, pno)	J.D. 5104	14/8/46 N.Y.C.

No.	Matrix	Title	Artist / accompaniment	Issue	Date	Location
			acc. Robert McCoy (gtr); Sonny Boy Williamson (hca)	De 7003	5/5/5?	Aurora
138	61794	Loving Heifer	Black Ace (B. K. Turner) (vo, gtr); acc. unknown gtr	De 7387	15/2/37	N.Y.C.
139	15216	Pony Blues	Charley Patton (vo, gtr)	Pm 12792	14/6/29	Richmond
140	WC 3765	Me And My Chauffeur Blues	Memphis Minnie (vo, gtr); acc. Little Son Joe (gtr); bs	OK 06288	21/5/41	Chicago
141	C 2485	Easy Towing Mama	The Yas Yas Girl (vo); acc. Blind John Davis (pno); gtr; dms	Vo 04830	10/2/39	Chicago
142	DAL 302	Coal Woman Blues	Black Boy Shine (vo, pno)	Vo 03757	–/6/37	Dallas
143	143941-1	New Jelly Roll Blues	Peg Leg Howell (vo, gtr); acc. Eddie Anthony (vln)	Co 14210	8/4/27	Atlanta
144	HTN 511	Morning Blues	Lightnin' Hopkins (vo, gtr)	Ald 3035A	25/2/48	Houston
145	81223	Corn Bread Blues	Texas Alexander (vo); acc. Lonnie Johnson (gtr)	OK 8511	12/8/27	N.Y.C.
146	140860	Kitchen Mechanic Blues	Clara Smith (vo); acc. Her Jazz Band: Bob Fuller (sax); Stanley Miller (pno); Buddy Christian (bjo)	Co 14097-D	20/8/25	N.Y.C.
147	150360	Coffee Grinder Blues	Jaybird (Burl) Coleman (vo, hca); acc. pno	Co 14534-D	22/4/30	Atlanta
148	3028	Pigmeat Blues	Ardell Bragg (vo); acc. Tiny Parham (pno); gtr	Pm 12398	–/8/26	Chicago
149	070473	Peach Tree Blues	Yank Rachell (vo, gtr); acc. Sonny Boy Williamson (hca); Washboard Sam (wbd)	Bb B-9033-A	11/12/41	Chicago

ITEM	MATRIX	TITLE	ARTIST AND ACCOMPANIMENT	CAT. NO.	DATE LOCATION
150	M 187	*The Dirty Dozen*	Speckled Red (vo, pno)	Br 7116	14/9/29 Memphis
—	C 5584½	*Dirty Dozen No. 2*	Speckled Red (vo, pno)	Br 7151	8/4/30 Chicago
151	C 954	*Feather Bed Blues*	Bumble Bee Slim (vo) acc. Myrtle Jenkins (pno); Big Bill Broonzy (gtr)	Vo 03446	4/4/35 Chicago
152	Vo 167	*Fool's Blues*	J. T. "Funny Paper" Smith (vo, gtr)	Vo 1674	10/7/31 Chicago
153	L-418-2	*Future Blues*	Willie Brown (vo, gtr)	Pm 13090	28/5/30 Grafton
154	20661-1	*Black Cat, Hoot Owl Blues*	Ma Rainey (vo) acc. Tub Jug Washboard Band	Pm 12687	–/6/28 Chicago
155	20712-2	*Fogyism*	Ida Cox (vo) acc. Dave Nelson (cnt); Jesse Crump (pno); bjo	Pm 12690	–/7/28 Chicago
156	BVE-36098	*Gwine To Have Bad Luck For Seven Years*	Elizabeth Smith (vo) acc. Morris (cnt); Bob Fuller (clt); pno	Vic 20297	6/9/26 N.Y.C.
157	D7/B/1062	*Hoodoo Lady Blues*	Arthur "Big Boy" Crudup (vo, gtr) acc. Ransom Knowling (bs); Judge Riley (dms)	Vic 22-0048-B	7/10/47 Chicago
158	W73821A	*Gypsy Blues*	Joshua Johnson (vo, pno)	De 48027	21/3/47 N.Y.C.
159	L-509	*Big Fat Mama Blues*	Charlie Spand (vo, pno)	Pm 13005	–/12/30 Grafton
160	77082	*Shootin' Star Blues*	Lizzie Miles (vo) acc. Porter Grainger (pno)	Or 1170	4/1/28 N.Y.C.

161	150305-1	*One More Time*	Barefoot Bill (vo, gtr)	Co 14561	20/4/30 Atlanta
162	U7275	*Louisiana Blues*	Muddy Waters (vo, gtr) acc. Little Walter Jacobs (hca); wbd	Chess 1441	c.-/50 Chicago
163	Vo 168/9	*Seven Sisters Blues Parts I & II*	J. T. "Funny Paper" Smith (vo, gtr)	Vo 1641	10/7/31 Chicago
164	62654A	*Hoodoo Woman*	Johnny Temple (vo) acc. Harlem Hamfats: Odell Rand (clt); Horace Malcolm (pno); Joe McCoy (gtr); Chas. McCoy (gtr); John Lindsay (bs); Fred Flynn (dms)	De 7385	6/9/37 N.Y.C.
165	L-1041-2	*Evil Woman Spell*	Charlie Spand (vo, pno)	Pm 13101	-/9/31 Grafton
166	D7-VB-1056	*Handreader Blues*	William Jazz Gillum (vo, hca) acc. Robert Call (pno); Willie Lacey (gtr); Ransom Knowling (bs); Judge Lawrence Riley (dms)	Vic 20-2964	2/10/47 Chicago
167	D6-VB-1924	*Root Doctor Blues*	Doctor Clayton (vo) acc. Blind John Davis (pno); Alfred Elkins (bs); Willie Lacey (gtr)	Vic 20-2323	2/8/46 Chicago
168	65658	*Voodoo Blues*	Fat Hayden (vo) acc. Sam Price (pno); Teddy Bunn (gtr); bs	De 7614B	26/5/39 N.Y.C.
169	5023-B	*The Jinx Is On Me*	Gabriel Brown (vo, gtr)	J.D. DA-5-6	2/5/45
170	B 8013	*Playing The Races (Dream a Number)*	John Lee Hooker (vo, gtr)	Mod 20-730	27/2/50 Detroit
171	L-647-1	*Playing Policy Blues*	Blind Blake (vo, gtr)	Pm 13035	-/12/30 Grafton
172	65421A	*The Numbers Blues*	Ollie Shepard (vo) acc. and his Kentucky Boys; Sam Price (pno)	De 7585	18/4/39 N.Y.C.

ITEM	MATRIX	TITLE	ARTIST AND ACCOMPANIMENT	CAT. NO.	DATE	LOCATION
173	C 91532	*Number Runner's Blues*	Jimmy Gordon (vo) acc. and his Vip Vop Band; Lonnie Johnson (gtr); pno; dms	De 7536B	18/10/38	Chicago
174	15248A	*Poker Woman Blues*	Blind Blake (vo gtr) acc. Alex Robinson (pno)	Pm 12810	-/7/29	Richmond
175	90857	*Gambling Man*	Red Nelson (vo) acc. poss. Richard M. Jones (pno); gtr; bs	De 7256	9/9/35	Chicago
176	60512A	*Coon-Can Shorty*	Peetie Wheatstraw (vo, pno) acc. Kokomo Arnold (gtr)	De 7159B	18/2/36	N.Y.C.
177	W145185-2	*Skin Game Blues*	Peg Leg Howell (vo, gtr)	Co 14473D	9/11/27	Atlanta
178	9548A	*Jack O' Diamonds*	Sippie Wallace (vo) acc. Louis Armstrong (cnt); Hersal Thomas (pno)	OK 8328	1/3/26	Chicago
179	15483-1	*Dice's Blues*	Bob Campbell (vo, gtr)	Vo 02830	30/7/34	N.Y.C.
180	C 4677	*Gambler's Blues*	Charles "Speck" Pertum (vo) acc. Eddie Miller (pno)	Br 7146	1/11/29	Chicago
181	91207	*Monte Carlo Blues*	Roosevelt Sykes (vo, pno)	De 7352	29/3/37	Chicago
182	17014-1	*Skin Game Blues*	Lucille Bogan (vo) acc. Walter Roland (pno)	Per 0329	8/3/35	N.Y.C.
183		*Gambling Blues*	Melvin "Little Son" Jackson (vo, gtr)	GS 668	-/-/49	Houston
184	401348	*St. Louis Fair Blues*	Texas Alexander (vo) acc. Eddie Lang (gtr)	OK 8688	20/11/28	N.Y.C.

186	21199-1	*Big Night Blues*	Blind Lemon Jefferson (vo, gtr)	Pm 12801	–/3/29	Chicago
187	C 4300	*Head Rag Hop*	Romeo Nelson (vo, pno)	Vo 1447	5/9/29	Chicago
188	C-3749	*House Rent Scuffle*	acc. Tampa Red (gtr); speech Lil Johnson (vo)	Vo 1410	27/6/29	Chicago
189	13593-2	*House Lady Blues*	acc. Charles Avery (pno); Tampa Red (gtr) Walter Roland (vo, pno)	Mlt 12762	19/7/33	N.Y.C.
190	L178	*Barrel House Flat Blues*	Mary Johnson (vo)	Pm 122996	–/11/29	Grafton
191	W140191-2	*Good Time Flat Blues*	acc. Ike Rodgers (tmb); Henry Brown (pno) Maggie Jones (vo)	Co 14055	17/12/24	N.Y.C.
192	404149	*Bootlegger's Blues*	acc. Louis Armstrong (cnt); Fletcher Henderson (pno) Mississippi Sheiks: Bo Carter (vo, gtr); Walter Jacobs (gtr); vln; bjo	OK 8820	12/6/30	S.A.
193	C 2292	*Alley Bound Blues*	Curtis Jones (vo) acc. pno; gtr; bs	Vo 04249	23/6/38	Chicago
194	C 91212	*Bootleggin' Ain't No Good No More*	Blind "Blues" Darby (vo) acc. Roosevelt Sykes (pno)?; bs	De 7816	30/4/37	Chicago
195	91775	*Beer Tavern*	Peetie Wheatstraw (vo) acc. pno; Lonnie Johnson (gtr); hca; dms	De 7657	14/9/39	Chicago
196	C-9386	*Jake Leg Blues*	Willie Lofton (vo, gtr)	De 7076	24/8/34	Chicago
197	C-4108	*Jones Law Blues*	Shorty George (James "Stump" Johnson) (vo, pno) acc. Tampa Red (gtr)	Br 7106	16/8/29	Chicago
198	C-5921	*Good Boy Blues*	Arthur Petties (vo, gtr)	Br 7182	25/7/30	Chicago

ITEM	MATRIX	TITLE	ARTIST AND ACCOMPANIMENT	CAT. NO.	DATE	LOCATION
199	47092-2	Better Leave That Stuff Alone	Will Shade (vo, gtr) acc. Jab Jones (pno)	Vic 21725	24/9/28	Memphis
200	D4-AB-321-1	One More Break Blues	St. Louis Jimmy (vo) acc. Ted Summitt (gtr); Roosevelt Sykes (pno); Armand Jackson (dms)	Bb 34-0727	14/12/44	Chicago
201	053986-1	I Stagger In My Sleep	Clara Morris (vo) acc. Blind John Davis (pno); Lonnie Johnson (gtr)	Bb B-8700	27/3/41	Chicago
202	C 3592	Junker Blues	Champion Jack Dupree (vo, pno) acc. Wilson Swain (bs)	OK 06152	28/1/41	Chicago
203	070405	Gotta Find My Baby	Doctor Clayton (vo) acc. Blind John Davis (pno); Alfred Elkins (bs)	Bb B-8901	11/11/41	Chicago
204	C 4081	Creole Queen	Little Bill Gaither (vo) acc. Horace Malcomb (pno); Big Bill Broonzy (gtr)	OK 06561	2/12/41	Chicago
205	21018-4	Hard Dallas	Ramblin' Thomas (vo, gtr)	Pm 12708	–/11/28	Chicago
206	71623-1	East Chicago Blues	Pinetop and Lindberg: Aaron Sparks (vo, pno); Milton Sparks (vo)	Vic 23330	25/2/32	Atlanta
207	142027	Old New Orleans Blues	Willie Jackson (vo) acc. Steve Lewis (pno)	Co 14136-D	14/4/26	N.O.
208	37975	Haven't Got a Dollar to Pay Your House Rent	Genevieve Davis (vo) acc. Louis Dumaine's Eight: Louis Dumaine (cnt); Earl Humphrey (tmb); Wally Joseph (clt); Louis James (sax); Morris Rouse (pno); Leonard Mitchell (bjo); Joe Howard (bs); James Willigan (dms)	Vic 20648	5/3/27	N.O.

			Huddie Ledbetter (vo, gtr)	Mus 227	1/4/39	N.Y.C.
209	GM 504	*Bourgeois Blues*				
210	070444-1	*Down South Blues*	Jazz Gillum (vo, hca) acc. Big Bill Broonzy (gtr); Horace Malcolm (pno)	Bb B-9004-B	24/7/41	Chicago
211	142137	*Jelly Bean Blues*	Clara Smith (vo) acc. Tom Edwards (tmb); Clarence Adams (clt); Stanley Miller (pno)	Co 14294-D	3/5/26	N.Y.C.
212	BB2	*Country Gal*	Smokey Hogg (vo, gtr)	Mod 20-532	–/–/47	Dallas
213	059205	*Crowing Rooster Blues*	Lonnie Johnson (vo, gtr) acc. Lil Armstrong (pno); Andrew Harris (bs)	Bb B-8804	7/2/41	Chicago
214	2288	*Maxwell Street Blues*	Charlie Jackson (vo, bjo)	Pm 12320·	–/9/25	Chicago
215	W 76712	*Owl Stew*	Cecil Gant (vo, pno) acc. bs; dms	De 48231	7/7/50	N.Y.C.
216	149538	*Elm Street Blues*	Texas Bill Day (vo) acc. Billiken Johnson (duet vo); pno; gtr	Co 14514-D	5/12/29	Dallas
217	9929A	*I'm a Mighty Tight Woman*	Sippie Wallace (vo) acc. Dave Nelson (cnt); Hersal Thomas (pno)	OK 8439	26/11/26	Chicago
218	146176	*Jacksonville Blues*	Nellie Florence (vo) acc. Barbecue Bob (gtr)?	Co 14342-D	21/4/28	Atlanta
219	11506	*Nut Factory Blues*	"Hi" Henry Brown (vo, gtr) acc. Charley Jordan (gtr)	Vo 1692	17/3/32	N.Y.C.
220	C 1346	*Fast Life Blues*	Bumble Bee Slim (vo) acc. pno; gtr	Vo 03446	2/4/36	Chicago
221	65316	*Easy Way Blues*	Peetie Wheatstraw (vo) acc. Sam Price (pno); Teddy Bunn (gtr); O'Neil Spencer (dms)	De 7641B	30/3/39	Chicago

ITEM	MATRIX	TITLE	ARTIST AND ACCOMPANIMENT	CAT. NO.	DATE	LOCATION
222	C 3885	*Two By Four Blues*	Merline Johnson (vo) acc. pno; bs	OK 06446	19/6/41	Chicago
223	15559	*Good Chib Blues*	Edith Johnson (vo) acc. Baby Jay (cnt); Ike Rodgers (tmb); Roosevelt Sykes (pno)	Pm 12864	7/9/29	N.Y.C.
224	45448-2	*Got Cut All To Pieces*	Bessie Tucker (vo) acc. K. D. Johnson (pno)	Vic 38018	30/8/28	Memphis
225	149535-2	*Ice-Pick Blues*	Whistlin' Alex Moore (vo, pno)	Co 14518-D	5/12/29	Dallas
226	70677	*Hijack Blues*	Walter Davis (vo) acc. Willie Kelly (pno)	Vic 23343	10/2/32	Dallas
227	1273	*Gutter Man Blues*	George Hannah (vo) acc. pno; gtr; dms	Pm 12788-A	6/6/29	Richmond
228	6822	*Gangster's Blues*	Peetie Wheatstraw (vo) acc. Jonah Jones (tpt); Lil Armstrong (pno); Sidney Catlett	De 7815	28/7/40	N.Y.C.
229	5694-2	*Mad Mama's Blues*	Violet Mills (Julia Moody) (vo) acc. Bubber Miley (cnt); Bob Fuller (clt); Louis Hooper (pno)	Dom 425	29/10/24	N.Y.C.
230	45424-1	*Furry's Blues*	Furry Lewis (vo, gtr)	Vic V-38519	28/8/28	Memphis
231	C 738	*Cold-Blooded Murder*	Bumble Bee Slim (vo) acc. pno; gtr	Vo 02865	20/10/34	Chicago
232	93571	*Lookin' For The Blues*	Jimmy Gordon (vo) acc. pno	De 7865	10/3/41	Chicago
233	D5-AB-350	*Maceo's 32-20*	Big Maceo (vo, pno) acc. Tampa Red (gtr); Tyrrell Dixon (dms)	Vic 20-2028	5/7/45	Chicago

234	147599-2	*Carbolic Acid Blues*	Bobbie Cadillac (vo) acc. pno	Co 14413	8/12/28	Dallas
235	U-4374	*Third Degree*	Eddie Boyd (vo, pno) acc. ?Crowder (sax); Willie Dixon (bs); dms.	Chess 1541	-/5/53	Chicago
236	149356-2	*Big Rock Jail*	Barefoot Bill (vo, gtr)	Co 14481-D	4/11/29	Atlanta
237	C 5076	*Workhouse Blues*	Leroy Carr (vo, pno) acc. Scrapper Blackwell (gtr)	Vo 1454	2/1/30	Chicago
238		*Jail House Blues*	Lightnin' Hopkins (vo, gtr)	G.S. 662A	c.-/-/49	Houston
239	9792	*Chain Gang Blues*	acc. Frankie Lee Sims (gtr) Kokomo Arnold (vo, gtr)	De 7069	12/2/35	Chicago
240	20343-2	*No Job Blues*	Ramblin' Thomas (vo, gtr)	Pm 12609	-/2/28	Chicago
241	2372	*Chain Gang Blues*	Ma Rainey (vo) acc. Joe Smith (tpt); Charlie Green (tmb); Buster Bailey (clt); Fletcher Henderson (pno); Charlie Dixon (gtr); Kaiser Marshall (dms); Coleman Hawkins (sax)	Pm 12338	-/12/25	Chicago
242	16429	*Eleven Twenty-Nine Blues*	Leroy Carr (vo, pno) acc. Scrapper Blackwell (gtr)	Vo 03157	14/12/34	Chicago
243	15449	*Prison Blues*	Alice Moore (vo) acc. Ike Rodgers (tmb); Henry Brown	Pm 12868	16/8/29	Richmond
244	81224	*Section Gang Blues*	Texas Alexander (vo) acc. Lonnie Johnson (gtr)	OK 8498	12/8/27	N.Y.C.
245	WC 2981A1	*Parchman Farm Blues*	Bukka White (vo, gtr) acc. Washboard Sam (wbd)	OK 05683	7/3/40	Chicago

ITEM	MATRIX	TITLE	ARTIST AND ACCOMPANIMENT	CAT. NO.	DATE / LOCATION
246	MEM-740	*Nashville Stonewall Blues*	Robert Wilkins (vo, gtr)	Br 7168	-/2/30 Memphis
247	SC 25	*Big House Bound*	Blind Boy Fuller (vo, gtr) acc. Sonny Terry (hca)	Vo 04897	29/10/38 Columbia
248	J.S.559	*County Jail Special*	Champion Jack Dupree (vo, pno)	J.D.5103	18/4/45 N.Y.C.
249	064192	*County Jail Blues*	Big Maceo (vo, pno) acc. Tampa Red (gtr)	Bb B-8798	24/6/41 Chicago
250	65408	*.44 Blues*	Roosevelt Sykes (vo, pno) acc. traps	De 7586	13/4/39 N.Y.C.
251	91195A	*Prisoner Bound*	Frank Busby (vo) acc. Honey Hill (pno)	De 7295	6/3/37 Chicago
252	91764	*Sing Sing Blues*	Bill Gaither (vo) acc. Honey Hill pno; bs	De 7784	13/9/39 Chicago
253	71981	*I've Got To Go and Leave My Daddy Behind*	Sara Martin (vo) acc. Sylvester Weaver (gtr)	OK 8104	24/10/23 N.Y.C.
254	4419-2	*Jailhouse Fire Blues*	Buddy Boy Hawkins (vo, gtr)	Pm 12489	-/4/27 Chicago
255	4651-2	*Greyhound Blues*	Alice Pearson (vo) acc. Freddie Coates (pno)	Pm 12523	-/7/27 Chicago
256	56732	*Bloodhound Blues*	Victoria Spivey (vo) acc. Luis Russell's Orchestra: Henry Allen (tpt); J. C. Higginbotham (tmb); Charles Holmes (sax); Will Johnson (gtr); Pops Foster (bs); Luis Russell (pno)	Vic 38570	1/10/29 N.Y.C.

257	20751	*Hangman's Blues*	Blind Lemon Jefferson (vo, gtr)	Pm 12679B	–/7/28 Chicago
258	G15514	*Dyin' in the Electric Chair*	Blue Boy (James Platt) (vo) acc. clt; Huerve Duerson (pno)	Vrs 16059	28/8/29 Chicago
259	11104-2	*The Judge Cliff Davis Blues*	Charlie Jackson (vo, pno)	Pm 12366	–/4/26 Chicago
260	07029-1	*G-Man Blues*	Curtis Henry (vo, pno)	Bb B-6845	15/2/37 Charlotte
261	064924-1	*Lawyer Clark Blues*	Sleepy John Estes (vo, gtr) acc. Son Bonds (gtr); bs	Bb B-8871	24/9/41 Chicago
262	C 90762	*Long Lonesome Day Blues*	Jesse James (vo, pno)	De 7213	3/6/36 Chicago
263	148708	*When The Levee Breaks*	Kansas Joe and Memphis Minnie Joe McCoy (vo, gtr), Minnie McCoy (gtr)	Co 14439-D	18/6/29 N.Y.C.
264	MEM-786	*Tallahatchie Rivers Blues*	Mattie Delaney (vo, gtr)	Vo 1480	21/2/30 Memphis
265	L59/60	*High Water Everywhere Part I and Part II*	Charley Patton (vo, gtr)	Pm 12909	–/10/29 Grafton
266	4491-5	*Risin' High Water Blues*	Blind Lemon Jefferson (vo, gtr) acc. George Perkins (pno)	Pm 12487	–/6/27 Chicago
267	13550-2	*Red Cross Blues*	'Alabama Sam (Walter Roland) (vo, pno)	Mlt 12753	17/7/33 N.Y.C.
268	91341	*Flood Water Blues*	Lonnie Johnson (vo, gtr)	De 7397	8/1/37 Chicago
269	62465	*Floating Bridge*	Sleepy John Estes (vo, gtr) acc. Charlie Pickett (gtr); Hammie Nix (hca)	De 7442	2/8/37 N.Y.C.

ITEM	MATRIX	TITLE	ARTIST AND ACCOMPANIMENT	CAT. NO.	DATE / LOCATION
270	C-097	Dry Spell Blues	Spider Carter (vo) acc. pno	Br 7181	13/9/30 Chicago
271	20192	St. Louis Cyclone Blues	Elzadie Robinson (vo) acc. Bob Call (pno)	Pm 12573	–/11/27 Chicago
272	91946 58-1	That Mean Old Twister	Lightnin' Hopkins (vo, gtr) acc. Wilson "Thunder" Smith (pno)	Ald 167	9/11/46 L.A.
273	V-9290	Florida Hurricane	St. Louis Jimmy (vo) acc. Muddy Waters and his Blues Combo: Waters (gtr); Sunnyland Slim (pno); sax; bs	Arst 7001	–/–/50 Chicago
274	1612	Southern Blues	Gertrude "Ma" Rainey (vo) acc. Lovie Austin and her Blues Serenaders: Tommy Ladnier (cnt); Jimmy O'Bryant (clt); Lovie Austin (pno); Jasper Taylor or Kaiser Marshall (dms)	Pm 12083	–/12/23 Chicago
275	63650	Fire Department Blues	Sleepy John Estes (vo, gtr) acc. Son Bonds (gtr)	De 7571	27/4/38 N.Y.C.
276	15557	Fire Detective Blues	Dobby Bragg (Roosevelt Sykes) (vo, pno)	Pm 12827	–/–/29–30 Richmond
277	C 93003	The Death of Walter Barnes	Baby Doo (vo) acc. Walter Davis (pno); Lee McCoy (hca)	De 7763	4/6/40 Chicago
278	C 93001	The Natchez Fire	Gene Gilmore (vo) acc. Walter Davis (pno); Lee McCoy (hca)	De 7763	4/6/40 Chicago
279	JAX-113-2	The Cockeyed World	Minnie Wallace (vo) acc. her Night Hawks: Will Shade (hca); Harry Chatman (pno); Robert Wilkins (gtr)	Vo 03106	12/10/35 Jackson

No.	Matrix	Title	Performer / Accompaniment	Issue	Date / Location
280	90635	*I'm Gonna Have My Fun*	Carl Martin (vo, gtr) acc. Chuck Segar (pno); gtr	Ch 50074	18/4/36 Chicago
281	99353-1	*Bonus Blues*	Joe Pullum (vo) acc. Chester Boone (sax); Rob Cooper (pno)	Bb B-6372	25/2/36 S.A.
282	053399-1	*Hitler Blues*	The Florida Kid (Ernest Blunt) (vo) acc. Bob White (pno); bs	Bb B-8589	7/11/40 Chicago
283	074170-1	*Pearl Harbor Blues*	Doctor Clayton (vo) acc. Blind John Davis (pno); Alfred Elkins (bs)	Bb B-9003	27/3/42 Chicago
284	C 3510	*That Old Number of Mine (Number 158)*	Big Bill Broonzy (vo, gtr) acc. Memphis Slim (pno); Ransom Knowling (bs)	OK 06080	17/12/40 Chicago
285	070861-1	*Give Me A 32-20*	Arthur "Big Boy" Crudup (vo, gtr) acc. Ransom Knowling (bs)	Bb B-9019A	15/4/42 Chicago
286	C 3791	*Million Lonesome Women*	Brownie McGhee (vo, gtr) acc. Jordan Webb (hca); George Washington (wbd)	OK 06329	23/5/41 Chicago
287	053976-1	*I Hate To Say Goodbye*	Walter Davis (vo, pno)	Bb B-8694	21/3/41 Chicago
288	C 4057	*Training Camp Blues*	Roosevelt Sykes (vo, pno) acc. poss. Alfred Elkins (bs)	OK 6709	21/11/41 Chicago
289	074071	*Baby Remember Me*	Lonnie Johnson (vo, gtr) acc. Blind John Davis (pno); Andrew Harris (bs)	Bb 34-0714	13/2/42 Chicago
290	WC 3144	*When You Are Gone*	Blind Boy Fuller (vo, gtr)	OK 05756	19/6/40 Chicago
291	D4-AB-326	*Win The War Blues*	Sonny Boy Williamson (vo, hca) acc. Blind John Davis (pno); Ted Summitt (gtr); Armand Jackson (dms)	Bb 34-0722-A	14/12/44 Chicago
292	102	*Build A Cave*	Mr. Honey (David Edwards) (vo, gtr)	ARC 102	–/–/51 Houston

ITEM	MATRIX	TITLE	ARTIST AND ACCOMPANIMENT	CAT. NO.	DATE LOCATION
293	SS1	*Back to Korea Blues*	Sunnyland Slim (Albert Luandrew) (vo, pno) acc. Snooky Pryor (hca); Leroy Foster (gtr)	Sun 101	–/–/50 Chicago
294	84973	*The War is Over*	Lightnin' Hopkins (vo, gtr) acc. Donald Cooks (bs); Connie Kroll (dms)	De 48842	29/7/53 Houston
295	D4-AB-323-1	*Bad Condition*	St. Louis Jimmy (James Oden) (vo) acc. Roosevelt Sykes (pno); Ted Summitt (el. gtr); Armand Jackson (dms)	Vic 20-2650	14/12/44 Chicago
296	WC 3110	*Warehouse Man Blues*	Champion Jack Dupree (vo, pno) acc. bs	OK 05656	13/6/40 Chicago
297	18733-2	*Silicosis Is Killin' Me*	Pinewood Tom (Joshua White) (vo, gtr)	Cq 8673	26/2/36 N.Y.C.
298	059483-1	*Don't Go Down Baby*	Robert Petway (vo, gtr)	Bb B-8756	28/3/41 Chicago
299	56733	*Dirty T.B. Blues*	Victoria Spivey (vo) acc. Luis Russell's Orchestra: Henry Allen (tpt); J. C. Higginbotham (tmb); Charlie Holmes (sax); Will Johnson (gtr); Pops Foster (bs); Luis Russell (pno)	Vic V38570	1/10/29 N.Y.C.
300	15669	*Pneumonia Blues*	Blind Lemon Jefferson (vo, gtr)	Pm 12880	24/9/29 Richmond
301	22674	*Pistol Slapper Blues*	Blind Boy Fuller (vo, gtr) acc. Sonny Terry (hca)	Vo 04106	5/3/38 N.Y.C.
302	C 1450	*I Can't Last Long*	Jane Lucas (poss. Victoria Spivey) (vo) acc. State Street Four: Lee Collins (tpt); Dorothy Scott (pno); Addie Spivey (pno); dms	Vo 03314	20/8/36 Chicago

No.	Matrix	Title	Performer	Issue	Date / Location
303	C 93846A	*Bring Me Flowers While I'm Living*	Peetie Wheatstraw (vo) acc. Lil Armstrong (pno); Chu Berry (sax)	De 7886	25/11/41 Chicago
304	C 1231	*I Done Caught My Death of Cold*	Bumble Bee Slim (vo) acc. Casey Bill Weldon (gtr); Black Bob Hudson (pno); bs	Vo 03767	6/2/36 Chicago
305	22064	*Hooting Owl Blues*	Dolly Ross (vo) acc. Porter Grainger (pno); chimes	Br 7005B	–/–/27 N.Y.C.
306	WC 2978	*Strange Place*	Bukka White (vo, gtr) acc. Washboard Sam (wbd)	OK 05526	–/6/40 Chicago
307		*Death Bells*	Lightnin' Hopkins (vo, gtr)	GS 646	–/–/48 Houston
308	90597	*Crying Mother Blues*	Red Nelson (Nelson Wilborn) (vo) acc. Cripple Clarence Lofton (pno)		4/2/35 Chicago
309	DAL 398-1	*Me and The Devil Blues*	Robert Johnson (vo, gtr)	Vo 0418	20/6/37 Dallas
310	064874-1	*Death Valley Blues*	Arthur "Big Boy" Crudup (vo, gtr) acc. dms; bs	Bb B-8858	11/8/41 Chicago
311	20374-1	*See That My Grave Is Kept Clean*	Blind Lemon Jefferson (vo, gtr)	Pm 12608	–/2/28 Chicago
312	2293	*Coffin Blues*	Ida Cox (vo) acc. Tommy Ladnier (cnt); Jesse Crump (pno)	Pm 12318	–/9/25 Chicago
313	17985-1	*Undertaker Blues*	Buddy Moss (vo, gtr) acc. Joshua White (gtr)	Vo 04380	21/7/35 N.Y.C.
314	64052	*Death of Slim Green*	Shorty Bob Parker (vo, pno) acc. Kid Prince Moore (gtr)	De 7470	6/6/38 Charlotte
315	85516	*Six Cold Feet In The Ground*	Leroy Carr (vo, pno)	Bb B-5963	25/2/35 Chicago

ITEM	MATRIX	TITLE	ARTIST AND ACCOMPANIMENT	CAT. NO.	DATE LOCATION
316	90033	*The Death of Leroy Carr*	Bumble Bee Slim (vo) acc. pno; gtr	De 7098	–/6/35 Chicago
317	C–37584–1	*Death of Blind Boy Fuller*	Brownie McGhee (vo, gtr)	OK 06265	22/5/41 Chicago
318		*His Spirit Lives On*	Joe Williams (vo, gtr) acc. Clifford Dinwaddie (wbd)	Chic. 103	–/–/45 Chicago
319		*F.D.R. Blues*	Champion Jack Dupree (vo, pno)	J.D. 5102	–/–/46 N.Y.C.
320	90922	*The World's A Hard Place To Live In*	Georgia Pine Boy (Joe McCoy) (vo, gtr) acc. vln	De 7828	5/9/35 Chicago
321	69409–2	*Happy Days Blues*	R. T. Hanen (vo)	Vic 23288	9/6/31 Louis
322	65423A	*Shepard Blues (Pig Latin Blues)*	acc. Willie Kelly (pno); Clifford Gibson (gtr) Ollie Shepard (vo)	De 7602	18/4/39 N.Y.C.
323	4017–2	*Mother Fuyer*	acc. and his Kentucky Boys: pno; sax; traps Dirty Red (Nelson Wilborn) (v)	Ald 194A	2/6/47 Chicago
324	WC 3204	*The Jive Blues*	acc. James Clark (pno); Lonnie Graham (gtr) Peter Chatman (vo, pno)	OK 05908	–/8/40 Chicago
325	U–7614	*Democrat Blues*	acc. hca; bs; Washboard Sam (wbd) Bobo Jenkins (vo, gtr)	1565	–/–/54 Detroit
326	P–53203	*Eisenhower Blues*	acc. Robert Richard (hca); Albert Witherspoon (gtr) J. B. Lenoir (vo, gtr)	Par 802	–/–/54 Chicago
327	64194	*Champ Joe Louis Blues*	acc. Lorenzo Smith (sax); Joe Montgomery (pno); Al Gavin (dms) Little Bill Gaither (vo)	De 7476	23/6/38

Atlanta

No.	Matrix	Title	Artist	Issue	Date	Place
329	144277-1	*Mississippi Heavy Water Blues*	Barbecue Bob (Robert Hicks) (vo, gtr)	Co 14222-D	15/6/27	N.Y.C.
330	63529	*The Train Is Coming*	The Honey Dripper (vo, pno) acc. dms	De 7483	1/4/38	N.Y.C.
331	15671	*That Crawlin' Baby Blues*	Blind Lemon Jefferson (vo, gtr)	Pm 12880	–/10/29	Richmond
332	93849	*Mister Livingood*	Peetie Wheatstraw (vo) acc. Lil Armstrong (pno); bs	De 7879	25/11/41	Chicago
333	BS 030828	*I Like The Way You Spread Your Wings*	Walter Davis (vo, pno)	Bb B-7978	19/12/38	Chicago
334	C 3790	*Key To My Door*	Brownie McGhee (vo, gtr) acc. George Washington (wbd)	OK 06437	23/5/41	Chicago
335	B 11499	*Midnight Hour Blues*	Leroy Carr (vo, pno) acc. Scrapper Blackwell (gtr)	Vo 1703	16/3/32	Chicago
336	C 1939	*Blues Everywhere*	Yas Yas Girl (vo) acc. Blind John Davis (pno); gtr; dms	OK 03638	22/6/37	Chicago
337	W147608	*Waking Blues*	Otis Harris (vo, gtr)	Co 14428-D	8/12/28	Dallas
338	20193	*Mister Blues*	Lucius Hardy (vo) acc. pno	Pm 12598	–/12/27	Chicago
339	BS 074101	*Blues Trip Me This Morning*	Tommy McClennan (vo, gtr) acc. prob. Ransom Knowling (bs)	Bb B-9037	20/2/42	Chicago
340	4449-2	*Jinx Blues*	Ora Brown (vo) acc. Tiny Parham (pno)	Pm 12481	c./3/27	Chicago
341	C 9428	*Milk Cow Blues*	Kokomo Arnold (vo, gtr)	De 7026	2/3/35	Chicago

ITEM	MATRIX	TITLE	ARTIST AND ACCOMPANIMENT	CAT. NO.	DATE LOCATION
342	DAL 394-2	*Hell Hound On My Trail*	Robert Johnson (vo, gtr)	Vo 03623	20/6/37 Dallas
343	02642-1	*The First Time I Met You*	Little Brother Montgomery (vo, pno)	Bb B-6766	16/10/36 N.O.
344	BVE-37945	*Rock Away Blues*	Sadie McKinney (vo) acc. Charlie Williamson (cnt); James Alsten (pno)	Vic 20565	24/2/27 Memphis
345	18219	*Sneaking Blues*	Scrapper Blackwell (Francis Black) (vo, gtr)	Ch 16370	24/11/31 Richmond
346	C 3907	*Conversation With The Blues*	Big Bill Broonzy (vo, gtr) acc. Memphis Slim (pno); Washboard Sam (wbd)	Cq 9932	17/7/41 Chicago
347	2294	*Rambling Blues*	Ida Cox (vo) acc. Tommy Ladnier (cnt)?; Jesse Crump (pno)	Pm 12318	–/8/25 Chicago
348	146191	*Sunrise Blues*	Will Day (vo) acc. gtr; clt	Co 14318-D	25/4/28 N.O.
349	02644	*Tantalizing Blues*	Little Brother (Montgomery) (vo, pno)	Bb B-6766	16/10/36 N.O.
350	70675-1	*Worried Man Blues*	Walter Davis (vo, pno)	Bb B-5129	10/2/32 Chicago

Acknowledgments to Discography

15 *Honey, I'm All Out and Down*   Huddie Ledbetter
Copyright Essex Music Ltd., 4 Denmark St., London, W.C.2. Quoted by permission.

19 *Saw Mill Man Blues*   Pleasant Joe
Copyright Milton "Mezz" Mezzrow, 12 rue Cadet, Paris 9e, France. Quoted by permission.

75 *Big Four Blues*   Leroy Carr
Copyright Leeds Music Ltd., 25 Denmark St., London, W.C.2. Quoted by permission

82 *De Kalb Blues*   Huddie Ledbetter
Copyright Essex Music Ltd. Quoted by permission.

150 *The Dirty Dozen; The Dirty Dozen No.2*
                                            Speckled Red
Copyright Leeds Music Ltd. Quoted by permission.

191 *Good Time Flat Blues*   Maggie Jones
Copyright Pickwick Music Ltd. Quoted by permission.

206 *East Chicago Blues*   Pinetop and Lindberg
Copyright Southern Music Publishing Co., Ltd. Quoted by permission.

209 *Bourgeois Blues*   Huddie Ledbetter
Copyright Cromwell Music Ltd. Quoted by permission.

226 *Hi-Jack Blues*   Walter Davis
Copyright Southern Music Publishing Co., Ltd. Quoted by permission.

242 *Eleven Twenty-Nine Blues*   Leroy Carr
Copyright Leeds Music Ltd. Quoted by permission.

256 *Bloodhound Blues*   Victoria Spivey
Copyright Southern Music Publishing Co., Ltd. Quoted by permission.

267 *Red Cross Blues*   Alabama Sam
Copyright Southern Music Publishing Co., Ltd. Quoted by permission.

299 *Dirty T.B. Blues*   Victoria Spivey
Copyright Southern Music Publishing Co., Ltd. Quoted by permission.

315 *Six Cold Feet of Ground*   Leroy Carr
Copyright Leeds Music Ltd. Quoted by permission.

341 *Milk Cow Blues*   Kokomo Arnold
Copyright Leeds Music Ltd. Quoted by permission.

335

Index of quoted blues singers

Blues singers who are quoted in the text are indexed in alphabetical order and the item numbers allocated in the Discography follow the names. Where a singer used a pseudonym the items are listed below it if the pseudonym is known more generally than the real name of the singer. Real names, where known, are also listed and cross-references made. All listed names are of vocalists, but instruments played are indicated where applicable.

Index

Blues singers are listed only when the references are other than to items listed in the Index of Quoted Blues Singers and the Discography of Quoted Blues

80 14

ARNULFO L. OLIVEIRA MEMORIAL LIBRARY
1825 MAY STREET
BROWNSVILLE, TEXAS 78520